SOUTHEAST ASIA
IN THE
NEW INTERNATIONAL ERA

FIFTH EDITION

Southeast Asia in the New International Era

ROBERT DAYLEY
The College of Idaho

CLARK D. NEHER
Northern Illinois University

A Member of the Perseus Books Group

Library of Congress Cataloging-in-Publication Data
Dayley, Robert.
  Southeast Asia in the new international era / Robert Dayley [and] Clark D. Neher.—5th ed.
    p. cm.
  Rev. ed. of: Southeast Asia in the new international era / Clark D. Neher. 4th ed. 2002.
  Includes bibliographical references and index.
  ISBN 978-0-8133-4404-1 (pbk. : alk. paper) 1. Southeast Asia—Politics and government—1945– 2. Southeast Asia—Politics and government—21st century. 3. Southeast Asia—Foreign relations. I. Neher, Clark D. Southeast Asia in the new international era. II. Title.

DS526.7.N45 2010
959.05'4—dc22

                                                                    2009005662

10 9 8 7 6 5 4 3 2 1

Contents

Preface and Acknowledgments

This book results from information gathered during many trips to Southeast Asia. I am grateful to the National Science, Ford, and Fulbright foundations, the United States Information Agency, and the United States–Indochina Reconciliation Project for their generous assistance during the lengthier stays. I am also indebted to the faculty and staff of Chulalongkorn University, Thammasat University, Prince of Songkla University at Had Yai and Pattani, Chiang Mai University, Payap University in Thailand, and the University of San Carlos in the Philippines for their intellectual and material support of my work at their campuses.

During my career as a student of Southeast Asian politics, I have learned much from colleagues who share my interest. I am especially indebted to M. Ladd Thomas, Danny Unger, and Dwight King in the Department of Political Science at Northern Illinois University. They have provided generous intellectual and collegial counsel. Similar support has come from Ronald Provencher, Judy Ledgerwood, Susan Russell, Constance Wilson, and Mai Kyi Win, all associates of NIU's Center for Southeast Asian Studies. April Davis, Karen Schweitzer, Sandi Holloway, and Nancy Schuneman contributed outstanding administrative support, and David Oldfield, Paul Chambers, Chandra Mahajakana, Bryan Hunsaker, Todd Culp, Ted Mayer, Robert Dayley, and Warner Winborne provided superb research assistance. Both undergraduate and graduate students at Northern Illinois University have contributed to this book as well through their enthusiastic interest in the Southeast Asian region. It is gratifying to have taught these students, many of whom are now among the new generation of scholars of Southeast Asia.

Although I accept responsibility for all errors and misinterpretations, many scholars of Southeast Asia will see their ideas reflected in *Southeast Asia in the New International Era*. Among those scholars who have helped shape my views are David Wilson, Donn Hart, Michael Aung-Thwin, Ansil Ramsay, Prasert Bhandachart, Bidhya Bowornwathana, Kusuma Snitwongse, Suchit

Bunbongkarn, Randy Fertel, Danny Unger, Gary Suwannarat, David Adams, Sheldon Simon, Chai-Anan Samudavanija, Tanun Anuman-Rajadhon, Sukhumbhand Paribatra, Proserpina Tapales, John McAuliff, Anek Laothamathas, Panitan Wattanayagorn, Carolina Hernandez, Ross Marlay, Nara Ganesan, and Narong Sinsawasdi.

CLARK D. NEHER

Preface and Acknowledgments
to the Fifth Edition

When Professor Clark Neher invited me to coauthor a fifth edition of *Southeast Asia in the New International Era,* I accepted without hesitation. My deep sense of gratitude to him alone would not allow me to decline. As his student and research assistant at Northern Illinois University, where I completed doctoral work in the 1990s, I was the recipient of his superior academic guidance and his fatherly interest in the well-being of my young family. Professor Neher is the consummate scholar and gentleman. For many of his former students, he is a model professor. Accepting the challenge to extend the life of this text beyond his retirement is a small token of my personal appreciation for his years of mentorship.

Having gone to press shortly after the events of September 11, 2001, the fourth edition of *Southeast Asia in the New International Era* was in need of considerable updating. The book now includes a chapter on Timor-Leste, the region's newest country, and it gives greater attention to the regional effects of the U.S. war on terrorism, political Islam, and the rise of China. It updates the analysis to include major developments throughout the region. Readers of previous editions will notice changes in the introduction. I have also added "Resource Guides" with each country chapter to encourage students to get beyond commonly used search engines and launch more effective Internet searches as they seek to explore topics further. In making revisions, I have tried to emulate Professor Neher's fluid writing style by balancing relevance with conciseness and retaining his analytical sensitivity to historical context, culture, and political leadership. With hindsight expanding, I have also made some modest revisions to existing text that appeared in earlier editions. Some of these changes are my own; others stemmed from feedback by three anonymous reviewers to whom I am very grateful. John Brandon also reviewed the fifth edition with useful comments. Necessary length restrictions may understandably leave some area experts troubled by relevant material not included in the book.

As best as possible I pitched information and analysis for readers new to the region.

In wish to thank The College of Idaho, Payap University, the National Institute of Development Administration (NIDA), and the Fulbright Foundation for supporting my research endeavors in Asia, where I have lived, taught, and researched for more than four years. Teaching opportunities at Davidson College, St. Lawrence University, Oglethorpe University, China Agricultural University, and Payap University's Thai and Southeast Asian Studies Program have allowed me to exchange intellectually with wonderfully curious colleagues and students. My students at The College of Idaho are a constant source of inspiration to me. The Asian Studies programs at Weber State University, the University of Oregon, and Northern Illinois University similarly deserve acknowledgment for supporting my area studies training. I especially wish to thank Carrie Dayley, my wife, for artfully producing the country maps that appear with each chapter. Garth Claassen provided art support. Evonne Earle supplied useful clerical support and Cassandra Painter of The College of Idaho's Heritage Scholar Program proofread many of the revised chapters for the new edition. Antoinette Smith and Annie Lenth provided excellent production and editorial support. From its conception to final publication, the fifth edition has enjoyed the guidance of Karl Yambert and Brook Kush at Westview Press.

ROBERT DAYLEY

Acronyms

ACFTA	ASEAN-China Free Trade Agreement
ADB	Asian Development Bank
AFP	Armed Forces of the Philippines
AFPFL	Anti-Fascist People's Freedom League
AFTA	ASEAN Free Trade Area
AIDS	acquired immune deficiency syndrome
AMP	Parliamentary Majority Alliance
APEC	Asia-Pacific Economic Cooperation
APU	Angkatan Perpaduan Umnah
ARMM	Autonomous Region in Muslim Mindano
ASEAN	Association of Southeast Asian Nations
AusAID	Australian Government Overseas Aid Program
BA	Barisan Alternatif
BSPP	Burmese Socialist Program Party
CGDK	Coalition Government of Democratic Kampuchea
CIA	Central Intelligence Agency
CNS	Council on National Security
CPP	Communist Party of the Philippines; also, Cambodian People's Party
CPV	Communist Party of Vietnam
CPT	Communist Party of Thailand
CRNT	National Congress for Timorese Reconstruction Party
CSO	Civil Society Organization
CVA	Timor-Leste Commission of Truth and Friendship
DAP	Democratic Action Party

DPR	Indonesian Parliament (lower house)
DPD	Indonesian Parliament (upper house)
ENC	Ethnic Nationalities Council
EOI	export-oriented industrialization
EU	European Union
Falantil	*Forces Amadas de Libertação Nacional de Timor Leste*
FDI	foreign direct investment
FTA	Free Trade Agreement
FUNCINPEC	United National Front for an Independent, Peaceful, and Cooperative Cambodia
Fretilin	Revolutionary Front for an Independent East Timor
GDP	gross domestic product
GMS	Greater Mekong Subregion
GNI	gross national income
GNP	gross national product
GRC	Group Representation Constituency
GSP	Generalized System of Preferences
HDI	Human Development Index
ICMI	Indonesian Association of Muslim Intellectuals
ILO	International Labor Organization
IMF	International Monetary Fund
INTERFET	International Force for East Timor
ISI	import-substitution industrialization
JI	Jemaah Islamiyah
JICA	Japanese International Cooperation Agency
JPDA	Joint Petroleum Development Area
JSOTF-P	Joint Special Operations Task Force-Philippines
KBL	Kilusang Bagong Lipunan
KNP	Khmer National Party
KPNLF	Khmer People's National Liberation Front
Lao PDR	Lao People's Democratic Republic
LDC	least developed country
LFNC	Lao Front for National Construction
LNG	liquified natural gas

LPRP	Lao People's Revolutionary Party
MAI	Multilateral Aid Initiative
MCA	Malayan Chinese Association
MDG	Millennium Development Goals
MFA	Multi Fibre Arrangement
MIA	missing in action
MIB	Malay Islamic Beraja
MIC	Malayan Indian Congress
MILF	Moro Islamic Liberation Front
MNLF	Moro National Liberation Front
MP	Member of Parliament
MPR	People's Consultative Assembly
NAFTA	North American Free Trade Association
NDF	National Democratic Front
NEFOS	newly emerging forces
NEP	New Economic Policy
NGO	nongovernmental organization
NICs	newly industrialized countries
NLD	National League for Democracy
NLF	National Liberation Front
NLHS	Neo Lao Hak Sat
NMP	Nominated Member of Parliament
NOC	National Operations Council
NPA	New People's Army
NPKC	National Peace Keeping Council
NU	Nahdlatul Ulama
NUP	National Unity Party
OECD	Organization for Economic Cooperation and Development
OIC	Organization of the Islamic Conference
OLDEFOS	old established forces
OPEC	Organization of Petroleum Exporting Countries
PAD	People's Alliance for Democracy
PAP	People's Action Party
PAS	Parti Islam Se-Malaysia

PAVN	People's Army of Vietnam
PDI	Indonesian Democratic Party
PDI-P	Indonesian Democracy Party-Struggle
PGNU	Provisional Government of National Unity
PKB	National Awakening Party
PKI	Communist Party of Indonesia
PKS	Prosperous Justice Party
POW	prisoner of war
PPP	People's Power Party; also, United Development Party
PRK	People's Republic of Kampuchea
RAM	Reform the Armed Forces Movement
RBAF	Royal Brunei Armed Forces
S46	Semangat '46
SARS	Severe Acute Respiratory Syndrome
SBY	Susilo Bambang Yudhoyono
SDA	Singapore Democratic Alliance
SEATO	Southeast Asia Treaty Organization
SLORC	State Law and Order Restoration Council
SMEs	small and medium enterprises
SNC	Supreme National Council
SRP	Sam Rainsy Party
SPDC	State Peace and Development Council
TNI	Tentara Nasional Indonesia
TRT	Thai Rak Thai Party
UMNO	United Malays National Organization
UNAMET	United Nations Assistance Mission in East Timor
UDD	United Front of Democracy against Dictatorship
UN	United Nations
UNDP	United Nations Development Program
UNESCO	United Nations Educational, Scientific, and Cultural Organization
UNICEF	United Nations Children's Fund
UNIDO	United Nationalist Democratic Organization

UNLD-LA	United Nationalities League for Democracy–Liberated Areas
UNMISET	United Nations Mission of Support in East Timor
UNMIT	United Nations Integrated Mission in Timor-Leste
UNOTIL	United Nations Office in East Timor
UNTAC	United Nations Transitional Authority in Cambodia
UNTAET	United Nations Transitional Administration in East Timor
USAID	United States Aid for International Development
USDA	Union Solidarity and Development Association
USSFTA	United States-Singapore Free Trade Agreement
UXO	unexploded ordnance
WTO	World Trade Organization

1

INTRODUCTION

Writing a book about contemporary Southeast Asia is a challenge because the region is no longer a primary focus of international attention. Weeks go by without any major news stories about countries that only decades ago dominated the discussions of government officials and ordinary citizens. Because of the end of the Cold War, as well as events put in motion on September 11, 2001, international observers now focus their attention on other parts of the world. Moreover, the lingering trauma, disillusionment, and cynicism of the Vietnam War have kept many journalists, political scientists, and policymakers from focusing on Southeast Asia.

International news coverage of Southeast Asia remains dominated by the superficial and sensational. Images of sunny beaches, soccer-playing elephants, and "exotic" cuisine are standard fare for the reporters of the globalization era. When periodic spurts of interest in serious stories do manage to enter the global news cycle, the images are typically of tragedy, violence, and exploitation—of cyclone victims, bandanna-clad kidnappers, or underage workers in sweatshops. Less frequent but more in-depth commentaries about Southeast Asia may center on the region's transformation from a "battleground to a marketplace" or on problems of environmental degradation, but for the most part Southeast Asia's story is persistently overshadowed by conflict in the Middle East, the movements of U.S. troops, and the global rise of China.[1]

Southeast Asia's recent story is obviously more complex than sensational headlines and stereotypical images suggest. In fact, as the world turns its attention elsewhere, the 500 million people who live in the region are experiencing unprecedented socioeconomic change. New forms of wealth and poverty are emerging across the region. Wrenching conflicts over rights, identity, social justice, and power have become the everyday experience of many Southeast Asians. Although it no longer draws the international attention as it once did, perhaps no region in the world is more dynamic.

A new era in international relations has arisen in the past several decades with lasting repercussions for Southeast Asia. Political, economic, and social forces of unprecedented scope are currently transforming the entire region. *Southeast Asia in the New International Era* analyzes contemporary politics in the context of these new international and domestic realities from the perspectives of both the Southeast Asians and the international community. This chapter introduces the region, describes changes accompanying the new international era, and explains how standard regime labels fall short in characterizing the richness and complexity of Southeast Asian politics. Eleven country chapters follow that evaluate each country in terms of basic political history, major institutions and social groups, democratization, economic development, the role of the state, and foreign policy. A small research guide follows each country chapter to assist readers in search of Internet-based bibliographies, socioeconomic data, research sites, and blogs on Southeast Asian countries. A comparison table of select figures appears after the final chapter.

INFLUENCES AND EXPERIENCES

Southeast Asia, a region of remarkable diversity, consists of eleven countries with differing histories, cultural traditions, resource bases, and political-economic systems.[2] Except for geographic proximity and a somewhat similar tropical ecology, few characteristics link all these nations into a coherent whole. Nevertheless, before the international era arrived, a broad shape to a Southeast Asian political economy had developed from a few generalized influences, experiences, and social patterns, which are described in this chapter. The influences and experiences include religious penetration by Hinduism, Buddhism, Islam, and Christianity; colonialism and introduction of political ideas from the West; the rise of nationalism associated with the struggle for independence; Japanese occupation; Cold War trauma, and regional economic transition. Shared social patterns, also outlined below, include a strong sense of the village as the primary unit of identity; agricultural economies overtaken by urban-based manufacturing and services; and patron-client systems that influence sociopolitical interaction.

An important force shaping Southeast Asia from ancient to modern times has been the arrival and expansion of non-native religions across the region. By supplanting local belief systems—or more often blending with them—exogenous religious influences evolved into today's endogenous value systems that contribute to the region's diverse cultural milieu. Hinduism and Theravada Buddhism, arriving from South Asian sources, brought to the region Brahmanical notions of the god-king (*deva-raja*), classic myths (*The Ramayana*), and karmic notions of rightful authority, thus shaping the concept of power and the royal structures that wielded it. Mahayana Buddhism, brought from India via China, also influenced political ideals in the region, particularly in Vietnam, where social order was believed to stem from hierarchal (Confucian) relations, Buddhist cosmology, and (Taoist) naturalism.

Islam arrived from merchants and traders primarily from South Asia subsequent to Hinduism and Buddhism. It did not enjoy a wide presence in Southeast Asia until the fifteenth century, about the time Europeans first began to arrive with Christian traditions. Throughout insular Southeast Asia Islam spread from island to island and from coastal ports to interior settlements. Christianity did not spread deep roots in the region, except for in the predominantly Catholic Philippines and East Timor, as well as among some enduring communities in Vietnam and Indonesia. Over the centuries of religious interaction, the eclectic, religio-royal traditions of Hinduism and Buddhism have sometimes clashed with the universalist, law-based religions of Islam and Christianity. However, tolerance and syncretism, not conflict, characterizes most of Southeast Asia's history of religious practice. Taken together, the diverse practices and beliefs of these religions, and their interaction, generate an array of cultural claims on how to organize societies politically and economically across the region.

Adding yet more complexity to this milieu of beliefs and practices was the gradual penetration of Western ideas of modernity, including "civilization," nationalism, capitalism, republicanism, democracy, and communism. Most of these foreign notions and ideologies emerged in the region during the nineteenth and early twentieth centuries, that is, during the final phase of nearly five centuries of European influence in the region. Many of the problems of political and economic development facing Southeast Asian leaders today can be traced to colonialism.[3] The grand strategic games of imperial competition and colonial rule brought the formation of national boundaries, which replaced the region's nonintegrated dynastic principalities that had only loosely governed rural populations. Foreign attempts to integrate these disparate populations often proved difficult. The imperialists eventually guaranteed new boundaries and imposed a Western sense of geographic and political order on the region.

By the late nineteenth century, national boundaries had been demarcated and the entire area of Southeast Asia, except Thailand, was in European hands. Over time, a money economy was introduced and resource extraction created large-scale industries that required skilled and unskilled laborers. Because the rural populations of Southeast Asia found industrial labor antithetical to traditional values, the colonialists imported Chinese and Indians to work in factories, tin mines, and rubber plantations. The Chinese and Indian communities, through their connections with Western imperialism and laws that pushed them into the commercial sector, subsequently enjoyed economic power in Southeast Asia disproportionate to their numbers. Urban life in colonial Southeast Asia was, in many respects, more Chinese and Indian than local or European. A discernable immigrant communalism evolved in tandem with urbanization. Hindu, Confucian, and European influences affected trade, urban architecture, art, and societal tastes and norms.

Among other changes, European colonists were responsible for the growth of the region's first economic infrastructure of ports, railways, and roads. Although they staffed their bureaucracies with local elites, offering education to the most gifted, the colonists failed to develop institutions of accountable governance. Serving European rather than local interests, imperial administrators exploited natural resources for export and neglected local socioeconomic development. Over time the cruelty, exploitation, and injustice of colonial rule bred popular resentment and put into motion a new force in the region: nationalism.

The rise of anti-imperial nationalism was the most consequential product of colonialism in Southeast Asia. Although deliberate movements against European control punctuated the early colonial history of Southeast Asia, it was the ideological battles of the twentieth century that fed the transformative nationalism that came to define the region's future.

A traumatic experience under Japanese occupation during World War II further fueled aspirations for self-rule and independence across the region. Following Japan's surrender in 1945 to Allied forces, Europe's postwar leaders disregarded attempts by Southeast Asian leaders to declare formal independence. Eager for resources to rebuild their own war-torn economies, the colonists audaciously returned to extend control over their previously held territories: the British in Burma and Malaya; the French in Indochina (Vietnam, Cambodia, and Laos); the Dutch in Indonesia; and the Portuguese in East Timor. To legitimize their ambitions, European administrators received international recognition for their actions through postwar treaties that excluded Southeast Asians from negotiations. Only the Philippines, vacated by its American occupiers in 1946, would join Thailand as an independent nation in early postwar Southeast Asia.

Resolve for independence hardened. In Burma, Indonesia, and Vietnam, nationalism became an especially potent and unifying force that led to fierce struggles for self-determination. In Malaysia and Singapore the struggle for *merdeka* (independence) was less violent but every bit as formative in cultivating a new sense of nationalist purpose. Across the region, experiences with colonialism had differed but the nationalist rhetoric for genuine self-governance emerged as a political *lingua franca* among anticolonial revolutionaries. Thailand, having escaped direct colonial rule, developed its own sense of nationhood stemming from its proud record of independence.

Hoping to bind the various peoples within the borders of its constitutional monarchy, modernizing Thai elites cultivated the nationalist creed "Nation, Religion, and King."

Relentless anti-imperial political activity and painfully violent episodes of engagement with colonial forces gradually produced two significant consequences for the region: the overdue withdrawal of the Europeans and the rise of a handful of charismatic, larger-than-life independence leaders including Ho Chi Minh in Vietnam, Sukarno in Indonesia, Aung San in Burma, Tungku Abdul Rahman in Malaysia, and Prince Sihanouk in Cambodia. But even as decolonization and courageous independence leaders offered fresh hopes under sovereign statehood, a new dimension of geopolitical struggle, the Cold War, entered the scene and overwhelmed the region.

The Cold War was fought in Southeast Asia along three related dimensions: internal ideological struggle; superpower rivalry; and interstate conflict. Leftist movements embracing communist visions for state control existed in every major Southeast Asian country during this period. Competing visions pitted communism against not only democratic capitalism (which scarcely existed in the region) but also right-leaning militaries, traditional monarchists, and neoimperial foreign influences. U.S.–U.S.S.R. superpower rivalry, expressed most clearly in the Vietnam War, was also colored by the Sino-Soviet split over global communist supremacy. Ever in search of international patrons, Southeast Asian communists sought to exploit this split to suit their largely nationalist purposes.

The meddling of three external Cold War powers in the region exacerbated existing conflicts and created new ones. The most tragic of these conflicts resulted in the rise of the genocidal Khmer Rouge, who, before the illegal U.S. bombing of Cambodia, had demonstrated few signs of serious might or the capacity to seize Cambodian state power. China, which had supported Vietnamese revolutionaries against both the French and the Americans, turned on its former communist ally by supporting the Khmer Rouge in an attempt to outmaneuver the Soviets, who maintained support for Vietnam. China's communist leaders count among the very few diplomatic supporters of the Pol Pot clique, which was responsible for the deaths of 1.7 million Cambodians during its three-year reign of terror.

With the 1975 withdrawal of U.S. military forces after the Vietnam War, China became a new guarantor of Thai security against possible Vietnamese aggression. China and Vietnam ended up fighting a brutal border war in 1979 after the latter invaded and occupied Khmer Rouge–controlled Cambodia. Vietnamese troops stayed in Cambodia until the United Nations brokered their withdrawal after the Cold War had ended.

The Cold War also produced new alliances and interstate conflict between Southeast Asian states. Thailand and the Philippines, both noncommunist states, joined the Southeast Asian Treaty Organization (SEATO), under the tutelage of the United States. In the 1960s and '70s, both countries provided troops and territory to the United States for staging actions in Vietnam. Vietnam and Laos looked to the Soviet Union and other communist regimes for support. Indonesia, led initially by the charismatic Sukarno, claimed Cold War neutrality only to invite an internal battle between left and right forces within the country. Sukarno's failed balancing act led to the rise of the anticommunist Suharto regime, which took power after a murky 1965 coup and countercoup. Cambodia too suffered the perils of neutrality only to see the rise of Pol Pot's Khmer Rouge. Soviet-backed Vietnam later occupied Cambodia, sending the Chinese-backed Pol Pot and his followers into jungle redoubts, where they stayed in hiding for almost twenty years. After the Vietnam War, and the reduction of U.S. commitment to the region, noncommunist states relied more heavily on the Association of Southeast Asian Nations (ASEAN) as a bulwark against Soviet-Vietnamese ambitions.

With the region split in so many directions in the 1980s, and with the only remaining U.S. presence in the region at military bases in the Philippines, the final phase of the Cold War experienced a welcome, but somewhat unexpected, transformative force in the region: the Japanese businessmen. Despite the fact that Japan had attacked and occupied all of Southeast Asia in World War II, and that lingering resentment and fear persisted, Japan's meteoric postwar economic success brought Southeast Asia into its orbit. Singapore was the first to benefit. As Japan's export-oriented economy grew, so too did its need for raw materials, petroleum, and other imports. Tiny Singapore obviously did not produce these resources, but its port facilities were geographically positioned in Asia to benefit from increasing oceangoing traffic to and from Japan. Singapore joined South Korea, Taiwan, and Hong Kong as models of third-world economic success, known collectively as the "Asian economic dragons."

In the mid-1980s, Japan's growing investments in Southeast Asia expanded rapidly as a result of the appreciating value of the Japanese yen, which made exporting from Japan expensive. Escaping the high yen, Japanese industrialists moved production to a number of Southeast Asian countries where cheap labor and favorable currency exchange rates made the region a prime export platform. All of this was timed with policy shifts in many Southeast Asian countries designed to emulate the successful export-oriented industrialization (EOI) strategies of the Asian dragons and their move away from import substitution industrialization (ISI). Southeast Asian governments aggressively courted ties with Japan and trade volume expanded. Thailand, Malaysia, Indonesia, and to a lesser extent the Philippines each moved toward a development model of activist state guidance of private sector–driven export growth. Malaysia's prime minister appropriately dubbed the new development approach the "Look East Policy."

As economies grew and middle classes began to coalesce, new interest in democracy and political reform began to surface across the region. In 1986, Ferdinand Marcos, a U.S. Cold War ally who had suspended democracy and manipulated law to extend his own rule, was ousted in a massive popular movement known as "People's Power." Thailand also moved closer to democracy by electing its first civilian prime minister since a previously failed period of democracy in the mid-1970s. Even economically autarkic Burma faced new prodemocracy forces. In 1988, demonstrators forced the country's ruling military junta to schedule elections for a representative parliament. The elections were held in 1990 but the losing generals did not honor the results. However, with the democratic genie now out of the bottle, aspirations for representative government in Burma have persisted ever since, often provoking brutal suppression.

Elsewhere in the region authoritarian leaders repressed growing aspirations for democracy even as the Cold War showed signs of thawing in Europe. On the communist left, Vietnamese leaders opened the economy but not its political system. On the nationalistic right, long-standing governments in Indonesia, Malaysia, and Singapore viewed greater democracy as a threat to budding economic success. Public pressure for political reform would emerge as a new force regional governments would constantly face following the end of the Cold War.

Shared Social Patterns

In addition to the religious influences, colonial history, nationalist movements, and Cold War experiences that have given shape to this otherwise diverse region, some observable social patterns also add definition to a Southeast Asian political economy. These generalized patterns are not universal but are widely shared across the region and contain elements of both "continuity and change"—a phrase used ad nauseam among Southeast Asian specialists who are forever attempting to characterize the enduring and dynamic patterns of socioeconomic behavior in the region.

Southeast Asian nations are characterized by an agricultural base that traditionally has been the heart of everyday life. Historically, the agricultural village served as the major unit of identity for the rural population, acting as its educational, religious, cultural, political, economic, and social center. Although urban growth expanded as trade increased over time—accompanied by Indian, Chinese, Arab, and European influences on the royal and colonial centers of power—the basic economic unit for most Southeast Asians (until recent decades) has been the peasant-style family-operated farm. Generally, the family farm was part of a village economy characterized by subsistence production, with most of the farm products being consumed by the family or within the village. Experiences differed but feudal-type arrangements across the region fed the development of landed elites, aristocrats, and royals who exploited the labor of rural populations for imperial projects—a pattern repeated later by European colonists (absent any local cultural foundations that historically ameliorated popular resentment of royal power).

Some areas of Southeast Asia today remain characterized by traditional village arrangements and subsistence agriculture but the socioeconomic picture has grown increasingly complex. The arrival of green revolution technologies, commercial agribusiness, and rising expectations of educational opportunity and material gain describes agrarian change today. "Farmers" are replacing "peasants" in the economic sense of these terms, and life inside most villages is now fully interdependent with life outside the village due to a host of transformative factors: rural-to-urban migration, expanding nonfarm work, globalized labor markets, remittance economies, new communication technologies, and rising consumerism. Over the past fifty years, the agricultural sector's economic importance has continued to decline relative to industry and services, although employment in the sector remains considerable.

In spite of these changes, the hierarchical structure traditional to the village still finds expression in the region's political life. Southeast Asian societies, generally speaking, remain fundamentally organized into networks of superior-subordinate (patron-client) ties. These networks form the basis of political structure and affect the allocation of resources and values. In their positive expression, these relations form "moral economies" where uneven but reciprocal relations bring mutual benefit to participants in a context of cultural appropriateness and meaning. Where there are marked inequalities in wealth, status, and control, and where resources are insufficient, those with limited access can seek alliances with individuals at a higher socioeconomic level or access to state resources. The relationship is reciprocal in the sense that the patron expects support, protection, labor, or some other service in return for dispensing benefits to the subordinate. In their pejorative interpretation, patron-client systems prop up authoritarian forms of government with vast networks designed for patrimony and capable of depoliticizing opponents through co-optation and participation. Such relational asymmetry can also foster exploitation and risks endless power struggles between elites who vie for each other's client networks.

Representative forms of government in Southeast Asia thus both benefit and suffer from these patron-client systems. Such networks can link those who wield state power with ordinary citizens and, potentially, link voting constituencies with elected officials. Left unchecked, however, patron-client partiality can threaten the legitimacy of democracy through favoritism, nepotism, corruption, and the abuse of official power. Throughout Southeast Asia rising demands by individuals and groups for increased governmental accountability, transparency, and recognition of civil and political rights clash with the deep-seated impulses of power elites to defend traditional forms of patronage. Citing cultural appropriateness, Southeast Asian elites have at times fashioned regimes that are, in the name of social order, structurally designed to institutionalize state patronage.

The influences, experiences, and social patterns lending shape to the Southeast Asian experience described above compose only a partial set of factors able to explain the various events and trends associated with the politics of Southeast Asian countries. The country chapters that follow illustrate this fact by employing much greater sensitivity to the particular conditions, events, individuals, groups, and institutions that make up political life. Nevertheless, in addition to these shared patterns and the common forces of colonialism, nationalism, and the Cold War that have shaped Southeast Asia, profound changes to the international system that followed the Cold War's end now influence the political economy of the region in unprecedented ways.

THE NEW INTERNATIONAL ERA

An extraordinary sweep of international change occurred following the end of the Cold War in 1989. The extent of these changes, occurring in rapid fashion, stunned the world and irrevocably recast international relations. The major catalyst responsible for causing a break with the past was Soviet President Mikhail Gorbachev, whose policies in the 1980s put in motion the end of the bipolar conflict that had structured world relations since World War II. Gorbachev, who took the helm of the U.S.S.R. in 1985, acted on the assumption that the economically stagnant Soviet Union could flourish only if it pursued comprehensive economic restructuring (perestroika) and an opening of Soviet society (glasnost). His reforms included a foreign policy of imperial disengagement, which U.S. presidents Ronald Reagan and George H. W. Bush welcomed. Populations across Western and Eastern Europe celebrated the Soviet leader's reforms. By the late 1980s a new global optimism emanated from events driven by a new agenda from the Kremlin.

In Asia, Gorbachev's policies meant the withdrawal of Russian troops from Afghanistan; demilitarizing the Sino-Russian border; ceasing aid to Vietnam and leftist insurgencies in the region; and abandoning military bases at Cam Ranh Bay and Da Nang in Vietnam. Vietnam responded to Gorbachev's changes by seeking to restructure its own economy. Pursing a new strategy dubbed *doi moi* (renovation), Vietnam's communist leadership began to permit free-market activity and foreign investment. These moves were in line with changes already sweeping communist China. China's leader, Deng Xiaoping, had previously broken from the failed development policies of his predecessor, Mao Zedong, and began to allow market forces to operate within communist China. During the 1980s Deng encouraged international trade and foreign investment and established ties with Asian businesses and Western multinationals. In the new international era overseas Chinese in Southeast Asia become major conduits for business between China, Asia, and the world. The People's Republic of China, a once feared Cold War power in Southeast Asia, enjoyed a new economic role as a regional economic partner and a formidable export competitor.

During the new international era the bipolar world of communists and noncommunists rapidly transformed itself into a more multipolar world where states, regions, international organizations, and nonstate actors would exhibit new forms of power and influence. Although the United States stood alone as the dominant global power in the 1990s, it soon learned that *relative power* was far from *absolute power*. Asia's own rising economic influence and Europe's deepening integration with the former communist states of the old Soviet bloc created new poles of economic and political power.

The new era also became defined by increasingly assertive international bodies such as the World Trade Organization (WTO), the International Monetary Fund (IMF), and the World Bank. These organizations established and enforced the rules of globalization, often coercing struggling governments to implement their policies of market fundamentalism in the process. Nongovernment organizations (NGOs) also proliferated across the world in the 1990s, promoting humanitarian, development, and rights-oriented causes. As for the United Nations, its increasingly visible blue-helmeted peacekeepers became symbols of a new activist (but often impotent) international community. Added to all of these new forces were powerful stateless actors tied to nefarious networks of terrorists, drug lords, and human traffickers. All of the new forces of globalization found their way into Southeast Asia during the new international era.

Although Japan had led Southeast Asia in its economic success in the closing decade of the Cold War, the East Asian economic superpower, paradoxically, began to sink into recession even as the new international era dawned. Nevertheless, ongoing Japanese investments continued to fuel Southeast Asia into a boom economy that came to enjoy global renown. South Korean and Taiwanese investors, fleeing higher labor costs at home, similarly poured investments into the region. Hot money from European and American traders found its way to the region's fast and furious "emerging markets."

Encouraged by Western governments, the IMF, and globalization advocates, Southeast Asian governments liberalized their financial markets, putting an end to many restrictions that formerly regulated the flow of capital in and out of their countries. As a result, joint ventures and foreign-financed enterprises expanded quickly and deliberately into textiles, footwear, electronics, automobile parts, cosmetics, agribusiness, petroleum refining, and other diverse industries and manufactures. Double-digit economic growth and trade balance surpluses soon characterized the Southeast Asian "tiger economies," as they came to be known. Thailand, Malaysia, and Indonesia, and to a lesser extent the Philippines and Vietnam, all participated in the rapid economic growth unleashed by the passing of Cold War tensions in the region.

The phenomenal economic growth rates the tigers experienced, as high as 10 percent per year during this period, fundamentally changed the Southeast Asian landscape. The most obvious change was in the increase in per capita gross national product (GNP). Per capita GNP in Thailand in 1977, for example, was $300; by 1997 the same figure had climbed to $2,970. Similar growth in per capita GNP occurred in the other countries over the same period: Malaysia, $660 to $3,531; Indonesia, $150 to $692; the Philippines, $310 to $1,049; and Singapore, from $2,120 to $24,664! (Hence its "dragon" status.) Corresponding figures for reforming but populous Vietnam and for economically stagnant Burma, Cambodia, and Laos indicated less improvement by contrast. By 1997 per capita GNP in these countries still averaged less than $500.

By the mid-1990s, so confident were Southeast Asians in their path to success that regional leaders began to engage the world in a debate that pitted "Asian values" against "Western values." The chief spokesmen in this debate were politicians from Singapore and Malaysia. Their contention was that because Asian culture valued social order over political freedom, it allowed economic markets to thrive even as societies remained orderly. Centuries of pent-up resentment against Western superiority unleashed itself in trans-Pacific rhetorical punches. The West's high crime rates, divorce rates, declining educational standards, and sedentary lifestyles of TV watching were cited repeatedly as evidence of American inferiority. "You Americans have this mantra about your high standard of living," argued a senior Asian diplomat, "but if standard of living means not being afraid to go outside after dark, or not worrying about what filth your children will see on all those TV channels, then our Asian societies have the higher standard."[4] The message was unambiguous: The world would be a better place if countries began to learn from Asia rather than the West. Journalists writing from New York and London countered by listing human rights injustices and corruption tied to Asian governments.

The "Asian values debate" symbolized the sweeping changes that had come to the region in the new international era. Political ideology, interstate war, and superpower meddling no longer served as central concerns to the modern states of Southeast Asia. Instead, the key issues became economics, development, integrated markets, and stable political development. Southeast Asian societies also became more concerned with the negative effects of rapid growth, such as deforestation, pollution, traffic, corruption, and (contrary to the rhetoric of some Asian politicians) increased drug use, criminal activity, and alienation among Southeast Asian youth. Still, in the bigger picture, Southeast Asian governments and their societies benefited by no longer building walls around their countries and isolating their economies.

The exception was Burma, which, after reneging on promised political reform and refusing to recognize election results unfavorable to the military government, persisted in its strategy of socialist economic autarky. Burma's dreadful standard of living, however, only reinforced the dominant view in the region that interaction, not isolation, was necessary for a country to flourish. Indeed, every Southeast Asian country that tested the open-market proposition experienced unprecedented economic dynamism. The results of openness included a phenomenal rise in the people's standard of living, but success was accompanied by widening gaps between the rich and poor.

The new international era also saw Southeast Asian societies transformed by new forms of communication. Television, mobile phones, Internet cafes, satellite communications, and the entire digital revolution changed the way information was spread from person to person in this new era. No longer could governments fully control information flow among the populace. In the new era, the challenge for governments became balancing the effects of technological change, foreign investment, international trade against political demands for greater openness and governmental transparency. Another challenge that emerged was, alas, the threat and reality of economic crisis.

A classic lesson of international political economy is that economic interdependence creates greater sensitivity and vulnerability to global markets. The globalization of Southeast Asian economies had made the region's countries increasingly vulnerable to external forces and the volatility of international markets. These vulnerabilities proved to be real when the region suffered financial disaster in 1997.

In the early 1990s, China's government, already advantaged by the country's seemingly endless supply of cheap labor, devalued its currency, making its exports even more competitive than those coming from Southeast Asia. With their currencies pegged to the American dollar, most Southeast Asian countries' exports consequently became more expensive than China's in international markets. China subsequently began to attract foreign investment more rapidly than Southeast Asia, and export growth in the tiger economies began to level off after a decade of breakneck expansion.

By the mid-1990s, the current account surpluses the Southeast Asian tiger economies had previously enjoyed turned into current account deficits. Initially this shift caused an increase in foreign products and luxury goods to enter local markets. With export opportunities slowing, Southeast Asians poured their own investment money into real estate speculation, lavish projects (such as five-star hotels and condominiums), and local stock markets. Capital inflows and easy credit also expanded, made possible by the earlier deregulation of financial and capital markets. Because local currencies were pegged to the U.S. dollar, many local borrowers denominated their loans in dollars to take advantage of lower interest rates. Over a few short years, debt obligations mounted across the Southeast Asian business community. Slowing revenues from declining exports and an oversupply of new housing development and high-rise office space caused the real estate asset bubble to burst. Debtors began to default on their debt. Stress on financial institutions grew and financial mismanagement of banks and investment firms began to make headlines. Corruption in both the public and private sectors drew increasing attention and government scandals invited public criticism, especially in countries such as Thailand and the Philippines where democratization had expanded freedom of the press since the end of the Cold War. In Indonesia, Suharto's thirty-year regime, built on performance legitimization, faced unprecedented signs of weakness.

By 1997 international investor confidence in Southeast Asia's tigers began to slip. Global currency traders, recognizing the shakiness of the region's economies, bet against the Southeast Asian currencies, undermining their worth even more. Government attempts to support the currency pegs proved futile. The result was a cascade of overnight currency devaluations from country to country, which in turn precipitated inflation, unemployment, and a massive outflow of capital from all the tiger economies. The sudden devaluation of local currencies combined with rapid economic contraction left local Southeast Asian investors saddled with massive loads of debt. Many investors faced the impossible task of meeting inflated repayment obligations in the face of declining revenues.

Leaders in Southeast Asia responded ineffectively to the economic crisis, allowing the downturn to spread throughout all of Asia, eventually hurting markets across the globe. Southeast Asia's politicians seemed incapable of making the difficult decisions necessary to resolve the crisis. Instead, they hunkered down, blamed Westerners, and continued to protect cronies and undermine public-spirited technocrats. The public, more educated and savvy than ever, knew better and realized that their own government leaders and their business cronies also shared the blame. The region's shell-shocked governments eventually turned to the IMF, the world's "lender of last resort," to help them finance their way out of the crisis. The IMF saw itself as the economic doctor of the new international era, ready and able to administer the treatments countries needed for financial recovery. It provided massive multibillion-dollar loans but only on the strict conditions that recipient governments would raise interest rates, increase tax rates, adopt strict budget austerity, and totally restructure their ailing financial sectors. It was the wrong medicine.

The IMF's ill-conceived rescue packages proved damaging to already-suffering economies. The cash liquidity the IMF provided to the stressed tiger economies largely went to pay off foreign creditors and financial institutions; it did little to spur economic growth. Government budget austerity measures exacerbated existing economic contraction, and local investment plummeted. Higher interest rates and tax burdens further inhibited local investment when it was most desperately needed. Rather than stimulate the economy with public spending, governments were bound by IMF conditionality to starve it further.

Social and political disruption followed. Rampant unemployment, rapid inflation, and economic hardship turned into antigovernment protests and disorder. As a result, the famed emerging markets and their proud political leaders saw the governments change in the wake of the crisis and IMF rescue packages. Only Singapore, with its more resilient economy, and Malaysia, whose leaders had opted to reject IMF money in favor of capital controls, survived the 1997 Asian financial crisis intact.

The 1997 Asian economic crisis shook Southeast Asia's confidence in open trade and globalization. Asian leaders stopped talking about Asian values. In fact, to a significant degree, the crisis set Southeast Asian countries on disparate courses that continue to the present day. Recovery patterns have differed markedly from one case to the next. Indonesia, which suffered the most severe setback, sunk into deep political crisis ending thirty years of rule under General Suharto, whose collapse led not only to greater democracy in Indonesia but also to the birth of East Timor, which had been under Indonesian occupation since 1975. Thailand, after cycling through rotations of parliamentary coalitions, eventually elected a new party (the Thais Love Thais party) whose billionaire leader turned to populist policies and ultimately ignited an ongoing political crisis. Philippine voters turned to an action-movie hero to manage recovery, only to throw him out of office for corruption a few years later in a reprise of People's Power. Vietnam stalled its pace of reform and became ever more sensitive to suppressing political opposition. In the wake of the Asian economic crisis and the political changes it spawned, the new international era grew even more complex as a result of terrorist attacks half a world away.

Southeast Asia's newly installed leaders faced a new, more complicated foreign policy matrix following the September 11, 2001, attacks in New York and Washington, D.C. Already worried about their sluggish economies, Southeast Asian officials now had to concern themselves with U.S. President George W. Bush's declarations of an international "axis of evil" that tied rogue states to stateless terrorist groups. His announcement that the countries of the world were either "with us or against us" put unwanted pressure on the region's governments. Predictions by the Bush administration that Southeast Asia would become the "second front in the War on Terror" caused even wider reverberations in the region.

Aside from the Philippines, which had long battled Muslim separatists in the country's south, none of the ASEAN governments enthusiastically embraced the Bush administration's view of a post-9/11 world. Thailand was a reluctant partner and Singapore turned to the United States pragmatically, especially after Islamist groups bombed hotels and embassies in neighboring Indonesia. Wars in Afghanistan and Iraq, however, turned much of Southeast Asia's large Muslim population against the United States. Only time and a 2006 change in leadership in Indonesia allowed for the degree of cooperation American leaders had earlier hoped to have received in the region. As of early 2009, the region had not experienced major terrorist attacks by radical Islamists in over three years. Correspondingly, analyst predictions of the region's becoming a second front of terrorist activity have begun to fade.

As government officials adjusted to a post-9/11 world and pursued policy packages with hopes of returning to the high growth rates of the previous decade, another global concern caught their attention: rising China. Southeast Asian countries continued to be outperformed economically by China throughout the first decade of the 2000s. Its economic competitiveness less affected by the Asian economic crisis because of its strict currency regime and regulated foreign capital markets, China had become Asia's new power. With respect to its relations with Southeast Asia, China's direct and indirect influence on the region came through new free trade deals, tariff reductions, business connections, and even increased cultural influence. With near universality, Southeast Asians were also enthralled by Beijing's impressive pageantry and execution of the 2008 Olympiad. By that same year, ASEAN's combined economies had come to rank as China's fourth largest trading partner. Adjusting to China's rise is now a top priority among all Southeast Asian governments.

Southeast Asia is now more than a decade beyond the 1997 economic crisis. Income figures from across the region show modest levels of economic recovery and even progress in overall development measures.[5] Nevertheless, in the new international era economic gains across the region indicate continued uneven economic progress. In terms of 2007 per capita GDP, when adjusted for purchasing power parity, microstates Brunei ($51,005) and Singapore ($29,663) lead the region. Malaysia ($10,882) follows at a distant third, with Thailand ($8,667) slightly behind. The Philippines ($5,137), Indonesia ($3,843), and Vietnam ($3,071) continue to rank in the middle of the pack, with the remaining countries farther behind: Cambodia ($2,727), Timor-Leste ($2,506), Laos ($2,039), and Burma ($1,039). Even with the most optimistic forecasts, it will take decades for Southeast Asia's poorest to reach the average living standards that the region's richest countries enjoy today.

With respect to human development, which measures a broader variety of demographic, health, and education data, Southeast Asia can currently be divided into four groups based on the Human Development Index (HDI), provided by the United Nations Development Program (UNDP):

Singapore and Brunei: *High-income/high human development microstates*

Malaysia and Thailand: *Medium-income/medium-high human development countries*

Philippines, Indonesia, Vietnam: *Medium-low-income/medium human development countries*

Cambodia, Laos, Burma, Timor-Leste: *Low-income/low human development countries*

In total, the dynamic forces of the new international era have reinforced and expanded the tremendous economic diversity of Southeast Asia. Generalizing across the entire region about its progress in economic and human development is increasingly a challenge (and increasingly meaningless). In spite of efforts to integrate the region's disparate economies, through initiatives such as AFTA (ASEAN Free Trade Area) and the GMS (Greater Mekong Subregion), the development trajectories of Southeast Asian countries seem to grow more disparate with each passing year. A similar trend of divergent paths characterizes the political regimes of the region.

COMPARING POLITICAL REGIMES

Because of the great diversity among Southeast Asian states, as well as the many influences and changes they experience over time, categorizing Southeast Asian political regimes is difficult and must be complemented by analyzing the unique attributes of each country's experience. Why this is the case is demonstrated below.

If one is primarily interested in identifying the regime types of Southeast Asia's countries, a standard approach would be to utilize accepted definitions of regime classification and to analyze which countries fit those definitions. By employing Larry Diamond's sixfold typology and the widely used Freedom House ratings (*free, partly free,* and *not free*), such an analysis is possible and fairly straightforward.[6] Diamond's typology distinguishes two types of democratic regimes (*liberal* and *electoral*); three types of authoritarian regimes (*competitive, hegemonic electoral,* and *politically closed*); and *ambiguous regimes,* a residual category for systems too difficult to classify due to changing conditions or ongoing instability. With respect to countries that label their own systems "democratic," Diamond encourages the distinction between regimes in transition that aspire to achieve liberal democracy from those that are *pseudo-democracies*, that is, systems where elections exist but institutional arrangements are deliberately designed to inhibit party competition, pluralism, or civil liberties.

From the perspective of Diamond's typology, Thailand, the Philippines, and Indonesia all fall within the general category of democracy. Each of the three systems, however, is an *electoral democracy* and falls short of meeting the criteria to be identified as an established *liberal democracy* (where political and civil liberties exist and endure, and where changing sets of elected leaders are chosen and accountable to an electorate through "fair" elections that are repeatedly held).[7]

Indonesia, an *electoral democracy*, is the only Southeast Asian country rated "*free*" by Freedom House in 2008. However, it is still a young and untested democracy.[8] Indonesia's political system remains deficient in some aspects of electoral fairness and durability but, having shed thirty years of hegemonic rule by Suharto, the country appears to be on a more visible track to *liberal democracy* than perhaps either Thailand or the Philippines as of early 2009.

Only a few years ago Thailand had a pluralistic system that was approaching the definition of *liberal democracy*. In fact, Thailand was classified by Freedom House as "*free*" for seven consecutive years (between 1998 and 2005). Once a democratic beacon in the region, Thailand has since suffered from multiple electoral-driven political crises, a coup d'état, constitutional legitimacy challenges, and politicized judicial intervention into the political system. In flux from one year to the next, Thailand has seen its freedom ratings swing from "*free*" to "*partly free*" to "*not free*," and back to "*partly free*" from 2005 to 2008. Unresolved political crisis has thus pushed the country into the netherworld of regime classification. Thailand, which saw its first democratic constitution appear in 1932, currently lies somewhere between an unstable *electoral democracy* and an *ambiguous regime*.

The Philippines, not in political crisis but accurately classified as "*partly free*" by Freedom House in 2008, is also closer to an *electoral democracy* than a *liberal democracy*. This fact is discouraging given the public aspirations for liberal democratic rule and the country's long experience under democratic constitutions that dates to the 1940s. Democratic institutions in the Philippines are semi-dysfunctional in that they often serve as a veneer for oligarchic rule. Corruption, lawlessness, forms of intimidation, and violence permeate politics and competitive elections for public office. The Philippine's *electoral democracy* serves elite interests over those of the broader public.

Under Diamond's typology, Malaysia is best classified as a *competitive authoritarian regime*, one where a significant parliamentary opposition exists but a dominant party is also able to retain governmental power for decades at a time. The country is often cited as an example of an "illiberal democracy." Recent developments indicate that the authoritarian features of the country's system are weakening and party dominance is under stress. The Malaysian political regime, under the weight of more intense parliamentary contestation and changing public attitudes favorable to liberal democracy, may eventually move beyond its current regime label.

In contrast is Singapore, where the ruling People's Action Party (PAP) has perpetually inhibited the development of a significant parliamentary opposition by restricting oppositional speech, harassing government opponents, and manipulating a politicized judiciary. Singapore is a *pseudodemocracy* or, more precisely, a *hegemonic electoral authoritarian regime*. Somewhat similarly, the Cambodian People's Party (CPP), under the tight grip of strongman Hun Sen, has used extra-electoral mechanisms to intimidate opposition parties, politicians, and activists to ensure ongoing rule. Cambodia is also classified as a *hegemonic electoral authoritarian regime* under Diamond's typology.

Due to the lack of competitive elections and serious restrictions of political and civil liberties, Vietnam, Laos, and Burma share classification as *politically closed authoritarian regimes*. In none of these countries does political pluralism exist, nor do institutional arrangements aspire to expand representative institutions along liberal democratic lines. Tiny Brunei, an absolute monarchy, also meets the definition of a *politically closed authoritarian regime*.

Timor-Leste, an infant state ever dependent on international support and succor, is best classified as an *ambiguous regime*. While the practice of parliamentary politics evolves, the country's most pressing problems are political disorder and weak state capacity. Democracy enjoys general legitimacy among Timorese but electoral instability, political violence, and growing regionalism on the island undermine state development and the rule of law.

Regime classification, as illustrated above, is useful for general comparisons, but it does not adequately portray Southeast Asian nations over time. Without supplementary analysis, regime labels are simply insensitive to the particular political structures, events, and behaviors that animate the political life of particular countries. Political repression in Burma, Vietnam, Laos, and Brunei, for example, is characteristically different in each country, yet all are classified as *politically closed authoritarian regimes*. Similarly, the political experiences and trajectories of Singapore and Cambodia could not be farther from each other in almost every way, yet both share typological classification as *hegemonic electoral authoritarian regimes*. Indeed, the difference in country experiences among those that share a regime label can be greater than countries with different regime labels.

The difficulties and limitations in categorizing the Southeast Asian political systems emphasize the importance of viewing them as highly diverse and worthy of analysis from the vantage point of their unique attributes. Only more specific examination and comparative analysis can get observers beyond stereotypical images, highly generalized economic development classifications, or regime labels that often obfuscate more than clarify. Building an appreciation for the political-economic realities that characterize the experiences of Southeast Asian countries requires case-by-case examination. The country chapters of this book are designed with this objective in mind and thus offer an introductory first step to such an exploration. The chapters begin with Thailand since it is the principal country of study of both authors. Otherwise, the order of the following country chapters follows no particular sequence.

Notes

1. The phrase to describe Southeast Asia's transformation "from a battlefield to a marketplace" was famously coined by Thai Prime Minister Chatichai Choonhavan in 1988.

2. The conventional short forms of country names are generally used throughout this book. On June 18, 1989, Burma's military rulers announced that the country's official name (in English) would henceforth be Myanmar and that Rangoon's name had been changed to Yangon. Because these name changes have not been accepted internationally, and to reduce confusion when referring to the country and its principal city prior to the name change, this book uses the names Burma and Rangoon.

3. Because this book focuses on contemporary politics, it unfortunately devotes little attention to precolonial and colonial history. Readers will need to search elsewhere for a better understanding of historical trends and cultural foundations of the region and particular countries. A common place to begin such a study is with the classic text edited by David Joel Steinberg, *In Search of Southeast Asia* (Honolulu: University of Hawaii Press, 1987) and a more recently published book, *The Emergence of Modern Southeast Asia: A New History* (Honolulu: University of Hawaii Press, 2005), edited by Norman G. Owen.

4. Quoted by Kishore Mahbubani, a Singaporean scholar and diplomat, from T. R. Reid, *Confucius Lives Next Door: What Living in the East Teaches Us about Living in the West* (New York: Random House, 1999), p. 62.

5. See the tables at the end of this book titled "Southeast Asia: Select Indicators" for figures used in the following paragraphs and for additional information on comparing development across the region.

6. Larry Diamond is the founder and editor of the *Journal of Democracy* and is a noted regime classification expert. The typology here is taken from his article "Thinking about Hybrid Regimes," *Journal of Democracy*, vol. 13, no. 2 (2002), pp. 21–35. Freedom House bases its ratings on a system that assigns values to indicators of "political freedoms" and "civil liberties." Visit www.freedomhouse.org.

7. "Fair" elections are defined as being administered in a transparent manner by neutral authorities and characterized by ballot secrecy, the impartial treatment of candidates and parties, impartial procedures for resolving complaints and disputes, and minimal political violence.

8. See the tables at the end of this book titled "Southeast Asia: Select Indicators" for 2008 Freedom House ratings for all Southeast Asian countries.

2

THAILAND

*T*hailand has become an exemplary case study of how third-world countries can advance economically while attempting politically to achieve stable democracy. The consequences of episodic political instability in Thailand have not undermined the capacity of its people to generate improvements in quality of life and maintain relatively peaceful conditions. Compared with their regional neighbors, the Thais have escaped brutal occupation, destructive revolutions, tyrannical dictatorship, and the setbacks of protracted war. Since 1932, when their country was still named Siam and they first adopted constitutional monarchy, the principal project of the Thai people has been to develop a modern economy in tandem with a workable democracy.

Today, Thailand ranks among Southeast Asian's "tiger economies" and is considered a success story with wide global recognition. This developmental success stems from a history of astute adaptation of those aspects of modernization and development that were appropriate to traditional Thai ways, especially adaptations that ensured the maintenance of two key cultural institutions: Buddhism and monarchism. Throughout their history, as citizens of the only Southeast Asian nation never to have been colonized, the Thais never had a foreign culture forcibly thrust upon them. Instead, they have searched, adapted, and struggled to create their own path to economic and political development amidst the dynamic influences of a global society.

Thailand's progress toward political liberalization and democracy is all the more striking given that for centuries the government was autocratic in form and spirit. Power was the privilege of a small elite as well as of absolute monarchs who were not accountable to the people and whose authority was enhanced by an aura of divinity attached to the highest levels of office. Those who ruled were believed to possess superior ability and moral excellence. Common citizens exhibited little interest in affairs beyond their own villages. Vestiges of elite rule remain embedded in Thai political culture, but rising expectations and new norms of democratic practice reflect a deepening

preference for political participation, accountable government, and recognition of human rights.

The Sukhothai Kingdom (c. 1238–1350) was the first Thai-controlled kingdom in history. In this formerly Khmer-ruled area, the Thais absorbed the cultures of the Khmers, Mons, Hindus, and Chinese and began the assimilation process that is important even today for understanding modern Thai society. Buddhism and Brahmanism flourished among the Thais during the Sukhothai era. The Sukhothai Kingdom expanded and retracted, depending on the fortunes of military campaigns, until the Ayutthaya period (1350–1767) began.

The Thais adapted much from the Hindu-influenced Khmers, who dominated the region from the ninth through fourteenth centuries. In particular, Thai kings were transformed from paternalistic guardians into autocratic god-kings with the attributes of a Brahmanic deity. The perception of the kings as god-kings, or *deva-raja*, remains even today as an important element of the veneration shown the king by his subjects. Notwithstanding this aura of godliness, Thai kings did not enjoy absolute power but were limited by court factionalism, competition for power, and an assumption of kingly virtue.

During the Ayutthaya period, important institutions were established that still influence Thai society. A *sakdina* (power over fields) system was introduced that provided structure and hierarchy to the social and political relationships of the Thais. Virtually all persons in the kingdom were given *sakdina* rankings according to the amount of land (or number of people) they controlled. The ranking determined the salary of officials, the deference due them, and their labor obligations to the state. Although the quantifiable character of the *sakdina* system had ended by 1932, the informal hierarchical nature of the system has endured as an element of Thai society.

The destruction of Ayutthaya by invading Burmese in 1767 was a traumatic event in Thai history. The political-social system was torn asunder. Despite the near-total destruction of the kingdom, the Thais displayed remarkable recuperative powers and in a short time resumed life under a new centralized government in Bangkok led by the Chakri Dynasty. Many of the Chakri kings were reform-oriented—systematizing administrative structures, freeing the slaves, bringing in highly educated technocrats, and ensuring the continued independence of the nation from Western colonialists. The present King Bhumibol Adulyadej is the ninth king of this dynasty.

Even after the 1932 revolt, which overthrew the absolute monarchy and established a constitutional monarchy, politics remained in the hands of a small elite group, now mostly civilian bureaucrats and military generals. The military, which emerged as the country's dominant institution, has controlled political power in Thailand for about fifty of the past seventy-five years. Since the revolt against absolutism, politics in Thailand has been predominantly monopolized by military leaders and a small number of government officials, with little competition or balance from forces outside the bureaucratic arena. From 1932 to 1973, Thailand's political system was a classic bureaucratic polity. The basis of political power was highly personalized and subject to informal political manipulations and loyalties. It was also very unstable. A cycle of military control followed by weak parliamentary government, constitutional crisis, and coup d'état began to emerge to characterize Thai politics over time.[1]

Thailand entered the modern period at the end of World War II in considerably better shape than most of its Southeast Asian neighbors. Having acquiesced to Japanese occupation (and thereby having suffered little war damage) and not having fought a debilitating struggle for independence, Thailand was relatively secure and stable. Initially after the war, Thailand seemed headed toward a constitutional system of parliamentary democracy, but the army soon took power.

The most influential of the postwar leaders was Marshal Sarit Thanarat, army commander in chief, who became prime minister in 1957, declared martial law, and ruled dictatorially for six years. He was the first prime minister to make economic development the cornerstone of his rule. His successor, Marshal Thanom Kittikachorn, followed in Sarit's footsteps by keeping the military in firm control of every aspect of government and by pursuing economic development. During both administrations, the legislature was impotent, political parties were for the most part forbidden to form, and corruption was rampant. These leaders also cooperated with the United States during the Vietnam War, providing logistical support, Thai troops, naval bases, and airfields that were used throughout the Cold War campaign against communists in the region.

In response to the low level of political accountability and the high level of corruption, the "great tragedy" of October 14, 1973, occurred when the citizenry rose against the Thanom government. Upon his orders, the military massacred hundreds of unarmed protesters at Democracy Monument in Bangkok, a bloody event that resonates in Thai society to this day. Thanom and his ruling partners were subsequently forced into exile at the behest of King Bhumibol Adulyadej, Thailand's revered monarch. The king then followed their expulsion by appointing the first civilian government since the immediate postwar period. Thailand's next experience with democracy thus began as a result of courageous student protests with the king's support.

The 1973 revolt raised the expectations of many Thais that fundamental economic reforms would be carried out. The succeeding three-year period, however, coincided with a worldwide recession and with inflation that temporarily ended the country's improving economic growth. Hence, the hopes of many Thais that democracy would improve their lives were dashed by an economic situation over which the new government had little control. Aside from establishing a minimum wage and some new funds for rural development, little was accomplished during this period.

The civilian government was also faced with an international and regional situation over which it had little control. The change to communist governments in Vietnam, Laos, and Cambodia and the rise of insurgency throughout the Thai countryside shocked many Thais, who felt that only an authoritarian, military-dominated government could deal effectively with these threats. Because Thailand's traditional security ally, the United States, was withdrawing from Southeast Asia, the civilian government renewed ties with China in hopes of counterbalancing a rising Soviet-backed Vietnam. This destabilizing state of flux added to the uncertainty many Thais felt. Thai society was polarized between left and right, driven by the effects of Cold War politics in the region.

Democratic civilian rule lasted only until October 1976, when the military again overthrew the government, proclaimed martial law, and abrogated the constitution. Sparking the takeover was another massacre of students at Thammasat University in Bangkok, in which scores of unarmed students were brutally executed, a crackdown jointly conducted by military and right-wing paramilitary forces. Predictably, the new military leaders adopted a strong anticommunist agenda. Many of its targets were leftist students and the civilian politicians of the previous government. Fearful of the military, thousands fled into the countryside, joining peasant insurgents. The leftist coalition of intellectual urbanites and rural revolutionaries, however, never materialized into the massive insurgency capable of usurping state power, as similar coalitions had in neighboring countries. The ongoing presence of the covert Communist Party of Thailand (CPT) and its associated insurgency, however, allowed for successive Thai governments, generals, and bureaucrats to justify strict national security policies and harass opponents in the name of anticommunism—a practice that continued until the end of the Cold War and was attempted even beyond.

The military remained the dominant government institution until 1988. Under General Prem Tinsulanond's prime ministership, the country began to liberalize politically into a type of semidemocracy. Prem included civilian technocrats in his cabinet and relied on the freely elected legislature for support of his programs. Despite two coup attempts against him, he remained in power from 1980 until 1988, when he voluntarily stepped down.

Chatichai Choonhavan was the first elected member of Parliament (MP) to become prime minister since the 1973 to 1976 period. Chatichai assumed his new position following the 1988 elections, when his political party, Chart Thai (Thai Nation), received the largest plurality of votes and Prem refused to accept another term as prime minister. The smooth transition from Prem to Chatichai reflected the new optimism about Thailand's evolution toward democracy. Chatichai had assumed power without relying on the army's support. The constitutional provisions for elections worked well in the transfer of political power.

Chatichai had served as minister of foreign affairs, minister of industry, and deputy minister under previous administrations. Because his reputation was that of a big-business playboy, most analysts believed his tenure as prime minister would be short. However, Chatichai initiated a number of highly popular policies, thereby enhancing his *baramee* (charisma) in the minds of the populace. He raised the salaries of government officials as well as the minimum wage for laborers, banned the indiscriminate cutting of trees, and stood up to the United States on trade and other economic issues. The decision to ban logging was particularly dramatic because conventional wisdom suggested that neither the cabinet nor the Parliament would ever agree to ban an industry in which many of the political and military elites had major economic interests. The ban was a first step in repairing ecological damage, but illegal logging activity persists to the present day.

Chatichai's idea to transform Southeast Asia from a "battleground into a marketplace" was especially popular with the business community, which sought to open economic ties with the Vietnamese. His call for increased trade with Vietnam and his invitation to Cambodian Premier Hun Sen to visit Bangkok reversed Thai foreign policy, which had long opposed normalization with either Cambodia or Vietnam. Chatichai also moved to improve ties with Laos after decades of intermittent border skirmishes and diplomatic conflicts.

Chatichai's policies were supported by his coalition majority as well as by military leaders, at least initially. Nevertheless, the problems of patron-clientism and corruption continued to be important parts of the political process, and the phenomenal economic growth rates of the late 1980s, fueled by East Asian investors, had brought large amounts of capital into the Thai economy. These new resources became the targets of public officials who sought them for private gain.

Thai citizens became increasingly skeptical about Chatichai's professed concern for the majority, which had not gained from the economy's high growth rates. Many Thais viewed his cabinet as primarily concerned with big-business interests. On February 23, 1991, hopes that Thailand was beginning to institutionalize democratic-civilian processes were dashed when a military coup d'état ousted Chatichai's government and restored military power.

The military claimed its primary motivation for the coup was the pervasive corruption of the sitting politicians. Thai newspapers, unencumbered by censorship, had been reporting for months on the rampant corruption among top-level cabinet members. Huge telecommunications projects, massive road and elevated commuter railway ventures, cable television contracts, and new oil refineries became well-known examples of multibillion-dollar deals arranged and managed (or mismanaged) by Chatichai government ministers whose primary aim was to perpetuate their own power base and personal wealth. Coup leaders announced these politicians had become "unusually wealthy." Coup leaders also cited the rise of a "parliamentary dictatorship" as another reason for the takeover, complaining in particular about rampant vote buying. A more direct cause for the coup, however, was a pattern of slights carried out by Chatichai and perceived by military leaders as threats to their traditional prerogatives.

Immediately after seizing power, military leaders abrogated the constitution, dismissed the elected government, and set up the temporary National Peace Keeping Council (NPKC). The NPKC, led by Army Commander in Chief Suchinda Kraprayoon, gave itself the powers of martial law and became the arbiters of public policy.

Initially, the people greeted the coup with acquiescence, though not enthusiasm, and there were no public protests or demonstrations. The NPKC moved quickly to establish an interim constitution and to name Anand Panyarachun, a distinguished civilian, as prime minister. His appointment was a sign that the military believed the populace would not tolerate direct military rule for long. Anand's appointment was universally praised, reflecting his impeccable status and reputation as a diplomat, administrator, and businessman. In turn, Prime Minister Anand appointed an interim cabinet consisting of technocrats, notable scholars, and senior military officials in the defense and interior ministries. The coup leaders emphasized their commitment to policy continuity in economic matters. Political parties were retained, and a national legislative assembly was established to approve a new constitution and arrange for an election. For the overwhelming majority of Thais, the coup changed nothing except the names of the kingdom's top government leaders.

New parliamentary elections were scheduled for March 22, 1992. During the interim, the junta gave Anand wide leeway in running the government but also asserted its views forcefully regarding the promulgation of the new constitution. The final document returned Thailand's legislative body to its former system, in which the appointed upper house of Parliament was given equal power with the elected lower house in matters of policymaking.

Nevertheless, Anand's independence from the military was unprecedented for a civilian who had been placed in power by a military coup. He blocked the military's request to buy additional weaponry and passed 127 new laws (compared to 105 for the thirty months of the preceding Chatichai government). His administration set forth measures supporting privatization, trade liberalization, deregulation of the economy, a value-added tax, infrastructure projects, and constraints on labor unions.

For the March 1992 polls, military-backed parties, which were close to General Suchinda, formed a joint campaign scheme, minimizing competition in order to elect promilitary candidates. On the other side were parties opposed to continued military dominance in Thai politics. If elected, they pledged to amend the constitution so it reduced the role of the military and bureaucracy.

A chief leader of this latter group of parties was Bangkok Governor Chamlong Srimuang, who had given up his gubernatorial position to lead a new party, Palang Dharma (Moral Force). Chamlong, a former military officer, enjoyed an incorruptible reputation unique among the Thai political establishment. He campaigned wearing a farmer's shirt and cultivated an austere image as a faithful member of Santi Asoke, a new Buddhist sect that rejected superstitious practices and demanded a strict lifestyle of celibacy, vegetarianism, and material sacrifice.

The campaign for the March 1992 elections reflected many of the problems that have surrounded Thai elections to the present day: party hopping, vote buying, and effectively monitoring candidate behavior. Hedging their chances for a cabinet appointment or seat with the ruling coalition, individual politicians, or whole party factions, will often switch parties before Thai elections in the hopes of attaching themselves to a rising party or political figure. Many parties woo candidates with lavish money incentives and promises of leadership positions. Despite the establishment of watchdog committees to monitor campaigning, political parties and candidates also buy votes. The March 1992 election included poll-watch volunteers who monitored individual candidates' campaign expenses, which were limited to $40,000. To discourage vote buying, radio, television, newspapers, and banners featured slogans designed to discourage people from "selling their freedom." Unfortunately, the government's campaign also suggested to voters that they should not accept money from a candidate but that if they did, they should then vote for that candidate's opponent. This more cynical response resulted in voters sometimes accepting favors from many candidates. Although vote buying occurred throughout the kingdom, poll watchers found only a few cases of outright fraud, such as ballot-box stuffing.

The March 1992 elections resulted in a narrow victory for parties aligned with the NPKC. Ironically, the coalition government the election produced included many "unusually wealthy" politicians of the ousted Chatichai government. Embarrassingly, the first nominee for prime minister this coalition proposed had his name withdrawn after the U.S. State Department confirmed it had denied him a visa because of alleged drug trafficking in the politician's business base in northern Thailand, in the vicinity of the famed Golden Triangle opium-growing area near Laos and Burma. The promilitary parties then nominated coup leader General Suchinda, who had previously promised that he would never seek the prime ministership. In what many Thais referred to as "the second coup" or "the silent coup," General Suchinda accepted the nomination and, in the process, reversed the steps Thailand had taken toward democracy. To express dismay, some 50,000 protesters demonstrated against the new government following the announcement of Suchinda's appointment.

The anti-Suchinda demonstrations grew larger in the days that followed, bringing well over 100,000 Thais onto Bangkok streets in May 1992. Led by Chamlong and opposition leaders, the mobile-phone-carrying urbanites, members of the middle class, and white-collared professionals demanded Suchinda step down. Many began a hunger strike around Democracy Monument. Although the Cold War in Southeast Asia had ended years before, Suchinda anachronistically claimed that the demonstrators were pawns of communist elements that sought to end Thailand's constitutional monarchy. Tension built, and the size and intensity of the protests grew.

In an episode eerily reminiscent of 1973 and 1976, Thai soldiers filed into Bangkok upon Suchinda's orders and began indiscriminately shooting into the defenseless crowds. Suchinda's troops also took control of the country's media and communications networks, but demonstrators with cameras and handheld video equipment recorded the violence and broadcast the images outside of Bangkok via fax machines and videotape. The unprecedented and effective method undermined the military's standard practice of propagandizing coup events to manipulate Thai and global opinion. Although the full count is not known, hundreds of people died from soldier-fired weapons in the crackdown of "Black May 1992," a tragic product of Suchinda's hubris and miscalculations.

The public's reaction to the massacre was one of overwhelming sadness and anger. Suchinda had not recognized that public expectations of civilian rule and participatory democracy had become the new norm. Many Thais were profoundly embarrassed by the violent turn of events. In the new international era when many countries were moving inexorably toward more open and liberal regimes, Suchinda had taken Thailand in the other direction by precipitating another military coup, manipulating post-coup elections to stay in power, and authorizing a Tiananmen-style crackdown on prodemocracy protesters.

After the violence, Prime Minister Suchinda was subsequently driven from office, his legacy a disastrous forty-eight-day reign. His welcome removal came after a globally televised rebuke by King Bhumibol, who made both Suchinda and Chamlong kneel before him on his throne. Suchinda was reprimanded for bringing death and shame to the country. Chamlong was scolded for forcing headstrong protests that put civilians at risk. The king succeeded in ending the crisis by dismissing Suchinda, agreeing to amnesty for all persons involved in the demonstrations, and supporting constitutional amendments designed to reduce the military's dominance in politics. As in 1973, the king's intervention during a political crisis was praised by an adoring public as timely, consequential, and historic.

In a second extraordinary royal intervention related to the May 1992 crisis, the king approved the return of Anand Panyarachun as prime minister. The king's decision occurred just before the Parliament overwhelmingly passed constitutional amendments requiring prime ministers to be elected members of Parliament and reducing the role of the military-dominated Senate. Anand's appointment was met enthusiastically by most Thais, who recalled the international praise he earned for running an honest and efficient government during the previous interim period.

Anand once again acted with admirable decisiveness as an interim leader. With the king's appointment legitimizing his authority, he demoted top military leaders responsible for the violence, removed important state enterprises from military control, and scheduled a new round of parliamentary elections, announcing he would remain in office for only four months, a promise he kept.

The September 1992 elections featured 2,417 contenders from sixteen parties contesting 360 parliamentary seats. Few of the candidates were newcomers, although many jumped parties. Some parties changed their names and distanced themselves from the tainted, "devil" parties affiliated with the military. The prodemocracy "angel" parties won the poll and formed a government under the leadership of a civilian politician as leader of the country. Chuan Leekpai, the soft-spoken, moderate leader of the Democrat Party from Trang Province in the south, assumed the position of prime minister. From his offices in Government House, the country's executive center, he led a 207-seat coalition in the 360-member House of Representatives.

Chuan's immediate challenge was to find a balance between democratic rule and sensitivity to the traditional prerogatives of the military. He also faced the challenge of keeping together his fragile administration, which included leaders of the coalition parties who themselves coveted the prime ministership. Opposition leaders pointed to Chuan's lack of charisma and leadership and his lack of policy initiatives and new programs.

Part of the difficulty for Chuan was that many of the problems his administration needed to solve were intractable. Even with a cabinet considered to be one of the brightest in Thai history, the first six months of Chuan's tenure generated few proposals for solving the problems of traffic congestion, pollution, environmental degradation, child labor, HIV/AIDS, centralized decisionmaking, water shortages, and ubiquitous corruption.

Despite these difficulties, Chuan attempted to democratize a corrupt, military-dominated political system. He led the country from September 1992 to May 1995, a long period of civilian control by Thai standards of political time. His parliamentary coalition fell apart due to a land reform scandal in the South (a Democratic stronghold) and conflicting demands among the ruling coalition of political parties. New elections were called.

In the July 1995 election, some twelve political parties and 2,300 candidates vied for the 391 House seats. About 40 million people voted. Predictably, campaign issues were vague because political parties in Thailand generally do not offer platforms or represent particular ideologies. Party hopping ensued with competitive candidates being offered up to 5 million baht ($200,000 in 1995) to switch parties. Voters were offered 100 to 300 baht ($4 to $12) if they promised to vote for a particular candidate.

The major personality in the campaign was Banharn Silapa-archa, leader of the Chart Thai party. Party members noted Banharn's vast experience: He was a billionaire business executive with six terms in Parliament and former minister of agriculture, industry, interior, finance, and transportation. Because he represented a rural constituency, he was viewed as someone who understood the average Thai. Banharn's campaign opponents charged that he was thoroughly corrupt, citing his nickname, "*khun ae thi am*" (Mr. ATM), for his impressive reputation for managing huge networks of patronage. Banharn was scorned by Bangkok voters and intellectual elites who viewed him as a country bumpkin.

Nevertheless, the elections resulted in a triumph for Banharn's Chart Thai party, which captured ninety-two seats. Banharn moved to mobilize a coalition of parties, while Chuan, whose Democrat Party won eighty-six seats, became the leader of the opposition. Banharn allocated ministerial portfolios to pro-military politicians as rewards for loyal service rather than on the basis of expertise. The new cabinet was highly factionalized and received negative assessments from Bangkok's outspoken press, mainly because old-style politicians dominated the cabinet rather than new-style technocrats.

Banharn's administration turned out to be a disaster characterized by corruption, a lack of direction, personal dishonesty (Banharn was discovered to have plagiarized his law thesis), and economic malaise. Though he was forced to call new elections in November 1996, little changed as a result. Rather than Banharn and the Chart Thai party, retired general Chavalit Yongchaiyudh, leader of the New Aspiration Party, won control, after benefiting from many members of Parliament who had defected from Chart Thai's waning star. Like Banharn, Chavalit was unpopular among Bangkok's elites and the leading newspapers, although he had achieved popularity in rural areas for his support of developmental projects, especially in the country's northeast provinces, or Isan region. Even so, his tenure would also be short-lived.

As prime minister, Chavalit faced two tremendous challenges: the passage of a new constitution, from a process that began prior to his tenure, and the 1997 Asian economic crisis, which began in Thailand during his watch. A major political crisis was averted when the Parliament overwhelmingly passed a new constitution on September 27, 1997. This approval represented the culmination of a long but inclusive process that had brought many segments of society into drafting the constitution. Many considered it to be the most democratic constitution in Thai history, the "People's Constitution." Chavalit's support for its passage added legitimacy to his leadership and bought him some time amidst otherwise crisis conditions owing to the collapse of the Thai baht in June 1997. As a result of the crisis, rising unemployment, inflation, IMF conditionality, and a failed financial sector, Chavalit's status became increasingly tenuous. Large demonstrations opposing his leadership began.

The protests centered on Chavalit's inability to resolve the economic crisis. Under his watch the baht had lost half its value against the dollar, the stock market had fallen precipitously, and the IMF had been forced to bail out the country with a loan of some $17 billion. Most Thais blamed the political system for the economic crisis, believing that politicians were more concerned about perpetuating their own power and profiting business associates than the public good. It was thus no surprise when the embattled Chavalit announced his resignation as prime minister, an office he had held for just eleven months. The mass protest that forced his resignation was indicative of the extra-parliamentary change agents of Thai politics: antigovernment demonstrations, coup d'état, royal intervention, or some combination of these three methods.

Because Chavalit's resignation came at precisely the time the Thai Parliament was acting on provisions to launch the new constitution, the country faced the prospect of an interim prime minister until elections could be called in 1998. Old names surfaced as options, including the king's trusted men Prem Tinsulanond and Anand Panyarachun, as well as Chuan Leekpai, the leader of the opposition Democrat Party. Chuan managed to forge a coalition majority and took over the top position for a second term. He instituted reform measures and mandated transparency and accountability, but the crisis continued to hurt the bulk of the population financially.

A new election in 2001 led to the rise of Dr. Thaksin Shinawatra, a telecommunications mogul and founder of the Thai Rak Thai (Thais Love Thais) political party. A former minister and estranged ally of Chamlong Srimuang, Thaksin was among Thailand's richest businessmen, having made his fortune selling computers to Thai government agencies and creating extensive holdings in the communications sector with mobile phones, pagers, broadcast television, and satellite communications. In a few short years, Thaksin's business empire spanned most of Southeast Asia's rapidly growing markets and his name appeared on *Fortune*'s list of the world's richest people. However, Thaksin was not a member of the traditional Bangkok bureaucratic or intellectual elite. His early career was in criminal justice, a field that had brought him to the United States for master's and doctoral degrees and then back to Thailand, where he worked in the Metropolitan Police Department. Of Sino-Thai origin and a proud son of silk traders in provincial Chiang Mai, Thaksin was ranked among the country's unrefined nouveaux riches in the eyes of Bangkok's urbane aristocrats.

Thaksin's business savvy and meteoric success, combined with his former political associations with Chamlong's Moral Force Party, seemed to combine the two qualities many common Thai voters believed were needed in an emancipator to free them from the economic crisis and dreaded IMF: competence and trust. What voters did not fully appreciate at the time was Thaksin's unmatchable political acumen and limitless political ambition. Indeed, his political genius enabled him to methodically create an unprecedented party machine with die-hard loyalists. The powerful Thai Rak Thai (TRT) proved so volatile that it ultimately led to another military coup, Thaksin's forced exile, and an intractable political crisis that continues indefinitely.

Thaksin's TRT election victory in 2001 came principally from public dissatisfaction with the slow pace and uneven distribution of Thailand's economic recovery. Chuan Leekpai's Democrats had held power for much of the 1990s, and Thais criticized their recovery policies for catering to international investors first. Many Thais believed it was time for a change. Thaksin, adopting a populist platform, promised to solve the economic problems, provide funds to villages, and grant debt relief for farmers. Critical of the Democrats' embrace of the IMF and the market fundamentalism of the Washington Consensus, Thaksin offered a more Keynesian approach, where the government would stimulate the economy with its own spending programs.

Where most new Thai parties eschewed specific policy platforms, centering instead on individual politicians or single-issue concerns such as clean government or national security, Thaksin embraced a multi-issue party platform. The TRT seemed to offer something for everybody. Although still orbiting around its leader as do all Thai parties built around patronage, the TRT brought into politics new faces from the ranks of the nouveaux riches and academia. Because the new constitution mandated that some seats in the Parliament be filled through a party list ballot, TRT was able to pull in many new loyalists. The Thais Love Thais party aggressively wooed established party bosses, provincial politicians, and members of erstwhile party factions who, after the failures of Banharn and Chavalit, sought to attach themselves to Thailand's newest rising star. Even many in the ever-expanding NGO community caught Thaksin's attention. He promised to support rural development and pledged to maintain a ban on the commercial use of genetically modified agricultural products.

The TRT thus built itself as a broad coalition tied to a broad array of promises. It projected an image of self-confidence, deliberateness, and dynamism. It projected an image of a "new Thailand," a party suited to lead the country in the emerging international era of economic dangers. At its ideological core, however, Thaksin's TRT was a walking paradox: It was fiercely nationalist, but not isolationist; it was populist but also favored the business elite; it was hedged with military allies, but it was not promilitary. The TRT was a classic patronage-based party network, but it offered a fresh message unwedded to staid notions of bureaucratism, moderation, or "Thai-ness."

Thaksin almost lost his seat shortly after taking it. In April 2001, a constitutional court opened a corruption case against Thaksin, whom the constitutionally mandated National Counter Corruption Commission alleged had hidden assets while serving as a cabinet member in 1997. He was accused of transferring shares worth billions of baht to his family, servants, and close friends. Thaksin claimed he had no knowledge of the transfer of assets. If the court had found him guilty, Thaksin would have been barred from holding office for five years and required to step down as prime minister. In its ruling, Thailand's highest court acquitted Thaksin on an eight-to-seven vote. Public opinion had favored his remaining as prime minister, so the decision was popular with the general public. This incident would not be the last time Thaksin and TRT leaders would force high drama involving the Thai judicial system.

Thaksin went on to become the longest serving civilian prime minister in Thai parliamentary history. Playing in his favor was the reformed 1997 constitution, which was purposefully designed to inhibit party hopping, foster more stable party competition, and strengthen prime ministerial authority—all in the hopes of ending the revolving doors of leadership that plagued the Parliament and Government House.

As prime minister, he won unprecedented support from upcountry provinces with his policies. His popular programs provided inexpensive medical care, gave loans and grants to villages, canceled and postponed debts owed by farmers, and established an asset-management agency to reduce corporate debt. He also developed programs to support small and medium enterprises (SMEs) and he encouraged every district in the country to develop at least one exportable product or handicraft. In the world of agriculture, he championed a policy to turn Thailand into "the kitchen of the world" by funding research and development in agricultural biotechnology and flirting with lifting the ban on genetically engineered crops.

Using weekly radio addresses and ensuring favorable media coverage, Thaksin worked relentlessly to propagandize the TRT's efforts to the public. By the end of his four-year term, Thaksin could boast of having engineered Thailand's economic recovery, reviving exports, and completing loan payments to the IMF ahead of schedule. Nevertheless, TRT's massive government spending drove concerns about the sustainability of so-called Thaksinomics. Many feared Thaksin's spending strategy was hollow and lacked investment potential, portending a false recovery. Public cynicism grew, especially in Bangkok.

Observers also took note that Thaksin's business networks were benefiting from the village loans and redistributionist schemes in rural areas. Unprecedented sales of pickup trucks, motorcycles, and mobile phones were accompanied by allegations of ties to TRT corruption and local-level scheming.

Programs such as the "million cows project," designed to give "one farmer, one cow," were disparaged by opposition politicians as mere vote-buying schemes veiled as antipoverty programs. Heavy criticism also came from human rights groups and the international community for Thaksin's brutal 2003 antidrug war, which included hundreds of extrajudicial killings. From the military's perspective, Thaksin also proved unable to keep his promise to end the ongoing separatist insurgency in Thailand's Muslim south, bordering Malaysia.

Having been sidelined and disturbed by TRT policies, middle-class urbanites, Bangkok's elites, human rights groups, academics, and bureaucrats formed a voracious oppositional bloc and began to demand Thaksin's removal. Thaksin responded to criticism by trying to muzzle the free media, further angering his accusers, who then charged him with dismantling democracy. In fact, some of Thaksin's most vocal critics were disillusioned TRT supporters who had turned on the party and its populist direction. Thaksin had become Thailand's most polarizing figure in decades.

In spite of mounting pressures, Thaksin Shinawatra was able to stay in power until his government's four-year term expired. With the economy back on track and rural constituents satisfied, TRT found itself in solid command for the scheduled 2005 general election. The small chance opposition Democrats had to unseat TRT and the Chart Thai party became even smaller after the 2004 Indian Ocean tsunami hit southern Thailand weeks before the election. Thaksin's actions during the disaster won him praise from both Thais and members of the international community. Even Democrat leaders conceded that Thailand's victims could thank Thaksin for his deft handling of the crisis.

In the February 2005 general election, TRT won big—bigger than any party in the history of Thai democracy, securing 375 of 500 seats. The opposition Democrats won only 96 of the 125 remaining seats, Chart Thai won just 27, and 2 went to a minor party. The TRT thus secured an unprecedented majority in the Parliament. Standard allegations of vote buying were drowned out by the obvious support rural voters expressed for TRT policies. Thaksin's party support and political machine appeared invincible. Bangkok's city voters could not foresee an election scenario in which Thaksin and the TRT would lose power.

Anti-Thaksin demonstrations began in Bangkok streets in late 2005, centering on allegations of official corruption. A few months later, in a gift to Thaksin's critics, a major scandal broke, with Thaksin unambiguously caught in the middle. Having used laws crafted by his own government, Thaksin benefited from a transaction where his family sold its $1.9 billion Shinawatra communications empire to a Singapore entity, tax-free. The news was more than his critics could bear. Street demonstrations mounted with slogans that Thaksin had not only benefited from the sale, but that his family had put the nation at risk with foreign control of Thailand's vast communications network. Thaksin, facing serious pressure, dissolved Parliament and called a snap election in an attempt to reestablish his legitimacy. Knowing that without upcountry support they would lose the election, Democrats and other opposition parties boycotted the election, publicly citing TRT vote-buying strategies and alleging that Thaksin held dictatorial ambitions.

Predictably, TRT won the April 2006 polls but was unable to establish a functioning Parliament due to the boycott and cries of illegitimate results. A deadlock ensued. With demonstrations for his ouster expanding, and a court ruling annulling election results, Thaksin was forced to take audience with King Bhumibol. Visibly shaken from the event, Thaksin agreed to step down. He arranged, however, to continue on as a caretaker prime minister, at least until new polls could be held. To his critics it was a false resignation; to his supporters it was a shrewd political victory.

His dissenters, organized under the People's Alliance for Democracy, or PAD, became enraged when they realized Thaksin would still run the country as a caretaker prime minister. Earlier contempt for Thaksin transformed into sheer hatred. Standing at the head of the anti-Thaksin movement were PAD leaders Sondhi Limthongkul, a media mogul himself, and Chamlong Srimuang, the resurrected leader of "angel" forces of Black May 1992 and founder of the defunct Moral Force Party, of which Thaksin was once a part.

Added to the growing list of Thaksin's alleged sins was the most serious accusation of them all—that Thaksin sought to eclipse the cultural charisma (*baramee*) of the king himself and even coveted republicanism. For evidence, the PAD pointed to Thaksin's increasing ceremonial activities that depicted him as a head of state rather than head of government. Rumors of the royal family's disdain for the prime minister circulated. The royal-yellow shirts regularly donned by the PAD faithful took on heightened symbolism; no longer did wearing yellow simply celebrate monarchy, as it had previously, it now implied support for its protection.

Thaksin had tried earlier during his tenure to form alliances within the royal camp but his meddling was viewed as calculating and disingenuous. King Bhumibol's most trusted adviser, Privy Councilor Prem Tinsulanond, emanated contempt for Thaksin.[2] The charge of republican ambition was political dynamite, upping the stakes of politics to a new level. Chatichai's "unusually rich" cabinet, Banharn's faked law degree, and Chuan's land reform scandal appeared as minor scandals in hindsight.

Thaksin's greatest ally amidst the rising controversy was the democratic principle of majority rule. In 2001 and 2005 Thai voters had overwhelmingly supported him, a point he cited often. Indeed, TRT enjoyed undying support in upcountry voting districts. The decision of opposition parties to boycott the April 2006 snap election was proof that Thaksin's opponents also recognized this fact. They knew that for all their charges labeling rural voters as un-educated, stupid, and foolish, little could be done to change electoral realities. They calculated that Thaksin's grip on power would hold as long as majori-tarian elections were in the picture.

The military denied coup rumors, but with another election pending in late 2006, and yet another TRT victory virtually assured, military coup d'état did indeed return to Thailand in the early morning hours of September 19, 2006. The event was quick, bloodless, and thoroughly welcomed by the anti-Thaksin minority in the country who had given up on constitutional means to remove the popular leader. King Bhumibol offered no disapproval of the junta leaders' actions. While seizing power, the military muzzled the media and streamed images of the monarch on television throughout the day of the takeover. Thaksin, in New York to deliver a speech at the United Nations, never returned to Thailand. TRT ministers inside the country were ordered to report to the junta leaders for temporary detainment.

The country was put under martial law for months. No groups of more than five people, including political parties, were allowed to gather and dis-cuss politics. Media restrictions were put in place. Armed troops were sent to Thaksin's home province of Chiang Mai as well as others, inhibiting any op-portunity for backlash by pro-Thaksin forces. The reasons cited for the coup included corruption, the need to restore political order, and Thaksin's failed se-curity policies over the country's restive south. The coup group announced it-self as the Council for Democratic Reform under the Constitutional Monarchy, shortened later to the Council on National Security, or CNS.

Though it was never revealed officially, Thailand's public and outside ob-servers knew the hands of Prem Tinsulanond had engineered the coup. As a longtime privy councilor, he emanated royal authority more than any other figure. The coup leaders garnered legitimacy shortly after events in personal visits to Prem's Bangkok home. Broadcasted images of top brass shaking hands with the smiling Prem on his home driveway delivered the desired message: The events had full royal sanction.

An appointed government was soon authorized. Its legitimacy rested on royal approval, Prem's backing, and support from the country's Bangkok-based, anti-Thaksin political minority. The majority voters who backed Thaksin privately expressed muted anger and disillusionment with Thai pol-itics. Martial law prevented organized dissent. Political scientists inside and outside the country shook their heads in dismay: "What had seemed like a firm march toward democratic consolidation from May 1992 onward had suddenly fizzled and relapsed into military-authoritarian rule."[3]

In the fifteen months of military rule between September 2006 and De-cember 2007, new initiatives enacted by coup leaders attempted to roll back Thaksinomics and set Thailand on a course of political reform. Nevertheless, the CNS (paradoxically) teamed new fiscal austerity policies with its own quasipopulist policies that attempted to win affection from provincial Thais and even outdo Thaksin himself. It announced totally free health care and offered extended village loan schemes. Then, in a move alarming to international investors, the CNS announced all government decisions, including those from economic ministries, would be based on the principles of Sufficiency Economy, the royal-inspired economic theory advocating Buddhist moderation, reduced consumption, and small-scale family farming. It was a clear signal away from Thaksin's pro-growth policies.

In its most substantial act, the junta abrogated the 1997 "People's Constitution," viewed as culpable in fostering Thaksin's rise. A new one was hastily drafted later by a select group of appointees and put up for approval by national referendum in 2007. The coup-crafted constitution barely passed by a weak 58 percent of the national vote; a majority of voters in the pro-Thaksin Isan voted against it.

Ironically, new elections in December 2007 proved that the coup had resolved nothing from the perspective of anti-Thaksin forces. Thaksin may have been in exile but his party lived on, and so did its majority support from Thai voters. Even a ruling by a constitutional court that forcibly dissolved Thai Rak Thai for past election violations could not prevent it from forming under a different name: the People's Power Party (PPP).

The PPP won the December 2007 general election and, in coalition with like-minded parties, formed a new government under Samak Sundaravej. Samak, seventy-two years old and flirting with political retirement, was a surprising choice. He was a veteran politician with an independent, tough-guy (nakleng) image long tainted by allegations of involvement in the 1976 Thammasat University massacre. During the Thaksin years, Thais viewed him as a loudmouthed TV gadfly, known for hosting a popular cooking show called Tasting and Complaining (chim pai, bon pai). With his appointment, however, the independent Samak appeared to have sold out to serve as Thaksin's puppet. After the coup, Thaksin took up residence in the U.K. and purchased the Manchester City Premier League football team.

By May 2008 Sondhi and Chamlong's PAD forces were back on the streets demanding Samak's resignation and the dissolution of Parliament. Yellow-clad protesters grew by the thousands when Samak sought to undo provisions coup leaders had put into the 2007 constitution. The PAD then introduced its proposal for New Politics, which called for reform of the country's Parliament to become 70 percent appointed and only 30 percent elected. The proposal also encouraged the full embrace of Sufficiency Economy and New Theory Agriculture—the royally conceived antipoverty strategy that recommended self-sustaining family farming and the avoidance of all debt, including investment debt for cropping. The New Politics proposal, which sought nothing less than the overthrow of majoritarian democracy, was considered a slap in the face to upcountry voters who would find themselves disenfranchised under the plan.

By August PAD protesters seized Government House, resulting in the brief arrest of its leaders. Demonstrations continued for weeks on end. The People's Alliance for Democracy disrupted parliamentary business, clogged Bangkok streets, and created a tense atmosphere in the city. Samak refused to resign but chose not to remove the protesters by force, claiming prudence and restraint. Coup rumors swirled. Just as events began to crescendo, a court ruling forced Samak to step down from his post. The charge: paid appearances on a TV cooking show while serving as prime minister.

Samak's departure resolved little. And to the astonishment of the anti-Thaksin movement, the PPP rallied around a new choice for prime minister: Somchai Wongsawat, Thaksin's brother-in-law. The audacious move by the PPP infuriated PAD supporters. It also proved to be a miscalculation on the part of the PPP. Somchai was unskilled and weak as PPP's leader. Among other failures, he bungled a tense standoff with Cambodia over a long-disputed Angkor-era temple near the Thai-Cambodian border. Politicizing the dispute as if Thailand's deepest national interests were at stake, Somchai's government, as well as the PAD, used the affair to attempt to make political hay.

The PAD, relentless in its efforts to force TRT remnants out of power, then acted by occupying the Parliament itself, trapping elected officials inside. Prime Minister Somchai was forced to jump over the back fence of the assembly compound to escape the siege. The PAD's risky actions pushed Somchai to the edge. He dispatched police, who then engaged protesters in a serious clash that led to the death of one female protester. Sensitive to crackdowns in 1973, 1976, and 1992, a Thai public nervous about government-ordered bloodshed viewed Somchai's use of force unfavorably. Queen Sirikit later attended the protester's funeral, an act that emboldened the PAD faithful.

By late 2008, PAD announced its "final battle" to remove the pro-Thaksin PPP government from power. By the thousands, "Yellow Army" protesters moved first to occupy a government-run television station and then both of Bangkok's airports, including Thailand's new Suvarnabhumi International Airport, a Thaksin project showcase. The PAD's foolhardy seizure became front-page news in Asia, Europe, and North America. Thailand's main artery of transportation with the world was shut off. Thousands of business travelers, tourists, Haj pilgrims, and others found themselves unable to get in or out of Bangkok because of the seizures. Airport authorities scrambled to accommodate the trapped travelers, sending some to a military transport center on the eastern seaboard. Days passed without any serious attempt to remove the protesters. Surreal images were broadcast globally of color-clad PAD protesters setting up food stalls, playing badminton, and waving plastic-hand clappers at speech rallies inside the Suvarnabhumi's space-age stainless steel terminal.

Prime Minister Somchai, forced to govern from Chiang Mai, refused to step down and issued calls for the PAD to withdraw before force would be employed. Subsequent orders for the police and military to remove the protesters were largely ignored. Thailand's crisis reached an impasse. Pro-Thaksin, red-shirt supporters of the sitting government, the United Front of Democracy against Dictatorship (UDD), began to stage counter-rallies around the city. Fears of confrontation grew. Expectations of a military coup to end the standoff rose with each passing day.

The siege finally ended in its eighth day, just prior to annual birthday celebrations for the monarch. As with Samak's expulsion, it was the courts that proved consequential. In an expedited case, a constitutional court ruled that the People's Power Party had violated election law during the 2007 elections, and the party was ordered dissolved. Dissolution meant Somchai was disqualified for office and had to begin a five-year ban from politics. The surviving PPP members reorganized themselves into yet a third incarnation of Thaksin's TRT, the Phuea Phandin party, but were unable to form a coalition government.

After the "final battle" of airport seizures, Sondhi and Chamlong declared victory and PAD protesters returned home. It was the end of what was essentially a three-year protest, begun by an unsuccessful effort to force Thaksin's resignation in September 2005. Since that time and in the name of "democracy," the anti-Thaksin movement (ignominiously) encouraged the boycott of a democratic election; a military coup d'état; the sacking of the 1997 "People's Constitution"; a proposal to disenfranchise the majority of the electorate; the unlawful seizure of Government House, Parliament, and the country's airports; and the politicization of Thai courts to force dissolution of the country's largest political party (twice) and the removal of three prime ministers who enjoyed the confidence of elected parliamentary majorities.

The intensity of the events left many members of Parliament weary. Party defections began spurring talks of a new government coalition led by Democrat leader Abhisit Vejjajiva, an Oxford-educated forty-four-year-old and protégé of Democrat veteran Chuan Leekpai. On December 15, 2008, Abhisit won enough votes in Parliament to become Thailand's new prime minister. Ironically, the possibility of a Democrat-led coalition surfaced only when a major faction of the twice-dissolved TRT-PPP opted to switch sides, denying the opportunity for the newly formed Phuea Phandin party to form a successor government. Some called the Democrats' capture of power a "silent coup." The pro-Thaksin UDD began to organize with the goal to remove Abhisit's government from office.

Red-shirted UDD demonstrators from upcountry provinces and Bangkok's urban poor launched protests in the capital that lasted over three months, largely at Thaksin's urging from abroad. His visa revoked by the United Kingdom months earlier, Thaksin now operated from countries that lacked extradition treaties with Thailand. In series of dramatic events the UDD protestors successfully disrupted the ASEAN summit hosted by the Thai government in the resort town of Pattaya. The UDD's actions forced Prime Minister Abhisit to embarrassingly request his fellow Asian leaders to return home. Crestfallen, Abhisit then declared a state of emergency and ordered the military to disperse the protestors who had grown in number to over 100,000. After a handful of deaths on both sides, the UDD's leaders called off the protests but pledged to continue their fight to restore Thaksin to power.

INSTITUTIONS AND SOCIAL GROUPS

Monarchy

Theoretically and legally above politics, the Thai monarch is the national symbol, the supreme patron who reigns over all, and the leader of the Buddhist religion. The monarchy's prestige and veneration have grown since the coronation of King Bhumibol Adulyadej, who is the kingdom's longest-reigning monarch and the world's longest-reigning contemporary monarch. In 2006 the Thai people celebrated King Bhumibol's sixtieth year on the throne. A year later they celebrated his eightieth birthday.

During the early decades of his reign, the king cultivated a role as a patron of rural development. He intervened publicly in politics on rare occasions, including in 1973. In the 1980s he supported the government of Prime Minister Prem Tinsulanond during two military attempts to overthrow Prem's administration. The king's strong resistance to these coups added to his public prestige and influence. He chose not to intervene in 1991 when a coup to oust Chatichai was successfully executed.

One of the king's most important interventions occurred during the May 1992 crisis when prodemocracy demonstrators called on General Suchinda to step down as prime minister. The military's violent response brought the country to the brink of civil war. King Bhumibol admonished the nation's leaders to settle the conflict peacefully, and he demanded the resignation of Suchinda and approved the return of Anand Panyarachun to be interim leader until elections could take place. In 2006 the king intervened again, this time admonishing Thaksin Shinawatra to step down as premier. Thaksin formally resigned but retained powers as a caretaker prime minister. Six months later, Thaksin was left in foreign exile as a result of the September 19, 2006, coup. The coup was viewed with approval by the king's most trusted privy councilor, Prem Tinsulanond.

Long-standing lèse-majesté laws shield the king and royal family from public criticism. On occasion Thai intellectuals (and in-residence foreigners) writing critically about the king or royal family members have faced charges and detention for offending the dignity of monarch. However, discretion, self-censorship, and self-imposed exile make these court cases fairly rare. Squaring the practice of lèse-majesté with liberal notions of free speech remains a sensitive subject in Thailand. Many Thais see no contradiction; others favor the stability it generates over democratic values. A London-style royal paparazzi media does not exist in Thailand.

The Thais' universal veneration for their monarch has raised concerns about a potential succession crisis. The king elevated his daughter, Princess Sirindhorn, to the rank of *Maha Chakri* (crown princess), thereby placing her in the line of succession along with her brother, Crown Prince Vachiralongkorn. The crown prince has often been criticized in Thailand's rumor mill for his lack of commitment and discipline, whereas the princess has been universally admired for her dedication. However, the crown prince has become involved in ceremonial duties and is being trained to succeed his father. Because the king is such a crucial cultural symbol, a contentious succession could undo the monarchy's stability by unleashing forces now held in check by the king's presence.

Constitutions

Thailand suffers from endless constitutional change and claims of constitutional illegitimacy. Nothing at the present time indicates its troubled history with constitutional change will resolve itself soon. Almost all of the major incidents in modern Thai political history (i.e., political crises, coups, mass protests) have included some dimension of constitutional crisis to them. While there is a value placed on the rule of law concept, enduring agreement on basic law has yet to be realized. Moreover, the impulse to resort to extraconstitutional means to resolve political crises (namely, military coup and royal intervention) undermines the consolidation of democratic constitutionalism and the rule of law in Thailand.

The Thai propensity for changing constitutions has been referred to as *faction constitutionalism*, whereby each successive draft reflects, legitimates, and strengthens major shifts in factional dominance. Thai constitutions have not been considered the fundamental laws of the land; rather, they have functioned to facilitate the rule of the regime in power. Since 1932, Thailand has been governed under seventeen constitutions, of which less than half were democratic and based on the parliamentary model with the executive accountable to a national assembly. Other constitutions did not require the prime minister to be selected from members of Parliament or did not have any elected Parliament or allowance for political parties.

Led by twice–interim prime minister Anand Panyarachun in 1996–1997, a "People's Committee" that included experts, academics, and members of civil society, drafted the 1997 constitution that was perceived to be the most legitimate, inclusive, and potentially sustainable democratic constitution ever promulgated in Thailand's long constitutional history. The drafting process was transparent and included input from the public. It was designed to reduce corruption, enhance human rights, decentralize the political system, make the Senate accountable (through direct elections), separate the executive from the legislative branch (by requiring ministers to resign from the Parliament), provide the judiciary with more authority, and strengthen larger political parties and discourage weaker ones. Under its provisions, one hundred members of the five hundred–seat Parliament were elected by a national vote from a list of party-nominated candidates, whereas the other four hundred members were elected by single-member constituencies.

Thaksin's TRT benefited from the 1997 "People's Constitution," which favored larger parties and stronger central authority. As one of its first acts, the 2006 coup group abrogated the constitution after stripping Thaksin of power. The 2007 constitution later drafted by the CNS returned Thailand to a half-appointed Senate, strengthened bureaucratic commissions, and empowered the judiciary over elected officials. When the constitution was subjected to a national referendum, less than 60 percent voted in favor of it. Prime Minister Samak's attempt in 2008 to reverse some of its provisions, sparking protests, was a predictable event.

Future political crises in Thailand will likely include elements of constitutional disagreement, claims of illegitimate provisions, promulgation, or abrogation, and the fundamental inability of enduring basic law to institutionalize. Resorting to extraconstitutional measures to resolve constitutionally driven political crises is likely to continue in the foreseeable future.

Patron-Client Ties

Historically, the key to understanding Thai society has been the patron-client relationship. Patron-client ties are hierarchical, face-to-face relationships of reciprocity. However, the relationship is not one of balance, as the superior has power over the subordinate. When individuals have few resources at their command but have various needs, people who can supply the resources and meet the needs attain power.

At every level, from the village to the central government in Bangkok, patron-client groups have disseminated information, allocated resources, and organized people. These groups have formed a network of personal relations that extends throughout Thai society and traditionally has formed the heart of Thai politics. Although both personalism and patron-client relationships remain important, in the past several decades Thai politics has evolved in the direction of decreased personalism and more formalized participation in political structures.

Military

Since the overthrow of the absolute monarchy, the Thai military has played the dominant role in Thai politics. Of the fifty-plus cabinets organized since 1932, more than half can be classified as military or military-dominated governments. The civilian governments, which have been the most unstable, are often replaced by military regimes following army coups.

The reasons for military dominance include the weakness of civilian governments and the fact that the military is the most highly organized institution in the kingdom. Because of perceived external and internal threats to Thai security, the military has proclaimed itself the only institution capable of protecting Thai sovereignty. Moreover, the hierarchical nature of the military is congruent with the tendencies of Thai political culture. Moreover, because Bangkok, as Thailand's primary city, dominates every aspect of the country's political and economic life, the military has needed to control only this one city in order to control the entire kingdom.

Civilian governments, especially those coalesced around provincial parties, face considerable difficulties maintaining good relations with top generals. Because the military factionalized itself, forging alliances with one set of generals can also pose trouble later. Due to their own previous military experiences, Chatichai, Chavalit, Chamlong, and Thaksin all bore ties with particular military factions that proved consequential later, altering the course of events during the political crises they each faced. Standing above all the military, of course, is the venerable privy councilor Prem Tinsulanond, the retired general with unparalleled approbation from the crown and singular influence over the direction of Thai political development.

The threat of military intervention during political crisis has remained constant in the Thai system, as indicated by events in 1991, 1992, 2006, and 2008. After Black May 1992 it appeared for a time that the Thai public had lost all tolerance for military intervention. However, the 2006 coup d'état was viewed as desirable by many Thais. PAD leaders even felt compelled to go abroad to explain why in Thailand, coups are needed to restore democracy.[4] Similarly, the PAD's attempts to spark a coup as a means to overthrow the remnants of Thaksin's political machine indicated a willingness among a certain segment of Thais to rely on the military as a political catalyst. The *de facto* insubordination army generals showed to Prime Minister Somchai, ignoring his orders to clear protesters from unlawful seizures of government buildings and Bangkok's airports, illustrates the enduring independent status of the military as a political actor.

Bureaucracy

For most of the contemporary era, Thailand has been a bureaucratic polity with the arena of politics within the bureaucracy itself. The bureaucracy has been the bedrock of stability in a political system where top leadership positions have changed unpredictably. Although coups may bring new factions into power, the bureaucracy continues its conservative policy role with little change in direction.

The bureaucracy's formerly exclusive role has been widened in recent years by the new role of technocrats, who have attained important positions and brought a more rational mode to policymaking. These highly trained and educated officials are more inclined to public-regarding values over traditional values of hierarchy, personalism, and security. The technocrats lost some of their luster in 1997 when the Thai economy collapsed, at least partly because they did not adequately interpret the warning signs of the coming disaster. Higher salaries in Thailand's growing private sector have increasingly depleted the talent pool in the bureaucracy that formerly boasted Thailand's best and brightest.

Over the past two decades, bureaucratic actors have lost policymaking power to extrabureaucratic groups such as Parliament, political parties, business groups, and even international financial institutions. Nevertheless, even if their past dominance of the system is gone, Thai bureaucrats remain major actors in the country's political life, as demonstrated by their sizable support for the anti-Thaksin movement and because of the stability they provide to a system with frequent changes of leadership at the top.

Parliament and Political Parties

At one time, elections in Thailand were held only when the ruling group became convinced it could control the process so that elections would merely enhance its power. Today, elections provide more meaningful choices among candidates who represent alternative ideas. Thailand's bicameral Parliament is not a rubber-stamp body for a ruling party or strongman. It became less peripheral to governmental decisionmaking thanks to a greater role granted it by Prime Minister Prem, under whose leadership the Parliament began to act independently, particularly on economic matters. Although characterized by frequent changes in its structure and membership, Thailand's national assembly is more active in engaging in public debate about important issues than other legislatures in the region.

One of the reasons Thai political life is so lively and contentious is that parliamentary power matters. Establishing a parliamentary majority and the corresponding right to choose a prime minister and government cabinet rank among the high-stake events in the Thai political system. Because governments change so frequently in the Thai system this function is more politically significant than the actual lawmaking function, which, though politically salient, is not prone to wide shifts in ideology following elections or change in configuration of coalition parties.

Though the Parliament was formerly dominated by bureaucrats, military figures, and local elites, in recent decades its membership has diversified with greater representation from the business community, provincial political families, women, and (owing to party-list ballots) technocrats, academics, and other public figures. As parties are not mass based and do not offer much by way of local-level politics, and because parties tend to center on powerful individuals with regional or national prominence, the activities of political parties increasingly go hand-in-hand with parliamentary activity.

It is not particularly useful to visualize Thai political parties as falling along a spectrum that runs from liberal to conservative, because most parties fall into the moderate or nonideological category. Ideological platforms are not paramount in Thai campaigns because voters tend to favor candidates who serve their district or regional interests first. Thai Rak Thai somewhat differed in this respect in that its populist message appealed across districts and regions. It conceived its patronage system as national rather than local or regional. To some degree, Thaksin wanted to do for all of provincial Thailand what master politician Banharn Silapa-archa of the Chart Thai party had done for his home province of Suphan Buri (winning for it development project after development project, year after year, and making it among the most livable rural provinces in Thailand). A key distinguishing feature of TRT thus was not ideology, but its desire to expand patronage in wider dimensions than previous successful parties had. Another key distinction of TRT was its new "professional party" approach to electoral politics; that is, it prioritized savvy marketing of the party as a media product over rigid commitments to ideals, platforms, or maintaining cumbersome membership rolls.[5]

The Democrat Party is the longest surviving party in Thailand, with over sixty years behind it. Its base was and remains in urban Bangkok and the country's southern provinces. Having institutionalized as a party, it weathers changes in leadership and can withstand long periods in the opposition. It tends to be a party that is either leading the government or leading the opposition. Almost no other parties in Thailand are institutionalized.

In longevity and institutionalization, the closest party to the Democrats has been the Chart Thai (Thai Nation) party. Founded in the 1970s, it drew support from military-business elites and from the central provinces of the Chao

Phraya River basin. Chart Thai also survived multiple leadership changes and lived beyond capturing and losing power in Parliament. Two of its leaders, Chatichai Choonhavan and Banharn Silapa-archa, rose to serve as the country's prime minister. It survived coups, periods when parties were banned, and numerous factional divisions and defections. What Chart Thai could not survive was the 2008 political crisis. Because of its association with the People's Power Party and support of prime ministers Samak and Somchai, the November 2008 court ruling dissolved Chart Thai on the similar grounds of vote buying and electoral fraud. Banharn's fate is sealed: at least five years banned from formal office; however, the fate of Chart Thai's surviving MPs remains uncertain. Some have gravitated to the Democrats, others to Phuea Phandin.

As 2009 begins, the Phuea Phandin party is the standing remnant (third incarnation) of Thai Rak Thai. It is likely that Phuea Phandin's Thaksin loyalists will survive and compete successfully in future elections. Although TRT's electoral success was phenomenal under Thaksin, it remains to be seen whether Phuea Phandin continues as a TRT-style, marketing-oriented "professional party" or whether rural voters will support TRT's remnants in Thaksin's ongoing absence. Where the People's Power Party (second incarnation) experienced little defection, the early days of Phuea Phandin do not bode well in terms of losing MPs to party jumping. After the PPP dissolved in late 2008, the "Friends of Newin" faction of the TRT-PPP defected to join the Democrats. Named after Newin Chidchop, a banned politician tied to Thaksin, the sudden marriage of former Thaksin allies to anti-Thaksin Democratic politicians speaks volumes about the nature of Thai party politics.

Party Jumping and Vote Buying

In Thai electoral politics, party jumping is virtually institutionalized into the system, as are the endless allegations of rural vote buying that accompany every election. Thai elites and others maintain that these practices are at the root of Thailand's political problems. The 2007 "People's Constitution" was designed to inhibit both practices.

Party jumping occurs due to political expediency and opportunity. Political parties wooing candidates often distribute money to attract MPs who are most electable. The practice of party jumping by candidates often falls on factional lines, where a veteran politician brings a network of client MPs to the new party with him. Party jumping and party factionalism are closely intertwined in Thailand's party system.

There is conflicting evidence as to whether vote buying is an effective means to garner votes. Losers in elections always believe it matters, but skeptical researchers maintain that no hard evidence exists to demonstrate that vote buying changes election outcomes.[6] What is generally agreed upon, however, is that the practice has been used extensively in past Thai elections.

Vote buying entails the following tactics: giving cash to voters in return for promises of support, offering food and alcoholic drinks free of charge, serving free food at village festivals, or even promising cash to voters if the candidate they were told to vote for wins. Vote-buying networks are run by candidate canvassers (*hua khanaen*) who have close ties with village leaders, teachers, and respected elders. Voters tend to vote for those candidates close to village or town leaders who have helped out the voters in the past. If these leaders have funds from candidates to divvy up, villagers are all the more likely to support the leaders' choice. A more audacious manipulation of the electorate is the creation of illegal election lotteries and inviting voters to bet on who will win in the election. Lottery agents working for candidates then rig the odds so that voting against the candidate is virtually the same as voting to lose one's own bet.[7]

DEMOCRATIZATION

The history of politics in Thailand is a history of authoritarian rule and attempted democratization. Thailand's traditional culture, with its emphasis on deference to authority and hierarchical social relations, has not proven conducive to stable democratic rule. In the past, the Thais' democratic orientations have been formalistic in the sense that they have had little depth. Other values—such as security, development, deference, personalism, and economic stability—have often taken precedence over values more directly related to citizen participation in governmental affairs. Thus, the status of democratization in Thailand has been tenuous.

The most pronounced cleavage emphasized in the study of Thai politics is between the conservative state, military, and technocratic elites (who defend bureaucratic autonomy from societal forces) and the rising extrabureacratic business class and provincial forces (who champion power for the Parliament, political parties, and electoral majorities). It is a mistake to translate this cleavage as one between preferences for authoritarianism versus democracy. The PAD's proposal for New Politics notwithstanding, the goal to develop Thailand into a democracy has not escaped the political discourse that emanates from all corners of state and society. A discourse of democracy in Thailand has evolved from political rhetoric into societal norms since 1973 and has been further fueled by events in Thailand since the end of the Cold War.

The presence of repeated coups is not evidence that Thais, on average, do not desire democracy. Results from opinion polls taken in 2002 and 2006 (four months before the coup) revealed that eight in ten Thais were generally satisfied with democracy and believed it was "suitable" for Thailand.[8] It is meaningful that Thais often justify the country's frequent military coups to foreign audiences as necessary to "save democracy"; that mass protests are viewed as rightful democratic expressions to advance "democratic political reform"; and that constitutions are tinkered with to "enhance democracy" or to "make democracy more stable."

Thus, expectations for democracy have not only grown in Thailand, they have become the norm. This development is not to say that desire for democracy is universal. Even so, to the vast majority of Thais (and many state elites), Thai regimes lacking representative government, civil liberties, or electoral accountability are at best accepted only as temporary, as legitimate only when viewed as necessary to resolve political crisis.

Generational considerations matter as well. For older generations with memories of the Sarit and Thanom periods, modernization brought higher levels of education, literacy, access to the media, and travel—all of which have heightened awareness among older Thais of democratic values and their international legitimacy. It is also crucial to note that the majority of Thais living today are under the age of forty and thus carry no memories of Thai authoritarianism before the 1973 democratic revolution. Their life experience in Thailand has taught them that coups happen but also that military rule is undesirable compared to well-functioning parliamentary rule, political party activity, an open media, and political participation.

If the issue of Thai acceptance of democratic values is not the source of Thailand's inability to consolidate democracy, other sources must exist. One source fueling Thailand's democratic instability may be the unrealistic expectations Thai society places on democratic governance. As successful democracies have learned, the utility in democracy is its ability to manage conflict, to demand government accountability, and to peacefully transfer power from one set of rulers to another. Democratic practice outside of Thailand has not escaped the hazards of abuse of power, corruption, and official mismanagement, nor does it necessarily produce democratic outcomes of equitable resource allocation. The difference between Thailand and established democracies is that the latter tend to resolve political crises without turning to extraconstitutional methods. Unrealistic expectations that democracy should be orderly, produce completely fair outcomes, and be devoid of political crisis produce disappointment and lead to justification of extraconstitutional means to solve political gridlock.

Another possible source influencing Thailand's democratic instability may be too little respect for the principle of the rule of law. Evidence for this source comes from the verbal justifications used to dismiss existing law by those who find its presence an obstacle to political goals (e.g., Thaksin's extrajudicial killings during his 2003 drug war, or elite support of military or royal intervention to resolve political crises). Such justifications can stem from a cultural milieu where power often justifies itself (through karmic beliefs of rebirth and fate) producing, in turn, a societal tolerance for *rule by law*, rather than the unyielding defense of the *rule of law*.

A final source of democratic instability may come from endless debate over constitutional arrangements. All sides in these debates tend to interpret their preferred arrangement as democratic. What the protagonists fight over are the precise institutional arrangements believed necessary to produce some magical, durable democratic order. The false assumption underneath this volatile debate is that institutional arrangements matter more than realistic expectations of democracy. It is possible that an enduring democratic order will escape Thailand as long as societal norms respecting the limits of democracy are overridden by unrealistic expectations that some perfect institutional formula for constitutional democracy actually exists. An enduring democratic order will exist in Thailand only when political losers transcend their impulse to turn to extraconstitutional military intervention, royal trump cards, or politicization of the judiciary *and* when political winners transcend the impulse to abrogate or reengineer democratic constitutions or disregard constitutional limits on executive power.

ECONOMIC DEVELOPMENT

In the postwar period, Thailand's economic performance was unimpressive until a 1957 military coup ushered in a new set of economic policies under the authoritarian leadership of General Sarit Thanarat. During much of the Cold War, Thailand's neighbors were embroiled in conflict and suffering economically. In this context it can be said that Thailand "won" the Vietnam War. Where the war left Vietnam, Cambodia, and Laos economically devastated and left the United States a weaker global power, Thailand emerged with improved economic infrastructure, roads, and airports, and with transferred technology—a result of over a decade of U.S. military aid, development projects, and circulated cash.

During the 1970s and 1980s Thailand sustained a 7 percent rate of annual economic growth, a pace equaled by only a few other developing nations. More remarkably, the kingdom's economic growth between 1987 and 1996 averaged close to 10 percent, higher than in any other country during that period. During these boom years, inflation also started under 5 percent. The 1997 Asian economic crisis, which began in Thailand, brought this rapid growth to a halt. Recovery under Thaksin returned Thailand to a pattern of growth, but a sluggish economy has been the consequence of political instability since the 2006 military coup.

Coincident with these high growth rates in the boom years was an increase in the export sector, which in the late 1980s grew by almost 25 percent each year. Foreign investment also grew rapidly, with Japan, Taiwan, the United States, Hong Kong, and South Korea the leading investors. Manufacturing also replaced agriculture during this period in terms of share of the country's gross domestic product.

Although 65 percent of the Thai people are involved in the agricultural sphere of the economy, the number of those in rice farming is decreasing. Thai farmers have diversified into crops such as vegetables, fruits, maize, tapioca, coffee, flowers, sugar, and rubber, as well as livestock. The rise of agribusiness processing and related industry has also pulled ruralites out of the fields. Although farming areas have not developed as rapidly as urban areas, the standard of living in the countryside has improved noticeably since the 1970s. Nevertheless, the urban bias of Thai economic development is clear from both the emphasis on manufacturing and the higher percentage of budget allocations centered on Bangkok.

The factors responsible for the kingdom's economic successes have included a commitment to free-market, export-driven policies carried out by highly trained and generally conservative technocrats, and general policy continuity. For the most part, these officials were not as steeped in personalistic, clientelist politics as were their peers in neighboring countries. Where corruption did exist, officials and politicians earning kickbacks or skimming from contracts generally plowed their ill-gained wealth back into the booming Thai economy. Moreover, although coups have been a standard mechanism for changing governments, they have rarely undermined the continuity of macroeconomic policy controlled by senior technocrats.

The vital involvement of Thailand's Chinese minority cannot be overstated as a factor explaining the vibrancy of the economy. This dynamic minority has provided leadership in banking, export-import manufacturing, industrialization, monetary policy, foreign investment, and diversification. The autonomy granted the Chinese has resulted in an entrepreneurial minority's reinvesting its profits into the kingdom, with comparatively little capital leaving the country. As investments in Asia have grown, the Chinese have used filial and cultural ties to China to expand Thai investments abroad. For much of the 1990s, the single largest foreign investor in China was a Thai agribusiness company, Charoen Pokphand, founded by overseas Chinese in Bangkok.

Population control is another factor influencing economic success. In just one generation, Thailand managed to lower its population growth rate from 3.0 percent to 1.4 percent. The decrease resulted from a massive government-sponsored education program that has changed attitudes about the optimum family size and made birth control products available throughout the kingdom. The lack of population pressure has resulted in a higher standard of living for families, higher educational attainment and literacy, and lower poverty rates. According to the UNDP, the percentage of Thai people living in poverty between 1990 and 2004 was 14 percent, compared to 27 percent in Indonesia, 29 percent in Vietnam, and 43 percent in the Philippines over the same period.[9]

During the economic boom, rules favoring the expansion of foreign investment made possible a capital influx from industrial nations. Thailand became further integrated into the world capitalist system and gained access to foreign credit and technical assistance in addition to enjoying flourishing trade relations throughout the world. Thailand has been a favorite site for production plants owned by Japanese, South Korean, and Taiwanese firms. Under pressure from foreign governments and international financial institutions, Thailand liberalized its capital markets too far, however, sowing the seeds of loose credit, bad loans, and shaky investments that contributed to the 1997 economic crisis.

The nearly three decades of sustained economic development came to an abrupt halt in mid-1997 after the Chavalit administration stopped propping up the Thai baht. Having futilely spent billions of baht from foreign reserves on a lost cause, on July 2, 1997, the government unpegged the baht from the U.S. dollar and allowed it to float. Within weeks, the currency had lost 40 percent of its value. Simultaneously, the stock market suffered a precipitous decline, losing 70 percent of its value. To strengthen the economy, the Thai government accepted a $17 billion bailout from the IMF along with strict conditionality to adhere to market fundamentalism.

Many reasons for the debacle were debated in government, business, and academic circles. The long list of culprits included poor political leadership, the refusal of recent governments to make hard decisions about fiscal responsibility, pervasive corruption that blocked important infrastructure projects and educational reform, and the undisciplined opening of the economy to foreign capital. During the boom, offshore debt had also grown steadily as Thais borrowed dollars at cheaper rates than they could borrow baht. Borrowed money was often spent on real estate and a wide range of investments that offered meager returns, such as convention centers, hotels, condominiums, and private hospitals. Bad loans flourished at the end of the boom. The baht became overvalued when the dollar gained value against the yen, making Thai labor and exports more expensive and therefore less competitive. Currency speculators then bet on the devaluation of the baht, borrowing baht at one price and selling the currency back at a devalued rate, thereby making tremendous profits.

The Thai government's hope was that the devaluation would boost exports, curb imports, and cut the current account deficit. To keep the budget balanced, the Chavalit government raised the value-added tax from 7 percent to 10 percent. Interest rates were also raised to guard against a surge in inflation. These policies were in keeping with conditionality the IMF set. Recovery did not return. Chavalit was ousted and Democrats, lead by Chuan, were given the opportunity to steady Thailand's sinking economic ship. Democrat leaders also followed the general IMF prescriptions of implementing budget austerity and restoring inflows of foreign capital. It was not until the election of Thaksin Shinawatra in 2001 that the Thai government noticeably changed its response to the economic crisis.

Once elected, Thaksin moved to set up a national asset management company to buy most of the financial system's remaining nonperforming debt, estimated to be about $30 billion. He moved to restructure the agricultural sector by providing debt relief for farmers and to provide funds to villages to promote income-producing activities. The debt restructuring featured a three-year suspension on debts owed by poor farmers to the state-owned Bank for Agriculture. Grants to villages were to be about 1 million baht ($23,000) to each of the nation's 70,000 villages. The stimulus policies worked. Inflation was generally kept in check, exports expanded, and the rural economy experienced an unprecedented flow of government money.

Following the 2006 coup, the rate of the Thai economy's recovery slowed into the 4 percent range. Concerns over the coup group's aggressive promotion of Sufficiency Economy waned, however, as the policies associated with its promotion proved to be vague goals rather than concrete measures.

More harmful to Thailand's economic prospects than policy changes have been the seemingly endless cycle of protests by pro- and anti-Thaskin forces that has existed since 2005. The recognized ability of demonstrators to disrupt government operations, to paralyze Bangkok's economic infrastructure, and to force scheduled ASEAN summits to be cancelled has fostered Thailand's image as a dysfunctional polity. Government instability, constitutional crisis, coup d'état, corruption, politicized courts, and constant threats of political violence have altered the political risk assessment of investors and tourists. More so than before, many outsiders now question the fundamental commitment to the rule of law in Thailand.

THE THAI STATE

Until the 1980s, scholars referred to Thai politics as a bureaucratic polity, in which politics took place within the bureaucracy and extrabureaucratic institutions were negligible. External institutions, such as the Parliament and political parties, were deemed to have little influence over the state's policy decisions. The bureaucratic polity included the military, as many of the generals held important government posts (including the position of prime minister). The state, then, was considered strong and autonomous, independent of such societal organizations as political parties, business associations, farmers' groups, and labor unions. When these groups began to emerge, they were initially co-opted, manipulated, or oppressed by the bureaucracy, which used the military as its controlling force. By integrating the military into the political process, the government established a broad-based regime. Utilizing both collaborative and coercive forces, the state increased its stability and capacity.

Since the student-led revolt against the military in 1973, however, Thai political institutions have increased in number and have broadened their bases considerably, strengthening the role of the legislature, political parties, and business associations while reducing direct military domination. As societal groups have come to play a more important role in Thai politics, the state has lost some of its autonomy and consequently become weaker.

Thai authorities expect autonomy from societal actors, especially rural citizens who have been relatively more politically passive than radical. Because rural citizens constitute about 65 percent of the population and have made relatively few demands on the central authorities, this notion of passivity has been central to the argument that the Thai state can (and should) act autonomously. Many state elites hold the rural electorate in contempt for increasing assertiveness in the political system, particularly through their participation in party politics, vote buying, and organized protests against state projects, such as rural dams. Among many state elites, the country's proliferating rural organizations opposing dams and state projects were pejoratively called *ngo*, a Thai word playing on the acronym NGO meaning stupid and ignorant.

A considerable degree of skepticism exists among state elites about the "cultural appropriateness" of majoritarian democracy. Thailand's constitutional and political battles, especially in the past decade, have pitted state elites and their values of state autonomy against elected officials who derive their authority and power from democratic institutions and rural voters. The expectation many Thai elites have for state autonomy stems at least partially from the past success of Thai authorities in preserving the state's independence and sovereignty; that having averted colonial rule, establishing a generally peaceful country, and meeting the basic needs of the majority of the citizenry, the Thai state had proven its effectiveness.

Nevertheless, if autonomy is a key variable for assessing strength, the Thai state is weak in the sense that officials who make authoritative decisions are not insulated from the patronage networks upon which they depend. Thailand's state officials are integrated into some of the country's most established networks of patron-client exchange. These relationships act as links between bureaucrats and societal groups in old business, agriculture, labor, the aristocracy, and the intelligentsia. Quasi-state enterprises, including public utilities and their organized employees, are also tied into long-standing networks of patronage that emanate from the state. The loss of these networks threatens the erosion of associated state institutions and, thus, state strength.

Thaksin Shinawatra's TRT network of patronage worked to displace and erode many of the traditional channels of bureaucratic and state patronage. Much of the resentment state elites held toward Thaksin was due to his disruption of the business-as-usual operations of a state-society patronage apparatus that had weathered so many changes in political leadership before. Thaksin's efforts to reprioritize state goals and create new state agencies caused antipathy and confusion among traditional bureaucrats. His bold attempts provoked a forceful response. As predicted by one Thai scholar well before Thaksin's rise, the conservative alliance of the military, technocrats, and old-style business elites, when threatened, may turn to "General Prem's influence to put pressure on any government which they deemed unpopular or unresponsive to their demands."[10] Thaksin, the most skilled and powerful political figure to challenge this conservative alliance, now lives in forced exile, a fugitive from the Thai justice system.

A state's legitimacy is a potent factor accounting for the strength of the state. Here again, the Thai state has managed to receive acceptance, even approbation, of the most important state institutions. The primary reason for this is that contemporary Thai authorities have basked in the aura of the king, the symbol of unity of the Thai state.

Thais have accepted the state's symbolic configuration within an ideology of king, state, and religion. Through socialization and the deliberate exploitation of the king's popularity by whichever regime is in power, the Thai state has become identified with the king and Buddhism, resulting in an extraordinarily high level of acceptance.[11] Questions about the strength of the monarchy (as an institution) in contrast to the strength of King Bhumibol (as an individual figure) will face Thai society in the future. Absent the aura of the king to bask in, state authorities could find challenges from elected governments far more difficult to repel in the future.

Constitutionalism is a possible alternative anchor of state strength in the absence or loss of royal aura due to succession. However, until common agreement on actual constitutional arrangements is achieved, implemented, and endures political crises, the strength of the Thai state will likely depend on the monarchy and of state institutions royal approbation.

FOREIGN POLICY

Thailand's current foreign relations must be seen in the context of the new international era brought on by the end of the Cold War. The most obvious manifestations of this new era include the perception that there are no regional or great-power threats to Thai security and that the U.S. security role in Southeast Asia has declined. Thailand's sustained economic development and the rise of nonbureaucratic interests in the political sphere have unambiguously pushed foreign policy into the economic realm. This development has caused the military to reduce its role in foreign policy in favor of the Ministry of Foreign Affairs, cabinet ministers, and political party leaders. The increased profile of Thailand's top economic diplomats has also brought the country unprecedented international esteem in recent years. As global economic integration replaced the Cold War, Thailand found itself in free trade agreement negotiations with the United States, the European Union, China, and Japan. Thailand's ASEAN partners are often partners at the trade negotiation table as well.

Thailand increasingly relates to the United States as an equal rather than as a client. As the Cold War ended, Thai foreign policy lessened security dependence on the United States, asserted a policy of equidistance in its relations with allies and adversaries, and launched a dramatically new Indochina policy without seeking U.S. support. In economic relations with the United States, Thailand became more assertive in bilateral negotiations over trade, intellectual property rights enforcement, and general economic policy independence (the exception being the IMF rescue package for Thailand during the 1997 economic crisis, which U.S. officials strongly encouraged).

Major aspects of Thai-U.S. relations also include joint military exercises; cooperation on suppressing narcotics trafficking, international crime, and terrorism; coordination on refugee matters involving Burmese activists and Hmong groups fleeing Laos; and ongoing support for educational exchange and the Peace Corps. Thailand provided some logistical support to the United States' war on terror but it never became a major military partner. Cooperation in tracking suspected terrorists proved worthwhile, however, when Hambali, a top al-Qaeda-linked bomb plotter, was discovered hiding in Ayutthaya and arrested in 2003.

The single most important issue in recent Thai-U.S. relations, however, has been negotiations over a United States–Thailand free trade agreement. Initiated by Thaksin and George W. Bush at an Asia-Pacific Economic Cooperation (APEC) meeting in 2003, the agreement showed some early progress. Business communities on both sides actively promoted it, countered by an equally active resistance from Thai and international NGOs. Political instability since 2006, nevertheless, stalled progress on the agreement.

The 2006 military coup removing Thaksin put the U.S. diplomats in an awkward position. They denounced the coup as undemocratic and harmful, yet at the same time tread carefully so as not to become the defenders, patrons, or saviors of the embattled exiled ex–prime minister. Thaksin's murky status that tied him to corruption, undemocratic practices, and alienation by Thailand's power elite weighed heavily on the U.S. position regarding the coup. The common refrain from Washington and the U.S. embassy in Bangkok was a call for the coup leaders to "return the country to democracy as soon as possible." After the country returned to elected government, Thai prime ministers Samak and Somchai had little time to spend on foreign relations with the country's old Cold War patron. Thailand's ongoing political crisis has taken its toll on Thai relations with Washington, even as the Obama administration opened new opportunities in early 2009. Snubbing Thailand in favor of a visit to democratic Indonesia, Secretary of State Hillary Clinton's first diplomatic trip to Southeast Asia left Thailand—and Abhisit Vejjajiva's fledging government—off the itinerary.

Since the passing of the Cold War, abrupt changes have come to Thailand's relations with its mainland Southeast Asian neighbors. Chatichai's initial efforts toward normalizing relations with Vietnam, Laos, and Cambodia were followed by support for the three countries' membership in ASEAN—a feat accomplished before the 1990s concluded. Lingering border disputes with Laos were also resolved as Cold War tensions dissipated. A symbol of improving relations between the two countries was the completion of an Australian-funded bridge across the Mekong River, which forms much of the border between the two countries. It was the first of three such bridges, all of far greater economic significance to landlocked Laos than to Thailand.

Thailand's relations with Cambodia also deepened in the 1990s. Foreign investment from Thailand brought Cambodia needed foreign exchange. Thai-driven investment in textiles, mobile phones, satellite communications, and other industries contributed to Cambodia's gradual economic recovery. Other areas driven by Thai investment—border casinos, brothels, and logging operations—proved less encouraging.

The degree of rising Thai foreign investment in Cambodia was demonstrated in 2003 when a popular Thai actress claimed Cambodia's famed Angkor Wat temple complex actually belonged to Thailand. The comment sparked unruly anti-Thai riots in Phnom Penh. Images of Cambodian youths vandalizing Thai-owned businesses and interests spread anger across Thailand. Mutual anger also erupted in 2008 over Khao Preah Vihear, another Angkor-era temple set on a cliff near the Cambodian-Thai border. Troops on both sides mobilized after Thailand objected to Phnom Penh's application to designate the temple a UN World Heritage site. Two Cambodian soldiers died in firefights near the temple and a number of Thai troops were temporarily kidnapped. The needlessly tense event sadly displayed how both governments sought to score points domestically with patriotic nationalism. Indeed, the legality of ownership of Khao Preah Vihear had long been settled in Cambodia's favor in the 1960s by the International Court of Justice. Nevertheless, both of these episodes demonstrate how Thai-Cambodian relations remain forever framed in terms of anxiety over premodern symbols of identity and power.

In the new international era, Thailand also supported Burma's application to ASEAN as part of its "constructive engagement" strategy with the Burmese regime. The purpose of this approach, which counters the policies of most of the world's nations, has been to reduce tensions between the two countries and to gain access to Burmese resources. The latter objective seems to transcend any particular government that controls Thailand. Thaksin enjoyed strong relations with Burma's ruling junta, and Burma was the first country the 2006 coup leaders visited following Thaksin's ouster.

Thai civilian leaders have not ignored threats to their territory. With some three thousand miles of borders with Burma, Laos, Cambodia, and Malaysia, there are constant (but generally small) border disputes and skirmishes. The situation is complicated by smuggling, weaponry, drugs, prostitution, and refugees—especially persons fleeing from oppression in Burma. In early 2000, God's Army, a ragtag group of Karen minority insurgents led by twin twelve-year-old boys, attacked a hospital in the Thai city of Ratchaburi. The Thais responded by killing the insurgents because they viewed the assault as a threat against Thai sovereignty and territory.

In regional affairs, Thailand strongly supported the post–Cold War initiative to create the ASEAN Free Trade Area (AFTA). A response to the European Union and the creation of the North American Free Trade Association (NAFTA), AFTA was viewed as a move to reduce economic dependence on Japan and East Asia. With a market of 320 million people in a rapidly growing region, AFTA sought to expand trade by lowering trade tariffs. AFTA's economic significance to individual countries, however, remained minimal because the partners shared similar economic and export profiles and the volume of bilateral trade each enjoyed with Japan, the United States, the European Union, and China far exceeded levels of intra-AFTA trade.

Of all the changes in the new era, China's rise as a power is arguably the most consequential international development for Thailand. Concerns about the Asian giant, however, are almost exclusively in the realm of trade competitiveness and economic relations, not security interests. Thailand's relationship with China improved markedly after the Vietnam War but even more so following the Cold War. In particular, the new environment expanded people-to-people contacts between Sino-Thais and Chinese business interests. Once a liability in Thai cultural circles, the Chinese heritage of prominent business families in Bangkok became a cause for celebration and resulted in visits to ancestral villages in China's coastal provinces. Cultural goodwill translated into good business.

As part of the ASEAN Plus Three process and China's initiative that launched the ASEAN–China Free Trade Agreement (ACFTA), Thailand enjoyed "early harvest" provisions of free trade with China in agriculture and other sectors by 2003, seven years before the FTA was scheduled to go into effect.[12] As a consequence, an increased flow of fruits and vegetables is transforming Thailand's agriculture markets, as well as stressing its environment. In northern Thailand, for example, small-scale tangerine producers have been pushed out by large, plantation-size tangerine exporters. The latter growers cannot clear land fast enough to plant ever more tangerine trees that are picked by Burmese migrants with fruit destined for shipment up the Mekong River to Chinese markets. Ubiquitous use of pesticides on tangerine orchards turned the area into Thailand's "ground zero" in the campaign against agrochemical inputs.[13]

Internationally, recognition for Thailand's economic success came symbolically in the new international era with the 2002 appointment of one of the country's top technocrats, Supachai Panitchpakdhi, as director of the World Trade Organization. An attempt to launch Surakiat Sathienthai, Thaksin's foreign minister, as Kofi Annan's replacement as UN secretary-general also brought Thailand international esteem, at least until the 2006 coup that overthrew Thaksin, thus tainting Surakiat's candidacy.

With respect to the UN, the new international era has witnessed Thai troops as part of UN peacekeeping forces in East Timor and praise from the organization for efficient handling of the 2004 Indian Ocean tsunami. Following the disaster, Thaksin Shinawatra led the international push to create an Indian Ocean tsunami warning system. In 2008, when Burma's military rulers initially refused foreign aid following Cyclone Nargis, Thailand convinced the regime to allow it to act as an intermediary to funnel aid to the country. Thai relations with Muslim states, on the other hand, were often strained due to perceptions of harsh, ineffective, and unfair policies toward Thailand's Muslim population in the South.

CONCLUSION

Thailand today is fundamentally different from what it was decades ago, when a military-dominated bureaucracy fully controlled society. Economic development, evolving expectations for democracy, and extended periods of parliamentary governance have brought new groups into the political system to challenge the traditional power elites. Conservative state elites still wield sufficient power to alter events but unless societal norms for representative government, accountable leadership, and civil liberties disappear, Thailand's technocrats, generals, and royals will find constant frustration in trying to undermine societal attempts to establish democratic institutions.

Whether a predominantly appointed national assembly under New Politics will find its way into a future constitution remains an open question. Whether it could survive if it became constitutional is a much easier question to answer. Constitutional history in Thailand suggests fierce contestation if such a reform is ever promulgated as basic law. The red-shirted UDD forces, politically disenfranchised by the arrangement, all too aware of the methods used by the yellow-shirted PAD and have begun to imitate them. Indeed, for New Politics to endure such protest, appointed elites would need to be more willing to physically suppress dissent than were the pro-Thaksin PPP governments. Ironically, the very choice they forced on Samak and Somchai (to shoot protesters or face eventual removal) would become their own to make. In the new international era with a twenty-four-hour news cycle always waiting, unleashing security forces against unarmed protesters wearing any color of shirt is a risky deal with the devil.

At best, Thailand's political future will see society muddle through yet more weak parliamentary governments, corruption scandals, demands from traditional state elites, and threats of military coup d'état. The struggle for democratic stability will continue under this scenario. At worst, the ailing health of King Bhumibol, and the uncertainty surrounding the events his passing will put into motion, will lead to an unprecedented degree of unpredictability.

Not to be forgotten is the still popular Thaksin Shinawatra, who remains a fugitive in exile. His comments following the end of the airport-seizure fiasco offered little comfort to those hopeful they had truly witnessed the "final battle," as promised by PAD. From his temporary exile home of Abu Dhabi, Thaksin ominously announced: "With me at the helm I can bring confidence quickly back to Thailand. We have to find a mechanism under which I can go back, that is why I must tell you that I will go back into politics."[14]

Thailand's future is nothing if not daunting. Reveals one Thai political scientist in the *Journal of Democracy*: "All Thais fear but do not dare say in public, that Thailand's future is up for grabs. What happens after the current king leaves the scene could be the most wrenching crisis yet."[15] Over their modern history the Thais have escaped brutal occupation, destabilizing revolutions, tyrannical dictatorship, and the setbacks of protracted wars. What they cannot escape is cyclical political crisis, perpetual constitutional change, and the uncomfortable sense that 1932's promise of democracy seems as distant as ever.

NOTES

1. Thai political scientist Chai-Anan Sumudavanija is famously credited for first describing this pattern, or Thailand's "vicious cycle" of coup d'état.

2. Paul Handley, *The King Never Smiles: A Biography of Thailand's King Bhumibol Adulyadej* (New Haven, CT: Yale University Press, 2006), pp. 425–426.

3. Thitinan Pongsudhirak, "Thailand Since the Coup," *Journal of Democracy*, vol. 19, no. 4 (October 2008), p. 143.

4. James Ockey, "Thailand in 2006: Retreat to Military Rule," *Asian Survey*, vol. 47, no. 1, p. 139.

5. Duncan McCargo and Ukrist Pathmanand, *The Thaksinization of Thailand* (Copenhagen: NAIS Press, 2005), pp. 77–79.

6. Robert B. Albritton and Thawilwadee Bureekul, "The State of Democracy in Thailand," paper presented at the Conference on the Asian Barometer, Taipei, Taiwan, July 2008, p. 1.

7. Pasuk Phongphaichit and Chris Baker, *Thailand's Boom and Bust* (Chiang Mai: Silkworm Books, 1998), pp. 250–251.

8. Albritton and Bureekul, "The State of Democracy," pp. 4–5.

9. See comparison tables at the end of this book titled "Southeast Asia: Select Indicators."

10. Chai-Anan Samudavanija, "Old Soldiers Never Die, They Are Just Bypassed: The Military, Bureaucracy, and Globalisation," in Kevin Hewison, *Political Change in Thailand: Democracy and Participation* (London: Routledge, 1997), p. 56.

11. Joel S. Migdal, *Strong Societies and Weak States: State-Society Relations and State Capabilities in the Third World* (Princeton, NJ: Princeton University Press, 1988).

12. Robert G. Sutter, *Chinese Foreign Relations: Power and Policy since the Cold War* (Lanham, MD: Rowman & Littlefield, 2008), p. 269.

13. See Robert Dayley, "The Sufficiency Ethic and Thailand's Agrarian Myth," paper presented at the Council on Thai Studies, Northern Illinois University, October 19–20, 2008; and "Imagined Futures: Sufficiency Economy and Other Visions of Rural Thailand," paper presented at the Tenth International Thai Studies Conference, Thammasat University, January 9–11, 2008.

14. "I'll Be Back," *Bangkok Post*, November 25, 2008, www.bangkokpost.com.

15. Thitninan, "Thailand Since the Coup," p. 149.

Resource Guide

Two useful tools for bibliographic and other information on Thailand are available from the University of Leeds at www.leeds.ac.uk/thaipol/thaibibl.htm and Australia National University's WWW Virtual Library: www.gksoft.com/govt/en/th.html. The University of California–Berkeley maintains a useful portal for digital and print resources on Thailand: www.lib.berkeley.edu/SSEAL/SoutheastAsia/seaelec.html. Northern Illinois University's Southeast Asia Digital Library includes a range of useful links that cover government, academic, and research institutions specific to Thailand: http://sea.lib.niu.edu. The University of Wisconsin–Madison Libraries similarly maintains a list of digital and print resources on Thailand: www.library.wisc.edu/guides/SEAsia/collections/UW.html.

The Royal Thai Government's official English language Web site is at www.thaigov.go.th/eng. An excellent source for economic and public policy information and statistics is the Thailand Research and Development Institute (TDRI), at www.tdri.or.th. For articulation and assessment of Sufficiency Economy, see the Thailand Human Development Report 2007 at www.undp.or.th/download/NHDR2007bookENG.pdf. For information on environment, agricultural, and international trade issues from a civil society perspective, visit BIOTHAI at www.biothai.org.

Daily online news sources in English include the *Bangkok Post* at www.bangkokpost.com and the *Nation* at www.nationmultimedia.com. Both of these sites have useful searchable archives of back issues. Useful blogs on Thai politics include http://bangkokpundit .blogspot.com and the *New Mandala*, an active blog on Thai politics maintained by researchers from Australian National University, at http://rspas.anu.edu.au/rmap/ newmandala.

Links to Thai television, including some broadcast news in English, are available at www.siamtv.info.

3

THE PHILIPPINES

*I*n the quest for political and economic development, the experience of the Philippines has been different from that of Thailand. Whereas the Thais have shown an ability to meld traditional cultural values with selected modern values to achieve an improved standard of living, the Filipinos have had considerably less success finding the appropriate blend. In contrast to the Thais, who have never had a foreign culture thrust upon them through colonialism, the Filipinos, colonized for four hundred years by the Spanish and then for forty-eight years by the Americans, were not as free to choose those aspects of westernization most conducive to development. Instead, the nation is beset even today by the same difficulties that arose during colonialism: oligarchic politics, personalism, and chronic economic inequality. In the Philippines, development and democratization are stymied by the diminished capacity of the political system to cope with the people's demands. The result is more often institutional decay rather than development, and authoritarianism rather than accountability.[1]

Close to 86 million people live in the Philippines, an archipelago inclusive of 7,107 islands. Nine of these islands including Luzon, the largest and most politically significant, comprise 90 percent of the population. Over 170 languages are spoken across the islands, with Tagalog serving as the lingua franca. The religious makeup of the Philippines reflects Spanish and U.S. colonial influences, as well as the country's proximity to Muslim neighbors Malaysia and Indonesia. Officially, over 81 percent of the current population is Catholic; Protestant and evangelical groups account for another 12 percent; Islam, at 5 percent, prevails across many of the southern islands.

On course to overtake Vietnam as Southeast Asia's second most populous country, the Philippines is largely poor with a gross national income (GNI) of $1,620. One in three Filipinos live below the national poverty line. Pockets of wealth and modernity do exist in urban areas of Manila and other principal cities. Despite political dysfunction, lawlessness, and endemic corruption, the

country's economy has experienced modest growth in recent decades and a middle class is emerging. A national audience favoring authority grounded in formal institutions rather than personalism exists, but "violence and guile" have tragically operated as the currency of social mobility.[2]

In many respects the experience of the Philippines parallels a Latin American trajectory more than Asian political history. The long Spanish and shorter (but also influential) U.S. domination of the Philippines left a mixed legacy. From the Spanish, the Filipinos inherited not only Catholicism but a highly inequitable system of land tenure dominated by a powerful land-owning class. The landed families and the hierarchical society, still powerful in Filipino politics, were rooted in clan warfare and Spanish feudalism. U.S. rule nudged the country's political structures toward competitive democracy, introduced a system of public education that vastly improved literacy rates (along with incorporating English as the national language), and fostered the rise of highly trained technocrats, bureaucrats, and entrepreneurs.

The U.S. presence from 1898 to 1946 (a consequence of the Spanish-American War) also provoked Filipinos to wage an unsuccessful war against their new occupiers. Politically, occupation helped nurture provincial leaders and a nascent oligarchy at the expense of the masses.[3] It also integrated the Philippine economy into the U.S. economy along colonial lines. The economic relationship between the Philippines and the United States was built on the primary goods produced for the American market, such as tobacco, sugar, and tropical fibers. In fact, the U.S. administration of the Philippines wasn't declared temporary until sixteen years after the initial occupation when President Woodrow Wilson pushed the Philippine Autonomy Act through the U.S. Congress. The act supported a transition to free, democratic government—an event delayed by further squabbling among American politicians, the Great Depression, commonwealth status in 1935, and Japanese occupation during World War II.

Philippine independence, proclaimed on July 4, 1946, began a period of semidemocratic rule within the context of a continuing oligarchy. A series of democratically elected presidents ruled over a society still pervaded by personalism and *compadrazgo* (godfather-based ritual kinship). The greatest democratic gains, however, were during the four years the country had under President Ramon Magsaysay, who died in a tragic plane crash in 1957. The magnetic Magsaysay, elected on his successful crushing of the communist Huk rebellion and his clean image, promoted civil liberties and enhanced Philippine democracy. His legacy remains larger than his successes in government as he struggled to manage the young postcolonial democracy. Violence perpetrated by the private armies surrounding the nation's elite families continued during his tenure and long afterward.

When Ferdinand Marcos was first elected president in 1965, the Philippines was experiencing economic growth and political stability. The vital Liberal and Nacionalista Parties, despite their fluid, nonideological nature, ensured the nation a lively competition for public office. At the same time, Philippine society suffered from problems that originated during the colonial era, the most salient of which were social and economic inequality, corruption, food shortages, and widespread violence.

In 1969 Marcos became the first president in postindependence Philippines to be reelected. His reelection was "bought" in the sense that he gave government funds to local officials who manipulated the vote in his favor. A constitutional provision precluded a third term, so Marcos planned to stay in power by abrogating the constitution and asserting that national crises demanded extraordinary measures. His proclamation of martial law in September 1972 ended formal democratic rule and began a fourteen-year period of authoritarian rule.

A majority of Filipino citizens supported Marcos's initial steps to end the breakdown of law and order, his promise of land reform, and his strengthening of the army against insurrections by communists throughout the archipelago and by Muslim dissidents in the southern islands. This support dissipated as it became clear that Marcos's achievements did not match his rhetoric and that the "temporary" period of martial law was merely a pretext to perpetuate his personal power.

Acting with the wholehearted support of the United States and using his martial law powers, Marcos was both executive and legislator. To give legitimacy to his regime, he instituted referenda, all of which turned out a 90 percent vote in favor of his continued tenure, and elections, all of which were fraudulent. Press censorship of antigovernment criticism, jailing of dissidents, lack of basic civil liberties, absence of a secret ballot, and control of ballot counting were the methods Marcos used to win approval for his rule.

By the mid-1970s, Marcos's so-named New Society initiatives under martial law began to disintegrate with the rise of lawlessness in the countryside, the realization that the "constitutional authoritarian" government was more authoritarian than constitutional, the imprisonment of respected political leaders such as Marcos's rival, Senator Benigno Aquino Jr., and the growing awareness of a mismanaged economy. Unemployment rose to over 20 percent and underemployment to 40 percent, real income shrank as inflation increased, and corruption reached an intolerable state under "crony capitalism," whereby Marcos's friends were placed in charge of business conglomerates despite their lack of business acumen.

The "lifting" of martial law in 1981 temporarily improved the image of the New Society but did not significantly change the authoritarian political order. The government continued to be based on personalism with no legitimacy granted to governmental institutions. Compared to the period before martial law and to conditions in neighboring countries, Philippine politics during the Marcos era was increasingly characterized by decay rather than by development. As the regime lost its legitimacy, the Armed Forces of the Philippines (AFP) became less professional, the economy worsened, and the Communist Party of the Philippines (CPP) and its military arm, the New People's Army (NPA), strengthened, thereby undermining the original rationale for martial law.

By 1983, after the hierarchy of the Philippine Catholic Church and business leaders had turned against Marcos and when Marcos's health was known to be precarious, Senator Aquino returned to the Philippines after several years of exile in the United States. Aquino, the single greatest challenger to President Marcos, was assassinated in August 1983 the moment he stepped out of the airplane that had flown him back to his country. The almost universal belief of Filipinos in the government's complicity in this assassination released long-suppressed grievances. The Marcos regime would no doubt have fallen even without Aquino's martyrdom, for Filipinos already knew that Marcos and his associates were responsible for the country's low vitality, whereas other noncommunist Southeast Asian nations were flourishing.[4]

After Aquino was assassinated, the Philippines suffered disastrous declines in industrial and agricultural production and in wages and employment as well as capital flight, high inflation, severe undernourishment for children in rural areas, a rich-poor gap wider than in any other nation in the region, and negative economic growth, while the other noncommunist Southeast Asian nations were boasting of the world's highest growth rates.

A momentous event in contemporary Philippine politics took place during three remarkable months, from December 1985 through February 1986. Bowing to intense pressure from the United States, wishing to take advantage of his improved health during a remission of his illness, desiring to end opposition attacks on him, sensing the disarray of potential opposition candidates, and confident about his capacity to engineer a mandate, Marcos called for snap elections to be held on February 7, 1986.

From the moment Marcos announced the elections, the key question was whether the opposition could unite around a single candidate, and the answer was unclear until the final filing day. Previously, the opposition had been able to unite only in its disdain for Marcos. Because of the highly personal nature of Philippine politics, the competing ambitions of potential leaders, and Marcos's ability to manipulate and co-opt rival forces, the opposition had a difficult time presenting a serious alternative.

Structurally, the opposition suffered from the disintegration of the two-party system during martial law. Instead, there were now many parties and organizations, each with an ambitious leader who wanted to be the candidate to run against Marcos. Corazon "Cory" Aquino, the widow of the martyred Senator Benigno Aquino Jr., emerged as the person around whom all the oppositionists could coalesce. Her genuine reluctance to lead added to her attraction as a sincere, honest, and incorruptible candidate, precisely the antithesis of the president. A grassroots groundswell of support culminated in a petition with over a million signatures from Filipinos urging her to run for the presidency. Mrs. Aquino met with Senator Salvador Laurel, himself a major contender for the presidency, and fashioned an eleventh-hour agreement whereby she and Laurel would be the presidential and vice presidential candidates, respectively, under the banner of Laurel's United Nationalist Democratic Organization (UNIDO). For the first time since 1972 when martial law was declared, the opposition had achieved unity.

Candidate Aquino proclaimed a "people's campaign," realizing that she could not match the president in financial or organizational strength. Marcos and his campaign had easy access to government money, which allowed him to raise officials' salaries, decrease taxes, and lower fuel and utility rates. By the end of the campaign, some $500 million from the government treasury had been spent to reelect the president. In contrast, the opposition spent $10 million, all of it raised from donations.

Whereas Aquino's first campaign speeches stressed her sincerity and honesty and her empathetic qualities as a sufferer under Marcos, her later speeches focused on issues and her program to reform the government. She vilified the president for his corruption and immorality as she cited evidence that the president had lied both about his role as a hero in World War II and about his fortune of several billion dollars in real estate around the world. The former issue arose after investigations of U.S. Army documents disclosed that Marcos's claim that he had headed a guerrilla resistance unit during the Japanese occupation of the Philippines was "fraudulent" and "absurd." U.S. congressional investigations also documented the president's wealth overseas. Aquino's major theme was that Marcos had brought economic ruin and political dictatorship to the nation and that she would restore integrity.

Marcos's campaign focused on his experience, including his wartime record, in contrast to his opponent's "naïveté." He stressed the need for strong male leadership rather than weak female leadership, suggesting that a woman's place was in the bedroom rather than in the political arena. Marcos, a staunch ally of U.S. President Ronald Reagan, accused Aquino of planning to cancel the Military Bases Agreement with the United States and to dismember the republic by giving away the southern island of Mindanao. He claimed that communists had taken over Aquino's campaign and that only he could handle the communist insurgency.

The voting was marred by fraud committed by Marcos supporters. When the "official" count gave Marcos 54 percent of the vote, the National Assembly—the final arbiter for voting controversies—proclaimed Marcos the winner, but the opposition launched a peaceful crusade of civil disobedience to bring down Marcos and allow the real winner, Aquino, to assume office. The U.S. State Department, official observers, journalists from dozens of nations, the Catholic Church, and most Filipinos agreed that Aquino had actually won the election by a large margin. In an embarrassing statement, Reagan indicated that Marcos's claim of fraud on the Aquino side deserved equal attention.[5]

As Aquino's civil disobedience campaign took hold, Defense Minister Juan Ponce Enrile and Lieutenant General Fidel Ramos, vice chief of the armed forces, defected from the Marcos camp and called for his resignation and for Aquino's ascension to the presidency. This rebellion by former Marcos supporters began a series of defections from the president, leaving him with only a small, hard-core group of backers.

When Marcos threatened to retaliate by bombing the headquarters of Enrile and Ramos, thousands of Filipinos—urged on by the archbishop of Manila, Cardinal Jaime Sin—surrounded the building, some even lying in the streets to keep the tanks from approaching. This display by students, farmers, nuns, and shop owners became known as People Power. The tank commanders eventually retreated, and many defected to the opposition. The United States signaled its support of the rebellion, thereby undermining Marcos's claim that only he enjoyed the confidence of the superpowers. On February 25, 1986, Aquino and Laurel proclaimed the people's victory and were sworn in as president and vice president. The next day, Marcos fled the country with his family to live in exile in Hawaii, where he died on September 28, 1989, at the age of seventy-two.

With little bloodshed, People Power had triumphed over a regime that had dominated the political, social, and economic life of the Philippines for twenty-one years. The republic was awash with optimism that a new era in Philippine politics had arrived. Indeed, in the first months of the Aquino regime the executive, legislative, and judicial institutions were revitalized, the military was curtailed, political parties were refurbished, electoral processes made honest and effective, the media freed, the Marcos cronies undercut, and the citizens given back their rights. However, the monumental problems faced by Filipinos remained: oligarchic politics, personalism, economic and social inequalities, and weak institutions incapable of meeting the people's needs.

In both the political and economic realms, President Aquino's administration achieved notable gains. Filipinos again could express pride in their country's government after years of corrupt and demeaning leadership. Governmental institutions were rejuvenated under a president whose commitment to democratic values and procedures was irrevocable. Even during Aquino's first year as president when she had virtually unlimited powers, she focused on restoring the democratic process. Civil liberties were reinstated, including the writ of habeas corpus, the release of political prisoners, and the holding of free and regularized elections. These gains came about through the promulgation of a new democratic constitution approved by over 75 percent of the Filipino people in a February 1987 referendum.

Contending with a desperately sick economy resulting from mismanagement by the previous regime, the Aquino administration achieved slow growth. The Philippine economic growth rate had been negative during the last years under Marcos, but the rate under Aquino was positive—6.7 percent in 1988 and 5.5 percent in 1989—while inflation decreased. Growth was highest in the industrial sector, as confidence in the economy grew and construction projects flourished.

Aquino had raised the people's expectations with promises of reform in all areas of life. She promised the end of the politics of personalism and the beginning of the politics of principle. Compared to the recent past in the Philippines, the Aquino administration earned high marks, but judged against higher standards, such as those of its Asian neighbors, its record was weak. Although the level of corruption and privilege decreased significantly under her administration, Aquino failed to change the system in a fundamental way. As with all Philippine presidencies during the country's postindependence period, the Aquino administration was characterized by oligarchic rule, economic and social inequality, desperate poverty, and the politics of personalism. Within four years of assuming the presidency, Aquino survived six coup attempts.

Aquino's initial and unsuccessful attempts to end communist insurgency were based on reconciliation, a policy the armed forces vigorously fought against, claiming the NPA insurgents were taking advantage of the military's soft line by strengthening their positions. To keep the military from rebelling, Aquino's counterinsurgency policy eventually moved toward a more conservative, harder line, including support for community vigilante groups established to repulse the rebels. These localized anticommunist self-defense organizations proliferated with the failure of peace negotiations between the Aquino government and the NPA. Aquino's endorsement of vigilantism was a sign that the communist movement was still extremely active, despite her administration's reforms. It also invited international criticism that her government was prone to "serious and unjustifiable" violations of human rights and had "turned the whole of the Philippines into a battlefield pitting civilian against civilian."[6]

In short, Aquino failed to institutionalize the overwhelming personal support she received from the populace. She did not develop a political party that could carry on her reform policies when she was no longer in office. Her followers expected that she would solve the nation's problems single-handedly. The proliferation of political parties during her administration weakened administrative discipline, as the leaders of various organizations vied for power rather than cooperated for the common good. Personalism once again triumphed over institutional legitimacy.

Personalism also became an issue when Aquino ineffectively dealt with allegations of corruption among her own family members. As a member of one of the wealthiest families in the Philippines, Corazon Cojuangco Aquino was raised in the tradition of family loyalty, and these ties precluded her from halting the improprieties of some of her Cojuangco relatives, several of whom had been Marcos cronies.

This familial problem was exacerbated by Aquino's reluctance to move more forcefully toward meaningful land reform. Because Aquino's family owned a six thousand–hectare hacienda, Luisita, in Tarlac Province on the island of Luzon, her detractors viewed this reluctance as self-interest. Aquino had the opportunity and power to put forth a comprehensive land reform program when she had revolutionary powers during her first year in office before the National Assembly was constituted. However, she waited to promulgate her Comprehensive Agrarian Reform Program until after assembly members had had a chance to gut those parts of the reform that were damaging to their own interests. Because 130 of the 200 elected members of Congress were leaders of established landowning families and 39 more were relatives of these families, the final land reform program was characterized by compromise and loopholes that guaranteed the continuation of the status quo. Even Luisita was not broken up and divided among its tenant farmers.

The post-Marcos period began to breed new disillusionment. Public opinion surveys showed that President Aquino's initial, almost universal support decreased steadily as her tenure in office lengthened. Beginning in December 1989 with a failed military coup attempt that temporarily destabilized the government, a series of dreadful events occurred that many Filipinos saw as ominous indications that the government's mandate was tenuous. A horrendous earthquake in July 1990, which devastated much of northern Luzon, was followed by the Iraqi invasion of Kuwait, which raised the price of oil in the Philippines, undermining the fragile economy. This was followed by a typhoon that swept over half of the archipelago in November, claiming nearly four hundred lives. The typhoon left half a million people homeless and ruined crops in a dozen provinces.

Even more devastating was the June 1991 eruption of Mount Pinatubo, a volcano in central Luzon that had been dormant for five hundred years. Considered the worst eruption in modern history, the volcano killed over five hundred people, caused hundreds of thousands to lose their homes and livelihoods, and affected weather patterns throughout the world. Unbearably, five months later the Philippines suffered through Tropical Storm Uring in the Visayas. The storm and consequent flooding caused some eight thousand deaths and the devastation of tens of thousands of farms. Much of the flooding could be attributed to the fact that many of the islands' mountains had been denuded from deforestation.

In the midst of these natural tragedies, the Philippine Senate rejected the Military Bases Agreement with the United States, ending America's military presence in the country. Clark Air Force Base, which was situated only about twenty miles from Mount Pinatubo, was buried beneath several feet of ash. The immediate effect was the loss of 70,000 jobs and $500 million in U.S. foreign aid.

After intense debate and speculation, Aquino decided not to seek a second term. (The constitutionality of a second term was part of the debate.) Seven candidates declared their intention to become president, all but one of whom (Miriam Defensor Santiago) represented traditional interests. The most notorious of the *trapos*, or traditional politicians (*trapos* is also a Tagalog word for rags), was former first lady Imelda Marcos, known worldwide for her 1,200 pairs of shoes. Aquino endorsed her minister of defense, Fidel V. Ramos, who was subsequently elected in May 1992 with only 23.4 percent of the popular vote. (No runoff is required among the candidates with the highest votes.) Ramos was known for his heroism in turning against his former boss, Ferdinand Marcos, in 1986 and for his competent leadership in defending Aquino against army-initiated coups. Nevertheless, he was laconic and careful to a fault.

Ramos faced many of the same crises Aquino had been unable to solve: chronic crime exacerbated by a string of kidnappings of Chinese children; continuing insurgencies by communists, rightist soldiers, and Muslim separatists; a debilitated economy with the lowest growth rate among the ASEAN countries; and daily brownouts, sometimes lasting most of the day. Ramos appointed commissions and directed his vice president to head up committees to solve these extraordinary problems. He also engaged in intensive travels around ASEAN to discover which of each nation's policies the Philippines could most effectively emulate.

During his six-year term (1992–1998), Ramos became known as the nation's most effective president of the postindependence period. Under his administration, the Philippines joined the rest of Southeast Asia as an economic tiger. Ramos took on the major oligarchic families and firms he believed restrained the nation's progress. He promoted a more open market system and strengthened the nation's sagging infrastructure. He gave foreign investors the right to 100 percent ownership in Philippine companies; transformed Subic Bay, the former U.S. naval base, into an enterprise zone with investment from American and other foreign companies; privatized state enterprises, including Philippine Airlines; and pushed through a fast-track mechanism for privatizing power companies, a decision that has helped solve the ubiquitous problem of electrical shortages.

Ramos's economic program was implemented under the slogan "Philippines 2000," indicating the target year for joining the ranks of the newly industrialized countries (NICs). Ramos's vision was to transform the Philippines into an economic power within the framework of a democratic political system. His success is shown by record growth rates approaching 7 percent, an end to the power shortages that had undermined the country's growth for decades, the privatization of huge firms that formerly had been controlled by the oligarchic families, and the growth of exports. Moreover, by continuing in his predecessor's spirit of political liberalism, Ramos proved that he was both a democrat and a developer.

Ramos's popularity was high as he approached the end of his six-year term. His major strengths were (1) a personal reputation for honesty; (2) a willingness to open the country to foreign investment, eliminate corruption, and create a workable tax system; (3) success in 1994 in forming a coalition between his party and the main opposition parties; (4) support from the business community, important factions of the military, and the U.S. government; and (5) an ability to nurture a commitment to democratic institutions among Filipinos. His weaknesses were (1) a lack of charisma and an unwillingness to make critical decisions; (2) an inability to break up the dynastic-controlled provincial economies; (3) impotence in coping with the horrible natural disasters that continue to devastate the islands; and (4) the lack of a mandate, after receiving less than one-fourth of the presidential vote to start off his term.

Ramos's achievements went beyond economic growth. He also kept the more professionalized military under wraps (not a small success, given that he was defense minister under Corazon Aquino), oversaw the reduction of crime in Manila (taking over as "anticrime czar" from Vice President Joseph Estrada), and brought the Philippines into the new international era through his trips abroad and his active role in regional associations. He was also primarily responsible for a 1996 peace accord between the government and Muslim insurgents of the Moro National Liberation Front (MNLF).

Because the constitution allows for only a single term in office, Ramos's friends began campaigning for a constitutional amendment that would allow him to run for a second term. This attempt was strongly opposed by numerous opposition groups and by Cardinal Sin, who viewed the effort as a throwback to the days of the Marcos dictatorship. Finally, in the face of massive protest demonstrations, Ramos was forced to announce publicly and straightforwardly that he would not seek a second term. Even many of his supporters believed that enacting a constitutional amendment to allow a second presidential term would set a bad precedent.

Winning a landslide victory in the next election was his vice president, Joseph Estrada (nicknamed Erap—the Tagalog word for friend, spelled backward), a garrulous populist known for his playboy lifestyle that included womanizing and gambling and for his starring roles in "B" movies. He was favored overwhelmingly by the rural poor and opposed vociferously by the urban intellectuals. He was viewed by the latter as the quintessential "patron," who was rude and crude and engaged in personalistic politics.

He began his six-year term of office auspiciously with a majority in both houses of the Philippine congress. The 1997 economic crisis had not affected the Philippines as strongly as it had Thailand, Malaysia, and Indonesia, at least partially because the economy was already a disaster. The nation continued to be viewed as the "sick man of Asia" because of its poor track record of development and its endemic poverty. Still, as the millennium began, the Philippines boasted positive economic growth rates, a significant change from the negative growth rates of its recent past. Estrada's rhetoric favored the poor during his first two years as president, but he did not succeed in producing policies that alleviated the difficulties of the poorer classes.

In 2000, Estrada was accused of gross corruption, and an impeachment trial began in the Philippine Senate. Evidence showed that Estrada had been involved in illegal gambling activities and that he had accepted public monies for his private gain. His personal life was vilified, especially regarding his lavish gifts to his minor wives and mistresses. For many in the poorer classes, the trial was viewed as the elite's attempt to undermine and overthrow their champion. Nevertheless, the evidence grew and mass demonstrations against him took place.

In January 2001, the impeachment trial collapsed when the Senate voted 11 to 10 not to allow bank documents to be shown to the Senate. This act was viewed as a virtual exoneration of Estrada. Hundreds of thousands of Filipinos demonstrated against Estrada, and the military and most government officials rose against him until he was forced to leave Malacañang Palace, the traditional home of the president. The Supreme Court declared that the office of president was vacant and that the vice president could legally assume the presidency. Although Vice President Gloria Macapagal Arroyo had resigned her cabinet post months before to protest the Estrada administration, she nevertheless replaced Estrada.

Estrada was later arrested and tried on charges of plundering $300 million in state funds. He was eventually found guilty and sentenced to life in prison. However, an official pardon in 2007 by Arroyo kept Estrada from serving his sentence, on the condition that the former president stay out of politics.

Under Arroyo, the Philippines continues to reverse the political stability won by Ramos but destroyed by Estrada. President Arroyo, the daughter of Diosdado Macapagal, former president and doyen of the Filipino establishment, was a classmate of Bill Clinton's at Georgetown University and holds a doctorate in economics from the University of the Philippines. She entered office facing a citizenry split over the constitutionality of the overthrow of

Estrada, an economic malaise lingering from the Asian economic crisis, and a refurbished military capable of attempting a coup d'état against her.

In July 2003, a rebel faction of the AFP seized a shopping mall and the Oakwood luxury apartment complex in Manila's financial district. They demanded that Arroyo and others in her administration resign, claiming corruption threatened the country. They also alleged top military brass had staged bombing incidents on Mindano to attract more U.S. military aid in the aftermath of the 9/11 attacks. The "Oakwood Mutiny," as it became known, ended hours later and resulted in the arrests of perpetrators and resignations of officials who had mishandled the affair. Most significant, it led to the resumption of the coup d'état as an extraconstitutional political tool, gone from Philippine politics during the previous fourteen years.

While completing the remainder of Estrada's presidential term, Arroyo publicly declared her desire to stay out of the 2004 presidential elections. Later reversing her decision, Arroyo ran and won against a field of weak candidates that included an Estrada ally, an anticorruption icon, and a broadcaster-cum-evangelist gadfly. The elections were marred by allegations of rigging and, later, the leak of an explosive election-time conversation between Arroyo and an election commissioner. Pollsters found that most Filipinos believed the elections were tainted. Calls for Arroyo's impeachment, thus far unsuccessful, have followed as her unpopularity has grown.

Arroyo's term expires in 2010. No viable contenders have emerged who are capable of unseating her before that time. In 2006, upon the twentieth anniversary of the People Power movement to oust Marcos, Arroyo, citing coup rumors, made the unpopular move of declaring a state of emergency. She deployed the military to Manila streets and barricaded Malacañang Palace with barbed wire. Scheduled marches were canceled and what was to be a celebration of Philippine democracy actually echoed Marcos's own 1972 imposition of martial law.[7] Arroyo followed the affair by lifting martial law three weeks later and then arresting suspected political enemies on specious charges.

A year later, the leader of the Oakwood Mutiny, Senator Antonio Trillanes, audaciously attempted yet another coup during his own court proceeding. A disorganized band of armed rebels stormed the courtroom and a nearby hotel and declared a new government. Following gunfire, the rebels were forced to give up hours later, and the coup was viewed as a publicity stunt as much as a serious attempt to seize power. Trillanes, who had only recently run for Senate from prison and won, waited in vain during the fiasco for a People Power uprising that never emerged.

As 2010 approaches, Arroyo maintains power via patronage to politicos and the military brass. It is a familiar but dangerous formula to Philippine politics. Another corruption scandal involving government communications contracts drew in Arroyo's husband, who eventually left the country. Also revealed was a secret meeting at the presidential place where bags of cash were handed to House members who had been told to first support and then derail a "sham" presidential impeachment proceeding to thwart the possibility of a genuine attempt.[8] Personalism, subornment, and guile, ever endemic to the country's politics, continue to shape events and the oligarchic characteristics of democratic rule in the Philippines.

INSTITUTIONS AND SOCIAL GROUPS

Patron-Client Relations

The Philippine government can be described as clientelist, a form of societal organization in which political life centers on relationships that are largely person to person, informal, hierarchical, reciprocal, and based on an obligation of indebtedness *(utang na loob)*. Because they are too weak, interest groups, political parties, the legislature, and other government institutions have been supplanted by clientelist relationships. Thus, political life in the Philippines has consisted of constantly changing coalitions of clientele groups that serve both to articulate mass interests and to ensure government control over the people.

The need for patrons to provide resources to their clients has been a major cause of corruption throughout Philippine society. Indeed, public office has been used both for private gain and for the support of clients. Clientelist systems rely neither on rational allocations of resources nor on market forces; their first priority is to perpetuate the power of those who already rule.

Under President Marcos, the clientelist nature of Philippine society was most evident in the president's grant of monopoly privileges to selected followers. Marcos put the control of numerous industries in the hands of his clients and assured them of immunity from loss; when the economy began to collapse and his authority lost legitimacy (after the assassination of Senator Aquino), Marcos lost control, first over the resources he used to reward his clients and eventually over the entire society.

With the rise of President Aquino, Marcos's clientele lost its source of favors, and new patronage groups emerged. This same pattern followed with subsequent presidents, albeit in a less corrupt manner than with Marcos. The biggest departure from cronyism has been Fidel Ramos, who sought to mitigate clientelist politics and worked to strengthen government institutions and laws. Even so, most Philippine politicians find it difficult to ignore these relationships and thus rely on their own clientele. This reliance undermines the importance and legitimacy of democratic institutions, resulting in the continued decay rather than development of Philippine politics.

Constitutions

The Malolos constitution of 1899, promulgated by Filipino nationalists under the leadership of Emilio Aguinaldo and the first democratic constitution in Asia, was based on South American and Spanish models and embodied the ideas of liberal democracy, representative government, separation of powers, and a system of checks and balances. This constitution endured only a short time before the United States ended the republic.

The U.S.-sponsored constitution of 1935 provided for a representative democracy based on the U.S. presidential model. Japanese occupiers set up their own constitution in 1943 for the Philippines but it was viewed as illegitimate and collapsed with the end of World War II. The 1935 constitution was subsequently restored and served the Philippines until 1973. In 1972, Marcos had convened a constitutional convention to draft a new constitution based on a parliamentary rather than a presidential model. However, Marcos's declaration of martial law silenced debate on his proposed constitution; a few months later a constitutional convention approved the new document, which called for a parliamentary form of government led by a prime minister and allowed the interim president (Marcos) to decide when to convene the interim national assembly, further allowing him to make and execute all laws until he convened the assembly. The constitution was then approved by people's assemblies (*barangay*) and went into effect on January 17, 1973.

President Aquino's victory led to a "Freedom constitution," a provisional document issued by presidential proclamation. It provided for presidential appointment of a constitutional commission to draft a new, permanent constitution. Meanwhile, until the commission presented a new constitution, which resembled the one of 1935, President Aquino held executive and legislative powers. A plebiscite on February 2, 1987, supported the new document, with 75 percent of the voters approving.

Under the 1986 constitution, the powers of the president are more circumscribed than under previous Philippine constitutions. The presidential term is six years, with no reelection permitted. To curb the familial patronage of the Marcos years, the president's spouse and all close relatives are barred from appointment as public officials. Martial law powers are also circumscribed, providing both the legislative and judicial branches the power to review legal bases for the imposition of martial law.

The Aquino constitution is among the most democratic in all of Southeast Asia, providing for citizens' civil liberties, a meaningful separation of powers, and rights of participation in choosing government representatives. The nation's success in bringing down Estrada exemplifies the reform nature of the constitution. Nevertheless, Arroyo has unsuccessfully sought to reform the constitution by instituting a parliamentary style government, echoing Marcos's reforms in 1972.

The Legislature

In the postindependence period, the Philippine legislature has been both a bulwark for freedom and a tool for legitimizing presidential decrees. The Aquino constitution gives numerous prerogatives to the Congress, including the sole power to declare war, to withdraw presidential emergency powers, and to determine revenue origination and appropriation. Whereas the Marcos constitution of 1973 allowed President Marcos to exercise both legislative and executive powers, in contrast the 1986 constitution clearly separates these powers. It includes a bicameral Congress, consisting of a 24-member Senate elected at large for six years and for not more than two consecutive terms and a House of Representatives of not more than 250 members, most of whom are elected from legislative districts apportioned on the basis of population.

Political Parties

The Philippines had a two-party system for most of its democratic period (1946–1972) when the Liberal and Nacionalista Parties alternately held power, with neither party ever able to get its presidential nominee reelected.[9] The ideological differences between the two parties were negligible, and neither party appeared to represent the interests of the vast majority of Filipinos. For the most part, the two parties functioned as mobilizers of votes for specific candidates.

Under Marcos, one party dominated the political scene. Marcos's New Society movement (*Kilusang Bagong Lipunan*, or KBL) was a noncompetitive, authoritarian party devoted to keeping Marcos in power and maintaining the support of the U.S. government. Through his magnetic personality, his dominance of the bureaucracy and the legislative and executive branches, his fraudulent plebiscites and referenda, and his manipulation of nationalist symbols, Marcos controlled every aspect of the party and its program.

In the post–martial law era after 1981, the KBL continued to dominate politics. However, as Marcos's support deteriorated, opposition parties began to emerge. The most important of these was UNIDO, formed in 1979 by Salvador Laurel, who had broken from the KBL. UNIDO, largely an alliance of establishment politicians who had lost out when Marcos took control, was united primarily in its opposition to his domination of the political scene. Thus, UNIDO became an umbrella organization encompassing a number of smaller parties under the leadership of prominent politicians such as Senator Benigno Aquino Jr., who established LABAN! (Fight!) while still a political prisoner of Marcos. These parties formed the core of support for Corazon Aquino when she ran for president.

After Marcos fell from power, KBL members scattered to different parties, including the once moribund Nacionalista Party. No one party emerged around Aquino's centrist-reform administration. Instead, a series of parties under the leadership of prominent politicians were established to enhance these politicians' political ambitions. However, in contrast to the two parties of the pre–martial law era, these new parties had ideological as well as personal causes. The centrist and left-of-center parties gave support to Aquino, although they disagreed among themselves over power sharing. The right-of-center parties, which opposed her leadership, also squabbled over a sufficient number of issues to prevent them from uniting.

Party politics remained largely an elite-establishment activity, based on patronage and personalism. Political parties play little role in presidential elections that are determined primarily by the general public's attitudes toward individual candidates. In 2004, Arroyo's party, Lakas-Christian Muslim Democrats, and the party of Fidel Ramos merged with a number of other parties only to find the combined party factionalized after victory.

Political violence in the form of bombings, assassinations, and voter intimidation haunts elections. For example, over 275 people were killed in violence related to the 2004 and 2007 elections for national and local offices. The latter, in fact, produce the most violence. Recent decentralization of fiscal authority continues to raise the stakes of local government, compounding the trend toward violence.[10]

The Military

Although long involved with supporting particular candidates for office, the military has never played the dominant role in Philippine politics. In contrast to Thailand's, the Philippine military has been subordinated to civilian leaders and given the orthodox task of providing external defense and security against domestic subversion. (Marcos exploited this second task to protect his personal interests.) Fidel Ramos is the only president to have been a military general.

The AFP had total personnel of 37,000 in the 1940s. Between 1975 and 1976 the number jumped from 90,000 to 142,000. Marcos expanded the army to three-and-a-half times its former strength during his tenure, which increased military involvement in civilian life, including the militarization of internal security forces.[11] Under Marcos, the military was deprofessionalized through his appointments of cronies and fellow Ilocanos (from northern Luzon) to the commanding positions. The clearest such example was Marcos's appointment of his cousin, Fabian Ver, as armed forces chief of staff. Ver, who was subsequently determined by a government-appointed investigatory commission to have helped plan the assassination of Senator Aquino, politicized the military, turning it into a security force for Marcos and the enforcer of his martial law. In return, Marcos gave military leaders access to financial benefits.

A group of reform-minded soldiers who reacted against the politicization of the military and its diminished professionalism organized into the Reform the Armed Forces Movement (RAM) and led the army rebellion against Marcos after the 1986 elections. Juan Ponce Enrile, a RAM leader, was awarded the position of minister of defense in Corazon Aquino's government for his role in ousting Marcos and supporting Aquino. Along with other RAM officers, he eventually turned against Aquino and led coup attempts against her government.

Despite attempts to reprofessionalize the military, or because of them, Aquino was constantly threatened by elements within the AFP. On December 1, 1989, members of the elite Scout Rangers and the marines instigated a violent and threatening coup attempt against Aquino. They captured air bases, the Fort Bonifacio army camp, and two television stations and attacked the presidential Malacañang Palace. Except for a call for President Aquino's resignation, no specific demands were made by the rebel forces. To repulse the attack, Aquino asked the United States to provide air support to forces loyal to the government. U.S. F-4 Phantom jets, flying from Clark Air Force Base, immobilized the rebel forces, who had occupied hotels and office buildings in Manila; the rebels agreed to a negotiated settlement. One of the principal rebels, Gregorio Honasan, leader of previous coup attempts and a RAM founder, once again evaded capture.

During the coup attempt, which was devastating to the Aquino regime, seventy-nine people were killed and six hundred wounded. Moreover, the image of stability, so important for the country's continued economic growth, was shattered. Also, Aquino lost face because of her decision to request U.S. support. Finally, the role of the U.S. military in this domestic issue complicated later negotiations on the American bases and exacerbated nationalist and anti-U.S. sentiments that were already near the surface.

During the Ramos and Estrada presidencies, no military coups were attempted. Ramos was the first Philippine president since Ramon Magsaysay to view security in broad terms, taking into account military, political, economic, societal, and environmental factors. Coup rumors have persisted under Arroyo's rule with actual weak attempts by a rebel AFP faction tied to the Oakwood Mutiny.

The AFP currently boasts 120,000 total troops but suffers from "institutional rot" due to poor organization and equipment, factionalism, and uncontrolled elements.[12] Top military brass maintain a distrust of politicians and still see themselves as the "nursemaid of change" in the milieu of Philippine politics.[13]

Women

Traditionally, women have played only minor roles in Philippine politics. Women have never held key positions of power in the legislature, cabinet, military, or bureaucracy. The rise of Imelda Marcos and Corazon Aquino to positions of immense power is anomalous rather than a pattern, as both were the wives of famous and powerful politicians. Marcos, who was governor of Metro Manila and minister of human settlements until her husband was overthrown in 1986, owed her claim to leadership to her husband's authoritarian rule. Aquino was the saintly widow of Senator Benigno Aquino. The power of these women is more a function of their familial ties to prominent male politicians than their successful surmounting of the formidable barriers that have traditionally kept women out of political positions of power.[14] President Arroyo became the Philippines' second female head of state, an event unprecedented in Southeast Asia.

The Church

As citizens of the only predominantly Christian country in Asia, Filipinos have felt themselves to be different from and even superior to their Asian neighbors. With over 12,000 priests and nuns throughout the archipelago, the largest land holdings in the nation, and control over thousands of parishes, schools, and hospitals, the Catholic Church is a significant political, economic, and social institution. Factionalized among conservative, centrist, and progressive forces, the church has played a crucial role in all areas of Philippine life.

The most politically active leader of the church in the Philippines was Jaime Cardinal Sin, archbishop of Manila and head of the centrist faction. Cardinal Sin, in conjunction with church bishops and clergy, played an important role in undermining President Marcos's administration and in fashioning the compromise that unified the opposition under Corazon Aquino.

In policy matters, church leaders have been outspoken in condemning corruption and other dishonest practices and in supporting programs that favor the poor and greater social justice. The church's condemnation of family planning, specifically the use of contraceptives, has kept the government from implementing a comprehensive plan designed to improve health standards and reduce poverty. The church's stand against homosexuality and artificial contraception has also made it difficult for condoms and sex education to be made available to those most in need. When Ramos, the first non-Catholic president in Philippine history, set forth an anti-AIDS program that included the distribution of condoms, Cardinal Sin denounced both the plan and the president himself. President Arroyo, alternatively, champions "natural family planning" and cites the nation's declining birth rate as supportive evidence.

Notwithstanding controversies, the church has emerged as a primary symbol of peaceful change, warning against political excesses by government and opposition groups alike. Cardinal Sin retired in 2003 and died two years later. His replacement, Gaudencio Rosales, has proven more politically moderate than his predecessor but remains willing to speak out against birth control legislation.

Papal visits play a significant role in shaping the Filipino Catholic church, its direction, and the standing of its local leaders. Pope John Paul II's second visit to the Philippines for World Youth Day in Manila, for example, produced a crowd of 4 million, the largest papal crowd to gather in world history. Filipino Catholics and Cardinal Rosales eagerly await Pope Benedict XVI's first Asian trip.

Communist Insurgents

With origins in the Soviet-supported Huk rebellion, the revolutionary opposition in the Philippines gained strength in the 1960s but became a meaningful threat to the nation's security during Marcos's rule. The Communist Party of the Philippines (CPP), the central organizational unit of the revolutionary opposition, is the largest communist party in ASEAN and oversees the New People's Army (NPA), the region's last remaining communist insurgency. The Maoist NPA controls about 5,000 troops spread throughout the archipelago's provinces. At its peak in the 1980s, the NPA had 20,000 loyalists who controlled some 20 percent of the country's territory.

The NPA's strength has come from disillusioned peasants, especially tenant farmers and day laborers, whose hopes for a better life were lifted by Marcos's announcement of a New Society and then dashed by unfulfilled promises and expectations. Similarly, the rise of Corazon Aquino initially weakened the NPA until her promises of meaningful land reform and improvement in the standard of living went unmet. Students and intellectuals were persuaded to join the NPA by the movement's claim to represent the nationalist struggle against imperialism and the peasant-worker struggle against feudalism and dynastic politics. Other citizens supported the NPA as the only viable force against the corruption and abuses of rights perpetrated by local dynastic politicians and military units.

Thailand's success in countering insurgency stemmed from combining a policy of reconciliation and amnesty with economic development. In the Philippines, however, reconciliation policies by Aquino, Ramos, and Arroyo have not been matched with a concomitant improvement in the standard of living. Although very little outside support is provided to the NPA, it was able to capitalize on the negative growth of the national economy and on the consequent extreme poverty suffered by nearly half of the population. The nation's interminable economic difficulties make it difficult to resolve the protracted, forty-year guerrilla war.

Moro Islamic Separatists

Fighting primarily for an independent state for Muslims in the southern islands of the Philippines, Moro nationalists launched an armed campaign in 1972. In 1975, the Moro National Liberation Front (MNLF) was formally recognized by the Organization of the Islamic Conference (OIC). Engaging in armed warfare, sabotage, and political violence, the MNLF struck agreements for autonomy under Marcos and Aquino that were never fully implemented. In 1984, a leadership struggle led to the creation of a second group, the Moro Islamic Liberation Front (MILF).[15] Also in the 1980s, a third group, Abu Sayyaf, formed with the assistance of Osama bin Laden's brother-in-law.[16]

In 1996, the Philippine government had established the Autonomous Region in Muslim Mindano (ARMM) as part of a historic peace agreement with the MNLF. Implementation, however, struggled and produced lingering resentment. The conflict waged on with the MILF but conditions changed following the 9/11 attacks and subsequent U.S. war on terrorism, which drew attention to all the groups in the area, their activities, and their affiliations. Abu Sayyaf's supposed connections with al-Qaeda and Jemaah Islamiyah (based in Indonesia) came under great suspicion and later question as the group adopted strategies of kidnapping tourists for ransom to finance their rebellion, activities belying notions that Abu Sayyaf acted as a tentacle of the well-financed al-Qaeda.

Eventually, over 7,500 U.S. troops were stationed in Mindano related to a military offensive to weaken the remaining Moro separatists and Abu Sayyaf Islamists. The use of military pressure was combined with political efforts led by Mahathir bin Mohamad of Malaysia, the OIC, and U.S. Aid for International Development (USAID) programs to help reintegrate Moro fighters into civilian life. A reduction in fighting occurred but local bombings still plagued the area. In December 2007, an agreement between the MILF and MNLF to put aside their decades-old animosity gave new hope that a political resolution with the Arroyo government was possible.[17] The Arroyo administration signed a controversial memorandum of understanding with the MILF to expand the ARMM into an ancestral homeland with wide-ranging self-government for the Moros. Drawing the ire of many Filipinos, the agreement was viewed by nationalist critics as a violation of the constitution and a threat to the republic. Fighting continued after the memorandum was signed, and the Philippine government eventually scrapped the deal.

DEMOCRATIZATION

The Philippines was once known as Southeast Asia's "showcase of democracy," and in terms of the formal institutions of government, that description is accurate. In the postindependence period up to the time of martial law, the Philippine government carried out its functions based on constitutional guidelines, through the separation of powers and adherence to a bill of rights.

Behaviorally, however, the picture is much different. Since the Spanish colonized the Philippines almost five hundred years ago, the nation has been ruled by a small number of family dynasties that have controlled both the economic and political spheres through decidedly undemocratic means. From the great haciendas of the Spaniards to the patronage politics of the U.S. period, these dynasties have ruled in a baronial, feudal manner, each controlling a particular area of the archipelago.

The country's archipelagic nature is partially responsible for the decentralized, dynastic system. Pervasive poverty also helps explain why the poor learn to rely on their wealthy patrons. Dynastic families sponsor the weddings of their laborers and tenants, pay for children's education, and care for the sick, thereby forming a tie of dependency that keeps the poor deferential and loyal. Without strong government institutions, patron-client relations develop to meet the needs of the majority poor.

The dynastic nature of Philippine politics is also due to cultural factors. A Filipino's loyalty is directed first to family, then to close friends, then to the local community, then to personally known political leaders, and finally to distant, impersonal governmental agencies. Although all of these concentric circles of allegiance place emphasis on the personal nature of loyalty, an individual's family and patron family demand the deepest loyalties.[18] In the *compadre* (godfather) system, a reciprocity is formed in which the higher-status *compadre* renders material benefits and prestige and the lower-status family provides loyalty, deference, and support. Thus, a candidate for office may be asked to sponsor a marriage or a newborn baby in return for a family's electoral support, and the family then has the right to seek political patronage from its new compadre.[19] Politicians are equally desirous of becoming sponsors to ensure a wide base of electoral support.

For democratization to take root in the Philippines, the formal institutions of government must become more than facades for oligarchic rule. Inasmuch as the overwhelming majority of newly elected senators and representatives are members of families who have dominated Philippine politics for centuries, the elections of Corazon Aquino and Gloria Macapagal Arroyo in reality extended the domination of certain families. Although the people in charge of the government have changed, and despite Fidel Ramos's efforts to reform the system, there have been too few fundamental changes in the character of the Philippine political system.

Under Arroyo a deepened sense of political malaise tinged by frustration afflicts the Philippines' electoral democracy, or what might better be described as dysfunctional democracy. Public cynicism has extended even to oppositional politics. People Power, once the essence of democratic spirit, is slowly becoming delegitimized as a useful political tool. Each time a popular revolt overthrows a corrupt president (e.g., Marcos, Estrada), a new set of elites take the reins of power only to extend oligarchic rule and, consequently, disillusionment.[20] Civil society has grown under Arroyo but a disturbing degree of violence and lawlessness persists at the local level. In 2006, Reporters Without Borders listed the Philippines behind Iraq as the second most dangerous country in which to practice journalism. Over thirty-two journalists were killed from 1991 to 2006 and only two cases have been brought to conviction.[21]

ECONOMIC DEVELOPMENT

If Thailand has been a favorite case study for capitalist development of agricultural societies in the past several decades, the Philippines became the model for what not to do. On a par with Thailand in the mid-1970s, when each nation had an annual per capita GNP of just over $300, the Philippines has slipped well behind, achieving a $1,192 per capita GDP in 2007 in contrast to Thailand's $2,750. Despite abundant natural resources, strong ties to the United States, and an English-speaking workforce, the Philippines has failed to realize its economic potential. Inequality remains the constant theme of the Philippine economy, even during periods of growth.

The Philippine economy has been skewed since the days of Spanish colonialism, which thrust a feudal economic system upon the Filipinos. When Americans refined the Philippines with their neocolonial system, the Philippine economy fell under the control of outside forces, including multinational corporations, and a group of fabulously wealthy Filipino families (mostly of Spanish or Chinese background). Neocolonial relations between Americans and Filipinos were characterized by exploitation rather than cooperation for the mutual good, with the bulk of the profits gained by businesses in the Philippines going to Americans.

The Philippine economy at the end of World War II was in a shambles because of the widespread destruction in Manila and of basic infrastructure throughout the archipelago. As with most Southeast Asian nations in the 1950s, the Philippines adopted an import-substitution industrialization (ISI) strategy to develop the economy. In essence, the ISI strategy restricted imports of foreign goods to improve the balance of payments and to generate new industries to make the nation more self-sufficient. The United States had already penetrated the domestic Philippine economy, so Americans did not oppose this policy.

Initially, ISI policies worked well in terms of benefiting domestic manufacturing industries, and between 1950 and 1980 the share of manufacturing in the total economy rose from 8 percent to 25 percent, whereas the share of agriculture declined from 42 percent to 23 percent.[22] Manufacturing accounted for more than half the value of Philippine exports in the 1970s, just a decade after accounting for only 6 percent. At the same time, however, every economic indicator showed the Philippines to have the least effective economy in the region. Moreover, only a small group of Marcos-centered industrialists and financiers benefited from this new form of state capitalism, while small businesses and labor groups were weakened.

In the agricultural and commodities sector, where most Filipinos were employed, the economy suffered ongoing maldevelopment. The concentration of wealth and land has been more pervasive in the Philippines than in any other Southeast Asian nation. Weak democratic institutions have proven unable to redistribute income or create new opportunities for Philippine voters.

The mixed success of ISI led international agencies such as the World Bank to change their advice and to recommend an export-oriented industrialization (EOI) strategy for economic development. However, interference by Marcos cronies kept protectionist measures intact, so the new strategy never worked effectively. In the commodities sector, reform was largely ignored. Marcos had given his best friends monopoly control over the sugar and coconut sectors, which led to their amassing fabulous riches. These riches ended up in Swiss and U.S. bank accounts and in real estate investments throughout the world, a capital flight that subverted the economy into an incurable state.

In the 1970s Marcos and his sugar barons made a costly bet on global markets by hoarding the commodity, only to see the price bubble burst by the end of the decade and render the country's sugar stock worthless. In the early 1980s, rising oil prices and the collapse of other commodities resulted in economic recession in acute economic hardship for many Filipinos. Farm prices had dropped so low that starvation was a real threat in the major sugar areas.[23]

Marcos's poor economic performance occurred simultaneously with the people's growing disenchantment with the New Society's authoritarian ways and gross corruption. Urban laborers grew increasingly angry about the erosion of their wages and the deterioration of working conditions, while employers found themselves losing profits because of the increased costs of energy and pressure from the Marcos administration to raise wages. Both of these groups, as well as the farmers, could see that President Marcos's family and cronies were living in ostentatious luxury.

All these factors so undermined the economy that only a spark was needed to bring Filipinos to the streets to demand change. That "spark" turned out to be the return home and assassination of Senator Aquino in August 1983. For Filipinos, the regime was not only a disaster economically but morally as well.

Economic growth rates since Marcos reflect participation in Asia's economic dynamism but at a slower pace due to chronic challenges in the Philippine economy. Aquino and Ramos helped economic growth return to the Philippines only to see it thwarted by dependence on oil imports, inflation, and the Asian economic crisis of the late 1990s. High population growth rates, which persisted well above 2 percent until the new millennium, combined with inefficient use of educational resources, have exacerbated the country's economic woes. Unemployment and underemployment have caused many Filipinos to travel abroad as guest workers in the Middle East, Hong Kong, Japan, and even fellow ASEAN states. Remittances topped $14 billion in 2007, about 10 percent of the Phillipines' GDP. Only the overseas workers from China, India, and Mexico send home more money than do Filipino expatriates and guest workers.

For his part, Fidel Ramos focused his presidency on improving the Philippine economy by liberalizing virtually every facet of the economy, allowing technocrats and the market system to prevail. By 1994 the economic growth rate had reached 5.1 percent, not outstanding by Southeast Asian standards but high compared to previous performance in the Philippines. By 1996, growth had reached 6.8 percent, an unprecedentedly high figure, helped by the lack of any major natural calamities during the year. Exports continued to grow, capital formation consistently increased, and the agricultural sector flourished. Inflation was under control. Many signs of growth were visible, most strikingly in Manila as new buildings were constructed, streets were repaired, tourists came in increasing numbers, and a middle class arose. The 1997 economic debacle that began in Thailand caused a devaluation of the Philippine peso, and the first signs in several years of an end to the growth period.

Arroyo came into the presidency when investor confidence was low. Estrada's cronyism had undermined the confidence of domestic business executives and foreign investors. He had coped incompetently with privatizing unproductive industries (mostly run by his cronies). The stock market was in tatters, and the peso continued to lose value. Despite Arroyo's political difficulties, her economic policies have produced strong results. Economic growth has averaged above 5 percent during her tenure. Outsourced international call centers have recently joined microchip processing and automotive manufacturing as promising areas for economic growth. Under Arroyo, an economist, the Philippine stock market is performing well and the peso has been among Asia's strongest currencies.

The problems besetting the Philippines in the post-Marcos period remain those familiar to the past: economic inequality, land disputes, monopolistic industries, corrupt leadership, and an elite class more concerned with self-interest than with the public good. These are problems that can be resolved only by fundamental changes in all areas of Filipino life, including the social, economic, cultural, and political realms. Over twenty years have passed since Marcos's ouster. Unfortunately, for most Filipinos, the standard of living remains lower than in much of Southeast Asia. With respect to the Millennium Development Goals (MDGs), growth in the Philippines is not producing results as in neighboring Vietnam. A 2006 report by the UN and Asian Development Bank identified the Philippines and Burma as Asia's worst laggards in achieving progress on MDGs.[24] The lack of development success is all the more galling considering that Filipinos have far more experience with democratic rule than their Burmese counterparts.

THE PHILIPPINE STATE

If autonomy from societal institutions is a key variable in assessing strength, the Philippine state is weak because its authorities are integrated into a web of patronage networks that limits their power. The Philippine state cannot establish a coherent program because its authorities are not free from the oligarchic connections that have been a major part of Philippine politics for five hundred years. In this respect, the post-Marcos years are little different from the Marcos era. Still, differences are noteworthy.

The Philippines under Marcos is an example of a state that intervened in the economic system with devastating results. President Marcos undermined market forces by setting up incompetent cronies in businesses, then providing them with subsidies that relieved them of the need for accountability and efficiency. However, Marcos's "crony capitalism" was different from that of his predecessors and successors primarily by degree. The result has been an economy of gross inequality, slow growth, and resistance to change; it has been unable to integrate with the international economy (except in an exploited manner). The state remains weak in its capacity to meet the needs of society.

As discussed in the chapters on other countries, the first condition necessary for state strength is massive social dislocation. Unlike Thailand, which had no colonial heritage, the Philippines experienced two colonial regimes, both of which had a massive impact on every aspect of the country's life. Moreover, the Japanese interregnum was a period of dreadful trauma and devastation, and as a result of the war Manila was all but destroyed. In terms of social dislocation, then, the Philippines has the necessary conditions for development as a strong state, but it has never fully developed.

A strong state is more likely to emerge when at a historical moment external political forces, such as a threat of foreign invasion, favor concentrated social control. In 1972 President Marcos used the internal threats of insurgency and civil war in the Muslim provinces to buttress his arguments for martial law. Insurgency and insurrection remained viable threats under Marcos's martial law as well as during Aquino's presidency. Thus, the experience of the Philippines should be conducive to the rise of a strong state. The protracted nature of the conflict, however, further demonstrates the state's poor capacity to develop institutions.

A social grouping that is independent of existing bases of social control and is able to execute the policies of state leaders is the third condition for a strong state. The economically powerful Chinese also have not acted as an autonomous class. The dynastic families, on the other hand, have a separate power base (their regional clientele) that is often at odds with state authorities. The Philippines does have strong autonomous societal groups whose primary loyalties are to their religious, regional, and economic clienteles. Catholic Church leaders play an important political role, and intellectuals, students, and insurgents also have interests that are opposed to those of the central authorities. In this respect, then, the Philippine state is weak, lacking legitimacy and the capacity to integrate independent groups that are skillful enough to execute the designs of state leaders.

Philippine leaders have differed in strength and accordingly have either strengthened or weakened the state. Marcos amassed tremendous powers for himself and his clientele, but he was sufficiently incompetent to jeopardize the fabric of the republic. Aquino reinstated democratic government, but she was unable (or unwilling) to form policies that undermined the oligarchic power structure. Ramos made some progress in building up the state but Estrada's subsequent populism and corruption undermined institutionalization of state organs. Under Arroyo's tenure, civil society has grown but she shows "no qualms about further undermining the country's weak political institutions."[25]

Thus, the Philippines has experienced the necessary conditions for the development of a strong state: massive social dislocation, external support, and antisystemic insurgency. However, the state has remained personalistic, characterized by ineffective leadership and a low capacity to meet the needs of the people.

FOREIGN POLICY

The United States, the Philippines' closest ally, also represents the republic's biggest foreign policy problem. Since the colonial period, the United States and the Philippines have had a "special relationship," a term that aptly describes the close and complex ties shared by the two nations for almost a hundred years.

The Philippines, as Asia's most Americanized country, shares a common Christian heritage and the widespread use of the English language. In fashion, music, art, education, and politics, Filipinos often emulate Americans rather than their Asian neighbors. The result, therefore, has been a love-hate relationship. Many Filipinos look to the United States as their hope and even their future home at the same time that they demonstrate against U.S. interference in their affairs. The classic illustration of this ambivalence is the equal number of Filipinos demonstrating against American policy in front of the U.S. embassy and the number of Filipinos waiting there in line for an immigrant visa.

U.S. support of President Marcos, which sustained and prolonged his rule, was applauded by some and denounced by others. The last-minute U.S. endorsement of President Aquino, after it became clear that Marcos was finished, together with help in persuading Marcos to leave the country (for safe exile in Hawaii) only partially helped to undo the damage.

The presence of U.S. bases on Philippine territory, which continued following Marcos' departure, intensified the conflicting emotions Filipinos felt toward the United States. Though most Filipinos were eager to shed their dependence on U.S. protection, an estimated 3 percent of the Philippine GNP was generated, directly or indirectly, by the bases: by the 30,000 U.S. personnel, by the 45,000 Filipinos who worked on the bases, and by Filipino businesses established near the bases, as well as by taxes paid by all these employees. An estimated $500 million, a huge amount in a poor country, was generated by the bases each year and fed into the local economy.

Negotiations commenced in 1990 to determine the future of U.S. bases in the Philippines. For U.S. negotiators, the issue was the continuation of the military's forward defense strategy in the Pacific; the bases were an integral part of a global network of alliance relationships and strategic facilities among the noncommunist countries of the world.[26] Subic Bay Naval Base was the largest naval supply depot outside of the United States, and Clark Air Force Base was the center of all air operations from Hawaii to the Indian Ocean and the Persian Gulf.

For the Filipino negotiators, the crucial points did not involve strategic advantage but rather issues of nationalism, constitutional principles, compensation, and social problems. Those who argued from a nationalist point of view stated that because the Philippines was no longer threatened by an outside adversary, the U.S. bases were no longer necessary to protect Philippine security and sovereignty. Another disputed issue was the impact the bases had on the quality of life in surrounding areas. From one perspective, the bases perpetuated a "moral cesspool" in Olongapo (near Subic) and Angeles City (adjacent to Clark). In Olongapo alone, some 16,000 prostitutes serviced sailors on leave; AIDS and other sexually transmitted diseases were rampant. Unfortunately, the economies of these towns had become dependent on socially undesirable activities, a situation that fostered a negative image of all Filipinos.

After months of negotiations, the Philippine Senate rejected the bases agreement and requested that the Americans leave Subic. Prior to this decision, the United States had already begun withdrawal from Clark Air Force Base as a result of the destruction from the eruption of Mount Pinatubo. The Philippine Senate's determination was based on the desire to move from a dependency relationship with the United States to a more nationalistic posture. The decision led to tensions and challenges as the nation substituted the traditional view of reliance for security on the United States to a more broadly based view.

Initially, the decision to oust the Americans worsened foreign confidence in Philippine stability, thereby worsening the already desperate economy. However, the long-term gain for the country's psyche was thought to be worth the short-term costs. Only after the Americans were gone could the government take responsibility for the nation's ills rather than blame "American dominance" for every difficulty that cropped up; at the same time expelling the Americans would undermine NPA propaganda about American "neo-imperialism." Shouldering sole responsibility for security and foreign affairs could also oblige Filipinos to look more creatively and determinedly for appropriate solutions to their problems.

For the Philippines, the Spratly Islands imbroglio became the next major flash point. Sitting in the South China Sea and believed to hold vast untapped resources, including oil and natural gas, the Spratlys are claimed by the Philippines, China, Taiwan, Vietnam, Malaysia, and Brunei. The South China Sea is also a strategic waterway for the vital trade routes linking the Persian Gulf with Japan, Taiwan, and South Korea, all of which rely on free passage for their oil imports.

Philippine interest in the South China Sea involves its claims to several of the one hundred Spratly Islands and to maritime jurisdiction over a wide expanse of the sea's resources. Philippine officials have defined the problem in terms of respect for Philippine territorial rights and sovereignty. The military, in particular, has made the dispute over the Spratlys a matter of national prestige and overall security. The Philippine military is much weaker vis-à-vis than China and Vietnam, and diplomatic concessions by Philippine presidents on the matter cause the issue to fester in Philippine politics. Hostile fire between Philippine forces and Chinese and Vietnamese boats in the area have occurred on occasion. China, in particular, sits as a formidable threat to Philippine interests in the South China Sea.

In 2002, at annual ASEAN meetings, a major agreement was struck between interested parties to lessen tensions. All countries agreed to a code of conduct regarding settling disputes. Later, in 2004, state-supported oil companies from the Philippines, China, and Vietnam agreed to seismic exploration of the area. A patchwork of claims on specific islands remains but the threat of direct conflict has abated. Diplomatic and economic relations between the claimant countries now eclipse narrower interests in the reefs and waters of the Spratlys.

Post-9/11 agreements between Gloria Macapagal Arroyo and U.S. President George W. Bush resurrected some of the mixed feelings Filipinos had toward the United States. Many Filipinos did not want to turn to the U.S. umbrella yet again, but evidence from the 9/11 Commission Report revealed al-Qaeda hijackers had met in the Philippines before the attacks. The troubled south took on international dimensions with new fears of international Islamists operating amidst Moro separatists, namely the al-Qaeda-linked groups of Abu Sayyaf and Jemaah Islamiyah (JI).

Arroyo offered the Philippines' full support for Bush's war on terrorism, and the United States gradually dispatched over 7,500 troops to assist with fighting rebellion and terrorism in the separatist Muslim south. By 2006, the U.S. State Department had officially declared certain areas of the South as "safe havens for terrorists." Months later, echoing the U.S. PATRIOT Act, the Philippine House of Representatives and Senate passed the Human Security Act to allow wiretapping of suspected terrorists.

Joint exercises are now commonplace between U.S. and Philippine troops, as are sporadic bomb blasts (and kidnappings) claimed by Abu Sayyaf and JI. The Joint Special Operations Task Force-Philippines (JSOTF-P), as it is known, remains the primary vehicle for U.S. involvement in the area. Operating with a counterinsurgency mission, the JSOTF-P emphasizes technical and humanitarian assistance to the AFP and local populations. U.S. military activity, some of it outsourced to U.S. defense contractors, includes arms sales to the AFP and cash rewards for local informants. Rumors of plans to reestablish a permanent U.S. base in the Philippines located in the South (expectedly) sparked new controversy. In the new international era, the Philippines remains wedded to U.S. protection and patronage, much as it did during the Cold War, World War II, and the Spanish-American War.

CONCLUSION

The contemporary Philippine political system is formally democratic, with structures and procedures conducive to an open polity. Informally, however, the system remains oligarchic, ruled by a self-perpetuating elite of landed families that has commanded the political and economic scene for centuries. Figuratively and literally, President Aquino symbolized this grand contradiction: commitment to democracy versus loyalty to her wealthy family. President Ramos began the long process of changing the political system into one that is more democratic, but his efforts were undermined by the return to personalism during President Estrada's short tenure. The rise of another figure from a prominent family, Gloria Macapagal Arroyo, was unsurprising.

The Philippines has not assimilated modern values with traditional ways in a coherent or harmonious manner. Although nominally democratic its leaders face constant challenges of legitimacy, allegations of corruption, and threats from the country's military. Moreover, the Philippine polity has rarely met the people's needs. Indeed, the standard of living of most Filipinos has deteriorated over the past several decades as a result of governmental mismanagement and the greed of the country's leaders. Philippine society has yet to develop an effective capacity to cope with changing demands and to assert the nation's destiny.

NOTES

1. This theme is the focus of David Wurfel's *Filipino Politics: Development and Decay* (Ithaca, NY: Cornell University Press, 1988).

2. John T. Sidel, "The Philippines: The Languages of Legitimation," in *Political Legitimacy in Southeast Asia: The Quest for Moral Authority*, ed. Muthiah Alagappa (Stanford, CA: Stanford University Press, 1995), pp. 165–168.

3. Paul Hutchcroft, "The Arroyo Imbroglio in the Philippines," *Journal of Democracy*, vol. 19. no. 1, (2008), p. 142.

4. William Overholt persuasively argues that, contrary to the established view that the assassination caused the collapse of the regime or even accelerated Marcos's decline, the assassination was a successful stratagem to delay the consequences of the Marcos regime's political, moral, and financial bankruptcy. See William Overholt, "The Rise and Fall of Ferdinand Marcos," *Asian Survey*, vol. 26, no. 11 (November 1986), pp. 1137–1163.

5. For a comprehensive look at U.S. Cold War support of Marcos, see Raymond Bonner's *Waltzing with a Dictator: The Marcoses and the Making of American Policy* (New York: Times Books, 1987).

6. Justus M. van der Kroef, "The Philippines: Day of the Vigilantes," *Asian Survey*, vol. 28, no. 6 (June 1988), p. 630.

7. Sheila S. Coronel, "The Philippines in 2006: Democracy and Its Discontents," *Asian Survey*, vol. 47, no. 1 (January/February 2007), p. 175.

8. Allen Hicken, "The Philippines in 2007: Ballots, Budgets, and Bribes," *Asian Survey*, vol. 48, no. 1 (January/February 2008), pp. 76–77.

9. One of the best overviews of the evolution of political parties in the Philippines is Luzviminda G. Tancangco, "The Electoral System and Political Parties in the Philippines," in *Government and Politics of the Philippines*, ed. Raul P. De Guzman and Mila A. Reforma (Singapore: Oxford University Press, 1988). The following paragraphs are based on her analysis.

10. Note Carlos H. Conde, "Election Violence Escalating in the Philippines," *International Herald Tribune*, May 6, 2007, www.iht.com/articles/2007/05/06/news/phils.php.

11. Felipe B. Miranda and Ruben F. Ciron, "Development and the Military in the Philippines: Military Perceptions in a Time of Continuing Crisis," in *Soldiers and Stability in Southeast Asia*, ed. J. Soedjati Djiwandono and Yong Mun Cheong (Singapore: Institute of Southeast Asian Studies, 1988), p. 169.

12. Michael J. Montesano, "The Philippines in 2003: Troubles, None of Them New," *Asian Survey*, vol. 44, no. 1 (January/February 2004), p. 96.

13. Coronel, "The Philippines in 2006," p. 77.

14. Raul P. De Guzman, Alex B. Brillantes Jr., and Arturo G. Pacho, "The Bureaucracy," in *Government and Politics of the Philippines*, ed. Raul P. De Guzman and Mila A. Reforma (Singapore: Oxford University Press, 1988), p. 180.

15. Michael Leifer, *Dictionary of the Modern Politics of South-East Asia* (London: Routledge, 1995), p. 162.

16. Simon Elegant, "The Return of Abu Sayyaf," *Time*, August 23, 2004, www.time.com/time/magazine/article/0,9171,686107,00.html.

17. Hicken, "The Philippines in 2007," p. 78.

18. Linda K. Richter, "Exploring Theories of Female Leadership in South and Southeast Asia," paper presented to the Association for Asian Studies, Chicago, April 1990, p. 7.

19. David Joel Steinberg, "The Web of Filipino Allegiance," *Solidarity*, vol. 2, no. 6 (March–April 1967), p. 25.

20. Coronel, "The Philippines in 2006," p. 178.

21. Hutchcroft, "The Arroyo Imbroglio in the Philippines," p. 148.

22. S. K. Jayasuriya, "The Politics of Economic Policy in the Philippines During the Marcos Era," in *Southeast Asia in the 1980s: The Politics of Economic Crisis*, ed. Richard Robison, Kevin Hewison, and Richard Higgott (Sydney: Allen and Unwin, 1987), p. 82.

23. Ibid., p. 83.

24. Coronel, "The Philippines in 2006," p. 182.

25. Hutchcroft, "The Arroyo Imbroglio in the Philippines," p.141.

26. Gregory P. Corning, "The Philippine Bases and U.S. Pacific Strategy," *Pacific Affairs*, vol. 63, no. 1 (Spring 1990), p. 12.

Resource Guide

A useful tool for bibliographic and other information on the Philippines is available from Australia National University's WWW Virtual Library: www.gksoft.com/govt/en/ph.html. The University of California–Berkeley maintains a useful portal for digital and print resources on the Philippines: www.lib.berkeley.edu/SSEAL/SoutheastAsia/seaelec.html. Northern Illinois University's Southeast Asia Digital Library includes a range of useful links that cover government, academic, and research institutions specific to the Philippines: http://sea.lib.niu.edu. The University of Wisconsin–Madison Libraries similarly maintains a list of digital and print resources on the Philippines: www.library.wisc.edu/guides/seasia/resarea.html. The Library of Congress maintains an Internet resource guide on the Philippines at www.loc.gov/rr/international/asian/philippines/philippines.html.

A government-sponsored and generic Web-based information portal about the Philippines is at www.pia.gov.ph. The official governmental portal is at www.gov.ph. A research institute that devotes itself to development issues with policy reports and scholarly articles is the Philippine Institute for Development studies: www.pids.gov.ph. The National Economic Development Authority provides similar material online: www.neda.gov.ph.

Daily online news sources include the *Manila Times*, over one hundred years old, with searchable archives at www.manilatimes.net, and GMA News at www.gmanews.tv. A news source especially devoted to the millions of Filipinos living outside the country is www.philippinestoday.net. Moro writers maintain a site dedicated to their cause at www.luwaran.com.

4

INDONESIA

*I*ndonesia, with its 230 million inhabitants, presents different challenges in its quest for economic and political development compared to its less populated neighbors. As an equatorial archipelago stretching as wide as the United States, Indonesia is the fourth most populous country in the world. Over one-third of all Southeast Asians live in Indonesia. Eleven major ethic groups and hundreds of minor ones inhabit 6,000 of the country's 17,000 islands.[1] Amazingly, more than half of all Indonesians live on the island of Java, one of the most densely populated areas of the world. Although 85 percent of the country's population is nominally Muslim, the variety of religious beliefs within this Islamic ambience suggests diversity more than unity. Thus, even as the world's largest Muslim country, Indonesia is continually shaped by geographic, linguistic, ethnic, and social heterogeneity. The population has overcome almost insuperable obstacles in achieving nationhood.

Indonesia experienced a daunting struggle for independence at the end of World War II. Having lived under Dutch control for 350 years and then Japanese occupation during World War II, Indonesians looked for a leader who could forge unity within diversity in the postindependence period. As spokesman for Indonesian independence, leader of the revolutionary struggle against the Dutch from 1945 to 1949, and first president of independent Indonesia, Sukarno became the charismatic "solidarity maker"—destined, it seemed, to forge a "new Indonesian person."

Postindependence Indonesia can be divided into four periods, separated by one- to two-year transition phases: (1) fragile parliamentary governance under Sukarno, 1950–1957; (2) "guided democracy" under Sukarno, 1959–1965; (3) the "New Order" under Suharto, 1967–1998; and (4) liberal democratic reform under multiple presidents, 1999–present. The first period featured numerous political parties, elections, and weak parliamentary government. These Western-style governmental forms—adopted to prove to Indonesians that they could govern themselves in a "modern" democratic manner—did not fit well with

traditional Indonesian culture, which placed little value on representation, group formation, and majority rule. Sukarno pejoratively referred to democracy as "50 percent plus one" governance. Eventually, westernized institutions were blamed for the government's inability to meet the people's economic needs.

As liberal democracy floundered, Sukarno moved toward a system based on traditional political concepts mixed and reformulated to meet goals of nation-building. The essence of "guided democracy" was *gotong royong* (mutual cooperation), where decisions could be arrived at with unanimous approval via collaboration rather than competition. Western-style voting was also replaced by *musyawarah-mufakat*—a traditional method of deliberation-consensus—with Sukarno himself as the ultimate and unchallenged arbiter.

To rally support for guided democracy, Sukarno made nationalism the cornerstone of his new ideology. Nationalism was defined as the submergence of regional and ethnic loyalties in favor of national ones, allegiance to Sukarno, indigenous patterns of governance (free from the mentality of colonialism), and the annihilation of neocolonialism. Loyalty to the greater interest was rooted in *Bhinneka Tunggal Ika*, a Javanese-derived phrase meaning "We are of many kinds, but one" (sometimes translated as "unity in diversity" or "*E pluribus unum*").

Fearful of disunity, Sukarno had brilliantly established *Bahasa Indonesia* (a minority Malay-based dialect) as the new national language upon independence. Although the country was home to over three hundred languages, demographic realities rendered Javanese the most commonly used language per capita. Nevertheless, by resisting the temptation to designate Javanese as the national language, and by favoring a minority *lingua franca* used by coastal traders, Sukarno ameliorated Javanese chauvinism, a force that continually challenges the unity of postcolonial Indonesia.

Sukarno also cultivated the idea of *Pancasila,* a term adopted from Sanskrit meaning "five precepts." *Pancasila*, the declared state philosophy of Indonesia, syncretically embraces the belief in one God, humanitarianism, nationalism, democracy, and social justice. Ambiguously defining each, often in long, fiery speeches, Sukarno's vision of "sociodemocracy" audaciously blended elements of liberalism, Marxism, theism, traditionalism, and modernism. The country's official emblem, the *Garuda Pancasila*, was unfolded by Sukarno as a mythical Hindu bird adorned with a coat of arms symbolizing the principles of *Pancasila*. A decorative ribbon held by the bird's talons declared the state motto.

Where *Pancasila* defined the scope of politics, *Marhaenism* functioned as the centerpiece of Sukarno's economic philosophy. *Marhaenism* targeted the rural experience as a type of subsistence socialism. Deriving its name from an apocryphal Sundanese farmer he supposedly met while cycling, Sukarno used it to emphasize "self-help" as the chief bulwark against "exploitation." By glorifying Indonesia's many small cultivators "who worked for themselves and no one else," Marhaenism's economic ideals thus belied any need for class revolution or organized struggle. It promoted, rather illogically, the development of an atomized but unified rural proletariat of national loyalists—a Sukarnoist dream of content, self-sustaining peasants neither radicalized into class consciousness nor corrupted by individualism or avaricious want.

By embracing *Pancasila, Bhinneka Tunggal Ika, Bahasa Indonesia*, and *Marhaenism*, Sukarno encircled the new regime with his own ideology, goals, and charisma, indistinguishably fusing his persona with the postcolonial state and regime. Recognized and celebrated across the third world for his postcolonial ideology and vision, Sukarno, similar to many of his contemporaries (Mao, Nasser, and Castro) was a one-man political institution.

After he banned most political parties, reduced the power of Parliament, and suspended civil liberties, Sukarno's political course under guided democracy became erratic. He moved ideologically to the left, embracing the Communist Party of Indonesia (PKI), and then to the right—strengthening the armed forces—when the PKI became too dominant. He tried desperately to balance the demands of numerous groups, including the PKI, Chinese entrepreneurs, students, rural farmers, rightist Muslims, outer-island groups, and the army.

Although guided democracy was initially supported as an Indonesian antidote to failed Western liberalism, deteriorating economic conditions and administrative chaos created disunity rather than erasing it. In practice, *Marhaenism* resulted in rural neglect, a disorganized attempt at state-led nationalization, and a large, free-for-all informal economy. Conditions of poverty thus worsened. Forever obsessed with foreign exploitation, Sukarno nationalized Dutch and British holdings, expelled 40,000 foreign expatriates, and demanded foreign-held territories in Borneo and New Guinea. As domestic problems deepened, he turned his attention abroad, pursuing a coercive foreign policy known as *Konfrontasi* (confrontation).

Under *Konfrontasi*, Sukarno moved beyond the Dutch to target the Federation of Malaysia, Britain, the United States, and the United Nations. Sukarno refused to recognize Malaysia with diplomatic relations upon its 1963 independence from the British and began to engage in guerrilla warfare with the new state over territorial claims. Then in 1964, Sukarno told the U.S. ambassador at a public gathering to "go to hell with your aid," despite Indonesia's dependence on Western military and financial assistance. Thoroughly convinced of a neocolonial plot and irate over international support of Malaysia, Sukarno spitefully withdrew Indonesia from the United Nations, rejecting its aid and antipoverty programs as well.

Sukarno's narcissistic obsession with his own international image exacerbated policy failure on the domestic front and rural neglect in particular. Under guided democracy, Indonesian society deteriorated precipitously. Government corruption turned flagrant and the cost of living index rose from a base of 100 in 1957 to 36,000 in 1965. Unemployment grew rampant and hungry peasants migrated en masse, forming a distressed population of urban homeless. Politically, the PKI gained strength supported by radicalized peasants and stressed urbanites who began to arm themselves with Chinese-made weapons.

Sukarnoism's final ideological piece, *Nasakom*, was perhaps more tactical than visionary. Introduced in the early 1960s, the acronym-slogan embraced a tripod of social values: nationalism, religion, and communism. With *Nasakom*, Sukarno openly embraced the country's communists as part of Indonesia's political future. With this move, the PKI's confidence surged even as revolutionary movements elsewhere in Southeast Asia were gaining strength. Images of the sickle and hammer and pictures of Marx, Lenin, and Mao began to appear proudly in public. Coinciding as it did with rising poverty, a faltering economy, and foreign policy zealousness, Sukarno's shift to the left sparked fear among right-wing military leaders, Western governments, as well as many pious Muslims throughout the archipelago.

On the night of September 30, 1965, in one of the seminal events in contemporary Southeast Asian history, a group of pro-Sukarno dissident army and air force officers launched a purge of their high command, alleging that a CIA-sponsored coup to topple Sukarno was being planned. In a dramatic abduction, six senior generals were murdered and subsequently dumped down a well at "Crocodile Hole" outside of Jakarta. An immediate and successful countercoup then followed, targeting the perpetrators. Within a matter of hours the coup leaders were captured and the putsch came to an end. *Gestapu*, as it was named, collapsed because the army united against the rebels and the population failed to rise in support of the coup.

The events of 1965 remain surrounded by shadow, rumor, and intrigue. Nebulous circumstantial evidence surrounding the coup suggests possible involvement by American or British intelligence. Some skeptics theorize the whole affair was orchestrated by the CIA and the anticommunist Suharto. Nevertheless, the precise roles of the dissident army rebels, the army generals, the PKI, foreign agents, and President Sukarno himself may never be known; evidence remains inconclusive and contradictory.[2]

What is clear is that *Gestapu* rendered Sukarno politically sterile, tainting his legacy and contributing to the emancipator's ignominious demise. It is also clear that General Suharto, the commander of the Strategic Army Reserve and one of the few surviving generals, assumed command of the army and, within two years, the entire country. The events of 1965 fundamentally changed Indonesia's political structure, decimated the PKI, led to one of the worst bloodbaths in history, and swept into power a military government that ruled Indonesia for thirty years.

In the months following the failed coup, hundreds of thousands of suspected communists and sympathizers were slaughtered, with the army's encouragement. This massive slaughter was aimed primarily at Sino-Indonesians, who were despised by many for having a disproportionately large role in the Indonesian economy and who were suspected of being more loyal to their Chinese homeland and communism than to Indonesia. Despite its enormity, the slaughter did not become the focus of international condemnation, perhaps because it occurred during the height of the Cold War and because the new anticommunist government in Indonesia was allied with the United States.

By 1967, Suharto had reduced Sukarno's power, banned the PKI, ended *Konfrontasi* against Malaysia, brought Indonesia back into the United Nations, and taken all power for himself. Suharto proclaimed a "New Order" for Indonesia, ending the twenty-year postindependence charismatic, ideological, and ultimately catastrophic leadership of Sukarno and beginning a period of development-oriented, authoritarian, and stable rule that endured until the Asian Economic Crisis of the late 1990s. Sukarno, at the age of sixty-nine and under house arrest, died of kidney failure on June 21, 1970.

The first task of the New Order was to create a stable and legitimate political system with control throughout the archipelago; the second task was to rehabilitate the shattered economy. Suharto used the military to accomplish the first goal, portraying the armed forces as the savior against the communist threat that had existed before the coup. To counter the problems of inflation, corruption, and poor economic growth, Suharto instituted a bureaucratic authoritarian state where power was limited to the state itself, led by the military, his close friends, some Western-trained technocrats, and eventually his family members. Suharto based New Order control primarily on co-optation and bureaucratic repression.

To enhance his nationalist credentials, Suharto mobilized the Indonesian army in 1975 to occupy East Timor, after the territory had declared independence from the Portuguese that same year. He feared that Catholic East Timor would be led by leftists and could become a beachhead for Soviet expansion. In 1976 East Timor became Indonesia's twenty-seventh province, but this was accomplished amid terrible carnage with fully 10 percent of the population killed during the invasion. Over time, Suharto's Indonesia developed East Timor with schools, hospitals, and infrastructure, but most residents continued to reject Indonesian control. Indonesian suppression of East Timorese dissent was brutal and, at times, merciless. In 1996, the Nobel Peace Prize was awarded to two East Timorese leaders, Catholic Bishop Carlos Filipe Ximenes Belo and exiled freedom fighter José Ramos Horta, for their "courageous" struggle against Indonesian aggression.

To consolidate power, Suharto also pursued a strategy to depoliticize all potential challengers. He purged the army of pro-Sukarno forces and made it the basis of his own strength. Suharto set up a "political organization" called Golkar (an acronym for *golongan karya*, or functional group), which was administered by officials at every level of government, from national to village. Suharto also restricted political association by forcing four Muslim political parties to merge into one: the United Development Party (PPP). The remaining secular and Christian parties were also forced to merge under the Indonesian Democratic Party (PDI). These two opposition parties, the only ones permitted by law, did not have access to the state resources available to Golkar.

Throughout Suharto's thirty-year rule, political freedom and civil liberties were subject to serious constraint. Journalists self-censored their work or were subject to harassment and detention. Business associations and NGOs operated under close supervision of Golkar's corporatist state. To keep Islamic claims on the state at bay, Suharto embraced *Pancasila* as the New Order's guiding political ideology. Later, as Islam's influence grew outside his control, he sought to co-opt Islam more directly by making a pilgrimage to Mecca and supporting the formation of the Indonesian Association of Muslim Intellectuals (ICMI), an organization loyal to the New Order regime.

Suharto also used elections to prop up his legitimacy for continued rule. Golkar's victories in these elections were guaranteed through institutional arrangements ensuring Suharto loyalists would maintain control of the People's Consultative Assembly (MPR). The MPR's membership was drawn from elected delegates, the military, and presidential appointees. Serving also as an electoral college, the MPR formally elected the president and vice president for five-year terms. Suharto thus handpicked much the delegatory body that elected (and reelected) him to office.

Over six general elections from 1971 to 1997, the vote for Golkar never fell below 62 percent and Suharto's claim on the presidency was never challenged. Golkar's electoral success was due to (1) a requirement that all governmental bureaucrats and employees join Golkar, (2) laws that restricted political parties and prohibited a free opposition, and (3) performance legitimacy with respect to improving economic conditions and post-Sukarno political stability.

Suharto was as successful in rehabilitating the economy as he was in stabilizing and legitimizing the political system. Following the advice of a group of Western-educated economic technocrats he had assembled, he cut government and defense spending and reaped revenues from the sale of oil. As a result, inflation was reduced, per capita income was greatly increased, and economic growth maintained a steady pace. Indonesia became self-sufficient in rice, and the availability of food improved. The success of Suharto's economic policy stood in stark contrast to Sukarno's failures. In 1967, when Suharto took full power, per capita GDP stood at $100; at the time of his ouster in 1998, it had risen tenfold to $1,080. Under Suharto's watch Indonesia became recognized as a Southeast Asian tiger economy, joining the new international era as a contending emerging market.

Economic growth brought Suharto legitimacy and undercut allegations made by his detractors about the authoritarian nature of his regime. These allegations included accusations of nepotism and corruption for allowing his wife and children to control lucrative monopolies. Critics also pointed to a widening gap between the rich and poor accompanying the country's tremendous economic growth. Over time, Indonesian students and intellectuals began to carefully criticize the New Order, push for increased democracy, and resist Suharto's autocratic rule. Human rights issues became central as living standards rose, a vibrant middle class emerged, and more and more Indonesians came to believe that military-dominated governments were anachronistic in an age of democratization.

By 1997, an election year, Indonesia's growing population was younger than ever. To a whole generation of Indonesians, Suharto was the only president they had known. Because of his advanced age, much discussion about the shape that post-Suharto Indonesia might take characterized the preelection period. Golkar (unsurprisingly) won a sweeping victory in Indonesia's general elections to seat representatives in the MPR, thus ensuring Suharto's reelection if he desired to stay in power. Suharto announced his availability for a seventh term even as the country confronted a growing regional economic crisis. By late 1997, Indonesia, following Thailand, faced a loss in investor confidence, capital flight, rising debt, and economic uncertainty.

As the economy soured, criticism of Suharto grew proportionally. The major criticism of Suharto's leadership concerned his family's and friends' domination of indigenous business and industrial conglomerates. More and more areas of the industrial economy—television stations, toll roads, telecommunications facilities, oil tankers—had become controlled by Suharto's children during his rule.[3] Because these monopolies arose through personal contacts with the president, the international business community became increasingly cynical about the economy.

Suharto rebuked foreign criticism and responded to detractors by using coercion, force, or denial. Free speech was continually suppressed as local and international journalists confronted restrictions. Many older Indonesians still remembered the dire poverty and chaos of the former regime and were willing to give the New Order much slack. But with a growing middle class, widespread literacy, and access to radio, television, and the printed media, the new generation of Indonesians was quickly growing into a dynamic force for change. The effects of the Asian economic crisis clashed head-on with Suharto's long-standing performance legitimacy.

With the twin pressures of economic collapse and political crisis bearing down, Suharto fretted, teetered, and balked in making needed policy adjustments during the ensuing months. An initial rescue package from the IMF was announced at the end of October 1997. This package stopped the economic slide only temporarily as new concerns over Suharto's ailing health kept investors nervous. The economy worsened and Indonesia's currency, the rupiah, dropped to 10,000 per dollar, where it had been 2,430 prior to the crisis. Inflation skyrocketed. Job losses increased. Pessimism flooded the archipelago nation. Charges of official "corruption," "collusion," and "crony capitalism" became common topics for the media and public.

After twice rejecting the conditions of another IMF rescue package, Suharto, still ailing, finally agreed to a second $43 billion bailout package in April 1998. Conditionality on the massive loan, however, not only cut subsidies on crucial goods that affected everyday Indonesians (cooking oil, instant noodles, paper, plywood, and cement) but further exposed the extent to which Suharto's family and tycoon partners controlled the public budget and every major sector of the country's economy. In May, Indonesia erupted when sustained street demonstrations turned violent. Antigovernment protests proliferated, and Sino-Indonesian businessmen were attacked, often brutally. The violence drove the rupiah down further, to 16,500 per dollar. Indonesia's thirty-year run of political stability and steady economic growth was over.

Amidst the disarray, on May 20, 1998, following ten days of antigovernment demonstrations led by students, Suharto resigned. B. J. Habibie, then vice president, was sworn in as the country's new leader, receiving the military's support. Because Habibie was viewed as a Suharto protégé, he faced the problems of distancing himself from the former president. The politically powerful in Indonesia viewed Habibie as an unpredictable gadfly unsuited for the presidency. While setting forth economic policies designed to resolve the crises of currency devaluation, inflation, and unemployment, Habibie indicated his support for reform and democratization. He called for new elections, free of the party constraints known under Suharto's rule.

Among Habibie's most significant decisions during his short tenure was to hold a referendum in East Timor offering an option of autonomy or independence. The result was an East Timorese majority of 78 percent favoring independence. The transition to independence was made difficult by the Indonesian military's continued oppression and violence against the East Timorese people. Massive intervention from the international community and the United Nations was eventually needed to assist Timor-Leste into its new era of independence.[4]

On June 7, 1999, democratic elections were held for the first post-Suharto Parliament in Indonesia. Some forty-eight parties competed for five hundred seats. Habibie, attempting to lead Golkar, had already lost the confidence of the population and received little support. With Golkar down, the elections resulted in a plurality victory for the Partai Demokrasi Indonesia-Perjuangan

(Indonesian Democracy Party-Struggle, or PDI-P), led by Megawati Sukarno-putri, daughter of the founding father and first president of Indonesia. Her party won 34 percent of the vote and 153 seats in Parliament. Golkar won only 22 percent and 120 seats, while Partai Kebangkitan Bangsa (National Awakening Party, or PKB) won 12 percent and 51 seats. The PKB was led by Abdurrahman Wahid, leader of the Nahdlatul Ulama (NU), the nation's largest Islamic organization. Other parties won fewer seats.

Ninety percent of eligible Indonesians voted in this first democratic election since 1955. Because the PDI-P won the greatest number of votes, many believed Sukarnoputri would become president. However, she chose not to campaign for the presidency. Her gender worked against her, as many devout Muslims indicated they could not abide a female leader, and she was viewed as a secularist among the more fundamentalist. Wahid ran for president and won; Sukarnoputri became his vice president.

President Wahid faced overwhelming crises, none of which he successfully resolved. His tenure as president failed to come to grips with any of Indonesia's modern problems. He proved incapable of running an economy and was ill-suited for the task of recovery. His failing health also kept him from being a vibrant leader. Legally blind and enfeebled by strokes, Wahid came across as a very old person who could not cope with the daily stresses of his position. He often dozed during his own speeches that were presented by his aide.

Under Wahid, the Indonesian archipelago looked as if it might disintegrate. Separatist movements, which had been bottled up by Suharto, hit Aceh in Sumatra, the Dayak region of Kalimantan, and West Irian Jaya (West Papua) on the eastern end of the archipelago. The resulting instability raised the question of whether Indonesia could reform and stabilize simultaneously. In 2001, after just nineteen months of his five-year term, Wahid was twice censured by the MPR as a prelude to full impeachment. The first rebuke was on February 1 and the second was on April 29. Sukarnoputri's party, PDI-P, supported censure. Wahid was asked to give a response to Parliament, but it was deemed unacceptable when he claimed the Parliament was acting unconstitutionally.

Finally, on July 22, 2001, the MPR met to debate Wahid's impeachment and to name Sukarnoputri president. The vote against Wahid was 591 to 0. Wahid responded by ordering an emergency rule, which he hoped would postpone or end the move against him, but Indonesia's security forces and the legislature defied him and did not follow the orders. Wahid warned that if he were forced from office, many provinces would attempt to separate themselves from Indonesia. But all that came to naught, and on July 23, 2001, Megawati Sukarnoputri became president of the world's largest Muslim country. Wahid initially refused to leave the presidential palace but then relented and went to the United States to seek medical treatment.

Sukarnoputri had not entered politics until the mid-1990s but rose to prominence after troops attacked her party's headquarters upon Suharto's orders. Raised in a presidential palace, a college dropout, and thrice married (including an annulled two-week elopement to an Egyptian diplomat), she was known to be taciturn, shy, and not particularly savvy regarding politics. She derived much of her support from Sukarno's charismatic aura, but her own style proved far different. "Mega," as she is commonly called, did not share her father's love for theatrical oration or his aptitude for political infighting. Upon assuming the presidency, her task was not to build a new nation but to reform Suharto's corrupt *ancien régime*. The effort was dubbed *reformasi*: an agenda to reform institutions, bring corrupt officials to account, and revive the ailing economy.

Immediately dictating the context of Megawati's rule were the events of 9/11, which occurred half a world away only weeks after her appointment. She soon found her country caught in the crosshairs of America's war on terrorism. She rejected claims by Washington that terrorists operated in her country until events proved her wrong. In 2002 and 2003, deadly terrorist bombings targeting nightclubs, hotels, and the Australian embassy rocked Bali and Jakarta. The plotters of the bombings, members of the Indonesia-based Jemaah Islamiyah (JI), were known communicants with Osama bin Laden's al-Qaeda. Megawati pledged to quell domestic terrorism but on her own terms, largely independent of the United States' antiterrorism framework, which was tainted by deep resentment among Indonesians, who universally condemned the U.S. occupation of Iraq.

The disconnect between the governments grew. The Bush administration viewed Indonesia as a terrorist haven but Megawati, like many Indonesians, viewed U.S. Middle East policy responsible for her own society's victimization at the hands of chauvinistic Arab-Islamists and extremists. Alternatively, street-level conspiracy theories claimed that Bush agents had perpetrated the local bombings to bring an anti-Muslim war to Indonesia. U.S.-Indonesian relations became more strained than they had been since the Sukarno era of *Konfrontasi*.

Although attending the UN-sponsored ceremony granting Timor-Leste full independence helped Megawati's standing with Washington and Canberra, cold diplomacy defined relations between Indonesia and its principal Western partners. Unlike leaders in Thailand, the Philippines, Singapore, and even Malaysia, who cautiously supported Western antiterrorism efforts, Megawati pursued a more reticent approach. For example, fearing alienation among Muslims and speaking too strongly against political Islam, Megawati refused to classify JI and similar groups as illegal organizations. Nevertheless, she apprehended suspects in the Bali and Jakarta bombings and sent them to court, where some received death sentences—although Abu Bakar Ba'asyir, the suspected mastermind and spiritual head of JI, served what eventually became a shortened prison term.

Beyond security issues and terrorism, Megawati's greatest troubles were in managing the domestic economy, controlling ethnic separatism, and delivering on her anticorruption agenda. Under her watch, foreign investment did not return to Indonesia's beleaguered economy at the rate it did elsewhere in Southeast Asia. Displaced workers continued to move into a growing informal sector and farmers struggled with drought support. Tourism, an early recovery sector, also fell sharply due to terrorist fears and the 2003 regional outbreak of Severe Acute Respiratory Syndrome (SARS).[5]

In both Aceh and Irian Jaya, Megawati's unprecedented attempts to establish greater autonomy backfired and resulted in further revolt and military suppression. Violent rioting between Christians and Muslims in the Moluccas islands also erupted in 2004, drawing unwanted international attention. Megawati also failed to bring to justice corrupt officials and military officers of the New Order era, including Suharto himself (deemed too ill to stand trial).

Megawati Sukarnoputri's most significant reform under *reformasi* proved to undermine her own political career. Amidst continued economic and ethnic troubles, the sitting president reversed a previous position and supported a constitutional change for direct presidential elections. Subsequently, in October 2004, she lost the presidency to Susilo Bambang Yudhoyono in the country's first direct election of an executive. Yudhoyono, a minister with a military background and security policy experience, pledged decisiveness on *reformasi* where his predecessor had failed.

Weeks later, on December 26, 2004, a 9.0 magnitude earthquake off the Sumatra coast caused the most deadly tsunami in recorded history.[6] Of the twelve countries affected, Indonesia experienced the greatest devastation: 126,804 dead; 93,458 missing; 474,619 internally displaced; and an estimated $5.4 billion in damage, a figure almost equivalent to Sumatra's entire GDP. International sympathy poured in, propelled by the media age and harrowing images of loss and destruction that were broadcast globally. Rescue aid from Asian, Western, and Muslim sources amassed with unprecedented speed and at record levels for a natural disaster. Former U.S. presidents Bill Clinton and George H. W. Bush became special UN ambassadors to raise funds for recovery and visited Sumatra. During the early months of 2005, the entire international community was consumed with addressing relief and recovery from the disaster in Sumatra and elsewhere.

Politically, the tsunami was significant given that areas partial to Aceh's independence movement were among the hardest hit. Multiple countries dispatched military units to take part in a broadly coordinated aid mission. Images of U.S. troops arriving in Aceh, unthinkable before December 26, symbolized the suspension of political concern in favor of humanitarian necessity. In August 2005, Yudhoyono, less than a year into his presidency, was able to reach a disarmament agreement with Aceh's depleted rebels that offered them greater autonomy—the three-decade-old separatist movement that had produced over 15,000 deaths finally concluded. A year later Aceh held its own direct elections, selecting a former rebel leader to serve as provincial governor.

On the other side of the archipelago, untouched by the tsunami, the story in West Papua followed a different track and Yudhoyono's efforts were less conclusive. West Papuans had been granted greater autonomy in 2002 by the government, including the shedding of the unwanted administrative name Irian Jaya in favor of West Papua. However, rough implementation of the agreement kept tensions festering and separatists hoping for an independence referendum.[7] Given the revenues West Papua's mining resources produce for the country's economy, the likelihood that Jakarta will allow such an event remains low.

Over the course of his presidency, Susilo Bambang Yudhoyono (popularly known as "SBY") skillfully reversed the direction of ailing Indonesia. Although a member of a minority party, Yudhoyono revived economic growth, quelled ethnic separatism, further depoliticized the military, and won praise from the United States and Australia for effective counterterrorism efforts. Using his specialized Detachment 88 force, funded in part by the U.S. State Department, Yudhoyono won credit for capturing Jemaah Islamiyah's top political leader, its top suicide-bomb recruiter, and its chief bomb-maker. Less impressive were SBY's results meeting public expectations regarding *reformasi*.

In spite of relative success, Yudhoyono saw his popularity decline during his tenure. Indonesia's open political environment, expanding civil society, and free press held the president accountable for failed promises. Much of the *reformasi* agenda remained elusive.

Ironically, Megawati Sukarnoputri and her PDI-P colleagues were counted among the biggest critics of Yudhoyono and his inability to execute trials against Suharto and New Order tycoons. Indonesia's judicial system remains the country's most corrupt governing institution, contributing to Indonesia's poor international reputation for honest government. According to Transparency International's 2007 corruption perception index, which ranks countries from the least to the most corrupt, Indonesia ranked 143rd out of the 179 countries measured, far worse than neighboring Singapore (4th) and Malaysia (43rd). After announcing her candidacy for the 2009 presidential elections, Mega and the PDI-P persisted in their criticism of the sitting government and gained ground in opinion polls over SBY.

If reelected in 2009, neither she, Yudhoyono, nor any other new president will ever be able to claim victory in bringing Asia's most corrupt chief executive to justice. Suharto died in January 2008, even as a civil suit against him lay pending. On behalf of the country, government prosecutors filed a lawsuit for $440 million in embezzled funds and $1.1 billion in damages—by all estimates a drop in the bucket of Suharto's ill-gained wealth.

At the time of Suharto's death, a full ten years after his overthrow, Indonesia has more than symbolically transformed itself into a new political system. Constitutionally correct party activity, lawmaking, and even budding leadership rivalries are encouraging signs. More important, political power is now gained, wielded, challenged, and transferred legitimately. It remains to be seen whether democratic advances will endure. A particularly encouraging sign is the development of the concept of loyal opposition in a plural political framework.[8] Today, in everyday Indonesian politics, the electorate's concerns focus on the rule of law and party competition, replacing past concerns about the legitimacy of the state or its regime. Indonesia is gradually democratizing.

INSTITUTIONS AND SOCIAL GROUPS

The Constitution

The 1945 constitution has been the primary legal document guiding contemporary Indonesia since its independence. Although manipulated by both Sukarno and Suharto to suit their respective purposes, the document has retained popular legitimacy. Since the collapse of New Order rule, the constitution has proven pliable to reform and undergone major changes affecting all branches of government. These changes, as part of *reformasi*, have been aimed squarely at addressing past political problems.

Indonesia's current constitution oversees a hybrid presidential and parliamentary form of government. Presidents today are not rulers in the manner of either Sukarno or Suharto. Although it appears to be a presidential system, executive power is now checked by more than just an electorate. The Indonesian legislature is also empowered to subject the president to votes of confidence. Elected presidents must also work with elected legislators to formulate policy. As executives are not necessarily from the largest political party, the legislature may feel no compunction to follow the president's policy agenda. Where the president holds greatest power is in appointing cabinet members, acting as commander-in-chief of the armed forces, and arbitrating foreign affairs as head of state. As now amended, elected presidents in post-Suharto Indonesia can serve only two five-year terms.

In 2004, during its first direct presidential elections, an open first round fielded five candidates, none of whom broke the 50 percent mark to ensure victory in the first round. As top vote-getters, Susilo Bambang Yudhoyono and incumbent Megawati Sukarnoputri combined for 60 percent of the vote, forcing a runoff. Yudhoyono subsequently won over 60 percent of the runoff vote to secure the presidency. Megawati and her PDI-P supporters stepped aside, and a constitutional change from one set of leaders to another proceeded peacefully.

Presidential elections scheduled for 2009 included a field of fifteen candidates from all major sectors of society. Megawati, the only viable candidate to seriously challenge Yudhoyono, trailed in pre-election polls by double digits. Polls also indicated that SBY might not receive a majority endorsement from the electorate, opening the possibility of another second-round showdown between the two prominent figures.

The present constitution establishes a 678-member People's Consultative Assembly (MPR) as the highest governmental body in the land. During most of the Sukarno period and all of the Suharto period, the MPR did not function as a free representative legislature. Only since the 1999 legislative elections and subsequent constitutional changes has the MPR begun to serve a democratic function embedded in pluralist, free party competition. Where the MPR formerly elected the president and vice president as an electoral college, a constitutional amendment in 2004 stripped the assembly of such power. Today the MPR holds powers to pass constitutional amendments and impeach the president (which Abdurrahman Wahid would attest is indeed functional). Day-to-day legislative activity, however, is handled by the country's recently reformed bicameral legislature, whose combined membership constitutes the MPR itself.

The lower house, the Dewan Perwakilan Rakyat (DPR), seats 550 members through national elections in a mixed system of district and proportional representation. Under the constitution, the DPR is the locus of legislative power. A body with regional representation, the 128-seat Dewan Perwakilan Daerah (DPD), was recently developed. The DPD cannot revise DPR legislation but can formulate legislation related to local autonomy, resource management, fiscal matters, and other issues concerning provincial relations with the central government. Though important, the DPD does not carry the standing or authority of an upper house, such as the U.S. Senate.

With proportional representation in the DPR, and separate assembly and presidential elections now functioning, it is questionable whether presidential and parliamentary power will again appear under a single party banner. Constitutional reform and new party pluralism combine to create an executive office formally accountable to multiple constituencies: the electorate, the president's party, the ruling government coalition, as well as opposition parties in the DPR and sitting members of the DPD who share the impeachment powers of the MPR. With so many audiences to please, the likelihood of a domineering executive to emerge, or for an executive to even last two five-year periods, appears small.

Pancasila

As the country's national ideology, *Pancasila* underpins the constitution supporting the basis of statehood and the ideals of legitimate government. It includes five principles:

1. Belief in one God (embracing religious belief and tolerance vis-à-vis secularism)
2. Humanitarianism (implying civilized society absent of oppression)
3. Nationalism (implying unity amidst ethnic diversity, or *Bhinneka Tunggal Ika*)
4. Democracy (defined as consensus-oriented decisionmaking, or *musyawarah-mufakat*)
5. Social justice (idealized as the economic welfare of all peoples of Indonesia)

To create a defense against Western liberalism as well as Islamic privilege, Indonesia's founders sought to develop an anticolonial political ideology that embodied republicanism and embraced Indonesian aspirations. Few have since questioned its validity, although its interpretation occupies the ideological center of Indonesian political debate. Islamic groups, in particular, are among those who challenge *Pancasila*'s secular dimensions. One such challenge came in 1980 when Islamic groups, the PPP, and a number of retired military figures submitted a petition known as the Petisi Kelompok 50 (Group of 50 Petition), criticizing Suharto and his administration for using *Pancasila* to undermine political opposition. Predictably, the government-dominated Parliament ignored the petition.[9]

Open to interpretation with changing conditions, *Pancasila* ideology has retained its legitimacy throughout the country's major political transitions. Although no longer required, most political parties still embrace *Pancasila* as their official party ideology. In the post-Suharto era, government manipulation of *Pancasila* has given way to increasing public contestation of its meaning.

Although attempts have been made, no Southeast Asian country can claim the success Indonesia has had in creating and maintaining its own state philosophy. Internationally, *Pancasila* has arguably proven less divisive than Turkey's secular-rationalist Kemalism, more internationally legitimate than Iran's theocratic imperative, and more compatible with modernity than the ultraconservative Wahabism currently animating antimodern Islamist movements from Algeria to Afghanistan.

Political Parties

Until the 1999 election, no party was able to realistically compete with Golkar, the official party of the government and the military. Golkar functioned simultaneously as the principal support of the government and as the representative of the Indonesian people. The military originally established Golkar in the 1960s to oppose communist organizations; thus, the party developed a national apparatus down to the village level. The only other permissible parties under New Order rule, the United Development Party (PPP) and the Indonesian Democratic Party (PDI), were destined to oppositional roles.

All of this changed in 1999 when Indonesia held open democratic elections with multiple parties. The biggest plurality of votes went to Megawati Sukarnoputri's Indonesian Democracy Party-Struggle (PDI-P), which garnered 34 percent of vote for the DPR. Golkar won only 22 percent, down over 40 percentage points from the previous election. At the time, the MPR still elected the country's executive. Although Megawati had rights to claim the presidency because of her party's plurality victory, too many legislators proved unprepared to elect a female chief executive. When a government coalition was formed, Abdurrahman Wahid managed to win a majority of votes to become president. Sukarnoputri was made vice president. The aftermath of the election was chaotic but the bigger picture was clear: For the first time in their lives, most Indonesians were able to participate in the political system and freely choose their own leaders. At campaign rallies, in print, and through diverse forms of public and private interaction, Indonesians became citizens able to express their complaints, opinions, and aspirations.

The subsequent 2004 election proved significant in its own right because it set the stage for the country's first direct election of its president. In the general election the principal parties included a reinvented Golkar, winning a meager plurality vote of 21.6 percent; Megawati Sukarnoputri's PDI-P, with 18.5 percent of the vote (down over one third from its 1999 victory); and the National Awakening Party (PKB) of Abdurrahman Wahid, with 10.6 percent of the vote. The remaining 49.3 percent of the vote was split between twenty-one parties, each with results in the single digits. Politically these parties ranged across the spectrum, but most were largely centered on a party chairman. Two minor parties, one bearing the banner of *Marhaenism*, boasted leadership from one of Megawati's sisters who made her own claims to the right to carry on Sukarno's legacy.

The multiparty system in Indonesia today functions similarly to those in parliamentary systems elsewhere transitioning toward democracy. With no party able to capture a majority of the DPR, coalition governments form as a result of intense bargaining; member parties are rewarded with positions in the presidential cabinet and access to the policy agenda. The politicking is high stakes for parties and their leaders. Ideology tends to give way to awkward political marriages, and politics becomes a messy affair. Thus far, the institutionalization of particular parties appears a long way off. With the exception of Golkar, most major parties operate around strong figures and their personalities.

Political Islam

As the largest Muslim country in the world, Indonesia has a relatively admirable record of integrating Islam into its secular political system. Political Islam, or the participation in political life motivated by Islamic values, has not produced the degree of instability, conflict, or antigovernment rebellion experienced elsewhere in Southeast Asia. Revolutionary Islam has proven more vexing to governments in Thailand and the Philippines. In these countries, Muslim minorities have been oppressed and have engaged in long-standing, Muslim-based separatist movements. In Malaysia, where large, non-Muslim Chinese and Indian minorities live side-by-side with a Muslim majority, political Islam has proven more divisive than in Indonesia.

Nevertheless, political Islam does animate Indonesian politics, and the more open period of post-Suharto politics has expanded the range and intensity of its recent involvement. Although religious and sectarian clashes erupt on occasion in parts of the archipelago (sometimes with deadly consequences), a broad-based, organized Islamic revolution on the scale experienced in Iran and Afghanistan or attempted in many Arab states is not featured in Indonesian experience. Thousands of varied religious institutions and strands of Islamic expression exist in Indonesia. This Islamic milieu weaves itself into the fabric of Indonesian society in a manner that defies traditional or monolithic characterization. Islam in Indonesia is temporally dynamic and socially contested.

Indonesian Muslims bear the reputation for a moderate, if syncretic, brand of Islam. About 99 percent of Muslims in Indonesia are Sunni. The heterogeneity that characterizes Islamic belief and practice in the country is rooted in the division between *santri* and *abangan* cultures within Java as well as other forces of *aliran* (i.e., vertical divisions across society produced by ethnolinguistic differences and identity politics). *Santri*, or pious Muslims, generally represent political Islam, whereas *abangan,* or nominal Muslims, lean toward secular politics and find cultural influence from *priyayi* traditions (pre-Islamic, Javanese-Hindu customs and supernatural beliefs). In Indonesian politics the dichotomy between *santri* and *abangan* drives much of political Islam, including much of the Islamic antipathy toward a hegemonic *Pancasila* ideology.[10]

Aliran forces influence how Islam is interpreted and practiced from group to group and region to region. Loyalties in Indonesia have traditionally been to the group first, exacerbating ethnic tensions but mitigating the formation of superior Islamic identity or a single Indonesian Muslim narrative. Because of these factors, Islamic revolution is unlikely to emerge or achieve a hegemonic role in Indonesian political life. Moreover, as Indonesia's rulers could attest, it is not easy to mobilize a diverse population of nearly a quarter-billion people for any cause, be it *Marhaenism*, communism, or some singular Islamic vision.

Since independence, Indonesia's leaders have nevertheless remained cautious about the potential for political Islam to coalesce into a larger political movement with revolutionary aims. By embracing the national ideology of *Pancasila*, radical Islamist aspirations have been suppressed by successive regimes that have embraced Islam's presence alongside the security imperatives of ethnic and religious diversity. Further, state patronage and regulation of Islam have often placed serious parameters around Islamic education and influences from outside Indonesia, especially under Suharto. By demobilizing Islam, Suharto, with an *abangan-priyayi* upbringing, began to co-opt Islam for seeming political gain. Suharto become a *hajji* (pilgrim to Mecca) and supported the creation of the Indonesian Association of Muslim Intellectuals (ICMI). He also developed a purposeful program to send the country's Islamic scholars to study at centers in Europe and North America, thus avoiding the more radical mosques in the Middle East.[11]

In Indonesia today, political Islam's largest role is found not in extremist movements but in political parties and mainstream social associations who champion Islamic values without pressing for the creation of an Islamic state. Prominent political parties include the PPP and the Prosperous Justice Party (PKS). While both claim Islam as their ideology, neither advocates Islamic republicanism or state-based sharia, or Islamic law. Together the PPP and PKS garnered over 16 million votes in the 2004 elections. These numbers are strong but pale in comparison to the more politically significant social organizations, such as Nahdlatul Ulama (NU) and Muhammadiyah.

Dating back to the 1920s, Nahdlatul Ulama formed in response to rising European Christian activity, secularism, and communism within Indonesia. During much of the Suharto period, Abdurrahman Wahid served as NU's leader. Wahid formally "removed" NU from politics in 1984 by withdrawing from the Suharto-forced coalition of Islamic parties that composed the United

Development Party (PPP). Concentrating instead on the organization's own development, Wahid's NU sought to assist Indonesia's Muslims through the religious and social concerns arising due to rapid economic change. Wahid later founded "Forum Demokrasi" in response to Suharto's creation of ICMI. At the time of Suharto's resignation in 1998, NU was poised to reemerge as a political force with its estimated 35 million members. Though it has thus far resisted the temptation to transform into a political party, NU does throw its support behind Islamic-oriented parties and candidates, such as Wahid himself. Widespread on Java, NU finds support among rural Javanese and in religious schools.

Muhammadiyah, and its female organizational arm, Nasyiatul Aisyiyah, claims membership of over 30 million. Muhammadiyah's primary goals are religious and educational. It sets up schools to promote Sunni Islam while also educating about democracy and public health. One of its most recent influential leaders, Amien Rais, helped force Suharto's resignation in 1998 and then later led the national assembly. Nasyiatul Aisyiyah, founded in 1917, has sought to define women's roles and, more recently, Arabism within Islam. Expressing disdain for fundamentalist Islam, women in Aisyiyah work against extremist ideologies that give little space for women within Islam.[12] The organization has even partnered with USAID to fund health projects and promote family planning with noted success.[13]

At the other extreme from parties and religious associations that engage Indonesian society through legitimate political channels are Islamist organizations that employ violence and terror to advance their chief cause: destroying the republic and creating an Islamic state. Although on the fringe of Indonesian society (socially and numerically), these groups create significant political problems for Indonesia and overall foreign relations. Some such groups, such as Laskar Jihad, instigate communal violence targeting nonbelievers; others, such as Jemaah Islamiyah (JI), seek international attention by targeting foreign interests.

Movements favoring the creation of an Islamic republic date back to the 1950s; however, the most radical groups in Indonesia formed within the past two decades. Jemaah Islamiyah was formed in 1993. The group was tied to five major bombings in Bali and Jakarta from 2002 to 2005 and later saw its top officials arrested and brought to trial. Yudhoyono in particular launched more aggressive efforts to weaken JI than his predecessors. In 2008, when JI bombers were convicted and executed and the organization finally declared illegal, few Indonesians came to its defense. Mainstream society within Indonesia, increasingly convinced of the pernicious effects of radical organizations, currently demonstrates a new willingness to allow elected officials political space to deal with extremist groups. As of late 2008, three years had passed without a single terrorist incident. Larger worries among the public center on concerns that the SBY government is too close to the United States or that new bans on extremist organizations may proliferate in scope, affecting the activity of mainstream associations. The election of Barack Obama, who spent some of his childhood years in Indonesia, was welcomed throughout Indonesia.

Military

For much of Indonesia's postindependence period, especially under Suharto, the military pervasively intervened in politics. Aside from Burma, no other Southeast Asian nation had experienced the same degree of military involvement in day-to-day governance. However, the political role of the Indonesian Armed Forces, or the Tentara Nasional Indonesia (TNI), has decreased dramatically in the post–New Order era, although its latent power to act remains strong and should not be discounted given the country's history.

Once the political role of the military was enshrined in state doctrine, its leaders set forth the notion of *dwi fungsi*, or dual function, ensuring for itself both a security and a sociopolitical role in Indonesian society. Through legislation this dual role legitimated the military's involvement as cabinet officers, governors of provinces, members of the legislative body, and leaders of Golkar. Until Suharto's overthrow, it was impossible to imagine an Indonesian administration without the active participation of army generals. The agenda of *reformasi* includes professionalizing the military and dismantling military *dwi fungsi* by removing generals from their designated seats in the assembly and their spots on corporate boards, where many "soldier-tycoons" amassed great wealth in the 1980s and '90s. Since 2004, no appointed seats for the military or anybody else exist in the MPR. Today, only elected representatives govern Indonesia's lawmaking bodies, as well as the republic's chief executive office.

DEMOCRATIZATION

Until 1999 liberal democracy had not flourished in postindependence Indonesia. The one attempt to fashion such a system, which lasted from 1950 to 1957, featured multiple political parties and a parliamentary government. However, that period was a time of great political unrest as the country moved from dependence on its colonizers, the Dutch, to independence. Sukarno, who was president during the transition, paid little attention to necessary day-to-day administrative tasks; nevertheless, the democratic system was blamed for the collapse of the economy and the country's infrastructure. Consequently, Sukarno's notion of a unique, indigenous form of guided democracy was readily embraced as more fitting for Indonesia.

Traditional Indonesian political culture is essentially hierarchical and authoritarian: Authorities at the center do not tolerate opposition or any individual gathering power resources independently, as this will endanger the potency of the state.[14] Sukarno's notion of democracy appeared to fit traditional Javanese value systems in which power is bestowed on one person, usually a sultan. From an Indonesian perspective, therefore, guided democracy was the most effective way to make policy, even if that process is not compatible with Western notions of representative and accountable government.

From a Western perspective, on the other hand, guided democracy ensured the perpetuation of Sukarno's power at the expense of the liberties and openness available under liberal democracy. From this vantage point, real democracy was not destroyed by a traditional culture but by corrupt, power-hungry politicians who established repressive policies and authoritarian institutions to retain their positions. Suharto's New Order was viewed from this perspective as the archetypal authoritarian administration that mouthed the virtues of democracy but practiced the politics of dictatorship.

Rejecting both of these extreme positions, a younger generation of educated officials emerged to suggest that accountability and civil liberties are not exclusive values of the West, and as Indonesia's population becomes educated, informed, and economically developed, there is no reason why Western democratic institutions cannot be adopted. Adding to the demand for a more open society were the numerous civil society governmental organizations (CSOs) in Indonesia, representing women's groups, trade unions, student organizations, labor, and various causes. Their growth in the 1990s represented rising disgruntlement with the lack of liberty and the suffocating restrictions under the New Order.

Emerging from the Suharto era, many Indonesians did not want Indonesia to be viewed as having an anachronistic political system in an era of democratization. The transition from Suharto to Habibie to Wahid was chaotic but set the stage for meaningful constitutional reform. The 1999 elections were a watershed development, setting the precedent for open party competition. Significantly, the willingness of Megawati and Yudhoyono to play by the rules and endure political failure without resorting to power grabs, a state of emergency, or extraconstitutional measures is the greatest contribution they could offer to Indonesia's democratic future. The contrast here with Thai elites and the never-dying impulse to turn to the king or the military during political crisis, and the Philippine practice of presidential-military alliances and martial law declarations, is indeed notable.

Across the polity, an expectation of constitutionally correct politics is taking root. As a state, the Republic of Indonesia has transcended serious challenges by ethnic groups, political movements, and undemocratic leaders. Following Sukarno's highly volatile balancing act, Suharto's authoritarian New

Order, and a wretched crisis-driven transition, Indonesia's young constitutionally based regime is showing potential and a will for consolidation. Such a feat, however, must be read against the history of previous regimes and their undoing. Events have overtaken Indonesia's political system before and may do so again in the future.

ECONOMIC DEVELOPMENT

The Indonesian economy is the largest in Southeast Asia. In the developing world only China, India, and Turkey have larger economies. Even as a demographic giant, Indonesia has had economic gains in recent decades that have rendered the country's per capita gross national income ($1,650) higher than less populated regional neighbors the Philippines, Vietnam, Cambodia, Laos, Burma, and Timor-Leste. Having averaged over 6 percent GDP growth each year from 1965 to 1997, during the Asian financial crisis Indonesia sunk to an alarming negative GDP growth of 13.1 percent. Since that nadir, economic growth has climbed slowly over the subsequent decade, returning to over 6 percent in 2007.

Sukarno's "revolutionary" economic system under his guided democracy was isolationist and xenophobic, skewed to meet ideological goals rather than the needs of the citizenry. Suharto's New Order economics sought to provide order to replace disorder and rationality to replace irrationality so that economic development would become the yardstick by which the success of his regime would be measured.

For the most part, the yardstick measured steady although not spectacular growth, but it was enough to buy a substantial share of popular support and political stability. The means to this end were a series of five-year plans to improve the public welfare, realize a financial bonanza from oil revenues, follow the advice of economic technocrats, repair the infrastructure, and begin to rely on the private sector for the necessary capital, structural change, and productivity.[15] The technocrats behind the recovery came to be known as the "Berkeley Mafia," a group of Indonesian economists trained at the University of California–Berkeley in the 1950s. Although the results were generally positive, some difficulties were encountered, including widespread income disparity, corruption, and mismanaged industries. A countertrend developed within the New Order for greater economic nationalism.

The most badly managed company was the government-owned oil industry, Pertamina, which went bankrupt in the 1970s. Led by President Suharto's colleague General Ibnu Sutowo, Pertamina incurred huge debts from lavish spending on useless projects. When oil prices dropped precipitously from $34 per barrel in 1981 to $8 per barrel in the mid-1980s, economic growth in

Indonesia fell correspondingly, ending a decade of greatly increased government outlays for education, infrastructure, and communications. The Indonesian economy's dependence on the oil sector in the 1980s was evident in that oil exports accounted for 78 percent of export earnings and oil revenues for 70 percent of government income at that time.[16] A decade earlier, by contrast, oil revenues had accounted for less than 20 percent of government income.

When oil prices fell again in 1986, the government was forced to enact drastic reforms to keep the economy from slackening. Suharto again mobilized his technocrats to bring order to the economy by making it less reliant on oil revenues, forcing austerity in budget expenditures to reduce the deficit, and opening the economy to foreign investment and joint ventures. A series of reform measures were established, such as creating duty-free zones, enacting liberal investment laws, and reducing bureaucratic red tape, all designed to encourage foreign investment.

The policy of promoting exports and foreign investment more aggressively replaced the policies of import substitution favored by economic nationalists and characterized by protectionism and heavy government intervention in distributing capital. The success of the new policy was shown by the fact that foreign investment commitments rose more than threefold over a three-year period, from $1.4 billion in 1987 to $4.7 billion in 1989.

Part of the reason for the great increase in foreign investment under Suharto was that Indonesia, like Thailand, became a major assembly area for manufacturers from Hong Kong, Singapore, Taiwan, South Korea, and even the United States. Most investments were in labor-intensive, low-technology industries such as footwear, food canning, textiles, and wood processing where Indonesia's low wages attracted entrepreneurs from higher-wage countries.[17] In addition, the indigenous Chinese, who have long been active in the economy, were given greater leeway in return for their support of Golkar. Officials and military officers provided Chinese business executives with protection and useful legislation, while in return the Chinese supplied capital and access to profits from their businesses. These Chinese businesspeople, called *cukong* (boss), were resented by Indonesian entrepreneurs, who viewed the *cukong* system as corrupt and exclusive.

In addition to growth tainted with corruption, other paradoxical legacies of Indonesia's rapid economy emerged. Although some new wealth trickled down to allow a small middle class to emerge, the rich quickly became richer. Absolute poverty declined markedly, but many Indonesians continued to live a subsistence existence. Foreign investment flooded in, but pleasing investors and ensuring their confidence came at the expense of labor rights and the local environment.

Although foreign investment leveled off in the 1990s as China and Vietnam became cheap-labor competitors, the cumulative effect of investment left the country vulnerable, as demonstrated by massive capital flight caused by the late 1990s "Asian Contagion." While the collapse of the Thai baht triggered a regional crisis, the depths to which Indonesia sunk were a result of the inherent weaknesses of the New Order economy exacerbated by international exuberance for emerging markets and reckless flows of hot money.

In the years before the crisis, the New Order administration moved in contradictory directions, sometimes supporting market mechanisms and liberalization and other times state intervention and the protection of conglomerates controlled by Suharto's family or cronies. The overall strength of the economy and the high rates of economic growth led to poor policies and regulation, including nationalist and protectionist policies Suharto engineered to protect those closest to him.

Hutomo Mandala Putra, known as "Tommy Suharto"—a favored son of the president—benefited greatly from his father's patronage at state expense. He was given rights to produce the "national car," the Timor (which is actually imported from South Korea). Tommy's exclusive tax exemptions and tariff concessions allowed him to sell the Timor at about half the price of competing vehicles. The United States challenged Suharto's support for Indonesia's national car on the grounds that to exempt it from taxes levied against imported cars was unfair. Domestically, many wealthy Indonesians refused to buy the Timor, citing its poor performance as an excuse that often masked their contempt for the family dynasty's use of its economic privileges to attempt to corner one of the most promising markets in Indonesia.

Tommy was also presented with lucrative contracts with the Burmese State Law and Order Restoration Council (SLORC) and was awarded Indonesia's trade monopoly for cloves. Suharto named him head of the Clove Marketing Board, a position that provided him with the ability to generate tremendous revenue. His siblings received similarly lucrative contracts. His eldest sister, Tutut Siti Hadijanti Rukmana, held a controlling interest in a company that collected revenues from Java's principal toll roads, occupied a senior post in Golkar, and was being groomed as a potential successor to her father. All of Suharto's six children, in fact, were involved in the nation's primary industries: automobiles, petrochemicals, computers, oil, and satellite communications.

Suharto responded to the national community only when the pressure to do so was particularly great. For example, in 1997 he stepped in to block a ministry recommendation that effectively would have forced parents to buy children's shoes from a company owned by the president's eldest grandson. The issue had been on the front pages of national newspapers since it was made public that the ministry had recommended that all elementary schoolchildren wear identical shoes, to be sold for $10.70 a pair. Indonesia's daily minimum wage is about $3. The shoes were dubbed "national shoes" by the public, in reference to the "national car" being manufactured by Tommy Suharto.

In 1997 and 1998, when the emergency packages were negotiated with the IMF, new details of Suharto family nepotism and corruption percolated to the surface. Public disdain for the Suharto family grew. The austerity measures imposed as part of loan conditionality proved painful for not only the Suharto family and his associates but also, by consequence, Indonesia's general population.

The IMF viewed the economic artifice Suharto had created as the cause of Indonesia's woes and dismantled it virtually overnight. In large part, the Suharto-tied monopolies as well as importer arrangements distorted prices of standard goods and items, not just automobiles, cloves, and satellite communications. The IMF-imposed lifting of subsidies, provoking a further slide of the rupiah, caused shortages and huge price increases on rice, cooking oil, instant noodles, paper, and cement. The economic crisis before the IMF measures, severely disrupting itself, demanded economic stimulus, not austerity. At the time when state capital was most needed to buoy an economy suffering capital flight and loss in demand, and when Indonesia's laid-off workers needed subsidized benefits most, IMF measures forced sudden price volatility and sudden budget austerity, and directed $43 billion in rescue funds to pay off international banks and creditors. Unemployment skyrocketed to 15–20 percent. Protesters turned their rage on Suharto's administration, Chinese businesspeople, and the IMF. Social disruption arose. The performance legitimacy of the New Order collapsed.

The Habibie and Wahid administrations suffered the burden of cleaning up the mess. Habibie's tenure, tainted by his Suharto connections, was dominated by political crisis and East Timor independence, and Wahid, whom many considered incapable of economic thinking, faced economic conditions that would frighten the most skilled policy managers. Sukarnoputri more capably brought stability to the economy, but it was not until Yudhoyono's presidency that "recovery" became more of a reality than a distant hope.

Yudhoyono implemented a set of economic policies designed to reduce unemployment, provide relief to the poorest Indonesians, and restore confidence in the embattled financial sector. To these ends, he invested in infrastructure development and sponsored cash packages and subsidies on rice and housing for the poorest strata. He also developed a deposit insurance scheme while also encouraging the growth of sharia banking. The outcome of these reforms and others has been mixed, but foreign investment confidence improved, as did perceptions related to business corruption.[18] Relative to neighboring countries, however, Indonesia's reputation as a difficult foreign investment environment persists. Indonesia's economic competitiveness with its Asian neighbors remains a priority. Symbolic of the dynamic nature of its large economy, Yudhoyono withdrew Indonesia from membership in the Organization of Petroleum Exporting Countries (OPEC) in 2008 as the country transitioned to a net oil importer. The country's economic outlook took a turn for the worse, however, as the global financial crisis deepened in early 2009.

Despite New Order corruption, severe economic crisis, and years of painful economic recovery, the quality of life of average Indonesians has improved significantly over the past four decades. Life expectancy, under fifty years in 1965, now stands at sixty-nine years. Primary school enrollment climbed from 41 percent to 94 percent. Astonishingly, over a forty-year period when its population grew by 75 million people (equivalent to two Californias), Indonesia saw its poverty rate lower from 60 percent to 27 percent. In terms of the Human Development Index, Indonesia's HDI value from 1975 to 2005 went from 0.47 to 0.73, a more dramatic swing than that experienced by any Southeast Asian country or other impressive developers such as China, Mexico, and Brazil.

THE INDONESIAN STATE

The diversity of Indonesia's population and its demographic character make the country difficult to control. Indonesia has had a history of social dislocation, which is the first condition for the development of a strong state. Like the Philippines, Indonesia experienced a long colonial rule (350 years as the Dutch East Indies), during which its economy served Dutch interests through the exploitation of Indonesia's natural resources. The impact of the Spanish and Americans on the Philippines was greater than that of the Dutch on the Indonesians, perhaps because there had been powerful indigenous empires in Sumatra and Java before the Dutch arrived, whereas there had been none in the Philippines before the Spanish arrived. The Japanese occupation of Indonesia, while not as devastating as in the Philippines, was an important event. Moreover, Indonesia waged a four-year war against the Dutch, who returned to retake their former colony after the defeat of the Japanese; thus, a revolutionary war led to rebellions and regional struggles between contenders for power.

Sukarno's fusion of his own political charisma and power to build a young state was effective until narrower economic and political failures undid his regime. The Indonesian state experienced a major bloodbath when, following the *Gestapu* coup of 1965, about half a million Indonesians were killed. The violence spread as racial, religious, ethnic, social, economic, and political differences were judged to be sufficient cause for mass killings. What began as a political cleansing to oust communists became an orgy of killing and a breakdown of law and order. The PKI, tallying 3.5 million members (and 23.5 million in affiliated organizations), was virtually annihilated. Together, these episodes suggest that Indonesia experienced the necessary dislocations to develop a strong state.

This strong, autonomous state emerged under Suharto. He brought various groups of people into his ruling circle who were independent of existing bases of social control yet skillful enough to execute his administration's designs. The technocrats brought order to the economy and thereby managed to strengthen Suharto's claim to power. Even more important, Suharto won the ongoing loyalty of military leaders who consolidated their power around the regime.

Under New Order rule, the strong state controlled all aspects of political and economic life and was not subservient to particular societal forces. Suharto depoliticized and co-opted all institutional and societal forces to maintain and enhance state power. Forever distrustful of politics, Suharto intimidated some societal groups with military coercion under *dwi fungsi*, emasculated others through administrative corporatism, and bought off others by giving them a stake in rapid economic growth. Consequently, the state's legitimacy found itself fused to Suharto's capacity to meet the economic needs of the citizenry and to his ability to protect the country's security both internally and externally. This troubled legitimacy caused close observers at the time to predict another episode of political tragedy.[19]

Today all potentially powerful groups are essentially integrated into the polity. The military, once overwhelmingly powerful, is now taking its place as a state-based interest group amidst an array of formal and informal pressure groups. The elected legislature is rising in its importance and proving capable of checking the abuse of presidential power. Even the most prominent societal groups once left out of the system (political Islam and Muslim parties) are now functioning freely and competing within a democratic constitutional framework. Although the state ideology of *Pancasila* is more openly challenged than in the past, the absence of forced allegiance to it is allowing for the organic development of its post-Suharto legitimacy.

Vis-à-vis society, Indonesia's state has weakened since the collapse of bureaucratic authoritarianism. Nevertheless, the state is not necessarily vulnerable to hegemonic control by a single group. Here, Indonesia's diversity and growing pluralism are assets to its political development. The current (albeit brief) trend embracing constitutionalism strengthens the durability of political order and state capability. The extent to which the diverse set of players in Indonesian politics further legitimate constitutionalism, the rule of law, and sanctioned authority will determine the possibility of a resurgent, strong state. Ethnic groups, political parties, political Islam, Javanese elites, the military, the business community, ruralites, non-Muslims, intellectuals, journalists, and

CSOs must find consensus in the rules of the game while simultaneously keeping state power at bay or falling prey to particularistic interests or dominance.

FOREIGN POLICY

As in other Southeast Asian nations, the primary goal of Indonesia's postindependence foreign policy has been to sustain the republic's security. Sukarno's means to this end relied on anti-Western nationalism; he was opposed to the old established forces (OLDEFOS) and allied with the newly emerging forces (NEFOS). OLDEFOS included the neo-imperialist nations and their allies, led by the United States. NEFOS, on the other hand, included the "progressive" third world and communist nations, locked in struggle against OLDEFOS. Sukarno's *Konfrontasi* against Malaysia, which began in 1962 and ended in 1965, was described as a classic example of a NEFOS struggle against an OLDEFOS lackey. Supporting Sukarno's foreign policy against the agents of neocolonialism, colonialism, and imperialism was the PKI.

When his New Order was inaugurated, Suharto ended *Konfrontasi,* banned the PKI, and reentered the international arena with a pro-Western, anticommunist foreign policy. New Order Indonesia's quiet support for ASEAN and the Zone of Peace, Freedom, and Neutrality in Southeast Asia reflected its leadership's lower profile in international relations. During the Suharto regime, Indonesia played only a minor role in international affairs, despite the fact that the nation is the fourth largest (in population) in the world and is of immense importance economically, geographically, and strategically.

The major exception to Indonesia's nonintrusive participation in foreign affairs was Suharto's decision to invade East Timor in 1975. This action exacerbated a vigorous guerrilla insurgency movement, which continued throughout East Timor's annexation. Habibie's decision to allow an independence referendum sparked further violence and resulted in a humiliating presence of international peacekeepers and UN authorities.

Relations between Indonesia and the People's Republic of China improved gradually following two decades of tension resulting from the *Gestapu* coup. As part of ASEAN, Indonesia gradually moved foreign policy closer to that of the other ASEAN countries. Sharing interests in checking Vietnamese power, Thailand and China made accommodations with each other in the 1970s. In the 1980s, Sino-Thais began forming connections with their ancestral land and a vigorous economic relationship began to grow. Indonesia, on the other hand, took until August 1990 to formally establish diplomatic relations with China, ending twenty-five years of hostility, and it was not until the presidency of Megawati Sukarnoputri that any significant bilateral efforts were made to expand trade between the two countries. The United States, Japan, Singapore, and other Asian and European countries have continued to be Indonesia's primary markets and sources of investment. Development assistance from the United Nations, the World Bank, IMF, and bilateral partners continue to shape macro- and micro-level economic policies.

Unlike Singapore, the Philippines, and Thailand, which emerged as overt and quiet partners in George W. Bush's war on terrorism, Indonesia proved a more reluctant partner and was instinctively leery of U.S. power and its misuse. Sukarnoputri's government publicly opposed the U.S. invasions in Afghanistan and Iraq following the 9/11 attacks. Susilo Bambang Yudhoyono later welcomed tsunami-related humanitarian assistance from the United States as well as resources to support counterterrorism within Indonesia. General foreign policy skepticism of the United States' relationship with Israel and its war on terrorism persisted through the end of the Bush administration.

Barack Obama's election in late 2008 opened a new door to improve relations between the third and fourth most populous countries in the world. Only days after the historic election, and before Obama had spent a day in office, President Yudhoyono had already called Obama's foreign policy "refreshing" and proposed a strategic partnership with the United States that included stronger people-to-people relations. Obama, he said, "spoke our language, knew our culture, ate our food, played with Indonesian friends . . . [and] experienced the inner soul of Indonesia."[20] In one of his first moves in crafting a new foreign policy direction for the United States, Obama sent Secretary of State Hillary Clinton to Asia in February 2009. Children from the Indonesian school Obama once attended welcomed Clinton with songs and flowers. In a press conference from Jakarta, she celebrated Indonesia's new stability as a Muslim-majority democracy and pledged to work toward a "comprehensive partnership" between the two countries.

Indonesia's regional role as a diplomatic mediator and Muslim world symbol continues to rise over time. It constructively helped to resolve the Cambodian crisis and maritime disputes among ASEAN states, and serves as a mediator between Burma and the international community. Internationally, Indonesia's status draws considerable attention among the global Islamic community for its successful economic growth and recent political reform toward political openness. Even as it fosters pan-Islamic unity, Indonesia also offers a moderating voice within the Organization of the Islamic Conference (OIC).

CONCLUSION

In terms of stability, democratic political representation, and civil liberties, Indonesia's political direction today is arguably more favorable than at any time in postindependence history. Although the country is forever challenged by geographic and demographic realities, inertia from its past record of economic growth raises the prospects for continued development. The disruption caused by the Asian economic crisis may have been deeper in Indonesia than elsewhere in Southeast Asia, but a favorable democratic dividend has resulted. Politically, Indonesia today stands in contrast to the troubled eras of instability and authoritarianism in previous decades.

Emerging from the tumultuous years of the Sukarno era, the New Order regime created conditions for economic growth but measured political development in terms of stability. The New Order proved institutionally weak and unable to transcend political crisis when economic growth halted. Of course, millions of Indonesians did see their lives improve during the thirty-year regime of Suharto, but ultimately performance legitimacy was a risky foundation for long-term rule. Suharto, like his predecessor, suffered an ignominious demise. The revelations of Suharto family privilege, cronyism, and corruption paraded before the world—coupled with humiliating, painful, and ill-conceived IMF rescue packages—were more than the Indonesian public could bear. It was thus from the ashes of the New Order's collapse that the country's rising expectations for democracy and demands for accountable government emerged.

How long the current trend in building institutions of representation and accountability will endure remains an open question, but signs of sustainability are undeniable. Unlike the Philippines (troubled by an entrenched oligarchy), Thailand (prone to constitutional crises and extraconstitutional impulses), or in Singapore, Malaysia, and Cambodia (controlled by illiberal, hegemonic parties), there is a growing consensus across Indonesia that democracy is desirable and possible. Representative government, parliamentary governance, and open party competition are now ideals embraced by ethnic groups, social classes, political Islam, and (importantly) the rising generation. Within this new framework of expectations, political winners are afforded legitimacy and political losers demonstrate a willingness to play a constructive, oppositional role. If the political system can be responsive to those receiving the fewest benefits of economic change, the consolidation of democracy in the world's largest Muslim country may be within reach. Sukarno's vision of *Bhinneka Tunggal Ika* (Unity in Diversity) remains Indonesia's central challenge, but the nascent institutions of the new era of liberal democratic reform show encouraging potential.

NOTES

1. In Leo Suryadinata, Aris Ananta, and Evi Nurvidya Arifin's *Indonesia's Population: Ethnicity and Religion in a Changing Political Landscape* (Singapore: Institute of Southeast Asian Studies, 2003), the authors use the Indonesian government's 2000 Census to identify eleven major ethic groups: Javanese (42 percent), Sundanese (15 percent), Malay (3.5 percent), Madurese (3.4 percent), Batak (3 percent), Minangkabau (2.7 percent), Betawi (2.5 percent), Buginese (2.5 percent), Bantenese (2 percent), Banjarese (1.7 percent), and Balinese(1.5 percent). Other ethnic groups compose the remaining 20 percent of the Indonesian population. Many scholars believe the 2000 Census underreported Indonesian-Chinese, who compose up to 3 percent of the total population (compared to the 0.9 percent officially reported). Given Indonesia's history of anti-Chinese activity and riots, the ethnic Chinese can also be considered a major ethnic group of Indonesia.

2. For a sampling of views of the *Gestapu* coup, see Benedict Anderson and Ruth T. McVey, *A Preliminary Analysis of the October 1, 1965, Coup in Indonesia*, Interim Report Series, Modern Indonesia Project (Ithaca, NY: Cornell University Press, 1971); Arnold C. Brackman, *The Communist Collapse in Indonesia* (New York: Norton, 1969); Peter J. Dommen, "The Attempted Coup in Indonesia," *China Quarterly*, no. 25 (January–June 1966), pp. 144–170; John Hughes, *Sukarno: A Coup That Misfired, A Purge That Ran Wild* (New York: McKay, 1967); Justus van der Kroef, "Origins of the 1965 Coup in Indonesia: Probabilities and Alternatives," *Journal of Southeast Asian Studies*, vol. 3 (September 1972), pp. 277–298; Tarzie Vittachi, *The Fall of Sukarno* (New York: Praeger, 1967); and W. F. Wertheim, "Suharto and the Untung Coup: The Missing Link," *Journal of Contemporary Asia*, vol. 1, no. 2 (Winter 1970), pp. 50–57.

3. David McKendrick, "Indonesia in 1991," *Asian Survey*, vol. 32, no. 2 (February 1992), pp. 103–105.

4. See chapter 13 for a more detailed account of Timor-Leste's independence from Indonesia.

5. Rita Smith Kipp, "Indonesia in 2003: Terror's Aftermath," *Asian Survey*, vol. 44, no. 1 (January/February 2004), p. 65.

6. According to the U.S. Geological Survey, the energy released from the earthquake causing the tsunami equaled 474 megatons of TNT or 23,000 Hiroshima-sized nuclear bombs. http://earthquake.usgs.gov/eqcenter/eqinthenews/2004/usslav/neic_slav_faq.html.

7. Damien Kingsbury, "Indonesia in 2007: Unmet Expectations, Despite Improvement," *Asian Survey*, vol. 48, no. 1 (January/February 2008), p. 46.

8. Ibid., p. 39.

9. Leo Suryadinata, "Indonesia," in *Politics in the ASEAN States*, ed. Diane K. Mauzy (Kuala Lumpur: Maricans, 1986), p.127.

10. Leo Suryadinata, *Interpreting Indonesian Politics* (Singapore: Times Academic Press, 1998), p. 29.

11. Michael Vatikiotis, *Indonesian Politics under Suharto* (London: Routledge, 1993), p. 127.

12. Pieternell van Doorn-Harder, *Women Shaping Islam: Reading the Qur'an in Indonesia* (Urbana: University of Illinois Press, 2006), p. 1.

13. Ulf Sundhaussen, "Indonesia: Past and Present Encounters with Democracy," in *Democracy in Developing Countries: Asia*, ed. Larry Diamond, Juan J. Linz, and Seymour Martian Lipset (Boulder, CO: Lynn Rienner Publishers, 1989), p. 455.

14. "U.S. Lauds Muhammadiyah Role in Indonesia," *Antara News*, April 3, 2006, www.antara.co.id/en/print/?id=1144054753.

15. Geoffrey B. Hainsworth, "Indonesia: On the Road to Privatization?" *Current History*, vol. 89, no. 545 (March 1990), p. 121.

16. H. W. Arndt and Hal Hill, "The Indonesian Economy: Structural Adjustment After the Oil Boom," *Southeast Asian Affairs 1988* (Singapore: Institute of Southeast Asian Studies, 1988), p. 107.

17. *Far Eastern Economic Review*, April 19, 1990, p. 42.

18. Kingsbury, "Indonesia in 2007: Unmet Expectations, Despite Improvement," p. 41.

19. Mochtar Pabottingi, "Indonesia: Historicizing the New Order's Legitimacy Dilemma," in *Political Legitimacy in Southeast Asia: The Quest for Moral Authority*, ed. Muthiah Alagappa (Stanford, CA: Stanford University Press, 1995), p. 255.

20. "Indonesia Urges Upgrading Ties with U.S.," *Bangkok Post*, November 15, 2008, archived at www.BangkokPost.com.

RESOURCE GUIDE

A useful tool for bibliographic and other information on Indonesia is available from Australia National University's WWW Virtual Library; visit http://coombs.anu.edu.au/WWWVLPages/IndonPages/WWWVL-Indonesia.html. The University of California–Berkeley maintains a useful portal for digital and print resources on Indonesia: www.lib.berkeley.edu/SSEAL/SoutheastAsia/seaelec.html. Northern Illinois University's Southeast Asia Digital Library includes a range of useful links that cover government, academic, and research institutions specific to Indonesia: http://sea.lib.niu.edu. The University of Wisconsin–Madison Libraries maintains a list of digital and print resources on Indonesia: www.library.wisc.edu/guides/SEAsia/resarea.html. The Library of Congress maintains a resource guide on Indonesia at www.loc.gov/rr/international/portals.html#t.

For governmental sites and information, the National Portal of the Republic of Indonesia is available at www.indonesia.go.id/en. For information on Indonesia's Parliament, some English-language content is available on its official page, www.mpr.go.id/index.php?lang=en. "Governments on the WWW" at www.gksoft.com/govt is not well-maintained but still contains useful links to political parties and subnational governmental institutions. Located in Jakarta, the Centre for Strategic and International Studies makes available to readers policy-oriented research on Indonesia and regional issues: www.csis.or.id.

A full directory of development organizations and CSOs operating in Indonesia is available at www.devdir.org/files/Indonesia.PDF. Other particular sites worth perusing include those of Nahdlatul Ulama, at www.nu.or.id/page.php?lang=en; the Free West Papua movement at http://westpapuafree.wordpress.com; and the University of Buffalo's Tsunami Disaster page, which covers all phases of the 2004 disaster: http://ublib.buffalo.edu/libraries/asl/guides/indian-ocean-disaster.html.

The *Jakarta Post*, Indonesia's most widely read English-language newspaper, maintains a site at www.thejakartapost.com. Tempointeractive.com is a valuable site to find political punditry and discussion, although content in English is somewhat limited. The Australian-based journal InsideIndonesia.com publishes interesting feature articles weekly and quarterly that span useful political and social topics.

5

MALAYSIA

*M*alaysia is Southeast Asia's most admirable achiever. Though generally classified as an illiberal democracy, Malaysia is more pluralist than Singapore, more politically stable than Thailand, and less corrupt than the Philippines. Malaysia has also more successfully managed ethnic and religious conflict than its geocultural cousin Indonesia. With a population of 26.2 million people and a per capita gross national income (GNI) of $6,540, Malaysia has achieved the status of a newly industrialized country (NIC). Only the citizens of microstates Singapore and Brunei enjoy a higher standard of living in the region. The Malaysian success story is especially noteworthy because of the country's geographic and racial diversity.

Malaysia consists of the peninsula (formerly Malaya) that is connected to southern Thailand, and Sabah and Sarawak on the island of Borneo, several hundred miles across the South China Sea. Three in five Malaysians now live in cities, and most of its territory remains forested. Less than 10 percent of Malaysia's land is arable.

There is no more powerful force in Malaysian society than communalism, or the division of the country into racial communities: 51 percent Malay, 26 percent Chinese, 7 percent Indian, and the rest smaller minorities and migrant populations. The Malays are Muslim, predominantly rural and agricultural, or *bumiputra* ("sons of the soil"). The non-Malays are urban and mostly non-Muslim, usually employed in industry, trades, and textiles. Urban centers are attracting more Malays from the countryside as the country grows wealthier.[1]

Immigrants to Malaysia from 1860 to 1940 were mostly impoverished workers and peasants from southern China or southern India who came during the British colonial administration to work the tin mines and perform labor the Malays scorned. As with overseas diasporic communities elsewhere, their separateness was reinforced even as they expanded their economic roles. The Chinese in particular became Malaysia's money lenders, middlemen, contractors, and manufacturers. Their primary stress on education and ambition provided

mobility so that at present the Chinese are the wealthiest businesspeople in most areas of the economy.

Communalism resulted in the stereotyping of Malaysia's ethnic groups. Malays routinely view the Chinese as aggressive, acquisitive, unscrupulous in business dealings, ritually unclean, and politically suspect. Chinese, on the other hand, view themselves as hardworking, progressive, competitive, and faithful to their families. To the Chinese, the stereotypical Malay is lazy and superstitious and without motivation for hard work or personal advancement, whereas Malays view themselves as scrupulous in their dealings with others and as more concerned with the quality of human relationships than with material acquisition.[2]

To mitigate ethnic differences, the British arranged the "Bargain" when they relinquished colonial authority over Malaya (not yet Malaysia) in 1957. The Bargain included such arrangements as constitutional advantages to the Malays; support for a Malay as head of state (*Yang di-Pertuan Agong*), chosen from among the sultans of nine peninsular Malay states; Malay as the country's official language; and Islam as the official religion. Also, the constitution provided special privileges to Malays in land acquisition, educational assistance, and civil service employment.

To meet the terms of the Bargain, the leading Malay, Chinese, and Indian political parties formed an alliance with the understanding that non-Malays would prevail in the economic sector while Malays would control the political sector. As long as that formula was accepted by all groups, the Malaysian political system was stable. When the formula was challenged in May 1969 following a national election, rioting ensued, causing the deaths of at least 196 people and precipitating the declaration of a state of emergency that lasted almost two years.

Great Britain continued to exercise influence over Malaya; over Britain's self-governing colony, Singapore; and over the dependencies of North Borneo (now Sabah), Sarawak, and Brunei (all situated on the island of Borneo). In 1963, Malaya joined with Singapore, Sabah, and Sarawak (but not Brunei) to form the Federation of Malaysia. All of these areas shared a common colonial heritage under Great Britain, and all feared that without collaboration, they could not function as viable and autonomous nation-states. To offset the integration of 3 million Chinese from Singapore into the federation, Sabah and Sarawak were brought in to maintain a favorable proportion of non-Chinese in the population. Singapore was given wide-ranging autonomy over its domestic affairs.

The federation lasted only two years, until August 1965, when Malaysia's first prime minister, Tunku Abdul Rahman, expelled Singapore for many complex reasons inextricably bound up with communal problems. The prime minister of Singapore, Lee Kuan Yew, called for a "Malaysian Malaysia"—that is, for a Malaysia with equal participation from all areas and groups. His call opposed and contrasted with Tunku Abdul Rahman's design for a "Malayan Malaysia," with special privileges reserved for the dominant ethnic group. When Lee Kuan Yew attempted to influence the larger area of Malaysia, Tunku Abdul Rahman regarded the attempt as a direct threat to continued political dominance by the Malays.

The 1969 communal riots were a watershed event in Malaysia's postindependence era, and their immediate cause was the erosion of support for Abdul Rahman's Alliance Party coalition in the 1969 elections. In the preceding two elections, in 1959 and 1964, the Alliance had won an overwhelming majority of the parliamentary seats. In 1969, for the first time the opposition parties won a majority (51.5 percent) of the votes against the Alliance Party's 48.5 percent. Although Alliance candidates still controlled a majority in the Parliament despite losing twenty-three seats, the 1969 election showed that the Alliance coalition's capacity to govern was seriously impaired. To celebrate their "victory," anti-Alliance forces paraded in the streets of the capital, Kuala Lumpur. Later, on May 13, Alliance supporters paraded, which led to communal tensions to the point of provoking mob action that raged for four days and tragically ended in 196 deaths (official count).

The Malaysian government viewed the race riots as a threat to the ethnic Bargain that had been the formula for civic stability. To ensure that Malays retained political power, a state of emergency was proclaimed, Parliament was temporarily disbanded, civil liberties were curtailed, and total authority was granted to a new body, the National Operations Council (NOC). The NOC worked to restore order and sought to return Malaysia to parliamentary democracy. The twenty-one-month period was a time of suspended democracy.

Believing that economic tensions were mainly responsible for the communal riots, Tun Abdul Razak, the new prime minister, proposed the New Economic Policy (NEP) to promote national unity, a just society, and to attack poverty by "reducing and eventually eliminating the identity of race with economic function." Under the NEP, the rights of Malays were extended by reserving for them a proportion of positions in higher education and certain businesses, and sedition acts were passed that prohibited discussion of such "sensitive issues" as the prerogatives of Malay rulers, special rights for Malays, and official status for the Malay language. In essence, this meant that Malay participation in the economic sphere was to be increased by granting special privileges in terms of business ownership, tax breaks, investment incentives, and employment quotas—a pro-Malay affirmative action program for the majority.

By 1972, parliamentary democracy returned, albeit within the constraints of the sedition acts and the reworking of the Alliance into the National Front (Barisan Nasional). Tun Abdul Razak established the National Front to ensure dominance of the political system by Malays and to preclude upheavals such as the 1969 riots. His party, the United Malays National Organization (UMNO), having co-opted most of the opposition parties, won 90 percent of the parliamentary seats in the 1974 election.

When Abdul Razak died in 1976 he was succeeded by Tun Hussein Onn, who, like his predecessors, came from prestigious ancestry and great wealth and had a Western education. He continued National Front policies until 1981 when, following a serious illness, he resigned and was succeeded by Deputy Prime Minister Datuk Seri Mahathir bin Mohamad. Mahathir, the first commoner prime minister, with no aristocratic ancestry or family wealth and with a local education in medicine, symbolized the new Malaysian technocrat. His brash and confrontational style was the opposite of that of his refined predecessors.

Dr. Mahathir became an articulate spokesman in modern Malaysia's bid to develop economically. His "Look East Policy" argued that Western nations were not appropriate models for Malaysia. He believed that Malaysia should emulate the methods of Japan, South Korea, and Taiwan, all Asian countries whose values were more in tune with those of Malaysia. He also introduced the concept of "Malaysia Incorporated," whereby business and government leaders would work together as in a modern corporation. His drive to privatize public utilities, communications, and transportation is an example of his attempt to encourage the profit motive and increased efficiency to the Malaysian economy.

In the 1982 parliamentary election, Mahathir and the UMNO-led National Front triumphed, winning 132 of 154 seats. Again in 1986, the National Front won a landslide victory, winning 148 of the 177 parliamentary seats, but this election marked the beginning of a period of political and economic difficulties. The leaders of the major parties in the Front fell into strife as the country underwent a major recession, which resulted in negative economic growth for the first time since independence.

The major problem was within UMNO, the dominant party of the National Front and the "home" of Mahathir (as well as all former prime ministers). Strife in UMNO led to the resignation of high-ranking officials, some of whom joined a faction known as Team B, who then challenged the leadership of Mahathir and his followers, known as Team A. In the elections for the leadership of UMNO in April 1987, Mahathir barely beat his challenger, Team B leader and Trade and Industry Minister Tunku Razaleigh Hamzah, when he won by only 43 votes, 761 to 718. In a shocking display of internecine factionalism, Team B officials accused Mahathir of blatant abuse of power, authoritarian leadership, economic mismanagement, and corruption.[3]

Razaleigh had run against Mahathir following five years of a recessionary economy, including a 1 percent decline in the GNP, which disillusioned the Chinese and the new Malay middle class. Mahathir's confrontational administrative style had also become controversial. The challenge to Mahathir was especially noteworthy because it is the custom of Malays not to challenge their leaders; generally, Malaysians believe in *taat setia* (absolute loyalty) to their rulers. It is considered a case of *kurang ajar* (impropriety) to question the leadership. The electoral challenge undermined this important custom in Malay politics.[4]

In response, Mahathir purged Team B members from his cabinet and from UMNO leadership, and he invoked the Internal Securities Act, ordering the arrest of persons critical of government actions. Also, three opposition newspapers were closed, and Operation Lallang was ordered: a sweep by the Malaysian police (on October 27, 1987) that took into custody 119 people who had been accused of threatening internal security by provoking communal conflict. All those arrested were members of religious, political, and social organizations that, merely by criticizing regime policies, had qualified themselves as "thorns in [Mahathir's] side."[5]

In still another stunning incident related to UMNO factionalism, the Malaysian high court decreed that since unregistered regional branches had participated in the UMNO elections, UMNO was an illegal organization. The high court's decision was a shocking development because UMNO had won every election since independence. Immediately there was a scramble to register a new party with UMNO in its name and to lay claim to the party's considerable assets. After rejecting Team B's applications, Mahathir was able to get UMNO Baru (New UMNO) registered. A dissident faction, again led by Razaleigh, formed a new party, Semangat '46 (Spirit of '46, the year of UMNO's birth), and allied itself with other opposition groups to form an alternative coalition known as Angkatan Perpaduan Umnah (APU), or the United Movement of the Faithful. Subsequently the National Front, led by UMNO Baru, won six of eight by-elections against the APU as well as the national election in October 1990.

Because of high-court decisions that Mahathir believed were against the interests of the National Front, he reduced the power of the courts by taking away their right to judicial review of executive decisions on internal security and matters concerned with the administration and operation of political parties. Indeed, in 1988 he forced a constitutional amendment through Parliament that eliminated the constitutional basis of judicial review and replaced it with "such powers as Parliament shall grant." Ostensibly, this reduction of the courts' power was to ensure that, in case of threat to the nation's security, an executive could move with dispatch rather than having to wait for the cumbersome courts to deliberate. Eventually, at Mahathir's instigation, a specially created tribunal removed a majority of court justices from office.

In early 1989, Mahathir suffered a heart attack and underwent a successful multiple coronary bypass operation. His rapid recovery restored him as the central figure in contemporary Malaysian politics, and he moved toward the

1990 elections with confidence as the National Front began to recover from factional struggles and the economy recovered from recession.

The strong economy was the principal factor in the overwhelming election victory Mahathir and the multiethnic National Front coalition achieved in October 1990. After only a ten-day political campaign, one of the shortest in contemporary Southeast Asian history, he won a two-thirds majority, thus ensuring control over constitutional amendments. The National Front won 127 of the 180 seats in Parliament despite an exceptionally strong opposition campaign.

The primary political issue of the early 1990s concerned the role of Islam in Malaysian society. Islamization had made inroads into the state of Kelantan, with the state assembly controlled by an Islamic-dominated coalition between the Parti Islam Se-Malaysia (PAS) and Semangat '46. Mahathir reacted against the notion of an Islamic state, which he deemed inappropriate for a multiracial society. The issue did not become a crisis because high economic growth rates provided a cushion that softened societal tensions.

In 1992–1993, a social reformation of great significance occurred when Mahathir decided to confront the nation's sultans, the traditional hereditary rulers of most of peninsular Malaysia's states, whose positions were largely ceremonial. The prime minister moved to reduce their power and prerogatives, notwithstanding laws and acts precluding discussion of the sultans' roles. By 1993, Mahathir had thus tamed the bureaucracy, political parties, judiciary, press, and sultans. Through confrontation and co-optation, he had successfully undermined the major forces once competing with him for political power.

The period from 1990 to 1996 was positive for the ruling National Front and for its leader, Mahathir. Winning its ninth general election in April 1995, with 64 percent of the popular vote, the Front enjoyed a two-thirds parliamentary majority. In addition, the Front won control of every state assembly except one (that of Kelantan), and the opposition was left in disarray. Both the Democratic Action Party (DAP) and Semangat '46 were shut out throughout the nation. The Barisan Nasional coalition of UMNO, the Malayan Chinese Association (MCA), the Malayan Indian Congress (MIC), and the largely Chinese Parti Gerakan were united after the election. Malaysians supported the Front because of the strong economy, the disarray of the opposition, and the Front's monopoly of the mass media. At seventy years of age, Mahathir had never been more secure in his position.

As Mahathir's health stayed strong and his international stature increased, few politicians were brave enough to question his preeminence. His main competition came from a former Muslim youth activist and deputy prime minister, Anwar Ibrahim, but Mahathir kept him off balance with intraparty rules that banned confrontations with the leader. Mahathir became Malaysia's longest-serving premier and the only Front chairman to lead his coalition through five successive elections.

Mahathir's international reputation widened after a series of speeches in which he praised the virtues of "Asian values" and condemned "Western values." He often spoke passionately about his nation's sovereignty and, appearing to revel in the role of "West-basher," about the Americans, whom he deemed to be neo-imperialist in their desire to control Malaysia and Malaysia's neighbors. In 1996 Mahathir was responsible for backing the construction of the world's tallest building, the Petronas Towers in Kuala Lumpur (eclipsing America's Sears Tower in Chicago). He built a gleaming high-tech research park, dubbed "technopolis," and a "Multimedia Super-Corridor" linking Kuala Lumpur with an immense new international airport. Mahathir has hosted numerous international conferences, including the thirtieth-anniversary celebrations of the ASEAN, and was primarily responsible for bringing Vietnam, Laos, and Burma into the association.

In 1997, when the Asian economic crisis hit Malaysia, Mahathir was in his sixteenth year of tenure and in sole command of his country. A new problem arose when the Malaysian ringgit lost much of its value as a result of the Thai currency's devaluation. For the first time, Mahathir was in the midst of a crisis he could not control directly because the crisis was caused by international and not domestic factors. His first reaction was to blame outsiders, and he ridiculously pointed his finger at the "Jewish conspiracy" he believed had long wanted to undermine Malaysia because of its predominantly Muslim population. Mahathir later explained that he was referring to only one Jew, Hungarian-born American financier George Soros, whom Mahathir accused of maliciously speculating on the Malaysian currency. Most of the world's press criticized Mahathir for refusing to accept that a large reason for currency crisis was domestic, and not external.

Mahathir turned his focus on "Vision 2020," a plan to lift Malaysia into the ranks of developed nations in the next twenty-five years. His goal was blunted by the economic crisis, which may explain the depth of his anger and his shocking anti-Semitic accusation. He was furious that his plans could be undermined by an economic crisis that was beyond his control. Mahathir rejected emergency aid from the IMF and, defying economic orthodoxy, imposed capital controls. Foreign investors, shocked by the announcement that their investment funds must remain in Malaysia for at least one year, reacted sourly. Although pundits predicted a policy disaster, Mahathir, who accused the IMF of trying to recolonize Asia, eventually won admiration for guiding the country through the turbulent Asian economic crisis without an IMF bailout.

By 2001, Mahathir had run Malaysia for twenty years and, like many overstaying leaders, he began to lose his edge and became surrounded by yes-men who failed him by pointing out only his successes and not his weaknesses. In

1999 Mahathir dismissed his deputy prime minister, Anwar Ibrahim, for alleged corruption and sodomy. Serious scholars of Malaysia believed that Ibrahim was sacked primarily because he was increasingly popular among Malaysians, a potential threat to Mahathir's continued leadership—hence the trumped-up charges of corruption that led to a six-year prison sentence when he was later was found guilty of both charges. The entire issue proved to be an immense international embarrassment to Mahathir and provided his critics with evidence that Malaysia was no longer a nation of laws, but instead a nation of personalities, many of whom were above the law.

Despite the debacle, Mahathir felt confident to set forth national elections for the Parliament in November 1999, six months before his term was even up. The short eight-day campaign led to the National Front's winning an overwhelming majority, 57 percent of the popular vote (down from 65 percent in 1995). Several provinces voted against the Front, choosing Islamic parties. Campaigning was minimal and many topics were banned. The election was an excellent example of electoral politics designed to perpetuate the leading party's power.

Mahathir's new term, beginning in November 1999, was for five years. The election was somewhat of a surprise because UMNO lost nearly half the Malay vote, although most of the loss among Malays was in the northeastern provinces. The Front still won a majority of the total votes and maintained Malays' support in key peninsular districts.

Four years after the 1999 elections, Mahathir stepped down as prime minister, believing it was time for new leadership. Mahathir left a paradoxical legacy from his twenty-two years in office. Because of his vision and leadership, the nation had enjoyed two decades of ever-improving living standards for all classes of people. With an intolerance of pettiness, disdain of opposition, and fervent commitment to Malaysian sovereignty, Mahathir sidelined rivals while lifting the country out of its third-world status. He embraced strategic alliances with Chinese and Indian elites but also left his UMNO colleagues (and his fellow Malays) as the beneficiaries of a political system stacked in their favor. During his tenure, Mahathir brashly disciplined the bureaucracy, political parties, judiciary, press, and sultans, all of whom once dared to challenge his political power.

Going out in true Mahathir style, the prime minister gave the world some parting thoughts. During a high-profile speech in 2003 at the Organization of the Islamic Conference (OIC), which Malaysia hosted, Dr. Mahathir claimed the U.S. invasion of Iraq proved the West's intention to recolonize the developing world. He also claimed Jews were controlling the world by proxy, adding defiantly that "1.3 billion Muslims cannot be defeated by a few million Jews." Then, as conference host, he turned on his OIC guests and rebuked the Muslim community for its backwardness, deriding its tolerance for religious fanaticism. "Islam is not just for the seventh century," he proclaimed. "Islam is for all times. And times have changed."

Abdullah Ahmad Badawi, a low-key but longtime UMNO minister, replaced Mahathir as prime minister only to struggle to find his own political style and support base. During his initial years as prime minister, a number of official scandals erupted and communalism reared its ugly head with resurgent Malay nationalism. Mahathir's party edifice was both crumbling and rallying at the same time. Caught in corruption imbroglios, UMNO elites came to one another's defense. Badawi's support suffered a blow in 2008, however, when Mahathir left UMNO, pledging not to return to the party until Badawi was relieved from his position.

Mahathir's dissatisfaction with his successor stemmed, in large part, from UMNO's poorest performance in general elections in twenty years. In March 2008 elections, UMNO won less than 30 percent of the vote and lost 30 seats in the 222-seat lower assembly. The National Front retained power but with its weakest coalition victory ever, and a slim 51 percent of the popular vote. The People's Front, a three-party coalition led by Anwar Ibrahim's People's Justice Party, secured 47 percent of the vote. In terms of assembly seats, the People's Front won 82 to the National Front's 140. The first post-Mahathir election had resulted in the National Front's loss of its previous two-thirds majority needed to pass constitutional amendments.

The changes in UMNO leadership caused by Mahathir's departure and party election woes opened new political space for democracy activists and opposition groups. Ibrahim, released from prison in 2004 when his previous verdict of sodomy was overturned, reemerged on the political scene. Wan Azizah Wan Ishmail, Anwar's wife, was elected by opposition parties as opposition leader. NGOs began to form coalitions and an increasingly vocal Internet community pushed for an end to UMNO's dominance. For the first time in decades, UMNO appeared vulnerable.

Parliament opened in May 2008 with a palpable sense that the government's majority was in jeopardy. Pledging to end government corruption, and the privileged position of Malay business oligarchs benefiting from the NEP, the opposition parties began wooing members to their side, hoping to shake UMNO's grip on Parliament. Facing a serious threat, UMNO leaders initially returned to harassing and intimidating their opponents. Activists and antigovernment Internet bloggers found police at their doorsteps and, amazingly, Ibrahim was rearrested, again on specious charges of sodomy. Subsequent criticism for Badawi to resign led the embattled prime minister to offer up a meager package of political reforms. In late 2008, UMNO's long record of National Front–led stability appeared more fragile than at any time since 1969.

Institutions and Social Groups

Political Parties

The Alliance (in the pre-1969 period) and the National Front (Barisan Nasional) are coalitions of parties, joined together by the common goals of winning elections and securing societal stability. These goals have for the most part been achieved. Three parties composed the Alliance: UMNO, the MCA, and the MIC. Representing the three major ethnic groups, these parties accepted the Alliance formula to legitimize the interests of these ethnic groups. The formula required that each group accept the basic societal division: Malays dominate the political sphere, and Chinese and Indians dominate the economy.

When the formula broke down in 1969, the Alliance was transformed into the Barisan Nasional, which consisted of the three Alliance parties as well as a coalition of former opposition parties led by the PAS, the country's strongest Islamic party. In all, Barisan Nasional was composed of eleven component parties, but UMNO remained the senior partner with final say over coalition decisions.[6]

In 1988, when the courts found UMNO unlawful on the grounds that the delegates sent to the assembly had not been properly chosen, the country was stunned. For most Malays, UMNO had embodied their culture, aspirations, and belief in their right to rule Malaysia. The rapid transformation of UMNO into UMNO Baru (with "Baru" subsequently deleted) was important to retain the country's legitimacy. For the first time since independence, UMNO was challenged by a party organization, Semangat '46 (S46), led by a Malay and strong enough to defeat the National Front. Having allied with Razaleigh's APU coalition (which included the PAS), S46 provided a viable alternative to the UMNO-dominated Front.

However, the APU's strength was found wanting in the 1990 elections, in which some 8 million registered Malaysians voted. Candidates representing the National Front capitalized on the issues of economic growth and political stability to achieve their electoral victory. The opposition's focus on issues of human rights, press freedom, lower taxes, and Mahathir's combative personality was not as credible to the voters.

Other efforts to develop a party coalition to oust the National Front have followed the APU's path but with increasing success. The Barisan Alternatif (BA) coalition formed in the wake of Ibrahim's arrest in 1999. The BA included the Islamic-oriented PAS, the Chinese-oriented Democratic Action Party

(DAP), and other Malay parties. BA parties, especially PAS, competed well in the 1999 general elections, but the DAP left the coalition shortly after September 11, 2001. PAS's platform included the goal of creating an Islamic state. The oppositional infighting was again put aside in the 2008 election when the People's Front coalition was formed to challenge UMNO. It included PAS, the DAP, and the People's Justice Party, led by Anwar's wife.

The National Front also has long enjoyed the advantage of UMNO's access to funds. UMNO has transformed itself into a huge business conglomerate with assets in numerous corporations. Although conglomerates throughout Southeast Asia rely on government patronage, no assemblage of companies owned directly by a political party appears to have benefited from government largesse to the same extent as UMNO's holdings.[7] Neither opposition nor allied parties in the Front have access to such funds. UMNO's greatest vulnerability, as demonstrated by intermittent scandals, rests in its own missteps in allocating the state budget.

The three-party People's Front coalition challenging UMNO and the National Front today is not an ideologically cohesive opposition but a tactical alliance. The People's Justice Party's main goal, for example, is to end preferential policies favoring Malays under the NEP. Offended by the corruption that preference has bred, the party of Anwar Ibrahim (de facto head) and his wife (official leader) is viewed as a viable alternative to UMNO for the federation's leadership. Anwar, a former Muslim activist, holds acceptable Muslim credentials for most Malays but his economic leanings have alienated economic nationalists in the People's Front coalition.

Parti Islam Se-Malaysia (PAS), or the Islamic Party of Malaysia, is a rising force in Malaysia. With an implicitly communalist platform, PAS is dedicated to advancing conservative Malay Muslim interests. Some within the party favor sharia-based administration at the state level. PAS enjoyed a brief stint in government coalition in the 1970s but soon parted ways with the business-oriented UMNO. Although it has jettisoned its objective to transform Malaysia into an Islamic state, many moderate Muslims, Chinese, and Indians remain leery of further PAS gains. PAS won control of five of Malaysia's thirteen states in recent local elections. With about 15 percent of the electorate secure, PAS may never dominate Malaysia, but its supporters remain committed partisans and the party's Malay identity threatens UMNO's core communal support.

The third party in the People's Front, the Democratic Action Party (DAP), is a secular, multiethnic party oriented toward furthering Malaysia's modernity. Advocating a "Malaysian Malaysia," the DAP is resurrecting jargon made prominent decades earlier by Lee Kuan Yew before Singapore left the federation. While the DAP platform is somewhat compatible with that of the People's Justice Party, the three parties of the People's Front share little more than anti-UMNO ambitions. If the parties were to someday replace the current UMNO-led government, the People's Front is unlikely to match UMNO's decades-long stability. A change in government may herald a new pattern of government instability.

Compared to political parties in Thailand, the Philippines, and Indonesia, UMNO is highly institutionalized as a party, which makes it a potent instrument of government. Unseating it will be difficult. Every Malaysian prime minister has reached that position because he has led UMNO, whereas leaders elsewhere in the region have reached the top governmental positions in other ways, reflecting the lesser importance of their parties and weaker institutionalization of their party systems. Highly institutionalized parties, nevertheless, can be dangerous engines of patronage; ongoing revelations of corruption and scandal render UMNO far from invincible in a system with an increasingly savvy and demanding public. A leadership change scheduled for 2009 will hand Deputy Prime Minister Najib Razak the reins of UMNO power and the premiership.

State Royalty

Malaysia's means of choosing its monarch is unique among Southeast Asia's constitutional monarchies. Nine states have hereditary rulers, the sultans, and the king, or *Yang di-Pertuan Agong*, is elected from this body (usually on the basis of seniority) for a five-year term. The king, who has ceremonial and religious duties and powers of appointment, can officially delay certain legislative bills (although this power has been circumscribed). The Malaysian king is not held in the same awe as the king of Thailand, who is venerated by the Thai public; nevertheless, he plays an important symbolic role as the head of state.

The sultans' role changed dramatically in 1993 when Mahathir moved to place them under the law. The prime minister's actions were precipitated by an incident in which the sultan of Johore allegedly assaulted a hockey coach with whom he was displeased. Mahathir proposed to lift the hereditary rulers' immunity from legal action. He also moved to revoke their right to grant pardons to themselves and their families.

Mahathir's moves were accompanied by daily press reports on the sultans' rampant corruption, philandering, and high living. These reports were shocking to the citizens both because of the extent of the alleged debauchery and because the reports appeared to break sedition-act regulations forbidding criticism of the sultans. Rural Malays were stunned to read such reports about their sultans, who had long commanded their loyalty and were viewed as their symbolic protectors.

Mahathir introduced amendments to the Parliament. However, amendments that concerned the "privileges, position, honors or dignities" of the rulers required their consent. The king eventually assented to a compromise bill that reduced the sultans' privileges. The compromise stated that the attorney general's consent was required before charges could be brought against the sultans and allowed for the creation of a "special court" that would rule on such cases. This measure would limit petty actions against the rulers. The larger point, however, was Mahathir's success in reducing the power and influence of one of Malaysia's oldest and most important institutions.

Serving as head of state in Malaysia's federative constitutional monarchy, the people's many rotating monarchs nevertheless bear the global distinction of rarely outlasting the government's prime ministers. Consequently, prominent prime ministers such as Tunku Abdul Rahman and Mahathir bin Mohamad became *de facto* symbols of the Malaysian state, both inside and outside of Malaysia. Political insignificance is thus the price of a system championing royal fairness.

Federal Parliament

Malaysia's political system is based on the British model, with a bicameral Parliament that elects one of its own members to the prime ministership. The prime minister must sit among the 222 seats in the lower House of Representatives (Dewan Ra'ayat) and must command majority support. The upper chamber, the Senate (Dewan Negara), has 70 members: 26 appointed by state legislatures and 44 appointed by the king after the prime minister's recommendation. Senators hold office for six years; representatives serve five years unless Parliament is dissolved sooner than that. Although representation is based on single-member constituencies, a weighting of constituencies in favor of rural areas traditionally enhances Malay representation—in effect almost guaranteeing Malay political power.[8]

The potential of Malaysia's Parliament to alter the course of the federation's politics is significant. Given the fragmentation of political interests in the party system, and the multitude of viable parties (seventeen with House seats in 2008), UMNO is more likely to lose its coalition partners in the Parliament before it loses general elections outright. The locus of political change in Malaysia's future is likely to be found in the parliamentary institution, that is, the electoral politics that determines who sits in it and the coalition governments it creates.

Political Islam

The religious element is central to Malaysians' political party orientations. Parties among the Malay majority are defined largely in terms of their degree of

Islamic orthodoxy. Although moderate Islamic parties have been dominant in the ruling alliance, the rise of the conservative Islamic Party of Malaysia (PAS) in many states, and as a major partner in the People's Front opposition coalition, is a noteworthy development.

In Malaysia, all Malays are Muslim by legal definition. Islam provides both legal and political privileges to Malays that, if lost, are tantamount to renouncing the Malay way of life. The state's new high-tech national identity cards, or MyKads, prominently list one's race and religion. Traditionally, Malay Muslims did not emphasize distinctions between secular and religious activities. Islam was tightly organized from the village up to the state level; hence, Muslims could be easily mobilized. Following the communal violence of 1969, proliferating Muslim revivalist groups (*dakwah*) made calls for Islamic fundamentalism, promoting rigid codes of conduct and the implementation of Islamic law. Many of these revivalist groups were filled with educated youth, often affiliated with the University of Malaya. Indeed, many of the movement's leaders came to hold radical Islamic ideas from the Arab world while studying in Britain.[9]

In the 1980s Mahathir sought to defuse the Islamic resurgence by a program of "absorption of Islamic values," but this fanned the contentious flames of communalism. Sentiment for an Islamic state grew as organizations found inspiration from movements in Egypt and Pakistan.[10] Even before the September 11, 2001, terrorist attacks, Mahathir aggressively applied pressure on Islamist fundamentalists groups with international ties. As Washington, D.C., launched its war on terrorism following the attacks, Malaysia cooperated with U.S. intelligence to uncover cells of al-Qaeda and Jemaah Islamiya in the country. Arrests, rumors, and discoveries of terrorist activity fueled anxiety in the region. The Petronas Towers were thought to be especially vulnerable to attack (authorities emptied the towers on September 12, 2001, for example). Terrorist bombings in neighboring Indonesia put Malaysian authorities on full alert about the nebulous threat the federation faced. Mahathir may have railed against Jews and the West in passionate speeches, but he also made no room for terrorists in Malaysia.

Similarly, Abdullah Badawi worked both sides of the Islamist extremism issue. Experienced in state security and antiterrorism as a former home minister, the unassuming new leader also carried strong Muslim credentials as the son and grandson of Islamic scholars. Advocating a policy addressing fundamentalism's "root causes," Badawi stepped up his government's antipoverty agenda for rural areas following bombings in Indonesia. Standing before the UN General Assembly, he also promoted the concept of Islam Hadhari (Civilizational Islam), or Islam compatible with both modernity and equitable development.

In Malaysia, Asia's newest NIC, Islam and modernity have generally evolved to complement each other. Because political Islam is largely moderate and finds expression through the party mechanism and other legitimate political channels, Islamist terrorism in multiethnic Malaysia has thus far remained limited. Malaysia's leaders also gain recognition for dampening the threat of communalism and the dangerous marriage between identity politics and Islamic fundamentalism. Nevertheless, the globalization of Islamist terrorism in the new international era leaves Malaysia exposed to pernicious influences beyond its borders.

DEMOCRATIZATION

As opposed to its neighbors, Malaysia has managed to sustain the institutions of democratic rule. The major exception, following the 1969 riots, was a temporary state of emergency, carried out less as a coup d'état than as an interlude during which parliamentary democracy could be rebuilt. Unlike Thailand, Indonesia, and Burma, the Malaysian military has not played a major role in politics. In the early years of independence, priority was given to socioeconomic development rather than to building substantial armed forces.[11] Despite significant upgrades in the military's profile in recent years and new purchases of fighter jets, submarines, and weapons systems, Malaysia's military remains far from a praetorian force.

In contrast to the Indonesians and Vietnamese, the Malaysians had the advantage of not having to struggle against the return of their colonialist ruler after the defeat of Japan at the end of World War II. The granting of independence by Great Britain was carried out peacefully and was received with some reluctance by Malaysians, who feared their country's viability would be jeopardized without British support. Nevertheless, the Malaysians adopted the Westminster model of governance, including regularized competitive elections, a representative Parliament, the separation of powers, civilian supremacy, and civil liberties. These adoptions are especially noteworthy because Malaysian elites tend to hold a formalized view of democracy that crumbles when it faces more deeply held values; stability and security, for example, take precedence over democratic values.[12]

Since independence, Malaysia has witnessed an impressive twelve national elections—in 1959, 1964, 1969, 1974, 1978, 1982, 1986, 1990, 1997, 1999, 2004, 2008. Remarkably, UMNO has won all twelve and the right to form a government, although sometimes with coalition partners. Although their numbers in the Parliament have been few, opposition candidates generally win about 40 percent of the votes. Over the course of these twelve elections there have been five orderly successions of power.

Despite this admirable election record, Malaysia is generally regarded as a quasi- or illiberal democracy because of serious limitations on civil liberties.[13] The country's Official Secrets Act, Internal Securities Act, and Sedition Act have imposed a culture of silence on citizens and prohibited discussion of "sensitive issues." Newspapers, television, radio, and the Internet are government (read: UMNO) regulated and generally compliant vis-à-vis all communalism issues. Web sites, magazines, and newspapers that overstep boundaries can be, and have been, shut down under the Internal Securities Act. "Religious freedom" for Muslims in Malaysia includes the criminality of apostasy and, in many states, conversion to another religion. In Malaysia's democracy, non-Muslims may not marry Muslims without converting first. Local sharia courts often hold authority over Muslims in such matters of marriage and conversion, or where federal law or state law is silent or ambiguous.

According to the system's defenders, the explanation for the necessity of quasi-democracy rather than full, Western-style democracy is that Malaysia's polycommunal situation is unique. Such a society cannot carry out its affairs in a fully democratic way if one segment of the society must be given special privileges of governance. In the context of communal issues, an election loss or coalition collapse by the National Front would mean the perceived end of the Malays' primary rights. Emergency rule became necessary in 1969, the argument goes, because Malays and Chinese reacted to that possibility.

The rules for Malaysian democracy, which had to be modified after 1969 to ensure that Malay political supremacy would continue, were changed to include opposition parties in the Alliance.[14] Dividing the nation along ethnic lines between those in power and those not in power would only worsen communal issues. To mitigate divisiveness, the National Front was created to accommodate a wider range of parties. Even the Islamic-based PAS was initially included in the National Front, but it later withdrew to join the Chinese-oriented DAP in leading the opposition. The Front formula was uniquely Malaysian, reflecting the difficult ethnic sensitivities that have long been at the core of Malaysian politics.

Malaysia's illiberal democracy, or what might be called a competitive authoritarian regime, has been sustained by the continuing strength of the economy, which mitigates extremist demands; by the growing urbanized middle class, which favors moderate policies; and by the country's modern history of British-style democratic institutions. Mahathir's emphasis on "Asian values" opposed democratic tendencies, especially regarding the rights to protest and question governmental leaders. Even so, most Malaysians seem to be content with the notion of quasi- or illiberal democracy, which they view as appropriate to their values. Nevertheless, the government's treatment of opposition politicians and UMNO corruption scandals are causing many to push for greater civil liberties and fuller democracy.

ECONOMIC DEVELOPMENT

Malaysia is one of the few success stories of economic development in the third world. With a per capita GNI now approaching $7,000, there has been a clear improvement in the standard of living since independence in 1957. In 1966, only 18 percent of households in a typical Malaysian village had piped water. By 1978, this figure was 71 percent and by 1993 close to 100 percent. Electricity was available to 45 percent of households in 1966; this increased to 79 percent in 1978 and 100 percent by 1987. In 1966, only 4 percent of Malay families owned a television; by 1997, the figure was just under 100 percent. During this period, dirt roads were paved, telephone lines were installed, and mosques were built.[15] By 2007, Malaysia's Human Development Index (HDI) global ranking was 63 (out of 177), higher than resource-rich Venezuela and Brazil, or former superpower Russia.

In 1971, by means of the unprecedented New Economic Policy (NEP), the Malaysian government initiated an extraordinary twenty-year plan designed to eradicate poverty and eliminate ethnicity as a function of economic prosperity. The plan was meant to change Malaysia's fundamental structures and ethnic divisions by directing the increments of rapid economic growth disproportionately to the Malay sector without expropriating Chinese assets or weakening the vigor of Chinese enterprise.[16]

The NEP was the government's response to the 1969 riots and the perceived need for a dramatic attack on the ethnic divisions in the economy. According to government data, in 1971 the ownership of share capital was 63 percent foreign, 34 percent non-Malay, and less than 3 percent Malay. The goal was to raise the Malay share of capital ownership to 30 percent and reduce the foreign share to 30 percent, while allowing the Chinese share to rise to 40 percent.[17] The means to this end were tax breaks, investment incentives, employment quotas, and the granting of special privileges in business ownership. The government required all banks to earmark a significant proportion of their business loans to Malays.

The NEP was to end in 1990; however, because the target of 30 percent capital ownership by Malays had not been met (standing at about 20 percent), the government appointed a commission to design a new twenty-year policy. The foreign share had fallen from 63 percent to 33 percent, and the difference was taken up by non-Malays, whose share increased from 34 percent to 47 percent. Other goals were substantially achieved, including the reduction of the poverty level, which had fallen from 30 percent in 1977 to 17 percent by 1987. Many more *bumiputra* Malays were engaged in businesses in which they had formerly been underrepresented. Investments in rural development and agricultural programs increased many times over during the twenty-year NEP.

Under Mahathir, Malaysia emphasized market-oriented mechanisms, featuring the privatization of public utilities, communications, and transportation; at the same time it also featured state-owned heavy industrialization and large state-managed holding companies. Mahathir's "Look East Policy" stressed the adoption of the work ethic and other principles followed by companies in Japan and South Korea as well as increased trade with Asian neighbors. The success of these programs led economists to claim Malaysia had joined Singapore, Taiwan, South Korea, and Hong Kong as Asia's fifth "tiger."

Malaysia became the world's largest exporter of semiconductors and one of the largest exporters of single-unit air conditioners, textiles, and footwear. Manufacturing accounted for one-half of total exports by 1990, compared to just 20 percent ten years earlier. These increases in manufacturing output, stimulated largely by export-oriented industrialization, have resulted in a much more broadly based economy.

In the 1990s, Malaysia's economic growth rate was one of the highest in the world, averaging 8.3 percent. The country enjoyed low unemployment and inflation rates along with increases in manufacturing production and foreign investment. However, Malaysia's economic success was mitigated by continuing reports that the percentage of Malays sharing in the new wealth had not increased appreciably, despite the stated goals of the NEP. Hence, in 1991, Prime Minister Mahathir introduced a ten-year new development policy, which sought to achieve 30 percent equity for Malays in the economic system. Mahathir set forth his ambitious goal for Malaysia: full development by the year 2020, with the gross domestic product (GDP) eight times larger than that of 1990. Such a noteworthy goal would require an annual growth rate of 7 percent during the intervening thirty years.

Despite the country's economic growth trajectory, several potential problems loomed. First, the growth rates to achieve the 2020 goal required importing plantation workers from Indonesia and Sri Lanka. Second, as wage rates improved, foreign investors looked for alternative sites for their assembly plants. Third, Kuala Lumpur was suffering from rapidly increasing traffic congestion, pollution, and environmental degradation. Fourth, the 1997 currency crisis undermined Malaysians' pride in their "miracle" economy and threatened to bring Mahathir's 2020 project crashing down. Indeed, the crisis meant the new millennium was greeted with nonperforming loans, large debts, rising unemployment, and lower than expected economic growth rates.

Malaysia's economy strengthened after the Asian economic crisis, notwithstanding Mahathir's refusal to accept IMF regulations. His decision to place controls on capital account transactions went against the decisions of other Southeast Asian leaders. But criticism of the capital controls ended when Malaysia's economy began to flourish again. From 2003 to 2007, Malaysia's GDP growth rate averaged above 5 percent.

Malaysia's economy today reflects increasing diversity founded on the base of its nationalized oil company, Petronas, manufacturing exports in electronics and information technology, and a natural-resources sector built on logging, rubber, palm oil, and liquified natural gas (LNG) (Malaysia is the world's leading exporter of tropical wood, natural rubber, and palm oil, and the world's second largest producer of LNG). Small and medium enterprises (SMEs) focusing on textiles, wood products, and services prosper in Kuala Lumpur, Penang, Johor Bahru, and other urban areas. A market capitalization of over $300 billion shores up the Kuala Lumpur Stock Exchange, one of Southeast Asia's oldest.

In negotiating free trade agreements with the United States (bilaterally) and with China (via ASEAN), Malaysia is forging ahead with a long-term internationalization strategy for its economy (although talks with Washington have stalled). Also, with Malaysia seeking to become a financial center for Islamic banking, the country's economic ties to the Muslim world are growing fast. After the United States, Malaysia is Saudi Arabia's largest trading partner, sending it and its oil-rich neighbors of the Persian Gulf furniture, electronics, and construction materials.

THE MALAYSIAN STATE

Malaysia was granted independence under peaceful circumstances and adopted and adapted British governmental institutions; thus, the country emerged from colonialism with a strong and stable political system. Because of the communal character of their society, Malaysian leaders adapted Western democratic structures in an attempt to provide Malays with dominance of the political realm. This required that the principal institutions of the society be merged with the state.

The clearest example of this close association is the integration of the Alliance (after 1969, the National Front) with the state. As in Indonesia, where Golkar was in essence a state institution, the National Front (led by UMNO) merged with the state—dominating the bureaucracy, the Parliament, the media, and the courts. This has set Malaysia apart from Thailand and the Philippines, where political parties are relatively autonomous from the state. If UMNO's control of Parliament is overturned, however, the state could achieve new separation from its long-dominant partner.

One characteristic of strong states is their ability to project their power into the countryside. Through the co-optation of local Malay elites and the provision of roads, financial credit, medical facilities, recreational programs, and other benefits, the Malaysian state has succeeded in tying local power brokers to the central authorities through either UMNO or local-level governmental agencies.

In economic affairs as well, the Malaysian state has asserted its control. No facet of the economy is excluded from governmental intervention, intended to ensure that the goals of the NEP are met and to provide resources to UMNO. The state has co-opted most of those who could challenge it. Indeed, oppositionists are established supporters of the state, differing only in terms of their desire to replace its political leaders. Thus, the Malaysian state is not subservient to societal forces, such as an autonomous military or insurgency, or to such external powers as a former colonial ruler or present-day international financial institutions.

Malaysia's status as a relatively strong state can be explained only partially in terms of its history of social dislocation. In contrast to Indonesia, which experienced a traumatic colonialism and a painful struggle for independence, Malaysia's colonial situation led to less dislocation. However, the Japanese interregnum; the evolution toward independence; the federation with Singapore, Sabah, and Sarawak; the ouster of Singapore; and the May 1969 ethnic riots provided sufficient dislocation for the development of a strong state.

A final condition for strong-state status is skillful leadership to take advantage of the prevailing conditions. Suharto in Indonesia clearly qualified as such a leader. Malaysia has also experienced strong leadership, from Tunku Abdul Rahman, the father of Malaysian independence, and Mahathir bin Mohamad, the manager of Malaysia's economic success. Malaysian leaders have not undermined the state's institutions in a manner similar to that of Marcos in the Philippines or Ne Win in Burma. Each prime minister has strengthened state institutions as a means to promote political stability, economic development, and ethnic harmony. In short, all these perspectives provide a context for assessing the Malaysian state as strong.

FOREIGN POLICY

Malaysia has not been an interventionist country, nor has it participated prominently in international affairs since its independence in 1957. During the Cold War, it joined the Non-Aligned Movement but it actively worked to eliminate communist insurgency along its Thai border. Regional cooperation through ASEAN has long been a first priority for Malaysia as a means to enhance both the nation's security and its economic objectives.

Following independence, Malaysia's main adversary was China because of the support the People's Republic gave to communists during the Emergency and because of distrust of Malaysia's indigenous Chinese. Nevertheless, in 1974

Malaysia normalized relations with China, although the domestic communal situation remained a concern in the relationship for decades.

Mahathir was principal spokesman for the ASEAN Free Trade Area (AFTA) and for Asian trade groups, which, he argued, could counter the North American Free Trade Agreement (NAFTA) as well as the European Union. Mahathir also became a third-world spokesman against "Western values," which he viewed as inappropriate for Malaysia and other third-world countries. He joined Singaporean leaders and others promoting "Asian values" as a superior alternative to the West's social disorder and moral indifference.

Malaysia supported the admission of Burma, Laos, and Vietnam into ASEAN. In 1996, tensions with Singapore increased when Singaporean Senior Minister Lee Kuan Yew made the comment that if Singapore ever was forced back into Malaysia, it would be a catastrophe for Singapore's ethnic Chinese because the Malaysian system was "racist." Eventually, the issue was handled diplomatically, but the disagreement reflected the long-running unease between the two neighbors.

In the new international era, Malaysia's policy focus has been economic. Its strategy for the twenty-first century is built on global trade and investment by enhancing direct links to three of the world's largest markets (United States, Japan, and China). Under Abdullah Badawi's watch, Malaysia became the United States' tenth largest trading partner. The governments of both countries pursued a bilateral free trade agreement designed to open new avenues for exchange. Japan, for its part, remains one of Malaysia's most important foreign investors and export markets. Malaysia's trade with China is now experiencing double-digit growth, although the balance is in the latter's favor. Despite surging energy sector exports to the mainland, Malaysia suffers a mounting trade imbalance with rising China.[18] The opening of the China-ASEAN Free Trade Zone in 2010 is destined to deepen Sino-Malaysian economic ties. China's appetite for Malaysia's palm oil, as well as its crude oil, continues to grow unabatedly.

Malaysia's global significance is now following its economic success. Its delicate position in the relations between the Muslim world and the West reflects its new role. Muslim commentators note that "the entire Muslim world views it [Malaysia] as a successful model of a modern Islamic state."[19] Indeed, of the most successful developers of the Organization of the Islamic Conference's fifty-seven countries (representing 1 billion Muslims), only Malaysia can boast that it is neither a petro-kingdom nor a microstate. Malaysia's increasing economic ties to the Muslim world are also complicating its relations abroad. After China, Malaysia is the largest foreign investor in Sudan's oil industry, drawing criticism that refined Malaysia supports a pariah, genocidal regime. Malaysia's foreign policy, moving beyond Asia-Pacific concerns, is now framed with a greater international dimension.

Conclusion

Since 1969, the desire for stability has kept Malaysians from relapsing into destructive identity politics and communalism. The political will of its Malay, Chinese, and Indian citizens to impose order on society found positive expression through political party alliances and by acquiescing to visionary leadership. Symbiotically, rapid economic growth and political order led Malaysia up the development ladder in tandem, hand over hand, foot over foot. By combining market forces, international openness, strong state guidance, and policies designed to benefit those most unlikely to benefit, Malaysia's leading party, UMNO, and its National Front alliance partners engineered enviable degrees of order, development, and equality.

Sacrificing certain civil and political liberties was, of course, a substantial price for stability and success. Mahathir, champion of "Asian values," often offended Westerners by gloating about Malaysia's brand of development, but it is difficult to imagine Malaysia's success in the absence of any trade-offs. As witnessed too often elsewhere, communalism does not generally escape asymmetrical structures of power and inequitable patterns of allocation.

Even as the National Front faces serious challenge in the wake of the 2008 elections, the formula for political success in Malaysia is perhaps more clearly understood than in any other Southeast Asian system: cross-communal alliances with willing Malay, Chinese, and Indian partners underpinned by a Malay-led "fidelity to the icons of indigenousness, protection, Malay unity, dominance, and Islam."[20] Existing institutions serve this formula well, but institutions are human creations that demand guidance and leadership if they are to endure. Malaysia's history suggests considerable risk for leaders who choose to alter this formula or the institutional legacies of Tunku Abdul Rahman and Datuk Seri Mahathir bin Mohamad.

Notes

1. In the study of Malaysia, the terms "ethnicity" and "race" are widely used to distinguish the same communities of Malays, Chinese, and Indians. In this chapter both terms are used loosely and are not intended to imply narrower definitions of either term.

2. Milton J. Esman, *Administration and Development in Malaysia* (Ithaca, NY: Cornell University Press, 1972), pp. 20–22.

3. Diane K. Mauzy, "Malaysia in 1987," *Asian Survey*, vol. 28, no. 2 (February 1988), p. 214.

4. Hari Singh and Suresh Narayanan, "Changing Dimensions in Malaysian Politics," *Asian Survey*, vol. 29, no. 5 (May 1989), p. 517.

5. Stephen A. Douglas, "How Strong Is the Malaysian State?" paper presented to the Association for Asian Studies, Chicago, April 1990, p. 2.

6. Zakaria Haji Ahmad, "Stability, Security and National Development in Malaysia: An Appraisal," in *Durable Stability in Southeast Asia*, ed. Kusuma Snitwongse and Sukhumbhand Paribatra (Singapore: Institute of Southeast Asian Studies, 1987), p. 125.

7. Doug Tsuruoka, "UMNO's Money Machine," *Far Eastern Economic Review*, July 5, 1990, p. 48.

8. Zakaria Haji Ahmad, "Malaysia: Quasi Democracy in a Divided Society," in *Democracy in Developing Countries: Asia*, ed. Larry Diamond, Juan J. Linz, and Seymour Martin Lipset (Boulder, CO: Lynne Rienner Publishers, 1989), p. 373.

9. Michael Leifer, *Dictionary of the Modern Politics of South-East Asia* (London: Routledge, 1995), p. 83.

10. Ibid., p. 83.

11. Zakaria Haji Ahmad, "The Military and Development in Malaysia and Brunei, with a Short Survey on Singapore," in *Soldiers and Stability in Southeast Asia*, ed. J. Soedjati Djiwandono and Yong Mun Cheong (Singapore: Institute of Southeast Asian Studies, 1988), p. 235.

12. For an in-depth analysis of this point, see James C. Scott, *Political Ideology in Malaysia* (New Haven, CT: Yale University Press, 1968).

13. Ahmad, "Malaysia: Quasi Democracy," p. 349.

14. Ibid., p. 358.

15. These figures come from Marvin Rogers, "Patterns of Change in Rural Malaysia: Development and Dependence," *Asian Survey*, vol. 29, no. 8 (August 1989), pp. 767–770.

16. Esman, "Ethnic Politics and Economic Power," p. 403.

17. Ibid., p. 403.

18. William Case, "Malaysia in 2007: High Corruption and Low Opposition," *Asian Survey*, vol. 48, no. 1 (January/February 2008), p. 53.

19. Abdulaziz Sager, "Saudi-Malaysia Alliance Could Help Reshape the Islamic World," *Arab News,* January 29, 2006, www.arabnews.com/?page=7&section=0&article=76990&d=29&m=1&y=2006.

20. William Case, "Malaysia: Aspects and Audiences of Legitimacy," in *Political Legitimacy in Southeast Asia: The Quest for Moral Authority*, ed. Muthiah Alagappa (Stanford, CA: Stanford University Press, 1995), p. 107.

RESOURCE GUIDE

A useful tool for bibliographic and other information on Malaysia is available from Australia National University's WWW Virtual Library, which has a specific page for Malaysia, at http://vlmy.geneva21.biz. Northern Illinois University's Southeast Asia Digital Library includes a range of useful links that cover government, academic, and research institutions specific to Malaysia: http://sea.lib.niu.edu. The University of Wisconsin–Madison Libraries, at www.library.wisc.edu/guides/SEAsia/resarea.html, similarly maintains a list of digital and print resources on Malaysia. Ohio University's Berita Database is also useful for resources on Malaysia: http://cicdatabank.library.ohiou.edu/opac/berita.php.

The Library of Congress maintains a resource guide on Malaysia at www.loc.gov/rr/international/portals.html#t.

Official government statistics for Malaysia are easily obtained at www.statistics.gov.my/eng. The Central Bank of Malaysia maintains useful economic information:

www.bnm.gov.my. To follow happenings of Malaysia's Parliament, visit www.parlimen .gov.my/eng-index.php. Two Malaysian bloggers who became parliamentarians continue their own blogs on Malaysia politics: http://parliament.jeffooi.com and http://tonypua .blogspot.com.

An excellent place to get a pulse for Malaysian political activism is Aliran Online: www.aliran.com. Associated with a magazine under the same name, the site provides links to its magazine issues, the NGO community, human rights reports, and reform agenda politics.

The *New Straits Times*, published from Kuala Lumpur, is the oldest English-language daily in the region, established in 1845: www.nst.com.my. The Malaysian National New Agency can be found at www.bernama.com. An excellent privately owned interactive Web site with real-time news, videos, and cultural features is www.malaysiakini.com; a similar Web site is also timely on current issues: www.themalaysianinsider.com. An English-language newspaper specific to East Malaysia is the *Daily Express*: www.dailyexpress.com.my.

6

SINGAPORE

The quest for survival, order, and prosperity is a dominant theme of contemporary Singaporean politics. Surrounded by nations hundreds of times larger in area with populations twenty to nearly a hundred times greater, this island city-state is in many respects a speck in a region of giant nations—even tiny Hong Kong is twice its size. As an urban entrepôt with virtually no agricultural base, Singapore stands alone, bereft of the resources and land of its Southeast Asian neighbors.

Singapore's principal resource is its people. Multiethnic and multicultural, Singapore's 4.4 million citizens are about 75 percent Chinese, 14 percent Malay, 9 percent Indian, and 2 percent other minorities. Singaporeans, who live in a densely populated city, are the wealthiest (with per capita GNI of $32,470), best-educated, best-housed, and healthiest population in Southeast Asia.[1] Literacy, for example, is over 95 percent, and among those under thirty years old it is 99 percent. Singaporeans have access to the most westernized conveniences and public services of the region as well.

In 1999, B. J. Habibie, then president of Indonesia, unflatteringly referred to Singapore as a "little red dot," just a speck on the map compared to its massive neighbors. Insulted as they were at the time, Singaporeans began to consider the contemptuous label as a source of pride, symbolic of the republic's remarkable economic success. The country's leaders, prone to strategies of cooptation, embraced the "red dot" label and Singaporeans, inside and outside of government, now celebrate their new soubriquet with affection.

Ironically, despite its achievements, Singapore has one of the highest rates of emigration in the world. In 1990, about 36,000 Singaporeans lived in other countries. By 2006, over 143,000 émigrés had formally registered with the republic's embassies abroad. A large number of unregistered exiles renders the Singaporean diaspora even larger. It is often Singapore's young and most talented who leave. The primary reasons emigrants give for leaving are advanced education and job opportunities, but for many, the city has become devoid of

SINGAPORE

MALAYSIA

Jahor
Strait

SINGAPORE ★

Singapore Strait

Main Strait

INDONESIA

spirit, heart, and vitality, characteristics that have been displaced by a materialistic coldness symbolized by the nation's ubiquitous rules and prohibitions.

No noncommunist society in Southeast Asia regulates its citizens' behavior as much as Singapore. For example, rules on traffic, street cleanliness, shops and markets, gum chewing, landscaping, and food preparation are strictly enforced by the authorities and rigorously followed by the citizenry. Regulation extends to residential choice. Land poor, Singapore's Housing and Development Board manages a large-scale program housing over 80 percent of citizens in multistory buildings. Since the 1960s, Singaporean authorities have engineered public housing allocations to diffuse ethnic-based residential clustering. Chinese, Malays, and Indians must live amongst each other in government-controlled, but affordable, "housing estates." The government's Central Provident Fund, derived from mandatory payroll contributions, functions as a compulsory savings program that supports the housing program as well as medical care and retirement pensions.

One might expect such bureaucratization would engender corruption. However, less corruption exists in Singapore than in any other Southeast Asian nation. Although a part of the political system, patronage is less salient in political recruitment and policymaking than is the case in the systems of Singapore's neighbors. The republic's clean reputation is reflected in Transparency International's annual rankings, where Singapore is listed among the five least corrupt countries in the world.

To achieve order, Singapore has fashioned one of the world's most effective and efficient governments. Characterized by democratic institutions but within the context of authoritarian order, Singapore's government has been controlled by a single party, the People's Action Party (PAP), since full independence was obtained in 1965. Until November 1990, Singapore had known only one leader, Lee Kuan Yew, who had led the island since 1957. Only two others, including Lee's own son, have ruled Singapore since 1990.

The themes of survival, prosperity, and order have become fused in Singapore to produce a unique style of politics and economic life.[2] The fusion stems from colonial times when the British controlled Singapore, making it dependent on British economic policies. After achieving limited independence in 1957, Singapore granted Britain control over its external affairs and security matters out of fear of a seizure of power by the communists or by external intervention. To achieve full independence, the Singaporean economic system established interdependence in the global economic system, and the country allied with its northern neighbor, Malaya, which complemented Singapore economically.

The concern for survival was the major impetus for the decision by Malaya and Singapore to forge the Federation of Malaysia in September 1963, which included Sabah and Sarawak as well. Tunku Abdul Rahman, Malaysia's founding prime minister, feared that Singapore might become communist, an "Asian Cuba." The solution was to accept the city-state as a member of the federation. From the Singaporean perspective, Malaya's agricultural resources were necessary for their own development. Lee Kuan Yew did not believe that Singapore was viable by itself.

The federation lasted only two years, until August 1965, because the Alliance government in Kuala Lumpur perceived that the Chinese in Singapore were threatening the Malays' privileged political position. Lee Kuan Yew had called for a "Malaysian Malaysia," with the implication that all Malaysians, regardless of race, could participate equally in all phases of life. This view was contrary to Tunku Abdul Rahman's belief that a "Malay Malaysia" was in the society's best interest. Unable to reconcile, the parties agreed to remove Singapore from Malaysia.

After separating from the federation, Singapore again faced the challenge of survival in an era of grave tensions, which stemmed mostly from the global Cold War and the *Konfrontasi* threat from Indonesia. Rather than seek a complementary alliance to attain security, Singapore fashioned policies designed to achieve rapid and far-reaching economic development to ensure its sovereignty. By 1969, the government had consolidated the republic's independence, stability, and viability, a consolidation that has lasted to the present. This success has depended on continued economic development and the inculcation of values supportive of a unified, highly educated, quality-oriented Singapore in people from diverse backgrounds.

When Lee Kuan Yew stepped down in November 1990, he sponsored his protégé Goh Chok Tong to become Singapore's second prime minister. Just nine months after becoming the nation's leader, Goh called a snap election to legitimize his administration. Goh needed to step out of the shadow of Lee, who continued in an official capacity as "senior minister." In contrast to Lee's more authoritarian style, Goh used a more consensual approach to governing. He did not yet have a popular mandate and wanted to take advantage of the country's excellent economy to ensure widespread support for the PAP.[3]

The August 1991 election resulted in a decisive victory for the PAP; only four of the eighty-one seats were won by the opposition Singapore Democratic Party. To shore up his administration even more, in December 1992 Goh stood in a by-election and received a significant victory, capturing 73 percent of the vote in his own constituency. There was special poignancy in this victory because in the previous month he had informed the populace that his two deputy prime ministers were both suffering from cancer. The better known of these two was Lee Hsien Loong, minister of trade and industry, the son of Lee Kuan Yew and presumed heir apparent to the position of prime minister. Indeed, many commentators suggested that Goh was only an interim leader until Lee Hsien Loong was ready to assume the top position. The other deputy prime minister diagnosed with cancer was Ong Teng Cheong. Both deputies were immediately treated with chemotherapy and were soon reported to be recovering.

Indeed, in 1993 both men made remarkable comebacks. Ong Teng Cheong was elected for a six-year term as the country's first executive president in August and Lee Hsien Loong returned as next in line for the prime ministership. Ong faced weak opponents, but he received only 58 percent of the votes cast (voting was compulsory). The PAP interpreted this as a rebuke from the public because candidates endorsed by the PAP are usually expected to win about 70 percent of the vote. The position of executive president was intended to be subordinate to the prime ministership, and it has not subsequently become more influential. In 1999, S. R. Nathan, a Hindu diplomat and the only candidate of the PAP, won a 70 percent majority for the presidency.

In 1995 and 1996, both Lee Kuan Yew and Goh Chok Tong engaged in a series of libel suits against their adversaries, winning every case and thus again demonstrating that the Singaporean judiciary has little autonomy from the executive branch. The PAP routinely wins multimillion-dollar defamation awards against political opponents and has even imprisoned some opposition candidates without charge.

In 1995, *New York Times* columnist William Safire described Singapore as a family dictatorship, characteristic of "old-fashioned European totalitarianism."[4] Goh responded with rhetorical shots of his own and a trans-Pacific debate about "Asian values" played out for months on editorial pages and in academic circles. Goh, Lee, and others (including Malaysia's Mahathir bin Mohamad) claimed Asian superiority over Western societies where crime, disorder, and corruption tainted economic success. They argued that a cultural emphasis on order, family, individual sacrifice, and hard work explained Asia's rising status. Critics responded by claiming that rule of law in Singapore was a sham and that "Asian values" justified strong-armed "authoritarian capitalism."[5] During this same time, the formerly impeccable Lee Kuan Yew and his son Lee Hsien Loong were revealed to have received discounts on two exclusive private condominiums. Lee explained that "it is an unfair world," which did little to mollify those who had supported the government's claim to meritocracy.

On January 2, 1997, parliamentary elections were held, but there was never any question about the outcome. The opposition contested only thirty-six of the eighty-three available seats, and the PAP won 63.5 percent of the total votes cast and eighty-one of the parliamentary seats. This strong showing reversed a downward trend that had reduced the PAP vote in 1991 to 59.3 percent. The Singapore Democratic Party lost every seat it had held. The victory was viewed as a vindication for Goh Chok Tong and his party's economic achievements.

Goh interpreted the result as a sign that voters had rejected Western-style liberal democracy; he also saw the outcome as his liberation from the long shadow of Lee Kuan Yew.

Similar election results in 2001 and 2006 perpetuated PAP legislative dominance, with winning margins of 75 percent and 67 percent, respectively. In 2004, Lee Hsien Loong took over as prime minister. Goh, credited for sound economic management and for bolstering education and medical assistance during his tenure, stayed on as senior minister. Lee Kuan Yew, ever present, took on yet another new title as "minister mentor." The 2006 election affirmed Lee Hsien Loong's new position, as the 1997 election had for Goh.

As in previous elections, the primary issues of the 2006 campaign concerned housing and charges of defamation. The PAP made it clear that areas of the city that did not support their candidates would be placed last in line for housing upgrades. Opposition candidates were ridiculed and sued for slander by the PAP before and after elections. Lee Kuan Yew and Lee Hsien Loong forced leaders of the Singapore Democratic Party into bankruptcy following a defamation lawsuit that judges (predictably) ruled in their favor.

Some noted that public outcry voiced against the PAP for manipulating the electorate with housing funds indicated rising interest in greater democratization. Yet, as 2010 approaches, Singapore's opposition remains effectually silenced and single-party rule has "reduced the parliamentary function down to passing the annual government budget and making new laws."[6] Elections, for that matter, remain loyalty tests and referendums on PAP performance, not contests between rival party platforms.[7] Under Lee Hsien Loong's leadership, Singapore continues the political patterns made familiar by his father: one-party dominance and technocracy, unapologetically focused on order, security, and material prosperity.

INSTITUTIONS AND SOCIAL GROUPS

Lee Kuan Yew

Few leaders in Southeast Asia have had the impact on their societies that Lee Kuan Yew has had in Singapore. Ho Chi Minh, Sukarno, Suharto, Ne Win, and Norodom Sihanouk had comparable influence, but none ruled a society with as much effectiveness as Lee. First in his class at both Cambridge and Oxford, Lee was a brilliant and pragmatic politician with more popular support than almost any other world leader.

By placing highly educated and technically proficient officials in charge of his development programs, Lee relied on his subordinates to establish effective policies free from corruption. By combining the advantages of Western-style democratic institutions with an Asian-style hegemonic political party system, Lee was able to dominate the country's politics and still achieve universal support and legitimacy.

In the late 1980s, Lee's consummate political skill lost some of its edge, as he moved toward authoritarianism and away from open and pragmatic policies. In a series of decisions concerning the jailing of dissident politicians and the restriction of newspapers printing articles critical of his administration, Lee veered from the careful balance he had achieved between civil liberties and order during the previous decades. Lee rationalized the new direction toward tighter order as necessary for the continued stability of the country and as appropriate for Asian culture.

Following his resignation as prime minister in 1990, Lee became senior minister and venerated statesman. He traveled extensively, advising developing nations on how to achieve the economic miracle he had overseen in Singapore. He stressed the importance of discipline and denigrated Western-style democracy as inappropriate for developing countries. He also gave up his position as secretary-general of the PAP to allow Goh to assume the legitimacy he needed to govern effectively.

In November 1991, the Parliament passed the Elected President Act, which provided for a stronger presidency but retained the cabinet, headed by the prime minister. Initially, it was believed that Lee would be nominated for the presidency, but he denied interest in a position he judged too subordinate. When his son Lee Hsien Loong assumed the prime ministership in 2004, Lee Kwan Yew became "minister mentor." Through this position Lee maintained a spot in the cabinet where his policy influence could continue. Well into his eighties, Lee commanded respect visiting with U.S. presidents, Chinese officials, and the world's powerful. Forever in shadow of the minister mentor, Lee Hsien Loong, a skilled leader in his own right, failed to exhibit his father's magnetism or visionary leadership.

Political Parties

The People's Action Party is virtually synonymous with Lee Kuan Yew and with governance in Singapore. The PAP has been in power since 1959; more striking than its uninterrupted rule, however, is that since 1968 the PAP has won all but a handful of hundreds of parliamentary seats, garnering as high as 84 percent of the vote.

The only party ever to provide credible opposition was the left-wing Barisan Sosialis (Socialist Front), which split from the PAP in the 1960s. Since that time, opposition parties have been allowed to function, but none have provided meaningful competition to the PAP. The reasons for the PAP's dominance

include the effectiveness and incorruptibility of most PAP politicians, the fac-
tionalization of the opposition, and the rigid rules that circumscribe the activities of political parties and opposition groups, which were especially important
in the late 1980s when newspapers were censored and suspected communists arrested. The other major reason for the PAP's success is the reluctance of the
electorate to risk undoing a system that has been working so well by voting in
alternative leadership. To many Singaporeans, the PAP is indispensable for continuing the extraordinary economic development and societal stability the city-
state has enjoyed since independence.

Unlike most hegemonic parties, the PAP does not have a large staff to perform research and stage functions.[8] Instead, civil bureaucrats outside the party
perform these functions, leaving the PAP visible only before general elections.
To ensure its continued dominance, the PAP has prepared for succession
through its self-renewal program, choosing young candidates who are more in
tune with the electorate. Between 1980 and 2006, the PAP's winning percentage in legislative elections fell below 60 percent only once. Fifty years following its first victory in 1959, the People's Action Party controls eighty-two of
eighty-four elected seats.

So overwhelming is PAP's dominance that opposition parties, such as the
Singapore Democratic Party and the Worker's Party, consider winning two or
three seats an electoral success. In 2000, the Singapore Democratic Alliance
(SDA) was formed from three opposition parties with hopes to put a dent in
PAP dominance. Such consolidation has yet to translate into more opposition
seats in Parliament.

Singapore's most visible opposition politician is Chee Soon Juan, a labor
rights advocate and secretary-general of the Singapore Democratic Party, an
SDA partner. Chee's activities include verbal attacks and publicity events often
alleging PAP corruption and undemocratic practices. Legal tangles with all
three of Singapore's prime ministers have landed Chee and his activist sister in
and out of jail and bankruptcy. Barred from international travel and running
for office until 2011, Chee draws support from Amnesty International and
other rights groups that contend Singapore's leaders restrict political speech
and abuse the judiciary to crush PAP opponents.

Legislature

Singapore's parliamentary system is a legacy of British colonialism, even
though its practice is much different from that of today's Great Britain. In contrast to the British bicameral system, the Singaporean parliamentary system is
unicameral and has presented no meaningful opposition to the administra-

tion. Legislators are elected to five-year terms, unless the prime minister dissolves Parliament before the term ends.

To ensure a semblance of bipartisanship, in 1984 the Parliament provided for three opposition seats, to be awarded if opposition candidates did not win at least three in constituency races. These three nonconstituency members would be appointed from among the highest-polling opposition candidates as long as they had won at least 15 percent of the votes cast in the constituency.[9] Nonconstituency oppositionists were not accorded full voting rights; they were prohibited from voting on motions relating to constitutional amendments, money bills, or votes of no confidence in the government. The opposition views this provision as tokenism rather than a meaningful commitment to open politics.

Another feature in parliamentary procedures is the "Team MP" scheme. Since the 1988 election, in certain constituencies, the electorate votes for a team of candidates instead of only one candidate. These constituencies are declared Group Representation Constituencies (GRCs), and each is represented by three members of Parliament. No more than half of the total number of constituencies can be GRCs. At least one of the three candidates in a GRC is required to be an ethnic minority (non-Chinese). The team that wins a plurality of the total vote is elected.[10]

The primary purpose of group representation is to institutionalize multiethnic politics by ensuring that minorities will be represented in Parliament by getting them elected on the coattails of others.[11] The PAP was confident that the change would not threaten its ability to win. Indeed, since 1988 minority population representation within the PAP has expanded while seats won by opposition parties remain rare.

In another attempt to bring alternative ideas to Parliament, nine distinguished individuals from the community, academia, the military, the professions, and trade unions are now appointed to serve as independent members, or Nominated Members of Parliament (NMPs). Nominated members are technically unaffiliated with any party, but a PAP-dominated committee makes their appointment. Voting rights of NMPs are restricted similar to nonconstituency members. Some NMPs have been active parliamentarians. The only non-PAP-initiated legislation ever to pass the Singapore Parliament came from a nominated member.

Nevertheless, Singapore's institutional tinkering of adding opposition quotas, ethnic diversity, and independent experts has done little to develop a consequential parliamentary opposition in Singapore. In the 2006 elections, for example, one nonconstituency opposition seat and nine nominated members were added to eighty-four elected delegates who came from fourteen GRC districts and nine single member districts, yet the PAP still controlled all but two elected seats. Almost half of the PAP's elected members ran unopposed, winning their seats upon nomination. Only two of the legislature's ninety-four total members were elected by Singaporeans to represent a parliamentary opposition. The voters in these districts face another five years of deprivation of public funds for their aging housing estates.[12]

DEMOCRATIZATION

The case of Singapore raises the question of whether a one-party state can be democratic. From a Western perspective, the governmental system of Singapore does not meet the criteria of full civil liberties and competitive choices of leaders. From the Chinese perspective, the government's paternalistic nature is appropriate, providing, as it does, law and order as well as economic achievement without relying on oppression. Lee Kuan Yew agrees with Sukarno's rationale for guided democracy in Indonesia and has said that Western-style majority rule leads to chaos, instability, dissension, and inefficiency. For Yew and his successors, legitimization is sought not through democracy but through performance, which is viewed as a technical matter. In Singapore, the critical factor in politics is the technocratic power of the elite, not the government's ability to ideologically mobilize its citizenry.[13] Technocrats, not democrats, characterize Singapore's one-party system, or more precisely, its hegemonic electoral authoritarian regime.

While building Singapore, Prime Minister Lee argued that in the Chinese tradition there was no concept of a loyal opposition. For example, it was not possible to support an opposition candidate without withdrawing total support from the government. This tradition stemmed from Confucian philosophy, which stressed the principles of centralized authority. Obligation to those in authority was the cement of the Confucian order. As long as the authorities were meeting the people's needs and leading according to moral principles, the ruler was considered to have the mandate of heaven and was therefore deemed legitimate by the public. From this cultural perspective, a strong one-party system is most conducive to effective rule.[14] Favoring conformity and predictability, Singaporeans do not swing back and forth from opposition to support for the PAP.

One-party systems can provide policy alternatives if there are differences in opinion among the party leaders. Moreover, if two-way communication between the government and the people is established, the citizenry can assert influence over public policy. In Singapore, a high degree of intraparty factionalism occurs, with varying points of view aired publicly; differences, nevertheless, tend to be issue specific, not ideological. In addition, the PAP has established grassroots organizations, including Citizens' Consultative Committees designed to elicit ideas from the public. These corporatist groups do provide input but do not indicate the development of an autonomous civil society, which the government views as potentially destabilizing. The government's claim to moral authority rests on public recognition of its performance record. Public compliance within this one-party system is rooted in a "broad-based recognition that politics is the business of the government, not the people."[15]

For five decades Singapore's technocracy has provided the republic with effective, but not always accountable, government, consistent with its traditions and history and supportive of the goals of development, order, and merit. Singapore's capacity to deliver on these goals over time is the fundamental question going forward. Founding father–cum–mentor minister Lee is the first to admit this fact, as he did in 2008 to a large crowd of Singaporeans and international delegates at the World Cities Summit. Speaking extemporaneously, Lee fretted that the island's voters might soon become bored and vote for a "vociferous opposition" out of "light-heartedness, fickleness, or sheer madness." A non-PAP government, he claimed, would ruin the city-state in as little as five years. "When you're Singapore," he clarified, "your existence depends on performance— extraordinary performance, better than your competitors—when that performance disappears because the system on which it's been based becomes eroded, then you've lost everything."[16]

Economic Development

It is impossible to make generalizations about Singapore's economic development because the nation's status as a city-state sets it fundamentally apart from its neighbors. With no agricultural base, Singapore is destined to become increasingly interdependent with the global economic system to ensure its survival.

Singapore is a mixture of capitalist and socialist economics, with emphasis on the former. The PAP leadership inherited a capitalist economic system from the British and has created state institutions to manage key aspects of the economy including housing, transportation, and shipping. Home to the world's busiest trans-shipment port, Singapore enjoys a geographic location that is its greatest economic asset. Although Singapore typically ranks among the world's most free economies, its government also controls large, state-owned holding companies that invest in manufacturing, communications, and foreign securities markets.

Singapore consistently posts the region's highest growth rates. These growth rates are largely the result of an outward-looking, export-oriented strategy begun after 1965 to accelerate the manufacture of consumer products, reduce unemployment, and obtain needed outside capital. Since 1965 Singapore's annual GDP growth has averaged above 8 percent. Only once, between 2000 and 2003, did Singapore experience more than two consecutive years with growth below 7 percent. Moreover, relatively low rates of inflation and unemployment have accompanied this growth. Inflows of foreign capital have been staggering. Foreign investment ballooned from $300 million in 1967 to a stock of over $300 billion in 2005.[17]

In anticipation of changes in the world economy, Singapore launched its "Second Industrial Revolution" in 1979, designed to restructure the economy toward high-tech industries. The plan was to manufacture exports of superb quality, win higher salaries for workers, upgrade job skills, and reduce dependence on foreign workers. The economy emphasized automotive components, machine tools, computers, electronic instrumentation, medical instruments, and precision engineering.

The revolution was a success until 1985, when the protectionist tendencies of developed countries hurt Singaporean exports. Low petroleum prices dealt a sharp blow to the ship-repair and shipbuilding industries (which made up one-quarter of the manufacturing sector), and high wages were not matched by growth in productivity.[18] Finally, the continued high rate of national savings (42 percent of GDP) could not become a part of productive domestic investments.

After state intervention had corrected each of these difficulties, the economy responded rapidly, leading Singapore to a period of remarkable growth. As the economy diversified, financial and business services displaced manufacturing as the economy's leading sectors. Not content with the level of economic development, Lee Kuan Yew set forth a controversial program to improve the country's gene pool. He determined that the quality of the people was the most important factor in a country's rapid development, and he arranged a program to encourage the marriage and procreation of the well-educated populace, giving incentives for educated mothers to have more children.

The early 1990s continued with solid 6–7 percent growth rates, although these percentages were down from previous years. Despite this record, the economy faced several problems. Seventy percent of domestic exports were produced by multinational corporations, perpetuating the nation's dependence on foreign-owned companies. Exports were not broadly based, with almost two-thirds of exports (in terms of value) in electronics and with the United States buying fully one-third of all exports.

Initially, the 1997 Asian economic crisis did not seriously jeopardize the Singaporean economy, because it was tied into the global rather than just the Southeast Asian economy. However, the worldwide economic slowdown in the United States and Japan that followed proved a challenge for the globalized economy. Singapore slipped into recession, with a -2.4 percent economic growth rate in 2001, a dramatic and significant drop from a remarkable 9.9 percent growth rate in 2000. Singapore recovered in 2002 only to find itself gripped by the SARS crisis that crippled the local economy, closed shopping malls, and devastated its Asian-based tourism sector.

The 2001 recession and economic effects of SARS raised questions about Singapore's export-oriented development model and recent efforts at regional integration. The PAP's answer: develop a knowledge-based economy highlighting financial services and cross-regional free trade agreements. By the mid-2000s, foreign investment in financial and insurance services surpassed manufacturing as the largest sector of foreign direct investment. The country also negotiated bilateral trade agreements with major economic players in the global economy: the United States, India, Mexico, Switzerland, Korea, Panama, Australia, and oil-rich states in the Persian Gulf.

Singapore has also pursued closer economic ties with China. China needs assurance that oil will flow freely through Singapore's ports. Two thirds of the world's oil flows through waters near Singapore each year, and only the port cities of Houston and Rotterdam refine more petroleum. As a new decade approaches, increasing demand for oil, particularly in Asia, leaves the city-state well positioned to benefit.

As a founding member of ASEAN, Singapore has supported efforts to further integrate the region's economies. Its economic relations with neighboring Malaysia are of vital significance. Singapore imports nearly half of its water supply from Malaysia, a fact Malaysian leaders frequently cite when relations turn sour. Singapore's investments in Southeast Asian countries are extensive and can invite trouble, such as when Temasek, a public holding company, bought Shincorp, Thaksin Shinawatra's telecommunications empire—a transaction that triggered the 2006 military coup in Bangkok and left the ousted Thai prime minister awash in legal troubles and Thailand in political turmoil.

The Singapore economy is interdependent with the global economic system. With a diversified economy, one of the best infrastructures for transportation in the world, superb medical care, the highest standard of living in all Southeast Asia, a highly educated population, and peaceful relations with its neighbors, Singapore's prospects for long-term economic growth are excellent. Even with domestic inflationary pressures on the rise, the prospects for Southeast Asia's wealthiest population look strong.

THE SINGAPOREAN STATE

Debate exists about how to best characterize the Singaporean state. Through a Chinese cultural lens, Singapore can be viewed as a "patriarchal state," where traditional elders wield influence over a compliant society. The country is also frequently characterized as a developmental state, due to the state's active management over investment and trade-oriented sectors. Its critics label it an authoritarian state, pointing to its high degree of centralization and power over dissenting voices. The island's own leaders may implicitly see their state in Hegelian terms, as an altruistic state prioritizing solidarity and order over interest group competition.[19] Debate notwithstanding, analysts agree that Singapore is, if nothing else, a strong state.

Upon first glance, Singapore does not have the requisites for a strong state. Geographically, the country is minuscule and has no important natural resources. Although it boasts the highest per capita income in Southeast Asia, its total GNP is far smaller than that of Indonesia, the Philippines, Malaysia, or Thailand. Singapore's military is capable of only minor defensive operations. Viewed in these terms, Singapore would not have the wherewithal to be a strong state.

Nevertheless, using standard criteria, Singapore's state can be considered strong. Its leaders use the agencies of the state to get Singaporeans to do what they want them to do. In no other Southeast Asian society do the citizens follow the state's dictates with the same regularity as in Singapore. Taxes are paid, young men accept compulsory military conscription, and traffic rules are followed. Few autonomous groups compete for influence in the society. Indeed, the state has co-opted the bureaucracy, the military, and interest groups, while the hegemonic PAP—itself a creature of Lee Kuan Yew—has co-opted the state.

In explaining or understanding the high capacity of the state in Singapore, it becomes apparent that the country's small size is a major advantage in strengthening the state. Although Singapore is heterogeneous in the ethnic sense, more important is that its society is quite homogeneous culturally. Singaporeans are urban and largely united in their goals for their society. Living in fewer than 225 square miles, citizens have little room for nonconformity. One need simply compare Singapore with Indonesia—where 200 million people live across thousands of islands and speak hundreds of languages—to get a rough idea of the vast differences between the two countries.

A necessary condition for a strong state is massive social dislocation that has weakened the capacity of a people or a society sufficiently to inhibit or preclude state strength.[20] This condition, evident in Indonesia under Suharto, has not occurred in Singapore. Singapore's post–World War II history has generally been stable, including its peaceful transition from colonial status to independence. Its expulsion from Malaysia was wrenching, strengthening the politics of survival, but it was not as traumatic as the anticolonial wars fought by Indonesia, Burma, or Vietnam. Rather than massive dislocation, continuity characterized Singapore's transition to full independence.

States are strengthened when external forces favor concentrated social control. As in most of Southeast Asia, where the international modus operandi in the postwar era was Cold War politics, Singapore was a recipient of Western aid to ensure that communism would not prevail. Also, during the Vietnam War and the 1980s, a tremendous growth in external investments occurred. The impact of aid and overseas investment was important for strengthening the role of the Singaporean state.

Serious military threats, whether internal or external, also facilitate the emergence of a strong state, and this condition was supportive of the strong state in Singapore. In the 1960s, when the PAP was factionalized into left-wing and moderate groups, Lee Kuan Yew's victory over the Left was interpreted as a victory over communism and, therefore, as a victory for the survival of the country's democratic system. Lee justified his "administrative state" as necessary to concentrate power and repress the state's internal and external enemies.

Another condition conducive to state strength is the presence of a social grouping, independent of existing bases of social control, that is skillful enough to execute the designs of state leaders.[21] The technocrats in Singapore are among the most educated and skilled in Southeast Asia. Lee Kuan Yew and his successors have turned policymaking over to these officials. Incorruptible and effective, they appear to be unbeholden to any particular societal groups. Instead, they are integrated into the state through the PAP or the ministries. Their lack of any mass political base reinforces their loyalty to the state.

The final condition for a strong state is skillful leadership, and here Singapore is the quintessential example. For many Singaporeans, Lee Kuan Yew *was* the state. His strength came less from charisma or repression than from his extraordinary capabilities to fashion an effective state. This condition alone appears to have moved Singapore into the ranks of the strong states, despite the absence of what was thought to be the necessary condition of massive state dislocation.

Singapore is the most disciplined society in Southeast Asia, in part because its citizens fear being fined or punished and in part because these citizens genuinely believe lawful obedience to be in the public interest.[22] Certainly, the government has set forth strict and often ridiculed measures to ensure orderly behavior (such as installing urine detection devices in housing block elevators that, if the rider urinates, lock the elevator door until authorities arrive). Although the Chinese heritage is one of discipline for the common good, at the time of independence, Singaporeans behaved no differently from their neighbors. The difference is that, since then, the Singaporean state has had the capacity to exploit that heritage to help it achieve its aims of survival, economic development, meritocracy, and order. The price it has paid is a lack of meaningful popular participation in the affairs of state and a sanitized society that has lost much of its soul.

FOREIGN POLICY

Singapore did not take charge of its foreign relations until 1965, when the republic was expelled from the Federation of Malaysia. Since then, the basic theme of foreign policy has been survival. As a small city-state with only minimal military capacity, Singapore has looked to Western powers and Japan to balance the influence of the Soviet Union (in the 1970s and 1980s) and China in Southeast Asia. Unabashedly anticommunist, Singapore supported the U.S. war in Vietnam and was a principal spokesman for a hard-line policy toward the Vietnamese government. More recently, Singapore has become a major investor in the Vietnamese economy and seeks close relations with China.

Despite its pro-U.S. stance, Singapore often enunciated a policy of neutrality, avoiding embroilment in major power conflicts. Nevertheless, certain issues have strained Singapore-U.S. relations. In 1988, Singapore accused Washington of interfering in its domestic affairs and expelled a U.S. diplomat who allegedly encouraged a high-profile dissident to organize a group of opposition candidates. Bad feelings also arose when President Ronald Reagan removed Singapore from the Generalized System of Preferences (GSP). The GSP had allowed selected goods to enter the United States duty free, but Singapore had attained the status of an NIC and was no longer eligible for this benefit.

Relations between Singapore and the United States reached a low in 1994 over the case of Michael Fay, an American teenager who was caned for an act of vandalism. U.S. public opinion polls indicated that most Americans supported Singapore's corporal punishment. The Clinton administration campaigned for a pardon for Fay, but Singapore's contemptuous response was to reduce his sentence from six lashes of the cane to four.

By the beginning of the millennium, Singapore had achieved its goal of survival. It was no longer threatened by internal insurgency or external intervention, and it was surrounded by large nations that had no capacity or desire to seriously intervene in the republic's affairs. But the events of 9/11 reopened old concerns and caused Singapore's leaders to imagine new ones.

As a porous hub of trade, oil shipments, and transportation, Singapore developed a renewed sense of vulnerability in 2001, which resulted in a warming of relations with the United States. In December 2001, an al-Qaeda sleeper cell, with plans to terrorize Western embassies, was discovered in Singapore. A year later, President George W. Bush traveled to the republic to sign a bilateral free trade agreement. The post-9/11, United States-Singapore Free Trade Agreement (USSFTA) proved to alter more than just economic relations between the two countries.

During the war on terrorism, Singapore has become a vital staging ground for U.S. operations in Afghanistan and Iraq (although it has prohibited the permanent establishment of a U.S. base). Goh Chok Tong even sent a token military unit to the Persian Gulf as part of U.S. Secretary of Defense Donald Rumsfeld's "Coalition of the Willing." Then, adding to its existing array of F-16s, Apache helicopters, and Harpoon missiles purchased in the 1990s, Singapore later inked an arms deal with Washington in 2005 worth upward of $1.8 billion. The USSFTA led to the purchase of twelve Boeing F-15SGs and millions of dollars' worth of missiles, ordnance, and other supplies.[23]

In addition to economic benefits and coordination on regional terrorist threats, Singapore's pursuit of stronger cross-regional relations with the United States hedged against an increasingly assertive China. Like its neighbors, Singapore both celebrates and fears China's rise. It is Southeast Asia's largest investor in China, fourth overall behind Japan. The massive Singapore-Suzhou industrial park in Jiangsu Province, negotiated at the highest levels by the two governments, typifies the countries' growing economic relations.

In the new international era, Singapore seeks to interpret China to the United States and the United States to China. Just before signing the USSFTA, it signed a strategic partnership agreement with China. At the same time it fears being perceived by its Muslim neighbors as an "unrepentant China beachhead."[24] Although fears of communism have disappeared, uncertainty about a rising China and new threats of Islamist terrorism keep Singapore desirous of a U.S. presence in Asia. By balancing economic and security interests between both powers, Singapore seeks strategic relations with each in a way that China and the United States could never imagine between each other.

Conclusion

Singapore's singularity does not always allow for meaningful comparisons with other countries. Indeed, the "little red dot" is an exception in Southeast Asia in terms of culture, ethnicity, geography, state capacity, and level of economic development. Only the less globalized citizens of oil-rich microstate Brunei, with one-tenth the population of Singapore, enjoy such a high income in the region. Singapore's small size notwithstanding, its geographic location remains significant. The city-state is destined to play a role in international trade, commerce, and finance as long as ships need the Malacca Straits to transport food, manufactures, and oil between Asia and the world. New bilateral trade agreements with major trading partners are likely to reap economic results in the future for Singapore. The smooth succession of power from Lee Kuan Yew to Goh Chok Tong to Lee Hsien Loong bodes well for continued PAP dominance and political stability.

NOTES

1. In terms of PPP, Singapore's per capita GDP figures lower at $29,663 (UNDP figures).

2. Lee Boon Hiok, "Political Institutionalization in Singapore," in *Asian Political Institutionalization*, ed. Robert A. Scalapino, Seizaburo Sato, and Jusuf Wanandi (Berkeley: Institute of East Asian Studies, University of California, 1986), p. 202.

3. This section relies on Shee Poon Kim, "Singapore in 1991," *Asian Survey*, vol. 32, no. 2 (February 1992), pp. 119–125, and Hussin Mutalib, "Singapore in 1992," *Asian Survey*, vol. 33, no. 2 (February 1993), pp. 194–199.

4. William Safire, "Honoring Repression," *New York Times*, July 10, 1995, A13.

5. Christopher Lingle, *Singapore's Authoritarian Capitalism: Asian Values, Free Market Illusions and Political Dependency* (Fairfax, VA: The Locke Institute), 1996.

6. Chua Beng Huat, "Singapore in 2006: An Irritating and Irritated ASEAN Neighbor," *Asian Survey*, vol. 47, no. 1, p. 208.

7. Cho-oon Khong, "Singapore: Political Legitimacy through Managing Conformity," in *Political Legitimacy in Southeast Asia: The Quest for Moral Authority*, ed. Muthiah Alagappa (Stanford, CA: Stanford University Press, 1995), p. 132.

8. Lee, "Political Institutionalization in Singapore," p. 207.

9. Chan Heng Chee, "The PAP in the Nineties: The Politics of Anticipation," in *ASEAN in Regional and Global Context*, ed. Karl D. Jackson, Sukhumbhand Paribatra, and J. Soedjati Djiwandono (Berkeley: Institute of East Asian Studies, University of California, 1986), p. 173.

10. Thomas Bellows, "Singapore in 1989," *Asian Survey*, vol. 30, no. 2 (February 1990), p. 146.

11. Lee Lai To, "Singapore in 1987," *Asian Survey*, vol. 28, no. 2 (February 1988), p. 203.

12. Chua, "Singapore in 2006," p. 208.

13. Khong, "Singapore: Political Legitimacy through Managing Conformity," p. 132.

14. *Asia Yearbook, 1991* (Hong Kong: Far Eastern Economic Review, 1990), pp. 214–215.

15. Khong, "Singapore: Political Legitimacy through Managing Conformity," p. 133.

16. Lydia Lim, "5 Years All It Takes to Ruin Singapore," *Straits Times*, June 26, 2008, available at www.straitstimes.com.

17. Figures from the Singapore Department of Statistics and the United Nations Conference on Trade and Development (UNCTAD).

18. Jon S. T. Quah, "Singapore in 1987," in *Southeast Asian Affairs 1988* (Singapore: Institute of Southeast Asian Studies, 1988), p. 249.

19. Terrence Chong, "Why Labels for the Singaporean State Fall Short," *Straits Times*, February 8, 2007, available at www.straitstimes.com.

20. Joel S. Migdal, *Strong Societies and Weak States: State-Society Relations and State Capabilities in the Third World* (Princeton, NJ: Princeton University Press, 1988), p. 269.

21. Ibid., p. 274.

22. Donald K. Emmerson, "Beyond Zanzibar: Area Studies, Comparative Politics, and the 'Strength' of the State in Indonesia," paper presented to the Association for Asian Studies, Chicago, April 1990, pp. 28–29.

23. Eul-Soo Pang, "Embedding Security into Free Trade: The Case of the United States-Singapore Free Trade Agreement," *Contemporary Southeast Asia*, vol. 29, No. 1 (April 2007), p. 10.

24. Ibid., p. 22.

Resource Guide

The National University of Singapore maintains a useful bibliography of major works on scholarly and governmental works on Singapore at www.lib.nus.edu.sg/bib/sh/. The Southeast Asia Digital Library maintained by Northern Illinois University includes a range of useful links that cover government, academic, and research institutions specific to Singapore: http://sea.lib.niu.edu. The Library of Congress maintains a resource guide on Singapore at www.loc.gov/rr/international/portals.html#t.

To get a full sense of the People's Action Party, browse its Web page: www.pap.org.sg. Useful economic information and news is available from Singapore's Ministry of Trade and Industry: http://app.mti.gov.sg. Official government statistics for Singapore are easily obtained at www.singstat.gov.sg; and to keep pace with Singapore's ever-expanding free trade agreements, visit www.fta.gov.sg.

Singapore's most well-known English-language daily, the *Straits Times*, was first published in 1845: www.straitstimes.com. Channelnewsasia.com provides an interactive Web site with real-time news, videos, and cultural features. Infopedia.nl.sg, maintained by the National Library of Singapore, covers a full range of political, economic, and social issues of interest to Singaporeans.

7

BRUNEI

*B*runei, known formally as Negara Brunei Darussalam (Brunei-Abode of Peace), is on the island of Borneo facing north to the South China Sea. It is divided into two sectors surrounded by the Malaysian state of Sarawak. With a population of only 390,000 and the second highest gross national income (GNI) per capita in Southeast Asia ($26,930), Brunei, together with Singapore, is unlike other nations in the region.[1]

About 70 percent of the people of Brunei are ethnically Malay, and most of this group works in the public sector. The Chinese community, which makes up nearly one-fifth of the population (but for the most part does not have Bruneian citizenship), supplies most of the nonpublic workforce. Indigenous, non-Muslim ethnic groups who live in the interior regions compose about 10 percent of Brunei's population. Imported laborers from neighboring countries supply additional labor to the microstate. Islam is the state religion.

Brunei achieved internal self-government in 1959 when the sultan promulgated the country's first constitution, thereby ending British administration and ensuring that power would be transferred to the ruling dynasty rather than to the people. The British still handled foreign and military affairs, however, until full independence was achieved in 1984. Ironically, the sultan was reluctant to accept independence because he feared his new nation would be vulnerable to attack from its larger neighbors, Indonesia and Malaysia.

Brunei's reluctance to assume full independence also stemmed from the monarch's fear that internal revolts could undermine the royalty's prerogatives. The most threatening incident occurred in 1962 when about a thousand followers of A. M. Azahari revolted. Shortly after attacking royal-owned oil installations, Azahari, who dreamed of an independent federation of Brunei, Sabah, and Sarawak, declared himself premier of Kalimantan Utara (North Borneo). Within two days the rebellion was crushed, supported by Gurkha fighters flown in from British bases in Singapore.[2] The sultan dismissed Parliament and declared a state of emergency, yet to be lifted four decades later. (Azahari fled to Indonesia, where he died in exile in 2002.)

South China Sea

BANDAR SERI BEGAWAN

Brunei Bay

BANGAR

SUKLANG

MALAYSIA

Borneo

BRUNEI

| 0 | 10 | 20 km |
| 0 | 10 | 20 mi |

Following independence, Brunei achieved political stability and economic development primarily because of enormous revenues from oil and natural gas. These funds allowed the government to establish a cradle-to-grave welfare system (facetiously known as the "Shellfare" state) that provided, among other things, free education and health care programs as well as subsidies for rice, housing, cars, funerals, and pilgrimages to Mecca. Moreover, there is no income tax.

The national ideology of Brunei is *Malay Islamic Beraja* (MIB), which means Malay Muslim Monarchy. The ideology emphasizes Malay-style Islam, with the monarchy as the defender of the faith and the people. MIB also discourages westernization and secularism. All public ceremonies and the school curriculum include MIB teachings.

When the sultan celebrated twenty-five years on the throne in 1992, he strengthened the concept of MIB, drawing from traditional Malay kingship and binding it with traditional Islam. MIB provides special status for Brunei's indigenous Malays and requires unquestioning deference to the throne. The purpose of MIB is ostensibly to keep unwanted foreign influences out of Brunei.

In honor of his jubilee year in 1992, the sultan built a new state mosque on the outskirts of Brunei's capital, Bandar Seri Begawan, at a cost of $30 million. Many Bruneians believed the sultan would establish democratic institutions during the celebrations. Instead, he announced that political parties and elections would remain proscribed and that the monarchy was the proper institution to bring benefits to the people. He tightened internal security, increased defense spending, purchased jet fighters from Great Britain, and announced plans to diversify the economy to lessen the nation's dependence on oil and gas.

Brunei joined ASEAN in 1984 and later supported efforts to create AFTA, the ASEAN Free Trade Area. In 2003, the sultan revived the moribund Legislative Council, which had not met since 1982. It then passed constitutional amendments to reform the Parliament, including the direct election of one-third of its forty-five delegates. Political parties were then permitted to organize and the sultan later began the construction of a new Parliament building. Still waiting for polls to be held, the partially elected Legislative Council had not convened as of late 2008.

INSTITUTIONS AND SOCIAL GROUPS

Sultanate

The sultanate is the embodiment of the state, and Sultan Sir Muda Hassanal Bolkiah—the twenty-ninth ruler in a dynasty that originated in the thirteenth century—is an absolute monarch whose legitimacy derives from his heredity, not from popular elections or accountability to Bruneians. He is the son of Sultan Haji Omar Ali Saifuddien Sa'adul Khairi Waddien, ibn Almarhum Sultan Mohammad Jamulul Alam, who was known as the Sultan Seri Begawan. Bandar Seri Begawan is named in his honor. Although the Seri Begawan abdicated in favor of his son in 1967, he attempted to keep ultimate power for himself so the present sultan was not able to rule unconditionally until his father's death in 1986.

The sultan has ceremonial responsibilities and, as the nation's prime minister and defense minister, administrative duties through which he exercises total control over the day-to-day affairs of the state. The legislative body remains appointed, and the cabinet is made up principally of members of the sultan's own royal family. There is no dissent from the populace because the sultan has absolute power. He recently amended the constitution to include his own immunity from any form of legal prosecution. His power is enhanced by the fact that he oversees the government bureaucracy, which employs an estimated two-thirds of Brunei's total workforce. The hierarchical nature of Bruneian society has made open communication with the sultan impossible for the common people. He is the head of state, head of government, and leader of the faith.

Despite announcements that Brunei would remain free from bourgeois decadence, the microstate has loosened up in an effort to attract tourism and Western business elites. Bookstores and movie theaters have opened, and satellite TV is ubiquitous. New Western-style restaurants (including McDonald's and KFC) have been established. Even hard liquor is available (although the nation is legally dry). In 1996, the American pop singer Michael Jackson presented a free concert for the sultan's fiftieth birthday, although he apparently was asked to swivel less than usual. Wealth is bringing new social problems to Brunei. A new generation of "bored youth" has emerged, as have graffiti, theft, and inhalant and methamphetamine use.[3]

There is no distinction between the state's wealth and the sultan's personal riches. Only four years after independence, the sultan was the richest man in the world, and he remains counted among its richest billionaires (worth about $30 billion). All the state's revenues and reserves are his, and he alone decides what portion goes for state expenditures.[4] The sultan of Brunei resides in a palace forty times the size of the White House, with 1,700 rooms. He rules in the style of classic potentates, albeit with modern tastes. Millions of dollars are spent on exotic collections of art, jewelry, and automobiles, including hundreds of Bentleys, Mercedes-Benzes, and Ferraris. He is surrounded by three wives (one divorced) and multiple children born over a forty-year span. With the sultan known more as a philanderer than a philanthropist, numerous stories of his activities have undermined his attempt to create an image of a responsible, benevolent ruler. In 1993, Filipino senators investigated reports that some of their country's best-known actresses, models, and singers had engaged in prostitution while visiting Brunei. The senators reported a "high-class white slavery ring." Also, a former Miss USA made headlines with allegations of sexual abuse by Bruneian royalty. The sultan has attempted to shed his playboy image and shore up his credentials as a devout Muslim with three pilgrimages to Mecca.

In 2000, the sultan issued a lawsuit against his brother, Prince Jefri, and about seventy other officials for allegedly having wasted billions of dollars of state funds. The prince was fired from his position as finance minister and cited for particularly gross corruption that included extravagant purchases of planes, yachts, and jewelry, and high-priced sex orgies. The prince entertains a retinue of wives and mistresses and is the father of thirty-five children.[5]

Prince Jefri fled Brunei and initially made an out-of-court settlement with his brother to repay losses and change his lifestyle. When he failed to live up to the agreement, a legal case was sent to Britain's Privy Council for further settlement. In full tabloid drama, the Bruneian royal scandal was followed with shock as court documents revealed how both royals had spent billions of dollars on selfish luxuries and services ($900 million on jewelry, $475 million on Rolls Royces, hundreds of millions on a family fleet of jets, and even $3.6 million on badminton lessons and acupuncture). When the court found the prince liable for $8 billion of the missing $15 billion, he fled to France. A 2008 warrant for his arrest from a London judge remains outstanding.

The heir apparent to the throne is Crown Prince Al-Muhtadee Billah, born in 1974, three years before his father's newest wife. After studying in England, Prince Billah married Pengiran Anak Sarah, a half-Swiss teenager thirteen years his junior. Their first son, Prince Abdul Muntaqim, born in 2007, is the youngest living person with rights to the world's oldest monarchical line.

Military

The Royal Brunei Armed Forces (RBAF), with about 4,500 members (the strength of a brigade group with support elements), is the smallest military force in ASEAN. This voluntarily recruited, highly paid national defense force represents a state that spends a higher proportion of its budget on defense than any other ASEAN nation.

Since 1962, the RBAF has been augmented by a battalion of British Army Gurkhas paid for by the sultan (the only permanent deployment of British troops in the region). This force helps to ensure that there will be no revolt against the sultan's rule. The RBAF regularly engages in joint exercises with U.S. Marine Corps, as well as armed forces from Malaysia and Australia. The RBAF also contributed peacekeepers to international operations in Cambodia, the Philippines, and Lebanon.

Political Parties

Brunei has no viable political parties, nor has the government mobilized its own party as have Indonesia and Burma. Brunei's sultan draws support through patrimonialist programs and by depoliticizing society. The country's short history is punctuated by failed attempts by actors outside the sultan's circle of patronage to effect change by forming political parties. The left-leaning, pro-independence Brunei People's Party, for example, briefly held seats in the Legislative Council in early 1960s but was forced into exile along with its leader, A. M. Azahari, following the 1962 rebellion. The Brunei National Democratic Party, established in 1985, sought to promote a moderate platform based on Islam and liberal nationalism. Its primary goal was to restore parliamentary democracy. When party leaders called for elections and asked the sultan to give up his position as prime minister, they were arrested and the party was forcibly deregistered.

The Brunei Solidarity National Party, formed in 1995, remains Brunei's only registered political party as of 2008. Outwardly supportive of the sultan's right to rule, its platform is vague beyond its support for small-business owners, from where it draws support. The party remains unconnected to the royal family or Chinese entrepreneurs and is essentially powerless. Its only hope is to compete for elected seats in the Legislative Council, assuming the sultan delivers on his 2003 pledge to permit elections.[6] Other parties, such as the Brunei National Solidarity Party and the Brunei People's Awareness Party, have been deregistered in recent years for technical reasons. They join the Brunei People's Party and the National Democratic Party on the growing list of defunct political parties in Brunei's meaningless party system.

DEMOCRATIZATION

There is no democracy in Brunei. The country's political system is an absolute monarchy, with no representative form of government, a politically closed regime. The 1984 constitution consolidated the monarchy's power by suspending parliamentary institutions. The reconvening of the Legislative Council in 2004 allowed for nonelected appointees to participate in some constitutional amendments and policy-level decisions at the sultan's behest. Even if the Legislative Council is re-formed with elected seats, as the sultan has announced, the capacity of elected representatives to exercise power would be limited at best. Thirty of the body's proposed forty-five representatives would still be appointed by the sultan. Elected village leaders are permitted some role in administrating state funds but have no policymaking function.

Civil liberties in Brunei include freedom of movement but little else. Journalists must practice self-censorship or risk charges of sedition. Labor rights are circumscribed and abuse of foreign workers by employers is rarely prosecuted. Brunei is considered "not free" by Freedom House, a rating shared in Southeast Asia by Cambodia, Laos, Vietnam, and Burma. Brunei remained under emergency decrees through 2008.

ECONOMIC DEVELOPMENT

Vast oil reserves make the dynamics of Brunei's economy different from the agriculturally based economies of other Southeast Asian nations. Oil and natural gas are the main source of government revenue, foreign investment, and employment. Together they account for about 90 percent of total export earnings, 80 percent of government revenue, and 40 percent of GDP. Although Brunei has benefited economically from rising oil demand and prices in recent years, its economy was hit hard by the Asian economic crisis in the late 1990s. Its top economic priority, therefore, is to diversify its economy to reduce vulnerability. The problem of oil export dependency is exacerbated by estimates that, at current extraction rates, reserves could disappear in twenty to thirty years. New drilling concessions established in 2008 may extend the life of the oil-based economy.

Over the past twenty years, officials have worried about which industries to pursue as oil and gas reserves are depleted. Formal plans were developed in the 1990s to promote the private sector, especially in pharmaceuticals, cement, steel, chemicals, ceramics, and high technology.[7] Garment manufacturing and cash crops were also pursued but largely failed after global quotas on textiles were abolished. Restructuring the economy has proven difficult, and investors have been slow to come to Brunei. A large industrial park aimed at downstream petrochemical industries is scheduled to open in 2009, drawing interest from European and Japanese investors.

Brunei's government views ecotourism as a promising alternative to the energy sector. Relatively untouched tropical forests make tourism attractive, but Brunei's remote location renders it unlikely that tourism will ever bring the economic returns that hydrocarbons now produce. Another initiative proposed by the sultan, following Malaysia's lead, is for Brunei to become a center for Islamic banking and finance. Outside investors have shown interest in Brunei, but the microstate's principal neighbor currently dominates Islamic-based banking in the region.

A final economic concern is employment. About 40 percent of Brunei's workforce is made up of foreign workers. Brunei's private sector, weak as it is, does not attract the country's own graduates. A rising rate of unemployment among younger Bruneians, often holding out for better government jobs, troubles officials. Increasingly, foreign workers are filling skilled positions in the private sector, adding to the already large base of immigrant laborers. Brunei's dependence on human resources from outside the country shows little sign of abating.

THE BRUNEIAN STATE

Brunei's small size makes governance far easier than in the larger and more diverse countries elsewhere in Southeast Asia. Moreover, the state has brought virtually all institutions into its fold, leaving no autonomous societal groups to compete with the state apparatus.

There is an essential identity between the state and the person of the sultan. The welfare state provides all basic needs of most Bruneians; thus, there is little dissension with the sultan's absolute powers. His lineage and royal aura and his leadership of Islam in Brunei further strengthen his position. Moves by groups calling for the formation of democratic institutions, and the relegation of the sultan to ceremonial rather than administrative functions, have failed.

Brunei has not experienced the massive social dislocation in the contemporary period that could explain its strong state status. The government has pointed to Indonesian and Malaysian support for past revolts as a major reason for the constraints imposed on the people's right to establish political groupings. However, the sultan's supreme role does not constitute a sufficient cause that clears the way to implement a new, state-sponsored strategy for survival. Brunei has experienced no event equivalent to the violent independence struggle in Indonesia, the destruction in the Philippines during World War II, or the First Indochina War.

Brunei has received considerable aid and support from its former colonial ruler, Great Britain, and the presence of the Gurkhas has strengthened the state by intimidating potential dissidents. There is no major external threat to Brunei's security today, nor has there been since 1962 when Indonesia supported the Azahari revolt. No dissident groups have been allowed to grow to the point that they pose a meaningful threat to the regime.

Almost every official, technocrat, and military officer in Brunei is related—directly or indirectly—to the sultan, his family, and his advisers. These people do not have another base of social control independent of the state; the sultan is the state, and all officials are part of his entourage. The lack of any mass political base in Bruneian society has reinforced these officials' loyalty to the state. Nevertheless, they are skilled and highly educated. Even the Chinese community is loyal to the state, despite the fact that most Chinese in Brunei are not even citizens. However, their businesses depend on the sultan's continued largesse and support.

Sultan Sir Muda Hassanal Bolkiah has grown in his position. He was in his father's shadow until 1986 and has only recently shown his leadership skills. His plans to diversify the economy into ecotourism and Islamic finance are far-reaching. However, his reluctance to move toward a more democratic government is effective in the short run but problematic in the long run, as increased communications and economic development bring the modern world to Brunei.

FOREIGN POLICY

Just one week after gaining full independence in 1984, Brunei joined ASEAN, strengthening its relationships with former adversaries such as Indonesia and Malaysia. Today, Brunei's foreign policy focuses on security attained through international legitimacy and expanding economic relations. ASEAN membership has been the primary means to that end. Brunei also cultivates relations beyond Southeast Asia with key partners.

Since independence, Brunei's relations with the United States have been close. Indeed, according to media sources, Brunei channeled some $10 million to help the U.S.-backed Contras in Nicaragua after depositing the money in a Swiss bank account in 1986, and the Bruneian government confirmed that "His Majesty the Sultan of Brunei Darussalam had made a personal donation to the United States to be used for humanitarian purposes in Central America."[8] This incident became part of U.S. President Ronald Reagan's "Irangate" imbroglio, and thus it was the first that most Americans had ever heard about Brunei.

In keeping with the country's generally pro-Western foreign policy, Brunei supported the U.S.-led liberation of Kuwait (an allied sultanate) from Iraq in 1990, as well as post-9/11 efforts at intelligence sharing to target Islamist terrorists. In December 2002, Sultan Hassanal visited President George W. Bush in Washington to personally pledge support for U.S. counterterrorism efforts in Southeast Asia.

Because Brunei is not threatened by any external power, the country has adopted a low-key foreign policy that is more reactive than proactive. Its main concerns are participating in ASEAN programs and building its diplomatic missions abroad to ensure trade and investment for the Bruneian economy. In recent years, Brunei successfully negotiated a free trade agreement with Japan, which imports 90 percent of Brunei's liquefied natural gas. It also became a member of the Trans-Pacific Strategic Economic Partnership, a free-trade body inclusive of Brunei, Singapore, Chile, and New Zealand that aims to eliminate all tariffs between members by 2015.

CONCLUSION

As is true of most other states in the region, there are discrepancies in the explanation of conditions for a strong state in Brunei, whose absolute monarchy is increasingly an anachronism in the changing world of Southeast Asia. As the world moves toward open societies and governmental accountability to the people, Brunei continues to more closely resemble a Middle Eastern kingdom. The country's capacity to sustain absolutism results from the great wealth brought in by the sale of oil and gas. In a country surrounded by agricultural societies in which most of the people are poor, the sultan has "bought" his legitimacy by providing his subjects with all of life's necessities and, indeed, with luxuries.

NOTES

1. In terms of per capita purchasing power parity, Brunei's per capita income is $51,005, fourth in the world (2007 UNDP figures).

2. Justus M. van der Kroef, "Indonesia, Malaya, and the North Borneo Crisis," *Asian Survey*, vol. 3, no. 4 (April 1963), p. 177.

3. William Case, "Brunei in 2006: Not a Bad Year," *Asian Survey*, vol. 47, no. 1 (January/February 2007), p. 192.

4. D. S. Ranjit Singh, "Brunei Darussalam in 1987: Coming to Grips with Economic and Political Realities," in *Southeast Asian Affairs 1988* (Singapore: Institute of Southeast Asian Studies, 1988), p. 63.

5. Seth Mydans, "Brunei: From Oil Rich to Garage Sales," *New York Times*, August 17, 2001, available at www.nytimes.com.

6. Case, "Brunei in 2006," p. 190.

7. Far Eastern Economic Review, *Asia Yearbook, 1990* (Hong Kong: Far Eastern Economic Review, 1990), p. 91.

8. K. U. Menon, "Brunei Darussalam in 1986," in *Southeast Asian Affairs 1987* (Singapore: Institute of Southeast Asian Studies, 1987), p. 99.

RESOURCE GUIDE

Readers can supplement this chapter with information and news on Brunei maintained by BBC News at http://news.bbc.co.uk/1/hi/world/asia-pacific/country_profiles/1298 607.stm. Links to government Web pages and the official policy line, updated daily, can be found at www.brunei.gov.bn. A list of active international development organizations in Brunei can be found at www.devdir.org/files/Brunei.PDF. Daily headlines and news are available from the *Borneo Bulletin Online* at www.brunei-online.com/bb. Because freedom of speech is strictly controlled by the Bruneian government, do not expect to find critical journalism or scholarship sourced from within the country.

8

BURMA

On June 18, 1989, the martial law government of Burma declared that the country's official name (in English) would henceforth be Myanmar.[1] Myanmar is a transliteration of what has been the country's official name in the Burmese language. The disadvantage of the name Myanmar (as well as of the name Burma) is that it has ethnic connotations, implying that the country is the land of the majority ethnic group—the Burmans. About fifteen major ethnic groups and dozens of smaller minorities make up more than one-third of the total population of 52 million; thus, there has long been ethnic sensitivity to the dominant position of the Burmans. The name "Myanmar" has not been accepted by most scholars of Burma who view the change as temporary until the illegitimate military government is fully reformed or overthrown.

As most of the nations of Southeast Asia move toward economic development and political liberalization, Burma is a clear exception. Characterized by ethnic conflict, economic stagnation, and political oppression, Burma has been unable to achieve *pyidawtha*—the ideal peaceful, pleasant, and prosperous society. Failure to reach this goal has been all the more tragic because the nation is rich in natural and human resources and because the Burmese came close to securing their political rights in 1988 when they revolted against their military leaders. Carrying out their own version of "People Power," the Burmese exalted in a short "Rangoon Spring" before the military brutally quelled the uprising.

The 1988 revolt was not the first time the Burmese have struggled for their rights. In January 1948, the Burmese won their independence after several years of demonstrations and often-violent opposition to British rule. The independence struggle was led by the Thakin movement, a group of anti-British nationalists headed by Aung San, the father of modern Burma and a fiery nationalist who received his training in Japan during World War II after the Japanese had occupied Burma. Subsequently, the movement turned against the Japanese as their occupation became increasingly repressive. Aung San,

who was expected to be Burma's first head of state, was assassinated in 1947 and thus became the nation's martyred hero.

The Thakin movement became the core of the Anti-Fascist People's Freedom League (AFPFL), a united front group opposed to the Japanese. AFPFL forces cooperated with the British to oust the Japanese and then turned against the British in the struggle for independence. The AFPFL negotiated independence and formed the country's first parliamentary government in 1948 under the leadership of forty-one-year-old U Nu.

The period from 1948 to 1958 was known as the "Time of Troubles." The well-organized minority ethnic groups opposed the government's move toward a national state and instead supported establishing autonomous states for each group. The Shans, Karens, and other groups rose against the central authorities, precipitating a struggle that began an ongoing civil war. Ethnic-based, antigovernment sentiment and conflict thus troubled the country in its early years of independence and remains a central element of Burma's military-dominated politics.

The second major postindependence problem concerned the poorly trained civil service, which was not able to carry out government programs effectively. U Nu's government had proclaimed a socialist policy that required a high degree of centralized administration, but the Burmese bureaucracy floundered, causing severe political and economic disturbances. U Thant, one of U Nu's closest advisors, was unavailable to fully assist in postindependence rebuilding, being tied up in New York as the third UN secretary-general. Absent independence martyr Aung San and the pragmatic U Thant, the charismatic U Nu struggled to guide Burma's Parliament and bureaucracy. Poor governance added fuel to ethnic resentments and a rising communist movement.

By 1958, Burma's political condition was so chaotic that U Nu turned the functioning of the government over to the military (Tatmadaw), led by General Ne Win, also a leader of the Thakin independence movement and a compatriot of Aung San. Following this "constitutional coup," a caretaker administration stabilized the cost of living and controlled the black market. Exports were increased and corruption was temporarily halted. Ne Win's government reorganized the bureaucracy to make it more efficient and restored a semblance of law and order. Corruption within the bureaucracy was uncovered, and violent crime and gangsterism were rooted out in the countryside. The caretaker military government also stepped up its campaign against ethnic rebels and a growing threat from communists. Throughout all of this activity, the press and courts remained free and independent.

Despite the success of the Tatmadaw's caretaker government in a number of areas, in 1960 the electorate chose to return to U Nu for leadership. Again, however, he was not able to control the economy. U Nu's leadership was based on his charismatic religious qualities and reputation for impeccable honesty, but he was a poor day-to-day administrator. The nation was reeling from multiple rebellions among minority groups, and therefore a large share of the central budget was allocated to internal security, but U Nu concentrated on establishing Buddhism as the state religion.[2] U Nu believed Buddhism was the best defense against rising sympathy for communism within Burma. His efforts to conceptualize an idealistic vision of a Burmese welfare state based on Buddha's teachings were not matched by a parallel plan for implementation and administration.

The military, which perceived that the civilian government was weak and dependent upon Western-style political institutions that were incompatible with Burmese culture, carried out a coup on March 2, 1962, led by Ne Win. This seizure of power, which was rapid, nonviolent, and without major challenge, began an era of military rule that has continued for over four decades. Ne Win disbanded the Western-style Parliament, banned political parties, and restricted civil liberties. Hundreds of thousands of ethnic Indians living in Burma, a legacy of British rule, were forced back to India and East Pakistan. He then devised a program of radical economic and political policies called the "Burmese Way to Socialism," which included nationalizing major industries, schools, rice mills, small and large businesses, and financial institutions. His program to install a centralized state monopoly of the means of production was designed to ensure control of a united Burma.

To mobilize support for the socialist program, Ne Win established the Burmese Socialist Program Party (BSPP), organized to reach down to the village level along hierarchical lines but with all power remaining firmly at the party's military-dominated top echelon. The party's main function was to legitimize army rule. To keep Western "bourgeois decadent" ideas from infiltrating into Burma, Ne Win arrested those who opposed his policies, restricted travel to Burma by foreigners, and ended academic freedom at the universities. His move toward a neutralist foreign policy took the form of isolationism.

In January 1974, Burma became the Socialist Republic of the Union of Burma after the electorate had passed the new socialist constitution. Although Ne Win discarded his military uniform in 1971 and became the "civilian" president of the new government, the military continued to be the dominant political force. Ne Win nominally stepped down as president in 1981 but retained his more powerful position as head of the BSPP. In that position he was able to continue his dominance over political and economic policymaking. Influencing Ne Win's decisions were his beliefs in astrology and numerology. The policies emanating from the military junta became increasingly erratic.

In the summer of 1988, hundreds of thousands of farmers, urban workers, students, monks, and civil servants took to the streets of Burma's major cities to demonstrate against their government leaders. This revolt was the culmination of years of frustration and disgust at the failures of the military government to bring development to Burma. Although rich in natural resources, Burma had been humiliated by the UN decision in 1987 to declare it one of the world's least-developed nations. The revolt was also a response to the pervasive suppression of the people's political rights since 1962, when the military had assumed all political power.

A more immediate cause of the revolt was the 1987 decision of Ne Win's administration to declare valueless some 80 percent of the Burmese money in circulation. Any kyat note over $1.60 in value became instantly worthless. As part of the policy, the junta unexpectedly ordered that old notes be replaced by new ones divisible by nine, Ne Win's lucky number. Kyat notes denominated in nine, forty-five, and ninety appeared in circulation. Sudden demonetization, justified as a measure to undermine black marketeers and control inflation, adversely affected the entire population, rich and poor. The bulk of the working economy was sustained by the black market (the government's socialistic economy having collapsed), so the demise of this unofficial market was seen as a great catastrophe. Moreover, no recompense was given to holders of kyat notes above the maximum allowed; in effect, then, the savings of the entire population were wiped out. The price of food skyrocketed and even government supporters began to grow restless with the country's direction.

The incident that sparked the 1988 revolt occurred in a tea shop, where students and other patrons squabbled over the choice of music tapes being played. When the police arrived, a student was killed. Thousands of his schoolmates later returned to avenge their colleague's death, but they were met by weapons and security police. In a particularly dreadful incident, forty-one students were herded into a police van, where they suffocated in the intense heat. More demonstrations and security clashes occurred during the ensuing weeks. Unofficial estimates of student deaths from beatings, bayonet stabbings, and suffocation were in the hundreds, but the government blandly announced a total of only two student deaths.[3]

In the midst of the unrest, General Ne Win gathered with leaders in a special session of the BSPP Central Committee. In an alarming speech, he took responsibility for the student deaths and resigned his post as party chairman in favor of General Sein Lwin. Most astonishingly, Ne Win called for a popular referendum on a return to multiparty democracy. He also warned, ominously, that future mob disturbances would invite the use of military force. The party rejected the idea of the referendum but agreed to accept his resignation and the appointment of Sein Lwin, known as the "the Butcher" for his 1974 decision to violently quell demonstrations by grief-stricken students honoring U Thant's death.

Ne Win's moves sparked more demonstrations and more killings by security police. Students, distrustful that Sein Lwin could ever lead reform, began to mobilize, joined by dockworkers, laborers, and members of the general population. Sporadic protests erupted in Rangoon and other major cities. Then, on August 8, 1988 (i.e., 8/8/88), the army followed through on Ne Win's warning. Sein Lwin ordered the use of lethal force on the demonstrators. Dozens were killed on the initial night of the crackdown but the violence simply hardened the protesters' resolve. Mass demonstrations continued for five consecutive days, as did the death toll. In yet another shameful incident, government soldiers shot and killed a group of exhausted doctors and nurses in front of Rangoon General Hospital.[4]

International outcry followed the junta's crackdown of the "8888 Uprising," as it became known. The U.S. government was one of the first to issue a protest and became a visible symbol of democratic government; thus, the grounds of the U.S. embassy in Rangoon became an important site for antigovernment demonstrations. Other governments condemned the crackdown as well. Demonstrations in Rangoon and in Mandalay grew to more than a million people.

Facing mounting protests, Sein Lwin abruptly resigned and the army began to withdraw from Rangoon five days after its slaughter had begun. Maung Maung, a civilian academic and Ne Win's personal biographer, was appointed president. For a brief time, a sense of victory swept the population and suggested that regime change was possible. Opposition politicians emerged after years of suppression and began to discuss plans for action. Aung Sun's daughter, Aung San Suu Kyi, visiting Burma from her home in London, began to offer public speeches encouraging reform. Top diplomats signed an open letter calling to end Burma's isolationism.

Then, just as systemic change seemed within reach, cascading events overtook themselves. The civil administration collapsed and the police went on strike. Prisoners were released and a sense of insecurity developed among the public. Revolutionary-style protests grew in size and audacity, and a number of government offices were stormed by unruly crowds. An attitude of recrimination surfaced. In a few cases, "suspected government agents were gruesomely beheaded or hacked to death in front of cheering crowds."[5] Burma faced the prospect of a bloody social revolution.

With the knowledge that the military's dominance was in jeopardy, army commander in chief General Saw Maung, ostensibly on orders from Ne Win, crushed the revolt and restored the military to power on September 18, 1988. The military's coup was not against an opposition government, as none existed, but was against the civilian facade government under Maung Maung that the army itself created. The violent coup was followed by the arrest of demonstrators, the censorship of all forms of communication, and the flight of tens of thousands of students to the nation's borders to escape the military and organize for a future rebellion. Altogether, some 3,000 Burmese lost their lives in their attempt to end military rule.

Saw Maung, taking his orders from Ne Win, established the State Law and Order Restoration Council (SLORC) to endure "until anarchy and demonstrations could be brought under control." SLORC consisted of generals who were loyal to Ne Win and were given responsibility for administering the state. Ruling by martial law, SLORC brutally suppressed regime opponents and began to initiate reforms. SLORC began to allow more open politics than did the military during the Ne Win years. In fact, political parties were able to apply for official recognition in anticipation of an election to be held in May 1990. However, when opposition party leaders spoke out against the regime, they were arrested.

SLORC argued that its harsh policies were necessary because of an alleged collusion between the Burmese Communist Party and the U.S. Central Intelligence Agency, which was the cause of demonstrations and antigovernment dissidence. Aung San Suu Kyi, who formed the National League for Democracy (NLD) in the days following the uprising, was placed under house arrest for having been "manipulated" by communists and foreign intelligence agencies. SLORC also argued that a highly centralized, military-oriented administration was necessary to ensure the country's continued unity in the face of potential rebellion by minority ethnic groups. None of these explanations were accepted by the vast majority of Burmese, who were extremely angry that their people's revolt had been crushed. The Tatmadaw, once a symbol of stability in Burma, became a hated organization.

Reports from Burma were few during 1989 and 1990 because SLORC did not allow foreign journalists or scholars into the country. However, sketchy reports suggested that SLORC was violating the Burmese people's human rights by silencing writers, banning assemblies, and forcefully moving some half a million people from their homes with the aim of breaking up prodemocracy neighborhoods and areas favorable to opposition leader Aung San Suu Kyi. The relocation of urban residents in late 1989 from cities to satellite towns was particularly egregious but was justified, according to SLORC, as a "beautification measure."

Despite these human rights violations, SLORC organized the May 27, 1990, election to choose legislators in the Pyithu Hluttaw (People's Assembly), the sole organ of legislative authority. Under the election law, each constituency was to elect one representative to the Pyithu Hluttaw. Some 492 constituencies, defined by population, were to choose representatives; seven constituencies of ethnic minorities, however, were not allowed to vote because of "security" threats in their regions. SLORC believed the election could be controlled to ensure that pro-government forces would prevail. In fact, the government was given the power to censor the speeches and publications of parties and candidates. Television time was limited to one ten-minute period per party during the entire campaign, and statements had to be submitted for approval seven days in advance. Candidates who gave speeches that had not been scrutinized and approved by the authorities were imprisoned.

Popular opposition leaders were harassed and kept from participating in the election. Aung San Suu Kyi, for example, was disqualified, as were former Prime Minister U Nu and another prominent opposition leader, former General Tin O. All of these leaders were placed under house arrest. Pro-government candidates who joined the successor party of the BSPP, the National Unity Party (NUP), received government funds for campaigning, but funds were not available to opposition leaders. The authorities banned outdoor assemblies and relocated citizens from their voting constituencies to ensure a pro-government vote.

Despite these measures, and in an extraordinary display of independence, the oppositionist National Democratic League won more than 80 percent of the seats (396 of 485) in the Pyithu Hluttaw. The NUP won only 10 seats, losing even in areas dominated by the army. Such a sharp rebuke of the martial law government was unexpected. Even months after the election, the military still refused to turn the government over to the newly elected legislators, even though the latter were ready to install a new constitution based largely on the country's last democratic constitution of 1947. Although the Burmese had expressed their anger toward the military government and their support for democratic rule through their vote, the regime in power was unwilling to act in compliance with the people's will.

Although world reaction to SLORC's oppression was strongly critical, the military continued to jail opposition leaders, to dominate every facet of society, and to isolate the regime from global currents. When in December 1991 Aung San Suu Kyi received the Nobel Peace Prize in absentia for standing up to the military junta, many believed that SLORC could not withstand the negative worldwide publicity. However, despite global condemnation and economic sanctions, SLORC dug in even deeper, claiming that freeing the Nobel laureate would threaten the nation's peace and tranquility.

In 1992, General Saw Maung stepped down as chairman of SLORC and was replaced by General Than Shwe, who was the nation's military commander and minister of defense. The new leader released some five hundred political prisoners, although the principal oppositionists were not freed. Colleges and universities were reopened, and a constitutional convention was called. The latter was viewed as a sham by both the Burmese people and foreign observers, who pointed out that the convention was dominated by the military and that the leading opposition leaders were still in jail. The convention met in January 1993 but did nothing to undermine military rule. Indeed, the conference specifically approved a leading political role for the army in the country's future governance.

During the postelection period, SLORC persisted in denying elected parliamentarians their rightful seats. In response, 250 would-be delegates formed a "parallel government" outside of the country in December 1990, the National Coalition Government of the Union of Burma. It called for the release of Aung San Suu Kyi and all political prisoners, the transfer of power to those properly elected, and a halt to the civil war. But the military rulers did not listen.

Sometime in 1994, the generals eventually realized that SLORC's policy of isolation had brought devastation to Burma. They allowed small openings in the economy, but the lack of capital, the poor infrastructure, and the disdain of much of the world made change difficult. Nevertheless, in the mid-1990s Burma's economic growth rate improved, ending the total stagnation of previous decades. Foreign entrepreneurs, mainly Asian, began setting up investments, and a "Visit Myanmar Year" promotional campaign was launched. New hotel projects changed the face of Rangoon. The opening did almost nothing to improve the standard of living of the people, among the world's poorest, most of whom led subsistence lives. Corruption, an inflated bureaucracy, political mismanagement, and the continued imprisonment of the democracy leaders were all reasons for the ongoing economic problems.

In July 1995, Aung San Suu Kyi was "released" from house arrest. In reality, she was guarded closely to ensure that she and her followers would not jeopardize SLORC's control over the nation. The government felt compelled to release her because of foreign pressures stemming from her extraordinary international reputation as a democrat. She was also released as an inducement to convince foreign nations to invest in Burma, and because the generals had decimated her National League for Democracy. Although thousands of Burmese citizens came to hear her speak, Aung San Suu Kyi was effectively silenced. Her talks were not allowed to be broadcast or printed in the government-controlled press. Indeed, the press attacked Aung San Suu Kyi daily. In 1997, when her British husband, Michael Aris, was near death from prostate cancer in Great Britain, Burma analysts believed the junta would show compassion by allowing him to spend his last days with his wife. However, he was denied a visa, and she was reluctant to leave Burma, fearing she would not be allowed to return. Aris died in Britain in 1999.

Throughout the 1990s, SLORC allowed no discussion of the key issue: Which was the more legitimate institution, SLORC or the NLD? The election results remained ignored by the government, which continued to rule in a despotic manner. Political opponents were jailed or executed. Military officers replaced civilians at all levels of the bureaucracy. Most political parties remained banned. E-mail and Internet communication was permitted in the country but only under tight control by censors. The military junta was able to sign cease-fire agreements with a number long-standing ethnic rebel groups, but for those still engaged in civil war, such as the Karens, the military stepped up its suppression, forcing hundreds of thousands to flee to Thailand, where they languished as refugees in terrible living conditions.

In an attempt to improve its international image, SLORC officials renamed the ruling council in 1997 the State Peace and Development Council (SPDC). SPDC policies have remained virtually the same as those of SLORC. Although the SPDC has partially liberalized trade and investment, most new foreign investment permitted into Burma explicitly benefits state officials who double as businessmen.

In 2000, a special UN envoy attempted to bring about talks between the government and the democracy leader, Aung San Suu Kyi, under house arrest for the second time. Speculation emerged that a new breakthrough and compromise could lead to an opening of the nation. By mid-2001, however, talks broke down. Months later, Aung San Suu Kyi was released from house arrest and allowed to travel within Burma. In 2003, while she was touring Depayin, a provincial town in upper Burma, a clash erupted between NLD sympathizers and the government. Opposition leaders claimed the confrontation led to seventy deaths, whereas the government reported only four. Prodemocracy groups accused the government of orchestrating the Depayin clash. Soon afterward, NLD leaders were arrested and Aung San Suu Kyi's third detention began.[6]

Intrigue within the military has also punctuated Burmese politics. Following an alleged coup attempt by Ne Win's son-in-law in March 2002, Ne Win was placed under house arrest by his own successor, Than Shwe. Months later, at age ninety-one, Ne Win died at his home on Inya Lake. The military junta refused to recognize Ne Win's passing with a state funeral or official salute of honor. In Burma's Tatmadaw, intergenerational despotism had fully arrived.

In August 2003, only months after the Depayin massacre, newly appointed Prime Minister Khin Nyunt outlined a seven-point roadmap for a transition to multiparty democracy. Reviving the moribund National Convention, the new leader aimed to redraft the constitution. The move drew some interest as Khin Nyunt, the former head of the military's intelligence service, had often brokered discussions with Aung San Suu Kyi. Burmese diplomats paraded the reforms at the United Nations. Still, very few inside or outside Burma viewed the process as legitimate. A year later, Senior General Than Shwe forcibly removed the former Ne Win protégé from office and placed him under detention. A purge of officials tied to Khin Nyunt followed.

In 2006, the SPDC announced a surprise relocation of the country's capital to an undeveloped rural area four hundred kilometers north of Rangoon. The decision is believed to have derived from consultations with the junta's favored astrologers. Naypyitaw, the new capital, required a massive construction effort and the relocation of government offices and residences. By literally distancing ministers and administrators from the population, the paranoid Tatmadaw resurrected the age-old court practice of isolating officials.

If intended to decrease the likelihood of antigovernment Rangoon activism, relocating the capital to Naypyitaw failed. In August 2007, the government imposed a drastic 500 percent hike in fuel prices. Protests followed, led by saffron-robed Buddhist monks and veteran leaders from the 8888 Uprising. The government reacted violently, using plainclothes goons at first and then uniformed soldiers. Protesters, including monks, were brutally beaten and arrested. The Buddhist clergy demanded an apology from the government, which never came. What followed became Burma's most significant mass protests since 1988, similarly drawing global attention.

On September 28, 2007, throughout the country thousands of monks went to the streets under the banner of the All Burma Monks Alliance, a hitherto-unknown group. As ordinary Burmese joined the monks, demonstrations grew massive in many parts of the country. In Rangoon, some protesters headed for the famous Shwedagon pagoda; others flocked to Aung San Suu Kyi's residence near Inya Lake. Still under house arrest, the Nobel laureate appeared at her gate engaging with monks and others. The blessing of the movement by Burma's leading dissident served as yet another catalyst. Within a few days, over 100,000 monks and laymen had paralyzed the country's major cities. Predictably, the Tatmadaw stepped up its brutality in return. At least thirty-one protesters were killed and many wounded. Pictures and video sent from digital cameras and cell phones flooded newswires worldwide; images of unarmed, shaven-head monks and students lying dead and bloodied on Rangoon streets produced shock. Despite an international outcry from Western governments, ASEAN ministers, and Hollywood celebrities, the ruling junta retained the upper hand. By October the protests had been suppressed. Temples were raided by security forces and monks detained. To reduce tensions, a UN envoy arrived to meet with junta leaders and Aung San Suu Kyi. The protests affirmed widespread discontent among Burma's population but they also exposed the weakened state of Burma's opposition to effect political change.

Undeterred by unrest, the SPDC announced plans for a May 2008 referendum on a new constitution, a document drafted exclusively by regime insiders to ensure the state's continued military dominance. NLD leaders organized a massive "No!" campaign that distributed leaflets throughout the country.

On May 2, 2008, eight days before the scheduled referendum, Cyclone Nargis hit Burma's populated delta region with devastating consequences; it was the worst natural disaster in the country's history. With massive force, Nargis caused over 130,000 deaths and left 2.4 million survivors stranded and desperate, according to UN estimates. Most disturbing was Than Shwe's initial reluctance to allow foreign aid and disaster relief to the cyclone's victims. Injured, homeless, and hungry, millions of Burmese suffered unnecessarily in the days and weeks that followed. Foreign journalists, restricted by the regime, produced underground reports offering the world a glimpse of the disaster's massive scale.

While Burma's leaders allowed millions to suffer by denying visas to aid workers and entry to supply ships, the SPDC audaciously went forward with its constitutional referendum, postponing voting in affected areas. State-controlled media announced weeks later that voters had approved the new charter with a 92.4 percent vote. International condemnation for mishandling the disaster and staging a farcical referendum on constitutional reform was nearly universal.

When the regime began to allow international aid to trickle in (via Thailand), only Burmese officials were allowed to distribute it. Ten days after Nargis, a new event gripped the world's attention: a 7.9 earthquake in southwest China that killed 90,000 people and left 5 million homeless. As the world watched the contrasting relief efforts in China and Burma, the true incompetence and paranoia of Burma's military junta was laid bare. For their quick action, Chinese officials, for example, won praise from UN Secretary-General Ban Ki-moon. Wen Jiabao, China's prime minister, earned the title of "Uncle Wen" from an affectionate Chinese public for his unrelenting efforts to coordinate earthquake relief efforts. By contrast, Than Shwe became the object of anger and bewilderment from inside and outside Burma. French diplomats called for the military junta to be charged with crimes against humanity and even raised the prospect of humanitarian intervention by the UN Security Council. Only following a face-to-face meeting with the UN secretary-general did Than Shwe relax entry restrictions on aid workers, although USAID workers were never allowed in. Burma's worst natural disaster was exacerbated by a tragic man-made catastrophe.

In 2008, ASEAN leaders took the opportunity to chide Burma's leaders, a rare event due to the regional body's noninterference principle. In a report at its ministerial meeting, it was announced that $1 billion would be needed for reconstruction. The cyclone had destroyed 450,000 homes, damaged 350,000 others, flooded 600,000 hectares of farmland, and severely damaged or destroyed 75 percent of hospitals and clinics in the region. For their part, Burmese leaders played down the report. They also claimed survivor reports had been faked and falsely portrayed government aid efforts. Gradually, the junta allowed more and more aid to trickle in to the worst-hit areas.

In the aftermath of Cyclone Nargis, government repression of political opponents continued unabated. Sixty-five-year prison sentences were handed down to fourteen prodemocracy activists just before 2009 arrived. Charged with instigating the 2007 protests were some of the veteran leaders of the 8888 Uprising. The extra-long sentences served as a message from the SPDC to future protesters that life in prison could be the expected price for political activism under the junta's watch. The charade of political reform continued with elections announced for 2010—only government-approved parties and candidates will be eligible to compete for seats in a new bicameral assembly.

INSTITUTIONS AND SOCIAL GROUPS

The Military

Since independence, the Burmese military has played the central role in governmental affairs. No other institutions or social classes have even been allowed to compete with the military. With the exception of Brunei, where the monarchy controls every aspect of society, no Southeast Asian nation has been ruled by a single institution to the same degree as Burma.

By the early 1960s, the Tatmadaw, which began as a popular pro-independence force under Aung San, was the only credibly unified force in the country. Ne Win, its undisputed leader, took over state power as a guardian who was above party politics. He ran the government by assigning leading governmental positions to military comrades.

Since independence, the army has intervened to assert its power on four occasions. In 1958, U Nu asked the army to step in temporarily, but in 1962 it took power without an invitation. In 1988, facing a social revolution, it reasserted itself by shuffling top leaders and engaging in a brutal crackdown on protesters. Yet another violent episode of military suppression occurred in 2007 that targeted monks, students, and ordinary citizens engaged in antigovernment protests.

The SPDC is a junta of fourteen high-ranking military officers led by Chairman Than Shwe. Other principal generals include Maung Aye, SPDC vice chairman and army chief since 1993, and Thien Sein, prime minister since 2007. Ne Win's favored protégé, Khin Nyunt, considered a moderate among top generals, served just a brief stint as prime minister before being purged by Than Shwe in 2004. Very little is known about how decisions are made among the ruling generals or within the SPDC junta as a whole. All their meetings are secret, and no one is allowed to report on how policy is determined.

The Tatmadaw grew rapidly from a force of 190,000 in the early 1990s to an estimated 400,000 by 2008. The joint U.S.-U.K. invasions of Afghanistan and Iraq confirmed the junta's belief that outside powers can and will team up to invade weak ones. Forever obsessed with security concerns, the Tatmadaw expanded its armed forces to a size in Southeast Asia second only to Vietnam. At such a pace, the quality of most new recruits is as sketchy as the outdated military hardware that Burma is eagerly trying to replace. Arms purchases have been brisk. Over the past fifteen years, arms deals with China, India, Israel, and other countries have upgraded Burma's weapons systems and doubled the size of its naval fleet. Now two hundred vessels strong, the naval fleet has a new-found mission of protecting the country's offshore oil and natural gas resources, which remain largely untapped.[7] Many observers believe a global arms embargo can be more effective in putting pressure on the regime than the long-standing economic sanctions that play into the hands of the government's autarkic economic development strategy.

Cease-fires with a number of ethnic insurgent groups in the 1990s served to lessen the Tatmadaw's domestic security concerns, at least those related to Burma's ongoing civil war (the longest-running in the world). Concerns over external security and foreign meddling, however, show no signs of abating. The September 2007 protests and Cyclone Nargis in 2008 soberly demonstrated the consequences of the junta's phobic security policies. Forty-five years after their seizure of power, the Tatmadaw's generals have retained institutional autonomy but at the expense of dubious comparisons to Kim Jong Il and the martial state xenophobes who rule North Korea. While such comparisons may exaggerate similarities (Burma is far more open socially and economically than North Korea), the fact they are made at all indicates the sad state of Burmese political life.

Legislature

The Pyithu Hluttaw, a unicameral body, was once elected by the people in single-member constituencies. Prior to 1989, the only legal party was the BSPP, which controlled the nomination of candidates so there would be no deviation from party policy. Twenty-nine members of the legislature were chosen to the Council of State, the supreme executive authority, whose chairman, Ne Win, served as president of the republic. The Council of State nominated a Council of Ministers for the Pyithu Hluttaw to approve. That council chose the prime minister and carried out day-to-day governing responsibilities. The role of the legislature under SLORC was negligible. When the new legislature elected in 1990 was won overwhelmingly by democratic forces, the military promptly shut it down altogether.

As a means to outmaneuver the NLD and bypass the legislative elections of 1990, the SPDC engaged in constitutional reform. The new charter, ostensibly approved by voters amidst Cyclone Nargis, plans for a new bicameral Parliament called the Pyidaungsu Hluttaw. One house, the Pyithu Hluttaw, will seat 440 constituency representatives; the other, the Amytha Hluttaw, will seat 224 representatives equally divided between Burma's regions and states. Of all seats in both houses, 25 percent will be designated for the military, a convenient number since the constitutional amendments will require over 75 percent approval in both houses. The constitution also mandates that Burmese married to foreigners are ineligible for candidacy or public office, blocking any possibility for Aung San Suu Kyi to be constitutionally elected. With the national referendum charter complete, elections for the new legislature are scheduled for 2010.

Political Parties

The only party allowed to function during the period of military dominance until 1988 was the BSPP. Committed to socialist policies, the BSPP became a national mass organization dedicated to supporting Ne Win as leader. In 1988 the BSPP was reborn as the National Unity Party (NUP), which inherited a strong organization and generous funding from its parent organization. The NUP had access to government resources, including transportation, and to government officials who supported the party. During the 1990 election campaign, NUP candidates were the only ones not harassed by government and military bureaucrats.

When political parties were sanctioned in 1989, nearly two hundred parties registered. Most were ethnically or regionally based and supported a particular person. Many small parties were formed, however, to qualify for access to telephones and rations of gasoline the government provided to political parties. Registration as a political party conferred the right to display a signboard, hold gatherings of fewer than five persons, and obtain extra gasoline. Nevertheless, governmental decrees made it impossible to hold meetings of more than five persons, print and distribute party literature, or say anything that might be construed as criticism of the military.[8]

The most important opposition party remains the NLD. Initially, the party was led by Aung Gyi, U Tin O, and Aung San Suu Kyi. Both Aung Gyi and U Tin O were dissident generals forcibly removed from the Tatmadaw before turning on the regime. Aung Gyi later turned on the NLD, resigning after accusing it of being infiltrated by communists. U Tin O, after spending years in prison after falling out with Ne Win in 1976, now spends stints in and out of detention along with Aung San Suu Kyi.

Aung San Suu Kyi, the daughter of independence hero Aung San, was schooled in Burma during her first fifteen years. A member of a prominent family, she was then sent to India, where her mother was ambassador, and to England to study politics, philosophy, and economics at Oxford University. She later published books on Burmese history and literature. Prior to 1988, she had no direct political experience and was known primarily as the daughter of Aung San.

Shortly before the 8888 Uprising, she returned to Burma from England to care for her ailing mother. She joined the opposition and, because of her name and superb oratorical ability, began to draw large crowds to her speeches. Burmese women imitated her hair and clothing style. She was cheered for her straightforward attacks against the government and against Ne Win. Her military adversaries, frightened by her mounting popularity, suggested that she was manipulated by communists. On July 20, 1989, the military placed her under house arrest and cut off all communications between her followers and the outside world. While still under arrest, she was awarded the Nobel Peace Prize in December 1991 for her courageous struggle against the military dictatorship. As a political prisoner she has suffered three detentions for a total of thirteen years of her twenty-year return. Attempts by UN Secretary-General Ban Ki-moon to initiate new talks between Burma's leaders and Suu Kyi have yet to produce results.

Her last detention followed the 2003 clash at Depayin, where she and her supporters were brutally attacked by over 1,000 plainclothes thugs, who held ties with the Than Shwe–founded Union Solidarity and Development Association (USDA). Organized in 1993 as a "social welfare organization," the USDA is now considered the "political arm" of the SPDC. With branches in major cities and towns throughout Burma, its grassroots presence is clearly on the rise, fronting for the regime's cooperative efforts with nascent civil society groups. Its followers often appear wearing white long-sleeved shirts and dark green sarongs. The regime dispatched USDA members for rehabilitation efforts following Nargis, its activities prominently displayed on a digital-savvy Web site. USDA members have privileged access to state resources and constituted the bulk of representatives at the constitutional convention, and its local bodies organized the May 2008 charter referendum.

The USDA is also slated to administer the 2010 legislative elections while running its own candidates in races, having formalized itself as a political party.[9] Echoing Golkar, Suharto's pro–New Order quasi-party that co-opted Indonesian interest groups in previous decades, USDA members now stand as the largest pro-junta organization in the country. The USDA's potential to serve as a public counterweight to the NLD is significant. Leery of the organization's veracity, prodemocracy advocates do not view it as a legitimate political party, pointing to its paramilitary thugs at Depayin and during the 2007 crackdown.

Monks

The military is threatened by Burma's 400,000 Buddhist monks, whose numbers are nearly the same as today's military. The monks are highly respected as teachers and religious leaders, and in the past their predecessors have toppled kings. Keeping the monks from rebellion is a key goal of SPDC policy.

The SPDC has even tried to infiltrate the monkhood with its own agents who report to the junta when dissidence arises.

The power of the monks to put political pressure on the junta was demonstrated in 2007. Led by the All Burma Monks Alliance and other groups, the monks brought a moral legitimacy to the demonstrations greater than that of Aung San Suu Kyi. At her gate, monks blessed Suu Kyi. Internationally, images of monks bloodied and beaten drew unique attention to what otherwise may have been lost as everyday third-world unrest. Past events render junta co-optation of Burma's monks unlikely, but Burma's monks are not necessarily a unified force either. As an opposition group that could threaten regime change, however, Buddhist monks do not seek to capture state power and remain destined to play only a supportive role in a broader movement.

Minority Ethnic Groups

During the postindependence period, Burma's minority groups have continued to view themselves primarily in terms of ethnicity rather than nationality. The Karens, Karenni Shans, Kachins, and other groups that fought for state autonomy do not trust the government. In their struggle for minority rights, these groups joined the National Democratic Front (NDF) in revolt. The NDF assumed that the peoples of Burma were members of ethnic-linguistic communities who voluntarily came together in 1947 to form the Union of Burma.[10] In this union, equality of communities was to be reflected in their organization as political units, each having power to govern itself, claim to a reasonable share of the nation's resources, an equal right to develop its land and society, and equal representation in the national government.[11] The states were to be strong and the central government weak. In reality, however, and despite promises to state leaders at the time of independence, the central government became strong and the separate states weak.

To achieve their goals, the minority ethnic groups organized armed insurgencies to protect their territories and to pressure the central government to accept a federated Burma, with ethnic states having autonomy under a federal umbrella government. Many opposition parties in the 1990 elections supported a federal system of government.

In 2001, the NDF and the United Nationalities League for Democracy–Liberated Areas (UNLD-LA) cofounded the Ethnic Nationalities Council (ENC). Moving the fight from armed insurgency to political diplomacy, the ENC's mandate has been to engage in a "tripartite dialogue" between Burma's ethnic minorities, the SPDC, and NLD. With the exception of a handful of rebel groups, armed conflict has largely given way to negotiation in recent years. However, Burma's ethnic minorities, with their long-held goals of state autonomy in a federalized system, await a full conclusion to the world's longest ongoing civil war.

Another problem is opium, which represented a traditional form of livelihood in areas where it has grown for more than a century. The British, of course, profited from the opium trade. Later, ethnic insurgents, as well as the Burmese Communist Party, relied on opium profits to finance their guerrilla activities. Ethnic Chinese brokers and Thai traffickers also became players in a drug-dependent civil war. In the late 1980s, Burma's generals got into the action through cease-fire deals where, in exchange for loyalty, they granted rebels autonomy and basic freedom to pursue narcotics. More deals in recent years, combined with rising Thai demand for methamphetamines, has left opium production in decline and the Burmese drug trade to criminal elements who operate with de facto impunity. To service Thailand's sex industry, human trafficking of Burmese women, often minorities, is dreadfully on the rise as well.

DEMOCRATIZATION

For almost all of its history, Burma has been ruled by autocratic monarchs, colonial administrators, or military leaders. Burma's only experience with democracy was a brief period under the 1947 constitution after independence, when U Nu supported representative institutions, free elections, and civil liberties. The ineffectiveness of U Nu's rule was used to rationalize the military takeover of the government in both 1958 and 1962. Since that time, democratic institutions and behavior, said to be "foreign to the traditions" of the Burmese and a rejected legacy of Western imperialism, have been suppressed. Burma is a politically closed regime.

Burmese political culture, with its emphasis on hierarchy and status, is not conducive to democracy. Paternalistic authority is inconsistent with democracy's reliance on equality of opportunity, freedom of speech and assembly, and representative institutions. Burmese leaders, like those in Thailand during periods of military rule, argue that the quest for modernization and for security from outside aggressors demands strong, effective government.

Burma's political culture may be changing as its people learn increasingly about life outside their country. The inability of the Burmese government to develop the nation economically, together with questions over the regime's legitimacy and methods of oppression, leads Burmese to frequently rebel against their leaders. Events in 1988 and 2007 suggest that despite their isolation from world events, many Burmese desire similar freedoms and opportunities now enjoyed by the once-oppressed peoples of Eastern Europe, East Asia, and other areas experiencing greater political liberalization and democracy. Learning about economic success and higher standards of living in neighboring Thailand, Malaysia, and rising India, the Burmese know that their government's claim that rigid authoritarianism is necessary for economic development is false. Despite the high-profile actions of its prodemocracy advocates, however, Burma has not begun a transition to democracy.

ECONOMIC DEVELOPMENT

The similarities between Burma and Thailand are striking. Both nations have had histories of absolute monarchy; both have practiced Theravada Buddhism; and both have comparable natural resources and fertile soils for agriculture. In the 1950s, Burma and Thailand also shared a similar size of GNP. In view of these similarities, why has Thailand had success in its quest for economic and political development while Burma has failed?

One answer stems from the most obvious difference between the two nations: The Burmese were colonized by the British, whereas the Thais have been independent throughout their history. The Thais, who did not develop an inferiority complex toward the West or antipathy to Western ways, were therefore more flexible about adopting and adapting westernization. In contrast, the Burmese consciously eschewed Western ways, including the materialism and commercialism of Western culture, which the Burmese generals believe have ruined Thai society.

Another answer is that the postindependence governments of Burma chose to isolate their nation from the global economic system, relying on government-controlled socialistic economics and autarky. Thailand, on the other hand, opened its economy through a policy of greater market freedom and export-driven growth. The results are dramatic: Thailand's per capita GDP rose from $100 in the 1950s to almost $3,000 in 2006, whereas in the same period Burma's rose from $100 to less than $300. Even when calculated in terms of purchasing power parity (PPP), Burma's per capita income in 2007 was only $1,039, the lowest in Southeast Asia.

"The Burmese Way to Socialism," which sought the marriage of Marxism and Buddhism, proved to be an economic failure; it led to neither socialism nor development. In addition to weaknesses inherent to state-controlled production, policies associated with the ideology repressed the Chinese and Indian minorities who served as the core of business and entrepreneurship in other Southeast Asian countries. It also led to a dual economy with a large unofficial black market. Black market prices in Burma have often been higher than official prices, creating incentives for those with access to state resources or imported goods to participate. On the other hand, sellers in the black market ironically benefit by increasing their incomes and by expanding supply, thus lessening consumer frustration. For example, telephones, gasoline, and entertainment products, in short supply, are often made available through the black market. But no country achieves overall development based on black market activity. Combined with poor educational and rural development programs, isolation has kept Burma poor.

Burma's economy reached its nadir in 1987 when the United Nations granted the once prosperous nation the ignoble status of least developed country (LDC), placing Burma in the same category as Chad, Ethiopia, and Haiti. Whereas Burma once controlled 28 percent of the world's rice trade, it controlled only 2 percent by 1970.[12] Years later, the brutal suppression of demonstrators in 1988 ended the few ongoing Western development projects, reducing the external capital that had been available to the government.

To counter this cessation of aid, Burma opened border trade with Thailand and China and promulgated more liberal foreign investment laws in the 1990s. Foreign investors were permitted to form either wholly owned enterprises or joint ventures in which the foreign partner was required to hold a minimum 35 percent stake. However, little investment was induced by the government's policy because of the country's political instability. What did arrive left quickly. Multinational firms such as PepsiCo, Wal-Mart, Levi Strauss & Co., Tommy Hilfiger, and Liz Claiborne pulled out after short stints. Unfavorable business conditions, pressure from human rights activists, and a 1998 U.S. government ban on new American investment in Burma further inhibited Western investment. In 2004, even more restrictive U.S. laws targeted Burmese imports and prohibited any payments into the country. China, Japan, and ASEAN governments, however, increased economic dealings with junta leaders through policies of "constructive engagement." Burma was permitted to join ASEAN in 1997.

Unable to compete with Southeast Asian NICs and China in textiles, manufacturing, and direct foreign investment (FDI), Burma's leaders shifted attention to natural resources. Extractive industries and the energy sector, they realized, were in high demand, and sector revenues often went directly to the state. Burma now exports natural gas and sells offshore exploration rights to Asian and Western partners. China, for its part, is fast becoming Burma's most interdependent trading partner. Seeking to bypass its Middle East oil shipments through the Malacca Strait, China will finance an oil pipeline from Burma's Western coast to Yunnan, in China's southwest. Burmese leaders are also expanding biodiesel production, coercing some farmers to plant biofuel-friendly physic nut trees. One program, with a goal to convert 8 million acres of farmland to physic nut production, resulted in forced land allocation and production quotas nationwide.[13]

It is difficult to be precise about economic growth in Burma because government figures are unreliable. Even so, confidence in the overall picture is possible. In the early 1990s, Burma's annual economic growth rate hovered around 1 percent to 2 percent, and the overall standard of living, especially among rural people dependent on agriculture, had fallen. Only the presence of a black market made the economy tolerable. In the mid-1990s, economic growth rates improved to the 4 percent to 6 percent level, as foreign firms flirted with in-country investments. Following its shift to the energy sector and natural gas exports, state revenues rose and civil servants experienced large pay raises. The country's trade surplus also grew. Since 2000, Burmese government officials commonly report double-digit growth rates, though many analysts estimate actual rates in the 5 percent to 6 percent range.

Whatever claims regime leaders make, Burma's overall socioeconomic picture remains bleak. Ordinary citizens struggle mightily through a chaotic maze of dual prices, inflation, shortages, bribery, and uncertainty. High inflation, caused in part by rapid salary increases for state employees, plagues the economy. To finance its chronic budget deficit, the government often resorts to printing money needed to cover imports of military matériel and luxury goods. At the street level, Burma's informal sector rivals its formal economy in size and a black market persists. The country's basic infrastructure is crumbling or nonexistent, especially in the countryside. Wasteful construction projects, such as rebuilding the country's administrative capital, create unnecessary opportunity costs on public funds. Corruption at all levels remains rampant. In its 2007 rankings of 179 countries, Transparency International ranked Burma dead last! By this measure Burma is home to the world's most corrupt government (tied with Somalia and well below the rankings of Nigeria and Zimbabwe).

Years of economic autarky and isolation have left Burmese far worse off than almost all of their Southeast Asian neighbors. Indeed, across the region very few people are worse off than the Burmese. The Human Development Index (HDI), which measures income, life expectancy, and education, now ranks Burma below Cambodia and Laos. Only the neophyte country of Timor-Leste ranks lower.

THE BURMESE STATE

The Burmese state has been dominated by a small number of rulers and institutions. Absolute monarchs and British administrators followed by a military general have made the authoritative decisions that have affected the entire Burmese citizenry. In the postindependence period, General Ne Win and the state became one and the same. Ne Win and his subordinates constituted the officials who decided public policy that is binding on the society. His domination of the state was impressive, but his capacity to meet the people's needs was weak.

Burma has poorly developed institutions outside the military. Junta leaders attempted to institutionalize pro-SPDC support through its subsidiary organization, the NUP, and the recent cultivation of the USDA. External institutions, such as a parliament, established political parties, and interest groups, have had little influence over the state's policy decisions. In this sense, the Burmese state has been strong and autonomous, independent of societal organizations.

Whereas in Thailand the integration of the military into the political process increased governmental capacity, in Burma the integration reduced capacity. In Thailand, the military worked in conjunction with the bureaucrats, the monarchy, and interest groups in responding to demands of the citizenry. Unlike Thailand's military, Burma's military used force rather than co-optation and coordination to retain its power. Only recently, through cease-fire agreements with ethnic rebels and coordination with pro-junta USDA, are signs of a co-optation strategy emerging.

In Thailand, the state authorities managed to achieve economic growth and rising incomes, primarily by allowing the nation's entrepreneurs to promote economic development. In Burma, however, the state authorities intervened in every aspect of the economy—nationalizing public utilities, industries, and agribusinesses and placing numerous obstacles in the path of entrepreneurs. The Burmese state has shown little adaptability to changes in the international and regional spheres and to the worldwide movement toward democratization. This lack of adaptability has undermined the legitimacy once enjoyed by the Tatmadaw. The military is no longer the respected unifier of the nation; instead, it is viewed as a tool for opportunism by supporters and a symbol of stagnation and oppression by its detractors. In this regard, the Burmese state at present is viewed as weak. It is a patronage operation with low capacity and legitimacy levels.

Burma's ongoing crisis is perhaps less about human rights than it is about the legitimacy of those who wield state authority.[14] Many within Burma, as well as many outside it, view the SPDC and Than Shwe as illegitimate. A final resolution of the legitimacy question remains the fundamental tension of Burmese politics.

Tatmadaw leaders harbor deep fears over challenges to their legitimacy. State leaders justify centralized authority on the grounds of national unity (under threat of ethnic separatism) and national sovereignty (under threat by foreign meddling and intervention). In Burma, civil society groups are viewed with suspicion. Following Cyclone Nargis, for example, Than Shwe equated the presence of foreign aid workers as akin to an erosion of state sovereignty. Unlike those of Thailand, Burma's rulers have not invited technocrats, politicians, intellectuals, or socioeconomic elites to participate in state affairs. The few outsiders brought into the polity have no autonomous political base or constituency. In this sense, Burma's state is weak. Burma does not meet the condition for a strong state requiring the presence of groups that are willing and able to execute the grand designs of state leaders.

Outside of Burma, UN membership provides state leaders a thin layer of international legitimacy. Top generals, of course, remain leery of UN intentions regarding Burma. Viewing it as obsessed with human rights, Burma wants little to do with the international community. Unlike that of Thailand, where, despite messy political quarrels, the state's legitimacy remains unquestioned internationally, Burma's state leadership remains surrounded at home and abroad by the deepest political questions over its rightful authority to state power.

FOREIGN POLICY

There are many good reasons why the Burmese have emphasized the importance of national security. Their colonial heritage and the Japanese occupation are reminders that Burma has been a victim of both imperialism and aggression. Burma is surrounded by nations with far greater populations and military strength, sharing a thousand-mile border with both China and India as well as with Thailand. Burma's ethnic minorities have been supported by outsiders, linked with the drug trade, and associated with elements of the Burmese Communist Party. Moreover, the nation's Indian and Chinese minorities have an influence in the Burmese economy disproportionate to their numbers. Finally, the government views westernization as a threat to Burmese traditional culture.

The government's response to this insecurity has been a policy of non-alignment. Earlier, Burma attempted to maintain an isolationist foreign policy by refusing to participate in the Indochina conflict, eschewing aid from various nations, and, until the late 1990s, forgoing membership in ASEAN. However, isolationism did not foster economic growth and, under the SPDC, Burma moved to a policy of modified isolationism. Relations with developed countries remain icy but Asian neighbors are reciprocating invitations from Rangoon to talk trade.[15]

Relations with Thailand have always been tense because of the history of conflict between the two nations. However, relations improved following the 1988 revolt when Burma, desperate for foreign capital, agreed to Thai requests to exploit its teak forests. Burmese concessions to Thai companies, prohibited from logging in Thailand due to new environmental laws, permitted extraction of 1.2 million tons of logs annually.[16] For the first time in decades, official and legal border trade was also established between Thailand and Burma.

Since the 1990s, several Thai politicians and military leaders have visited Burma to coordinate trade, drug eradication, and offshore oil exploration. The leader installed by Thailand's 2006 military coup made his first foreign trip to Burma. Elected Thai Prime Minister Samak Sundaravej, who replaced the coup-installed prime minister, made an official visit to Burma months after the 2007 mass demonstrations, only to return praising Than Shwe as a good Buddhist and throwing his support behind the SPDC's constitutional reform process. Unsurprisingly, Thailand was the first country Burmese generals permitted to offer (belated) relief aid for cyclone victims.

Relations with Burma's other major neighbors, India and China, are warming as well. Earlier, following the 8888 Uprising, the Indian government expressed support for the Burmese people's resolve to achieve democracy. The two countries now trade in arms and share interests in Burma's offshore gas and oil. China, even more aggressively than India, has cultivated relations with Burma during the post-1988 period of modified isolationism. Border trade, energy interests, the prospect of a trans-Burma oil pipeline to Yunnan, and common interpretations of state sovereignty bring the two countries together. General Maung Aye, second to Than Shwe, made a state visit to Russia in 2006 to enhance relations. In fact, improved relations with Thailand, India, China, and Russia are bolstering the junta's confidence to handle domestic issues on its own terms.[17] All of these countries remained conspicuously absent from the international criticism that followed the Tatmadaw's 2007 crackdown on monks and protesters. Only Japan, another principal partner, withdrew aid in response to the protests and the death of a Japanese photojournalist covering the event.

Earlier, in 1990, the United States downgraded its representation in Burma from an ambassador to a chargé d'affaires but did not sever relations following antigovernment protests. To the extent any cooperation between the two governments has since that time occurred, it has been primarily to address narcotics trafficking in the region. Otherwise, it has been one tough measure followed by another. The Clinton administration condemned Burma's oppressive system, imposing visa restrictions on junta members and their families. These acts were followed by increased restrictions on trade and imports and, in 2007, executive orders from George W. Bush directed at blocking the assets of twenty-five top Burmese officials. To an international audience, First Lady Laura Bush publicly chided junta leaders following Cyclone Nargis. On her first trip to Asia as President Barack Obama's Secretary of State, Hillary Clinton announced that the U.S. policy on Burma was under review in hopes of encouraging "more effective" political and economic reform to "help the Burmese people."

Burma's new modified isolationism brought it into the orbit of regional cooperation, but ASEAN, a body committed to noninterference, struggles with the junta's ongoing repression. One caucus of ASEAN state parliamentarians has even proposed Burma's expulsion from the body following the violent events of 2007. ASEAN leaders had hoped Burma's membership would pull the nation away from its most important ally, China, but this hope remains unrealized. Many ASEAN states themselves, like Burma, are seeking closer cooperation with rising China.

To the relief of many ASEAN ministers, Than Shwe's government declined its turn to chair ASEAN in 2006. Burma's presence in the organization is forever troublesome. ASEAN leaders argue that international sanctions isolate Burma and that democratic reforms in the country would come about most readily through constructive persuasion. How long each of its members can remain committed to this policy remains uncertain. Events such as the 2007 crackdown and dreadful mishandling of Cyclone Nargis are causing parliaments and legislatures in the region to put pressure on foreign ministers to abandon policies of noninterference.

CONCLUSION

Burma's future is unclear because the state is in a period of traumatic transition. Although the move from socialism to capitalism appears to have begun, the move from authoritarian military rule to democracy is still problematic. Most significant, the Burmese will continue to resolve their problems at their own pace, refusing to become dependent on outsiders. While the authorities' first goal is to perpetuate their power, they maintain that Burma's development will be based on indigenous values and not on crass westernization.

In 2012, the Burmese military junta will reach fifty years in power. Than Shwe, at seventy-four, is increasingly ill, suffering from chronic diabetes, coronary disease, and failing kidneys, which require dialysis on a daily basis. Signs of divisions within the Tatmadaw have been slow to emerge. Maung Aye, a septuagenarian himself, is viewed as more pragmatic than Than Shwe, but among Burma's generals, pragmatism is a relative term. The military leaders who follow Than Shwe and Maung Aye will likely take the same slow path to change. For them to reverse course and allow Aung San Suu Kyi and the NLD a path to power is virtually unthinkable. For their part, opposition leaders find SPDC measures to alter constitutional rules unacceptable, portending more clashes that pit prodemocracy demonstrators and monks against junta leaders and security forces. A Burma that is governed by a legitimate, democratically designed and elected legislature, however desirable, appears only as a distant dream.

Expanding membership in the pro-junta USDA could provide new channels for patronage and popular participation. In the most positive scenario, Burma's future may find more peace under a corporatist pattern akin to Indonesia under Suharto. The real enigma lies in how the SPDC, under current policies, could ever achieve the degree of economic success that extended New Order rule for thirty years. To move from a coercive system to one built on performance legitimization would be a remarkable achievement for Burma's generals.

The Burmese polity will not lose its authoritarian character overnight, nor will Western-style democracy immediately flourish if Aung San Suu Kyi were to suddenly find a path to power. Patron-client politics, factionalism, and oligarchy have been essential elements of Burmese politics and will continue to be important factors. Outside observers might do well to recognize that a politically balanced democracy is not the sole alternative for Burma. A more benign form of authoritarian control could prove more stable. The current patterns of Tatmadaw military control, however, are no longer acceptable to many Burmese.

NOTES

1. The "r" in Myanmar is not pronounced but serves to lengthen the "a" sound. The word is pronounced approximately as "Bamah" (as if the My and B were fairly indistinct). As "Burma" was the universally accepted English-language name for the country until 1989, and to reduce confusion resulting from the use of two names, this chapter will use the name "Burma" throughout. Because no sitting legislature in Burma approved the change at the time it occurred, the U.S. government did not recognize the name change.

2. Burma's population is predominantly Theravada Buddhist (89 percent), found particularly among Burmans, Shan, Mon, and Karens. Christianity (4 percent) is widespread among some Karen groups, Chins, and other upland groups in Northern Burma. Islam (4 percent) exists in pockets among lowland Burmans, Indians, Bengalis, and the predominantly Muslim Rohingya minority of Western Burma. Many upland groups along Burma's borders practice traditional indigenous beliefs, commonly shared with transnational ethic relations scattered throughout Southeast Asia and southwest China.

3. Burma Watcher, "Burma in 1988," *Asian Survey*, vol. 29, no. 2 (February 1989), p. 174.

4. Thant Myint U, *The River of Lost Footsteps: A Personal History of Burma* (New York: Farrar, Straus and Giroux, 2006), pp. 32–34.

5. Ibid, p. 35.

6. Kyaw Yin Hlaing, "Myanmar in 2003: Frustration or Despair?" *Asian Survey*, vol. 44, no. 1 (January/February 2004), p. 88.

7. Aung Zaw, "A Growing Tatmadaw," *The Irrawaddy*, vol. 14, no. 6 (March 2006), www.irrawaddy.org/print_article.php?art_id=5537.

8. Josef Silverstein, "Aung San Suu Kyi: Is She Burma's Woman of Destiny?" paper presented to the Association for Asian Studies, Chicago, April 1990, p. 10.

9. Wai Moe, "USDA to Organize Referendum, Election," *The Irrawaddy* (11 February 2008), http://www.irrawaddy.org/article.php?art_id=10260.

10. Josef Silverstein, "National Unity in Burma: Is It Possible?" in *Durable Stability in Southeast Asia*, ed. Kusuma Snitwongse and Sukhumbhand Paribatra (Singapore: Institute of Southeast Asian Studies, 1987), p. 80.

11. Ibid., pp. 80–81.

12. Maureen Aung-Thwin, "Burmese Days," *Foreign Affairs*, vol. 68, no. 2 (February 1989), p. 150.

13. Ardeth Maung Thawnghmung and Maung Aung Myoe, "Myanmar in 2006: Another Year of Housekeeping?" *Asian Survey*, vol. 47, no. 1 (January/February 2007), p. 197.

14. Chao-Tzang Yawnghwe, "Burma: Depoliticization of the Political," in *Political Legitimacy in Southeast Asia: The Quest for Moral Authority*, ed. Muthiah Alagappa (Stanford, CA: Stanford University Press, 1995), p. 191.

15. Kyaw Yin Hlaing, "Myanmar in 2003: Frustration and Despair?" *Asian Survey*, vol. 44, no. 1 (January/February 2004), p. 90.

16. James F. Guyot and John Badgley, "Myanmar in 1989," *Asian Survey*, vol. 30, no. 2 (February 1990), p. 191.

17. Thawnghmung and Aung Myoe, "Myanmar in 2006," p. 198.

RESOURCE GUIDE

A useful tool for bibliographic and other information on Burma is available from Australia National University's WWW Virtual Library: www.gksoft.com/govt/en/kh.html. The University of California–Berkeley maintains a useful portal for digital and print resources on Burma: www.lib.berkeley.edu/SSEAL/SoutheastAsia/seaelec.html. Northern Illinois University's Southeast Asia Digital Library includes a range of useful links that cover government, academic, and research institutions specific to Burma: http://sea.lib.niu.edu. The University of Wisconsin–Madison Libraries maintains a list of digital and print resources on Burma: www.library.wisc.edu/guides/SEAsia/resarea.html. The Library of Congress maintains an Internet resource guide on Burma at www.loc.gov/rr/international/portals.html#t.

The government-controlled newspaper of Burma, the *New Light of Myanmar*, is available online at www.myanmar.com/newspaper/nlm/index.html. The Union Solidarity and Development Association (USDA) promotes its activities on its official site (in English): www.usda.org.mm/eng/index.php.

A number of Internet news sources are also available from Burmese in exile and human rights organizations, including *The Irrawaddy* at www.irrawaddy.org; *Mizzima News* at www.mizzima.com; and the *Burmese Digest* at http://burmadigest.wordpress.com. Aung San Suu Kyi's own site is www.dassk.com (often not functional).

Sites devoted to ethnic minority groups include the Ethnic Nationalities Council at www.encburma.org and the Karen Human Rights group at www.khrg.org. Voices for Burma is an organization that promotes "responsible tourism" as a means to support local communities and ethnic minority areas within Burma: www.voicesforburma.org.

9

VIETNAM

Stretching some twelve hundred miles from its border with China to its southernmost point in the South China Sea, Vietnam is shaped like two rice baskets at either end of a pole. The bulk of the population lives in the two "baskets": the Red River Delta in the north and the Mekong River Delta in the south. The "pole" is the mountainous stretch of territory in the central, sparsely populated part of the country.

Vietnam, with more people than France, Germany, or Egypt, is the world's thirteenth most populous country. The majority of Vietnam's 87 million people work in agriculture. Formerly, most Vietnamese practiced Mahayana Buddhism, but Vietnamese society has been secularized since independence so that most residents do not actively practice or pursue religious beliefs. Among those who do, Buddhism still predominates, although about 7 percent are Roman Catholics, a religion brought to Vietnam during the French colonial period. Confucianist principles from the nation's Chinese heritage remain widespread across society and stress centralized political authority, duty, and subordination to superiors: ruled to ruler, son to father, and pupil to teacher. Many minority religions also exist in Vietnam, including the indigenous Cao Dai and Hoa Hao sects, with over 1 million adherents each.[1]

Nationalism has been the key concept for understanding Vietnamese politics. Indeed, Vietnam's search for a national identity received its greatest impetus during the thousand-year Chinese domination (111 BC–AD 939). The ability of the Vietnamese to emerge from that period with many of their traditions intact is a clear indication of the nationalist urge that has pervaded the country's history. Similarly, the struggle against French colonialism, Japanese occupation, and U.S. intervention reflects the importance of that nationalism.

Vietnam has not always been united. During the era of French colonialism, the country was divided into three areas: Tonkin in the north, with Hanoi as the capital; Annam in the middle, with Hue as the capital; and in the south, Cochin China, whose capital was Saigon. Traditionally, the northerners have

seen themselves as modern, progressive, and efficient, and they have viewed the southerners as lazy. The Annamese have seen themselves as highly cultured, the northerners as grasping, and the southerners as rustic. Southerners have regarded themselves as pacifistic and their northern neighbors as aggressive and violent.

In addition to these differing regional perceptions, national unification had to overcome the cultural and political dichotomy between the rural areas and the cities. Such interaction as there was consisted largely of the exploitation of the peasantry by the mandarin class. Moreover, Vietnam is populated by minority groups that have traditionally been treated with disdain by the Vietnamese majority.

Despite the divisiveness that has characterized much of Vietnamese history, a nationalist continuity has remained in the form of anticolonialism and anti-neoimperialism. Following the Japanese defeat in 1945, Ho Chi Minh—the leader of the League for the Independence of Vietnam, known as the Vietminh—proclaimed the country's independence and set up a provisional government that he headed. The first lines of Ho's historic speech of Vietnamese freedom were lifted directly from the U.S. Declaration of Independence. The French and representatives of the newly established Democratic Republic of Vietnam, led by Ho, initially agreed that a new independent state existed and that the French would not move to reclaim their former colony. However, the agreement broke down, and a series of clashes ignited the First Indochina War, which lasted eight years and became an object of U.S. Cold War interests.

The military defeat of the French led to the Geneva Conference of 1954, which sought to separate the rival French and Vietminh forces by setting up a temporary military demarcation line at the seventeenth parallel. This line was not intended to be a political or territorial boundary. In addition, the Geneva agreements called for eventual national elections to establish a single administration throughout the country. During the Geneva Conference, an anti-Vietminh administration emerged below the seventeenth parallel, led initially by the former Annamese emperor Bao Dai and subsequently by the strongly anticommunist Catholic mandarin Ngo Dinh Diem. On October 26, 1955, Diem proclaimed the Republic of Vietnam, better known as South Vietnam, with its capital in Saigon and himself as the first president; he had the support of the United States. He repudiated the Geneva agreements, specifically the provision for national elections.

Ho Chi Minh had agreed to the Geneva agreements at least partly because he believed that national elections would ensure reunification under communist Vietminh leadership. Ho, who was both a nationalist and a communist, saw the two ideologies as inseparable. His goal of a united Vietnam was scuttled when it became clear that Diem had no intention of merging with the north.

During Diem's increasingly repressive rule in the late 1950s, South Vietnam became the site of a guerrilla insurgency against his government. The political arm of the guerrilla activity was the National Liberation Front (NLF), which was initially an autonomous southern-based movement. The military arm was known as the Viet Cong (Vietnamese Communist). A large number of northerners who had moved to the south following the Geneva Conference joined these guerrillas. In the early 1960s the North Vietnamese provided increasing military support to the NLF. The People's Revolutionary Party— South Vietnam's communist party, which was controlled by the north— gradually came to dominate the NLF until ultimately the two organizations were indistinguishable.

To counteract the insurgency, Diem relied on U.S. advisers, weaponry, money, and soldiers. U.S. support began in 1954 with 1,000 advisers, which increased to 5,000 by 1960. Despite this support, Diem's own position deteriorated until U.S. President John Kennedy acquiesced to a coup d'état against Diem by South Vietnamese generals. The coup, which took place in October 1963, and Diem's concurrent death paved the way for a dozen ineffective and unstable military governments, which were less interested in economic or social reforms than in a military victory over the Viet Cong and the North Vietnamese.

U.S. involvement continued to escalate. In February 1965, the United States began massive bombing of the north to interdict North Vietnamese supply lines, erode morale, and provide time for the south to strengthen its forces. None of these purposes was achieved. By 1968, half a million U.S. military personnel were in Vietnam, but the Tet offensive by the north, which involved coordinated attacks on all major cities and towns in the south, demonstrated the ineffectiveness of the U.S. bombing policy, demoralized American troops, and fully revealed the communists' unyielding will to suffer mass casualties for their cause. Opposition to the war in the United States intensified, and President Lyndon Johnson announced he would not seek reelection.

Ho Chi Minh's death in 1969, meanwhile, hardened his followers' resolve to realize the vision of a unified country. A collective leadership arose in Ho's absence with Le Duan the first among equals. No one could replace Ho, for his stature was too vast to be inherited by a single person. The leadership transition proceeded smoothly without major shifts in war strategy or destabilizing factional purges. The Soviet Union, China, and other countries of the communist bloc continued giving the north material support. The guerrilla warfare tactics of General Vo Nguyen Giap thoroughly frustrated U.S. troops and commanders. U.S. losses mounted from month to month.

South Vietnam had increasingly become a client state of the United States. To reduce this dependency and to blunt rising U.S. protests against the war, in the early 1970s President Richard Nixon began a policy of "Vietnamization"—

the gradual withdrawal of U.S. troops from Vietnam—while escalating the bombing against the north. In May 1970, U.S. and South Vietnamese troops invaded Cambodia, ostensibly to halt Viet Cong use of Cambodian "sanctuaries." The result, however, was a massive escalation of the war to all of Indochina, unparalleled demonstrations in the United States against the war, and the unification of insurgent forces in Cambodia.

Following Nixon's historic 1972 visit to China and the Christmas bombing of Hanoi later that same year (in which 40,000 tons of bombs were dropped), the Paris Peace Accords were signed by the contending powers in January 1973. North Vietnam agreed to a cease-fire, while the United States agreed not only to a cessation of bombing in the north but also to withdrawal of its troops. The Paris Peace Accords were essentially a victory for the north because North Vietnamese troops were able to stay in place. Without U.S. bombing support and financial aid (the United States had spent over $112 billion in Vietnam since the 1950s), South Vietnam could not withstand the pressure from the north.

The rationale for U.S. intervention in Vietnam had several foundations. The first concern was the perceived national interest of the United States itself. Most U.S. policymakers saw the fall of Vietnam to communism as one more stage in the growth of a cancer that could eventually spread to America itself. Thus, South Vietnam became a testing ground for communist wars of national liberation. It was believed that anything less than a committed stand against communist aggression would be tantamount to an invitation for further aggression in other parts of the world. American policymakers also cited the commitment of five presidents, the terms of the Southeast Asia Treaty Organization (SEATO), and agreements with South Vietnam as justification for U.S. involvement; they believed that American credibility as a world power was at stake.

Finally, decisions regarding Vietnam were also a function of internal pressure. Each president feared a political backlash if he were seen as soft on communism or responsible for the defeat of South Vietnam. Therefore, Vietnam became the test of presidential strength, especially for Johnson and Nixon, both of whom articulated the need for total victory.

U.S. rationale for intervention was in part a function of the ignorance and arrogance of American policymakers at the time. A lack of appreciation for Vietnamese history, society, and culture, combined with a blind belief in faulty theories of democracy and mistaken assessments of U.S. power, doomed U.S. policymakers from the start. U.S. policy in Vietnam was the unfortunate result of several small steps, gradual escalatory moves that by themselves seemed restrained to strategists but that in sum committed American blood and treasure to an unwinnable war. Policy decisions resulted in a war in which over 2 million American soldiers fought and 58,000 died.

In April 1975, North Vietnamese troops moved swiftly through the south, conquering province after province and eventually capturing Saigon. A war for Vietnamese independence that had endured for three decades came to a swift close. The cost of victory was over 2 million Vietnamese dead, with millions more injured and displaced. Cities, towns, and rural villages were left devastated from years of conflict. More bombs were dropped during "the American War"—as the Vietnamese refer to it—than were dropped in all past wars combined. About 4 million Vietnamese (as well as thousands of U.S. veterans) would also become long-term sufferers of the crippling effects of Agent Orange, a toxic defoliant dropped from U.S. planes to clear forests for war.

The immediate causes of the communist victory included the corruption of the South Vietnamese army and the end of U.S. support. Longer-term reasons for the communist success included the artificiality of the south's political system. The South Vietnamese government, which did not meet the needs of the people, was viewed by northerners as well as many southerners as a lackey of the United States. The war was also never fully understood by U.S. policymakers, who underestimated the importance of nationalism and the tenacity of the Vietnamese people to withstand great pressure. Moreover, the war never received the wholehearted support of the American public or of even a large element of the government. As the war continued, more and more Americans became convinced that the means used by the U.S. government were disproportionate to the stated goals.

The North Vietnamese moved swiftly to consolidate their power. Not since the 1860s, when the French began appropriating Vietnamese territory, had Vietnam been fully unified and absent foreign occupation. The newly united nation was named the Socialist Republic of Vietnam. Ho Chi Minh's goal of a united Vietnam under communist rule was reached, and in his honor Saigon was renamed Ho Chi Minh City. Hanoi became the nation's capital. Plans were carried out to transform the south's economy from capitalism to socialism, and "reeducation camps" were established to indoctrinate former partisans of the South Vietnamese government with socialist values. An estimated 2.5 million Vietnamese were sent to these camps, which lasted into the mid-1990s.

The southerners did not take well to the economic programs of their new rulers, and many fled the country in a first wave of refugees. They resisted efforts to collectivize and redistribute the land. Moreover, the Vietnamese economy deteriorated, worsened by drought and the diversion of resources to its military in Cambodia and along the Chinese border. Poor management and planning by the central authorities were also responsible for the economic catastrophe the new revolutionary government faced.

As the Vietnamese government ended the traditional free-market system in the south, the indigenous Chinese, long the mainstay of entrepreneurship in Saigon (now Ho Chi Minh City), fled the country. The government's reform of the monetary system had wiped out the savings of these shop owners. The result was a second wave of refugees, this time ethnic Chinese who fled by sea and thus became known as "boat people." During 1978 and 1979, 75,000 refugees per month fled Vietnam, arriving on the shores of Thailand, Malaysia, Singapore, Indonesia, the Philippines, and Hong Kong, overwhelming those countries' humanitarian resources.[2] Close to 1 million Vietnamese of all ethnic backgrounds left the country in the years following the communist takeover.

On December 25, 1978, with the concurrence of the Soviet Union, Vietnamese troops invaded Cambodia and established a new government led by an unknown Vietnamese-trained Cambodian named Heng Samrin. The Vietnamese claimed that they launched their invasion to restore order and security in border areas by punishing Cambodia for a long series of border incursions and for intransigence in negotiations. The Vietnamese also insisted that they were liberating Cambodians from the genocide and repression of the Pol Pot regime. The invasion acted as an impetus for the subsequent Chinese invasion of Vietnam in February 1979. The Chinese hoped their own offensive would force Vietnam to withdraw its occupation force of 200,000 troops from Cambodia. China desired to "teach Vietnam a lesson," to convince the Vietnamese that China was not a paper tiger, to punish the country for its harsh treatment of overseas Chinese, and to send a signal to the Soviet Union that China would not acquiesce to growing Soviet influence in Southeast Asia. Although neither country was able to claim clear-cut victory, Vietnamese forces remained in Cambodia.

Vietnamese expectations that independence from foreign exploitation for the first time in over a hundred years would bring them a better life were dashed by the continued deterioration of the economy. In the 1980s, a decade after their defeat of the United States—the world's mightiest and most technologically sophisticated nation—the Vietnamese people's standard of living was worse than before the war. Indeed, the economy had advanced little since the French colonization of Vietnam in the late nineteenth century.[3]

The Sixth Congress of the Communist Party of Vietnam (CPV) realized the seriousness of the economic malaise and met in December 1986 to implement a plan to remedy the problems. Nguyen Van Linh, a prominent reformer, was named CPV general secretary. His appointment and the retirement of such old-guard communist revolutionary leaders as President Truong Chinh, Premier Pham Van Dong, and Foreign Minister Le Duc Tho signaled a significant turn in Vietnamese politics. The leadership shift to the more pragmatic, economically oriented, reform-minded younger officials from the ideologically conservative, security-minded party leaders was the first major break in leadership patterns since Ho Chi Minh came to power after World War II.

At the December 1986 party congress, Linh set forth a policy of renovation (*doi moi*), a plan publicly approved by the CPV leaders, all of whom agreed that the policies of the previous eleven years—since the end of the war—should not be continued. Renovation called for major economic and political changes with the proviso that the party-led dictatorship of the proletariat remain sacrosanct. The move was timed, not coincidentally, with Gorbachev's decision for the Soviet Union to reduce support for client states and move domestically toward perestroika, or economic restructuring.

Nevertheless, despite past failures, reform was difficult because a strong coalition of conservative party leaders felt threatened by the changes. CPV leaders feared that the party's dominance would be lost, and military leaders—who played an important role in the politburo—believed that renovation threatened national security because it diminished the importance of military strength in favor of economic development.[4]

The changes included rapid movement away from the centrally planned economy and development of a more market-oriented model. The shift built upon the economic reforms that had begun in the late 1970s when a contract system was introduced and decentralization of various sectors of the economy was carried out. The contract system had allowed peasants to sell a small portion of their crops after meeting their obligations to the government. That system had stagnated when peasants refused to cooperate because their profits were so small that they had no incentive to produce more. The new plan provided greater incentives, including the leasing (and later purchasing) of land formerly nationalized by the government.

Renovation also called for more public debate and more power for the National Assembly, the main legislative branch of the government. Many political prisoners were released and corrupt officials ousted from their positions. The press was allowed to criticize government policies more aggressively, at least until the Seventh Party Congress in 1991. The destabilizing protests in Burma (1988) and China (1989) that preceded the CPV's five-year congress, and the collapse of the Soviet Union that followed, cemented party resolve: *Doi moi* would go forward but open political expression would not.

Although popular, renovation met with sharp criticism when new policies initially failed to improve the economy. In 1988, for example, famine was barely averted in the northern provinces, and inflation increased to almost 1,000 percent. Vietnam's reformers increasingly found themselves on the defensive.

As Vietnam entered the 1990s, the government was in transition from the old-guard revolutionary forces, who had held power in the north since independence, to younger (although still elderly) reform-minded communists, who were more willing to try new means to achieve their aims. Dramatic and far-reaching changes in Vietnam occurred in 1995, when the country normalized diplomatic relations with Washington and became a member of ASEAN, an alliance originally formed to oppose "Vietnamese intervention."

Vietnam's Southeast Asian neighbors, eyeing Vietnam's large market, had accepted Vietnam's economic rebirth.

Economic ties were also the impetus for reconciliation with the United States. Conservative American politicians and business leaders, having seen the advantages to American business from the 1994 lifting of the U.S. embargo against Vietnam, threw support behind plans to support new ties. There was virtually no negative reaction by Americans to the new policy, except for minor complaints against President Bill Clinton himself for not having participated in the war thirty years earlier. The first U.S. ambassador to the Democratic Republic of Vietnam, Douglas "Pete" Peterson, had spent six years in Hanoi as a prisoner of war. Reconciliation, not recrimination, became the new standard in U.S.-Vietnam relations.

Doi moi has created new challenges for the CPV, but from the mid-1980s to the present, the effects of new policies, on balance, have been positive for the Vietnamese. A major challenge has been reform's disproportional benefits. Vietnam's northern and southern regions, once divided and at war, soon found themselves competing under *doi moi* policies for foreign investment, largesse from the state, and political influence. Whereas the north had followed communist economic policies since the 1950s, the south had experienced communist planning for only ten years, from 1975 to 1986. These differences meant many southerners were better equipped with entrepreneurial skills and business acumen as *doi moi* began. Foreign investors, sensitive to business climate and government meddling, also preferred the expansive Ho Chi Minh City and its more hands-off investment zones to smaller and more bureaucratic Hanoi. By 2004, Ho Chi Minh City, with 5 percent of the country's total population, was producing over 20 percent of Vietnam's GDP. The party's top positions increasingly began to favor southerners with track records of reform success.

After a decade of fits and starts and many frustrations by foreign investors, Vietnam's policy shift began to produce dramatic results. Following the south's lead, the Red River Delta region in the north, including many rural provinces, began to experience rapid economic growth. Remarkably, between 1993 and 2004, overall poverty rates in Vietnam fell from 59 percent to 20 percent.[5] Political life remained circumscribed but individual freedoms were expanded. Socially, a new youth culture emerged, symbolized by rock music, fast motorbikes, and high levels of material consumption. The country's first generation raised in a unified, postwar Vietnam found common ground not in Uncle Ho's vision of simple living but in pop culture, music television, and designer logos.[6]

Beyond strong economic growth, ASEAN membership, and normal relations with the United States, Vietnam's final mark of *doi moi* success came in 2006 when it achieved membership in the World Trade Organization (WTO).

At the CPV's 10th Party Congress, held that same year, party business was confined largely to reshuffling leadership positions and staid pledges to enhance government efficiency. Nevertheless, indicating a measured shift toward greater rule of law, the party allowed unprecedented preconference openness and increased transparency of party business.[7] Vietnam's party of reform-minded communists was now more concerned with growth-related official corruption than corrupt policies unable to produce growth. Vietnam's track record of economic success and poverty alleviation was in fact drawing praise from the international community.

Economic growth in Vietnam has produced inequality but at lower levels than in Thailand, Indonesia, and China. Although 70 percent of Vietnamese still reside in rural areas, it is not uncommon for particular provinces to report double-digit growth, driven by food production and agriculture exports. Changes to budgeting procedures have also permitted local authorities more autonomy to allocate expenditures to suit local needs.[8] Improvements in rural development are also credited to Vietnam's collaborative programs with the World Bank and international agencies tied to the United Nations. Vietnam, unlike many of its globalizing neighbors, has not achieved economic growth by abandoning its rural majority.

Unfortunately, Vietnamese leaders have not heeded all the lessons from their neighbors' experiences with boom and bust capital markets. Vietnam's young stock markets in Ho Chi Minh City and Hanoi reached new heights only to collapse precipitously. Between January and June 2008, Vietnamese stocks lost 60 percent of their value. Ho Chi Minh City's market, catering to foreign money, dropped every day it traded in May. Inflation soared over 25 percent and angry consumers reacted by hoarding goods and abandoning the Vietnamese currency. While the experience did not repeat the full effects of the 1997 Asian economic crisis, it raised new questions about the sustainability of *doi moi*–driven growth and CPV governance of the economy. Vietnamese officials were forced to battle inflation and devalue Vietnam's currency while simultaneously trying not to cripple growth or incite social unrest.

In the more than twenty years since reforms began, Vietnam's economic achievements remain noteworthy, especially in terms of overall development. Vietnam today is a different country than it was the decade following "the American War." Before *doi moi*, 60 percent of Vietnamese lived in poverty, forced to suffer in a hopeless economy and with a government unable to provide basic services. Today, less than a fifth of Vietnam's large population lives below the poverty line, and almost everyone has access to basic education, health care, decent employment, and economic opportunity. In comparative terms, over 80 percent of Vietnamese enjoy a standard of living currently unknown to the one in three Burmese, Cambodians, Filipinos, Laotians, and East Timorese who continue to languish below the poverty line, stuck with governments who fail them from year to year. Vietnam today is a Southeast Asian success story—a story of success qualified nonetheless by the cost single-party rule imposes on civil liberties, political freedom, and official justice.

INSTITUTIONS AND SOCIAL GROUPS

Ho Chi Minh

On May 19, 1990, the people of Vietnam celebrated the one hundredth anniversary of Ho Chi Minh's birth. As the founding father of independent, communist Vietnam; the victorious leader over the Japanese, French, and Americans; and the founder of the CPV, Ho is the most important Vietnamese of contemporary times and perhaps the most important leader in recent Southeast Asian history. He was and remains a central institution—the symbol of united, nationalist, communist Vietnam. Pictures of "Uncle Ho" are ubiquitous in Vietnam, statues and busts of the leader adorn public places, and millions of people have viewed his embalmed body in the Soviet-built mausoleum in Hanoi.

Ho was the son of a Confucian scholar who was active in anticolonial activities, and his mother died when he was ten. Throughout his life he used numerous pseudonyms (the name Ho Chi Minh means "he who enlightens"). He spent thirty years abroad, living in and traveling to the Soviet Union, China, New York, London, and Paris. He became a committed communist and founded the forerunner parties of the CPV, including the Indo-Chinese Communist Party in 1930 and the Vietminh in 1941. His tastes were simple, even ascetic, yet he was tenacious and sometimes ruthless in the means he used to achieve his goals.

Ho died six years before the nation was reunited. His last testament requested that at his death there be a one-year moratorium on farm taxes and that his ashes be placed in urns in the three parts of Vietnam: Cochin China, Annam, and Tonkin. However, these requests were not heeded by Ho's successors. Instead, taxes were raised, and his body was embalmed in a massive building similar to Lenin's mausoleum in Moscow. No Vietnamese leader has subsequently received the adulation Ho received during his life, although every leader has attempted to wrap himself in Ho's mantle. "Ho Chi Minh Thought" is the party's guiding philosophy.

Communist Party of Vietnam

Although the communist party rule in postwar Eastern Europe was imposed from without by Soviet arms, the Communist Party is indigenous to the Vietnamese and was the vehicle for the independence struggle against the French colonialists and, later, the Americans. In modern Vietnamese history, the CPV has had an almost exclusive claim to represent the broader ideals of nationalism and patriotism. For many Vietnamese, the CPV and nationalist struggle are identical.

Party membership numbers 3 million, more than 3 percent of the population. After stagnating membership in the 1990s, the party quickly expanded membership, raising questions by some about whether quantity has reduced quality. A recent decision to allow businessmen into the party rankled revolutionary party purists, in particular.

Vietnam's constitution gives the party the leading role in society, enforcing a unified Marxist-Leninist policy line for the state and society. In effect, the CPV controlled state government until the era of renovation, when the state was given more authority. Today, tensions exist within the party between ideologues and pragmatists and businessmen and bureaucrats. These tensions inhibit a single policy ideology to completely dominate political life, as once was the case.

Vietnamese politics as practiced in the politburo is best understood by an analogy to the great game of *bung-di*, or faction bashing.[9] Party factions, long prevalent in the communist party, form around individuals but traffic in issues. They are enduring but not permanent, and they can divide and reform to meet changing needs. Despite attempts to contain factionalism, they remain ubiquitous. In the early *doi moi* period, Vietnam's politburo divided into four major factions: reformers, neoconservatives, bureaucrats, and the military.[10] Today, the divide between reformers and neoconservatives has softened with successful economic growth. Flickering signs that political liberalization is on the table for discussion have emerged. However, the range of discussion excludes any suggestions of radical reform to multiparty democracy. In Vietnam, no alternative parties are allowed to form and challenge the CPV for state power.

Nationalism remains the glue that binds the CPV's generations, factions, and regional interests together while underpinning the party's ongoing legitimacy to govern. The party's elevation of Ho Chi Minh thought to official ideology in 1989 was designed to buttress this legitimacy amidst policy reforms. At that time the party claimed its *doi moi* policies were consistent with Ho's views about how socialism could be built in Vietnam—views that, they qualified, had been previously kept from the public. Citing rediscovered "original" documents, the CPV used Ho's "view of socialism" to justify market-oriented *doi moi* and to "delegitimize the policies of the leadership from 1975 to 1986."[11]

Since Ho's death, collective leadership has characterized Communist Party rule in Vietnam. Today, the party politburo is made up of more younger members than ever before. These leaders are better educated and concern themselves more with Vietnam's economic productivity and technological improvement than with revolution and ideology.

In a system where party and state overlap extensively, top party leaders hold all significant offices of state government. From the party's Tenth Congress in 2006 emerged an all-powerful fourteen-member politburo, inclusive of Vietnam's current ruling triumvirate: (1) Party Secretary Nong Duc Manh, a northerner in his second term distinguished in the foreign media as Vietnam's most cosmopolitan leader; (2) President Nguyen Minh Triet, an enthusiastic reformer from the south who functions as head of state; and (3) Prime Minister Nguyen Tan Dung, a southerner known for his anticorruption agenda. Northerner Nguyen Phu Trong, another politburo member, is chairman of the National Assembly. This position wields less power than the other three but plays an important role in Vietnam's party-controlled governmental rule.

The National Assembly

Formerly insignificant, the National Assembly of the Socialist Republic of Vietnam is beginning to perform functions similar to legislatures elsewhere in Southeast Asia. The CPV revamped the National Assembly's role at its Seventh Party Congress in 2001. Increased attention to the rule of law in the Vietnamese system is requiring the National Assembly to do more than simply rubber-stamp party dictates. Changes have included greater participation in law-based policy formation and new constitutional powers that permit votes of no-confidence in ministers and officials appointed by the assembly.[12]

National Assembly delegates are chosen through national elections. These elections involve more candidates than available seats but the CPV dominates the candidate selection process. Nonparty candidates may run for office, and many do win seats, but all candidates must first be vetted by the Vietnamese Fatherland Front, an umbrella political organization controlled by the party. No parties opposed to the CPV or Ho Chi Minh ideology are free to compete in assembly elections. In 2007, Vietnamese voters elected delegates to the Twelfth National Assembly. A total of 875 candidates competed for 493 seats; almost 10 percent of delegate winners were nonparty candidates.[13]

Military

The Vietnamese army is the CPV's creation, and the leading generals are members of the party leadership. The 4.4 million–member People's Army of Vietnam (PAVN) is the largest in Southeast Asia and includes one of the world's largest reserve forces. After 1975 the PAVN, initially given the mission of reunifying the nation, was charged with defending Vietnam from external attack, such as when the Chinese crossed Vietnam's northern border in 1979. In contrast to armies elsewhere in Southeast Asia, the Vietnamese army has not threatened a coup against the communist leadership. Its role remains subordinate to that of the party.

DEMOCRATIZATION

In 1989, the central committee of the CPV, alarmed by developments in Eastern Europe, Burma, and China, rejected appeals for political pluralism in Vietnam. President Nguyen Van Linh stated that the party rejected calls for "bourgeois liberalization, pluralism, political plurality, and multiopposition parties aimed at denying Marxism-Leninism, socialism, and the party's leadership."[14]

From the Vietnamese perspective, Western democracy represents all that their own leaders have rejected: unstable regimes led by bourgeois leaders for their own interests against the interests of the masses. The Vietnamese also reject the "arrogance" of democratic countries that are critical of the Vietnamese government. Vietnamese leaders have stated that conditions in the country are not appropriate for democracy. They also point to democratic instability in Thailand, Indonesia, and the Philippines following the Asian economic crisis. They argue their own approach is vindicated by economic growth and a reduction in poverty.

In the economic domain, democratization is not such a pejorative term. Decentralization and accountability are accepted as necessary for an effective economy. Economic principles such as "the market" and "competition," once viewed as decadent bourgeois concepts, have become the centerpieces of renovation.

Vietnam has no history of democracy. Its traditions are Confucianist, stressing hierarchy and order, and more recently communist, emphasizing the party's unquestioned supremacy. There have been few popular demonstrations for democratic rights, and the Vietnam War was never a struggle for civil liberties and representative government. The movement of the Eastern European communist governments toward democracy has not impelled the Vietnamese leadership or the people to initiate a similar transformation of their own government.

With respect to progress in civil liberties, the government's record is mixed. Conflict over religious freedom occurs, for example, between dissident Buddhist monks and communist government officials. Many Buddhists wish to establish the Unified Buddhist Church in place of the Vietnam Buddhist Church, long under the dominance of the CPV. The exiled Vietnamese monk Thich Nhat Hanh (once nominated for a Nobel Peace Prize by Martin Luther King Jr.) has been permitted to return for visits to Vietnam in recent years but tensions between Communist Party leaders and Vietnam's Buddhist community remain.

On the other hand, Vietnamese Catholics, initially persecuted by communists, practice with less fear than in the past. Unlike in China, where allegiance to the pope in Rome is disallowed, Catholics in Vietnam are permitted to engage with the Roman Church. In 2010, in celebration of the jubilee year of the local church, Vietnamese Catholics are hopeful Pope Benedict will make an unprecedented visit to Asia's fourth largest Catholic population. Such a visit would do much to improve Vietnam's human rights image, troubled by a long record of allegations and charges.

In the post-1975 period, Amnesty International documented cases of detention without trial of many former civil servants and members of the South Vietnamese armed forces in reeducation camps. Also documented were unfair trials of alleged opponents of the government and prisoners of conscience and reports of torture and ill treatment of prisoners in police custody and in prisons. Today Amnesty International admits treatment of dissenters has improved since renovation but that Vietnam's record is still unacceptable.

Freedom of the press does not exist in Vietnam. The Internet functions more freely than in China but antigovernment sites are blocked, nonetheless. Press accounts exposing government corruption and even criticism of policy are increasingly permitted but also permit top leaders to showcase "anticorruption" campaigns. Vietnam is a politically closed regime.

Labor rights, a major target of the international rights community, are slowly improving. In the early 2000s, the government entered programs with the International Labor Organization to reform labor laws and practices. Collaboration has yet to produce labor protection in line with global standards—organizing unions, for example, is still limited by party approval. Nevertheless, in the first six months of 2006, a record 303 wildcat strikes erupted and were not forcibly suppressed. Observers believe they in fact prompted the government to raise the minimum wage 40 percent for factory workers. New laws have also made it easier for migrant workers from rural areas to obtain benefits once denied them.[15]

ECONOMIC DEVELOPMENT

After the end of the war in 1975, the Vietnamese economy declined for a full fifteen years. Inflation rates were astronomical, and unemployment hovered at about 20 percent. Infrastructural essentials such as ports, roads, and electricity were primitive, and housing abysmal. Vietnam's banking system was barely viable, partly because there was so little managerial expertise. Annual per capita income was estimated to be $200, making Vietnam one of the poorest nations in the world. Famine, which threatened the northern provinces in 1988, affecting 10 million farmers, forced Vietnam—a country once self-sufficient in rice—to appeal for international food aid. Ho Chi Minh's favorite aphorism, emblazoned on red banners strung across streets throughout Vietnam— "Nothing is more precious than independence and freedom"—was interpreted in an ironic and sardonic sense. In unguarded moments, Vietnamese stated that "nothing" was exactly what they had.

Given Vietnam's superb natural resources, the country's poverty was all the more shocking and embarrassing to Vietnamese leaders. However, there were important reasons why the country was unable to develop in parallel fashion to the neighboring ASEAN nations. A major reason is the extensive war damage, which required tremendous resources to repair. In the south alone, the war produced 20,000 bomb craters, 10 million refugees, 362,000 invalids, 1 million widows, 880,000 orphans, 250,000 drug addicts, 300,000 prostitutes, and 3 million unemployed. Two-thirds of the villages and 5 million hectares of forests were destroyed.[16]

The U.S. involvement in South Vietnam created a dependent economy, and the billions of dollars spent on the war brought a surfeit of capital that ended abruptly when the United States disengaged. Hanoi had expected to receive some $3 billion in reparations aid, which had been promised by U.S. Secretary of State Henry Kissinger but was later refused when the United States maintained that North Vietnam had not carried out the terms of the Paris Peace Accords. Soviet aid did not make up for the loss of Western aid and trade lost to the Vietnamese because of the U.S.-sponsored trade embargo. Moreover, the Soviet Union's technological aid was insufficient in many ways.

Adding to Vietnam's woes was mismanagement by its leadership. Alternating between reform and orthodoxy, Vietnam's leaders "displayed a paranoid world view, a low adaptability level, perfidy consistently perceived in the motives of others and perpetuation of a cult-type leadership capable of believing the illogical, the irrational, even the absurd."[17] Nationalization and collectivization, thrust upon the south after reunification, were unfailingly disastrous, largely because of southerners' refusal to adhere to socialist policies.

Peasants refused to meet their obligations to the state when the state's prices for their crops did not cover even the costs of production.

To overcome the crisis, the CPV's Sixth Congress in December 1986 proposed major reforms under *doi moi*. Rice output in 1986 was far below 1942 levels, and northern farmers, as members of state-organized cooperatives, produced 52 percent less than farmers from the south who resisted collectivization. To alleviate this situation, land laws were modified to guarantee farmers a ten- to fifteen-year tenure on land they cultivated, although the expectation was that land could henceforth be owned in perpetuity and be inherited. This policy change signaled the end of efforts to collectivize agriculture in the south.

The 1986 reforms gave farmers the legal right to sell their produce on the free market after each paid a tax based on his or her output. Approximately 10 percent to 20 percent of the tax went to the state for the farmers' use of cooperatively owned machinery and for fertilizer and other necessities. Under the new system, farmers could keep a far larger percentage of their output than under the former contract system. Although it took several years for the policy to have a positive impact, Vietnam reemerged in 1989 as a major rice exporter for the first time since the 1950s. Vietnam became one of the world's three largest rice exporters along with Thailand and the United States; most of its rice was exported to West Africa, the Philippines, India, Sri Lanka, and China.

Vietnam's foreign investment code was also revised to attract more foreign investors. To draw joint ventures, the government liberalized tax policies and extended guarantees that investment capital would not be expropriated or joint ventures nationalized.[18] The 1987 investment law offered a two-year tax moratorium for joint ventures and established export processing zones in which foreign companies could import materials, use low-cost local labor for assembly, and export final products. A large proportion of the new investors were overseas Vietnamese.[19] The new code increased trade with Japan, Singapore, Hong Kong, France, Indonesia, and India but did not bring in the amount of capital hoped for because of the continuing U.S. trade embargo. More and more countries, however, broke the embargo to take advantage of the liberalized trade and investment opportunities, especially regarding offshore oil exploration.

The reforms made a dramatic difference in Vietnam's everyday economy. Construction of homes, buildings, bridges, roads, and schools, for example, burgeoned throughout the country, even in the north where the economy had been stagnant for many decades. Privately run restaurants and shops opened and flourished. Inflation dropped to more manageable levels as a result of the devaluation of Vietnam's currency, the dong, to the free-market rate, and government austerity measures—recommended by the IMF, with which Vietnam hoped to restore relations—were adopted to attract investment, credit, and technology from the West. Vietnam also reformed its meager, Russian-based tourist industry by investing in new hotels and encouraging more airline traffic from Western countries.

Vietnam remained impoverished, but for the first time since the end of the war there was economic development. In a sense, however, the country remained divided because development was more rapid in the south than in the north (partly as a result of the millions of dollars sent back to relatives from the 2 million southern Vietnamese living abroad). Unemployment remained high, especially among those considered "unreliable" because of their involvement with the former Saigon regime. Peasants, who continued to farm within a small margin of error, risked devastation by natural disasters, such as drought or flooding, or by the possible imposition of orthodox socialist economics less favorable to small-scale agriculture under a new administration.

It was initially believed that the loss of the Soviet Union as a major financial supporter would undermine the Vietnamese economy irrevocably. However, by 1992 the economy had improved, with increased rice production and controlled inflation. Both exports and imports increased dramatically, and trade with Japan as well as Singapore and the other ASEAN countries more than made up for the Soviet loss.

The ending of constraints on the IMF's assistance to Vietnam in 1993 and the lifting of the American embargo in 1994 were responsible for a huge increase in foreign direct investment. These openings represented the breakdown of the last external barriers to Vietnam's goal of becoming an Asian "tiger." GNP growth rose to an annual 8.2 percent with progress in all economic sectors. The politicians remained committed to *doi moi*, so the mid-1990s became an era of fundamental economic change. Ho Chi Minh City's economy grew by an astonishing 15 percent, and the new free-market system inexorably affected every sector of the economy. Vietnam was increasingly viewed as the "new economic frontier," capable of achieving extraordinary growth rates because of its disciplined workforce, cheap labor and materials, and zealous goal to join the global capitalist system.

In 1995 and 1996, annual economic growth rates stood at 9.5 percent, the highest in the world. Given the country's remarkable growth and the enthusiasm of the world community for the "new" Vietnam, the subsequent difficulties of 1997 were surprising. Suddenly the economic boom hit a plateau, and growth rates actually declined to 7 percent (still high in comparison to growth rates in industrialized nations). The number of tourists declined rapidly. Confidence in reform dropped. Foreign entrepreneurs, citing frustration with Vietnam's Byzantine bureaucracy, reduced their investment by about one-third from the previous year's total. Bureaucratic waste and corruption made it almost impossible for investors and entrepreneurs to move forward with dispatch. Even low-level policy decisions required the approval of those highest in the CPV hierarchy, wasting a tremendous amount of time and talent.

Added to these problems were underdeveloped economic institutions and government corruption. The banking system remained primitive, virtually incapable of making or collecting on loans. The dong was overvalued, especially during the 1997 currency crisis that struck the rest of Southeast Asia. Vietnamese exports were becoming more expensive even though the products were often of low quality. Foreign companies shut down their factories in the absence of legal contracts and to protest the emphasis on under-the-table payments demanded by both private business elites and public officials.

Vietnam's late 1990s economic decline was driven by underdeveloped institutions, corruption, and policies that failed to improve its business climate. Amidst slower growth, Vietnam also successfully navigated two external crises as the century turned: the 1997 Asian economic crisis and the early 2000s global recession. Less integrated with the global markets than its more economically advanced neighbors, Vietnam was spared from the worst effects of the Asian economic crisis. Emphasizing stability over growth, Vietnamese leaders saw a domestic slowdown continue through 2002, but GDP rates never dropped below 5 percent. In fact, during the early 2000s global recession, Vietnam's growth was among the strongest in the world.

Part of Vietnam's success at the time was due to a U.S.-Vietnam bilateral trade agreement signed in 2000 that enhanced manufactured exports and invited new investment. Growth rates pushed upward to nearly 7.5 percent by 2003 and export growth again reached double digits. Observers noted, however, that much of this new growth was taking place in the state sector, driven by heavy state investments of "low quality" and tainted by official corruption.[20] Questions also persisted about how Vietnam could again handle continued rapid growth without quickly upgrading the country's infrastructure and educational system. Low-quality investment and structural limits notwithstanding, Vietnam's GDP climbed back into the 8 percent range by 2005.

WTO membership in 2007 further accelerated Vietnamese exports to the United States, Japan, South Korea, and Singapore. Investment growth improved as well. Intel Corp., for example, selected Vietnam for its new $300 million chip-testing facility. Vietnam's economic performance seemed to be moving from strength to strength. Then "securities fever," as it was called, hit local and foreign investors. For a couple of years, Vietnam's stock market was among the world's most promising. Ordinary Vietnamese, many for the first time in their lives, began to float money on exchanges in Ho Chi Minh City and Hanoi. However, poor government regulation made the fledgling Asian bourses vulnerable to manipulation, misinformation, and fraud. The government, with many state enterprises listed on the Hanoi exchange, grew increasingly nervous and hastily passed securities laws it had no capacity to actually enforce.

In 2007, the two-decade-old reform movement produced one of the country's highest GDP growth rates, 8.5 percent. Crude oil, textiles, seafood, coffee, rubber, and rice were pouring out of the country. Vietnam's economic winners looked for places to both spend and multiply their new earnings. Consumption of import luxuries ballooned due to lower import taxes. Vietnam's growing class of the insatiable super-rich gobbled up European luxury cars, designer cosmetics, and high-priced mobile phones. Winners also poured money into land. Commercial real estate in Hanoi and Ho Chi Minh City soared, fetching higher prices per square meter than in New York, Singapore, or Tokyo. By the end of the year, the economy was racing. Vietnam's two stock exchanges reached a combined value of $29 billion, about $28 billion more than just three years earlier.

This peak of investor exuberance was followed, as many predicted, by a spectacular collapse of Vietnam's stock markets in 2008. Vietnam's rapid growth had generated a growing trade imbalance and rising inflation. In a matter of weeks, the world's hottest stock markets became the world's worst performing. Consumers, many with memories of hyperinflation in the past, began to hoard commodities and buy gold, exacerbating inflationary pressures. Vietnam's currency also fell under pressure. Ominously, observers pointed to parallels with Thailand and Indonesia in 1997.

Vietnam's shell-shocked government, facing its first real capital market crisis, tightened the reins on the economy. It moved quickly to raise interest rates and announce a total ban on the importation of gold. Import taxes on luxury goods also were adjusted upward. Also, hoping to ward off black-marketeers and currency speculators, officials quietly devalued the dong by 2 percent against the dollar. International investors took the devaluation as a bad sign, as the beginning of much larger devaluations accompanied by a serious economic crisis. Local and foreign enterprises faced new uncertainties. Vietnam's twenty-year, *doi moi*–driven ride of rapid growth was now shifting into lower gear.

THE VIETNAMESE STATE

Until recently, the Communist Party of Vietnam has been the state. All authoritative decisions were made by the party and then disseminated to the populace through a tightly controlled organization that allowed no dissent. Civil liberties have been curtailed to ensure that the party is uncontested. Only since 1986 have new institutions emerged that have real power, such as the National Assembly.

Vietnam is the archetypal example of a nation that endured major social disturbances that uprooted the traditional bases of social control and cleared the way for new state leaders. For Vietnam, a succession of wars and revolutions led to fundamental organizational changes in everyday life, concentrating social control into a single agency—the CPV.

These social dislocations occurred at a time when support and shelter for Vietnamese state leaders were provided by the world communist movement. Since World War II, Vietnam has never been free of either potential or actual aggression by outsiders. The Japanese, French, Americans, and Chinese have all intervened, compelling state leaders to mobilize their forces and concentrate their power and capabilities. Vietnam is therefore a classic example of a country in which war and the threat of war induce state leaders to take risks to consolidate social control and thereby create a strong state.

The legitimacy of the Vietnamese state is rooted in its communist revolution, which expelled foreign occupiers, unified the country, and established the Socialist Republic. This legitimacy has not been seriously challenged by the Vietnamese since 1975. Channels through which the people could mount such a challenge have been limited by strict, one-party rule. As a member in good standing in the world's most established international organizations, the Socialist Republic of Vietnam enjoys universal international legitimacy as well.

As for the party's own legitimacy to govern (distinct from the legitimacy of the Socialist Republic itself), disastrous economic results of the 1975–1986 period portended a serious domestic legitimacy crisis. *Doi moi* policies breathed new life into the party. Today, the CPV leans on performance legitimization, combined with official interpretations of Ho Chi Minh thought, as the bulwark against a possible domestic challenge to its legitimacy.

In contrast to elected leaders in open, pluralistic democracies, Vietnam's governors have fewer constituencies to satisfy. The party, in its supreme position, must be heeded; but the highest government leaders are generally one and the same as top party leaders. Fortunately for Vietnam's governors, bureaucratic loyalties lie primarily with the state rather than with autonomous religious, ethnic, or class interests. Vietnam's rulers do not face the social diversity and ethnic nationalism that endlessly challenge leaders in Burma, Indonesia, Malaysia, and the Philippines. Intellectuals, monks, and business entrepreneurs form political constituencies of some significance but have largely been depoliticized, co-opted, or otherwise silenced.

Ironically, *doi moi* has increased the state's role. Where the party formerly ruled through dictates generated by its own governmental apparatus, Vietnam today is home to a complex state apparatus dependent on institutionalizing procedures, processes, and law. External demands to comply with UN programs, World Bank projects, and WTO membership differentiate the nature of the state's active role from its pre-reform past. Moreover, Vietnam's unprofitable state enterprises, gradually being divested, are being replaced by new efforts to emulate successful state-owned companies elsewhere. The party announced in 2007, for example, that the hundred-plus enterprises the military owned must be transferred to civilian rule. At the same time, government leaders openly acknowledged their desire to create a government-owned holding company, along the lines of Singapore's Temasek, and to bring all state enterprises under its management.

Foreign Policy

Before 1986, the major goal of Vietnamese foreign policy had been to secure the sovereignty of the nation against all aggressors. To meet this goal, Vietnamese foreign policy sought to ensure a cooperative, nonthreatening Indochina firmly allied with Vietnam; prevent an anticommunist front from threatening Vietnamese interests; limit the role of the United States, China, and the Soviet Union in Vietnam's sphere of influence; and establish working relations with neighboring ASEAN countries. These latter, more specific goals were met with varying degrees of success.

In the post-1975 period, Vietnamese foreign policy was framed by fundamental Marxist-Leninist principles. The nation's reliance on socialist solidarity versus the interventionist, exploitative capitalist world narrowed its options and reduced the flexibility that the conduct of foreign relations requires in a world of fast-moving change. Foreign policy was carried out in *dau tranh* (struggle) terms, in which diplomacy was treated strategically—like protracted military conflicts—over an extended period of time.[21] This approach made negotiations with allies and adversaries difficult because Vietnam's arguments were presented as statements of superior virtue, not as expressions of national interest.

After 1986, ideological fundamentalism decreased, and policymakers stressed the need for Vietnam to play a greater role in the global economic system. Vietnam's leaders saw that communist governments were failing around the world, that Vietnam was economically isolated, and that the nation had become too dependent on the Soviet Union; thus, they moved in fundamentally new directions in foreign policy.

Politburo liberals argued that keeping Cambodia as a friendly neighbor was important but not to the point of threatening Vietnam's economic collapse. These reformers argued that a withdrawal from Cambodia would end Vietnam's international isolation by leading to the normalization of ties with the United States, halting the multilateral trade embargo against Vietnam, and inviting Western aid.[22] Adding to pressure to withdraw was the restiveness of

Vietnam's armed forces, demoralized by the military stalemate in Cambodia that had cost some 55,000 Vietnamese lives.

However, withdrawal from Cambodia, begun in September 1989, did not bring the expected international gratitude. Instead, ASEAN and the United States faulted the troop withdrawal for not being part of a comprehensive peace plan for Cambodia and for not allowing monitoring by an international control mechanism. It was not until July 1990, when U.S. Secretary of State James Baker announced that his government would begin direct negotiations with Vietnam relating to the Cambodian situation, that the withdrawal elicited a positive response from the United States. Meanwhile, no moves were made toward normalizing relations, and the trade embargo continued.

Vietnam also moved to improve relations with Asian and Western nations interested in developing economic ties. Hundreds of trade and investment delegations from Japan, Taiwan, South Korea, Thailand, and various European countries arrived to set up business ventures. Relations with China also improved, partly because of the vast border trade between the two nations.

For the United States, Vietnam had been a low foreign policy priority since the end of the war. The American foreign policy establishment was no longer concerned about Vietnam or its fate. The noncommunist countries of Southeast Asia, however, were flourishing in the 1980s and no longer viewed themselves as potential victims of Vietnamese aggression. Many agreed with the sentiment of a Thai prime minister that the time had arrived to turn Southeast Asia "from a battlefield to a marketplace."

In the United States, memories of the war were fading, and Vietnam soon became more cooperative on the issue of unaccounted-for American prisoners of war. Hanoi accepted a standing U.S. offer to conduct joint U.S.-funded searches in provincial areas where the remains of MIAs were thought to be located. It was during this period that the question of normalizing relations between the United States and Vietnam was brought to the fore.

From a Vietnamese perspective, normalization was desirable, notwithstanding the government's negative view of past U.S. involvement in Indochina. Soviet aid to Vietnam had decreased and Soviet President Mikhail Gorbachev confirmed his country's intention to give up its military bases in Vietnam. Russians were not liked in Vietnam, and there was a surprising feeling of warmth for Americans in both the northern and southern areas. Vietnam was still very poor, and normalization with the United States could open doors to international aid from the West.

On the U.S. side, one argument for normalization viewed Vietnam as the next economic frontier. Japan, South Korea, Taiwan, and Thailand were already investing heavily in the country, taking advantage of its inexpensive labor and disciplined workforce. With its liberal new foreign investment code, Vietnam had become more enticing to business ventures. The Washington business lobby became increasingly supportive of normalization so the trade embargo could be lifted. Political arguments followed economic ones. It was believed that closer economic relations with the Vietnamese (the so-called engagement thesis) would help spur political liberalization and even democracy in Vietnam. Military arguments for normalization stressed U.S. strategic interests. The need to deepen U.S. ties in the region seemed timely, given the uncertain status of bases in the Philippines and China's ambitions now that the USSR was withdrawing from the region.

Arguments against normalization stressed that diplomatic relations with Vietnam would legitimize a repressive government. Indeed, many Vietnamese refugees in the United States opposed normalization for that reason. In their view, the North Vietnamese had brutally and illegally taken control of the south, and they should not be rewarded for that action. Many U.S. veterans' groups were also embittered by talks of normalization, emphasizing the unresolved POW-MIA issue.

Most observers believed that Vietnam and the United States would establish diplomatic relations in 1992 before the end of President George H. W. Bush's administration. Because Vietnam had withdrawn its troops from Cambodia, had supported the Cambodian peace process, and had begun to cooperate on POW-MIA issues, officials in Hanoi believed the embargo would be lifted and diplomatic relations restored. Indeed, the Bush administration began the process by softening the terms of the embargo and allowing telephone links with Vietnam to resume, a welcome event to the 1.5 million Viet Kieu (overseas Vietnamese) living in the United States. U.S. firms were allowed to sign contracts, which could quickly be executed once the trade embargo was lifted. They could also open offices in Vietnam and carry out feasibility studies. President Bush announced that "we can begin writing the last chapter of the Vietnam War." Nevertheless, the Bush administration did not follow through.

Bill Clinton announced early in his presidency that diplomatic relations would not be restored until "every MIA and POW is accounted for." This impossible condition discouraged supporters of improved ties between the two nations. They surmised that Clinton might be more hesitant than Bush to open relations with Vietnam, given allegations during the presidential campaign that Clinton had dodged the military draft during the Vietnam War. Meanwhile, virtually every other Western nation was involved in various economic relationships with the Vietnamese. It was not until 1994 and 1995 that the embargo was lifted and diplomatic relations were established, respectively.

The demise of the world's socialist nations undercut Vietnamese foreign policy, which was based on solidarity with the Soviet Union and its allies. This dramatic change made improving Vietnam's ties with the Western capitalist world the best means of future economic aid and trade. At the same time, Vietnam mended fences with its traditional adversary, China; leaders of the two nations attended a summit and restored many crucial ties. Although these improved relations were damaged by Chinese claims of sovereignty over the Spratly Islands in the South China Sea, the positive aspects largely outweighed the negative ones. The two communist neighbors, once enemies battling over the fate of Cambodia, normalized relations in 1991. Cooperation and noninterference increasingly defined their relationship in the 1990s. By the early 2000s, a mature stage of "normalcy" came to characterize Sino-Vietnamese trade relations, symbolized most importantly by Vietnam's lucrative exports of crude oil to China. Although the relationship is asymmetrical, Vietnam is merely deferential, not subordinate to rising China.[23]

Vietnam also basked in its new status as ASEAN's seventh member; the country's recent foreign policy moves indicate that the development of economic ties has become far more important than the security considerations of the past. The language of Vietnam is increasingly about markets, investments, intellectual property rights, trade, and credits.

Most symbolic of just how far Vietnam's foreign policy had taken the country since its redirection in 1986 was a November 2006 event in Hanoi, when twenty heads of state gathered in Hanoi for the annual Asia-Pacific Economic Cooperation (APEC) meetings. As is customary at APEC meetings, state leaders took time for a photo dressed in the traditional local attire of the host country. For the Vietnamese people—recent survivors of European colonialism, Japanese occupation, a U.S.-USSR proxy war, and a Chinese border war—the image of George W. Bush, Vladimir Putin, Shinzo Abe, and Hu Jintao adorned in colorful, silk woven *ao dai* gowns, and standing side-by-side with Vietnamese President Nguyen Minh Triet, symbolized more than cordial relations. Rather, the image stood as evidence to the respect the Vietnamese had won from decades of struggle. As Uncle Ho had promised, freedom and independence from foreign control was indeed precious.

CONCLUSION

Vietnam's future is linked to the ability of the Vietnamese Communist Party to balance economic reform with strict one-party rule. With rich natural resources, a large, disciplined workforce, and a long tradition of entrepreneurial activity, Vietnam has the capacity to become Asia's newest economic frontier. From 1975 to 1986, the communist government undermined Vietnam's advantages with its oppressive policies and mismanagement. The regime's realization of this fact has brought about major economic reform, which bodes well for the nation's future, but the development of expectations of political liberalization could prove destabilizing. For the foreseeable future, however, Vietnam's Leninist party structure is poised to remain one of the lone survivors of the collapse of global communism.

NOTES

1. The Cao Dai religion, founded in the 1920s and located in South Vietnam, eclectically blends Buddhism, Taoism, Confucianism, Christianity, and other beliefs into a single, monotheistic religious system. Hoa Hao, founded in the 1930s and also located in the Mekong Delta region, is a variant of Buddhism that deemphasizes monastic temple worship in favor of lay practice.

2. Frederick Z. Brown, *Second Chance: The United States and Indochina in the 1990s* (New York: Council on Foreign Relations, 1989), p. 39.

3. David G. Marr and Christine P. White, eds., *Postwar Vietnam: Dilemmas in Socialist Development* (Ithaca, NY: Southeast Asia Program, Cornell University, 1988), p. 2.

4. Ronald J. Cima, "Vietnam's Economic Reform," *Asian Survey*, vol. 29, no. 8 (August 1989), p. 789.

5. Figures from *Vietnam Country Brief*, World Bank, February 2007, available at www.worldbank.org.

6. For an excellent account of social change related to Vietnam's youth, see Robert Templer, *Shadows and Wind: A View of Modern Vietnam* (New York: Penguin Books, 1998).

7. Vo X. Han, "Vietnam in 2007," *Asian Survey*, vol. 48, no. 1 (January/February 2008), pp. 33–34.

8. *Vietnam Development Report 2005: Governance*, joint donor report to the Vietnam Consultative Group Meeting, December 2004 (Hanoi: Vietnam Development Information Center, 2004) p. *i*.

9. Douglas Pike, "Political Institutionalization in Vietnam," in *Asian Political Institutionalization*, ed. Robert A. Scalapino, Seizaburo Sato, and Jusuf Wanandi (Berkeley: Institute of East Asian Studies, University of California, 1986), pp. 49–51.

10. Douglas Pike, "Change and Continuity in Vietnam," *Current History*, vol. 89, no. 545 (March 1990), p. 118.

11. Thaveeporn Vasavakul, "Vietnam: The Changing Models of Legitimation," in *Political Legitimacy in Southeast Asia: The Quest for Moral Authority*, ed. Muthiah Alagappa (Stanford, CA: Stanford University Press, 1995), p. 277.

12. *Vietnam Development Report 2005: Governance*, p. *i*.

13. Vo, "Vietnam in 2007," p. 34.

14. *Asia Yearbook, 1990* (Hong Kong: Far Eastern Economic Review, 1990), p. 241.

15. Hy V. Long, "Vietnam in 2006," *Asian Survey*, vol. 47, no. 1 (January/February 2008), p. 170.

16. Marr and White, *Postwar Vietnam*, p. 3.

17. Pike, "Political Institutionalization in Vietnam," p. 43.

18. Ronald J. Cima, "Vietnam in 1988: The Brink of Renewal," *Asian Survey*, vol. 29, no. 1 (January 1989), p. 67.

19. Cima, "Vietnam's Economic Reform," p. 797.

20. Adam Forde, "Vietnam in 2003: The Road to Ungovernability," *Asian Survey*, vol. 44, no. 1 (January/February 2004), p. 124.

21. Douglas Pike, "Vietnam and Its Neighbors: Internal Influences on External Relations," in *ASEAN in Regional and Global Context*, ed. Karl D. Jackson, Sukhumbhand Paribatra, and J. Soedjati Djiwandono (Berkeley: Institute of East Asian Studies, University of California, 1986), p. 240.

22. Ronald J. Cima, "Vietnam in 1989: Initiating the Post-Cambodia Period," *Asian Survey*, vol. 30, no. 10 (January 1990), p. 89.

23. Brantley Womak, *China and Vietnam: The Politics of Asymmetry* (Cambridge, UK: Cambridge University Press, 2006), p. 29.

Resource Guide

A useful tool for bibliographic and other information on Vietnam is available from Australia National University's WWW Virtual Library: www.gksoft.com/govt/en/vn.html. The University of California–Berkeley maintains a useful portal for digital and print resources on Vietnam: www.lib.berkeley.edu/SSEAL/SoutheastAsia/seaelec.html. Northern Illinois University's Southeast Asia Digital Library includes a range of useful links that cover government, academic, and research institutions specific to Vietnam: http://sea.lib.niu.edu. The University of Wisconsin–Madison Libraries similarly maintains a list of digital and print resources on Vietnam: www.library.wisc.edu/guides/SEAsia/resarea.html. The Library of Congress maintains an Internet resource guide on Vietnam at www.loc.gov/rr/international/portals.html#t.

The government Web portal of the Socialist Republic of Vietnam is available in English at www.chinhphu.vn/portal/page?_pageid=439,1&_dad=portal&_schema=PORTAL. The Communist Party of Vietnam is at www.cpv.org.vn/english/index.html. Official economic news and information are available at the Ministry of Finance Web site: www.mof.gov.vn/DefaultE.aspx?tabid=197.

A list of active international agencies, NGOs, and organizations operating in Vietnam is available at www.devdir.org/files/Vietnam.PDF. As Vietnam is a pilot country for the UN One Program, a useful site is www.un.org.vn.

For daily news in English, try *Vietnam News*: http://vietnamnews.vnagency.com.vn/default.php and VietNamNet Bridge at http://english.vietnamnet.vn. Nhan Dan provides news directly from the Vietnam Communist Party: www.nhandan.com.vn/english.

10

CAMBODIA

The many names under which Cambodia has lived in the past few decades reflect the turmoil this country has undergone. Cambodia was once known as the Kingdom of Cambodia, but the country became the Khmer Republic when the military came to power in 1970. From 1975 to 1979, the period of fanatic Khmer Rouge leadership, the country's name was changed to Democratic Kampuchea, followed by the People's Republic of Kampuchea when the Khmer Rouge was replaced by a Vietnamese-backed government. In 1989, the country became the State of Cambodia only to return to its former name, the Kingdom of Cambodia, when the country restored royal institutions under a constitutional monarchy in 1993.

Cambodians trace their heritage to the great Khmer civilization, which culminated in the twelfth century when the Khmers ruled over most of modern-day Cambodia, Laos, Thailand, and Vietnam. This magnificent civilization, symbolized by the great temples at Angkor, lasted over five hundred years and reached a level of military, technological, political, and philosophical achievement that was unmatched at the time in Southeast Asia. Angkor eventually fell in the fifteenth century to Ayutthaya, and subsequent kingdoms suffered from instability and external pressure until 1864, when the French took over a weak Cambodia as a protectorate.

The great Khmer civilization has now become the Kingdom of Cambodia, with 14.6 million residents. Most Cambodians are rural farmers who live in poverty. Theravada Buddhism predominates among the population. As a nation, Cambodia personifies tragedy, its people having suffered unspeakable horrors during the Khmer Rouge era from 1975 to the beginning of 1979. Indeed, neither the people nor the nation has fully recovered from these horrors. Signs of improvement are emerging but progress remains inhibited by corrupt leadership, a plundering of the country's natural resources, and a deep dependence on foreign assistance.

THAILAND

LAOS

Mekong

Khao
Preah
Vihear

Angkor Wat

BATDAMBANG ●SIEM REAP

Tonle
Sap

Mekong

KAMPONG
CHAM

PHNOM
PENH

VIETNAM

Gulf
of
Thailand

CAMBODIA

South
China
Sea

0   50 100 km
0   50   100 mi

Cambodia's search for identity and nationhood, once the country was freed from French colonialism, was dominated by Prince Norodom Sihanouk, whom the French had placed on the throne in 1941. In 1955, one year after Cambodia's independence was granted, King Sihanouk abdicated, named his father as king, and entered politics directly as Prince Sihanouk. His unrivaled dominance of Cambodian life from the end of World War II to 1970 was due to the way he had achieved leadership, which was by plebiscite, and to the unsurpassed loyalty of rural Cambodians. He was revered as a god-king in the tradition of the Angkor kings, and his authority rested on charismatic, traditional, repressive, and legal foundations.

Sihanouk, who controlled all important policymaking institutions, exhibited a remarkable capacity to keep each major sector of society in check, thereby maintaining political stability. His overthrow on March 18, 1970, was therefore a surprise to most analysts of Cambodian politics. On that date, while Sihanouk was in the Soviet Union, the Cambodian National Assembly—charging Sihanouk with abuses of office—unanimously condemned him to death for treason and corruption. His position was assumed by General Lon Nol, the premier in Sihanouk's government.

Sihanouk's downfall stemmed from the presence of North Vietnamese and Viet Cong forces in the so-called Cambodian sanctuaries. Against his army's wishes, Sihanouk had allowed the Vietnamese to use this territory, although his trip to Moscow was to request Soviet aid in ousting the Vietnamese. The Vietnamese presence in Cambodia had become so permanent that by mid-1969 they had built a base of support in a region that encompassed nearly one-fourth of Cambodia's total area. Sihanouk had also allowed shipments of Chinese arms across the country from the Cambodian port of Sihanoukville.

Sihanouk's relations with the United States during this time were both acrimonious and supportive. He opposed U.S. involvement in Vietnam, although as the North Vietnamese established themselves in Cambodian territory, he reversed policy and argued the need for an American force in Asia to provide a balance of power to the communist nations. From the U.S. perspective, Sihanouk was mercurial and untrustworthy; thus, his ouster was welcome. Although it remains the subject of much speculation, no definitive evidence has yet proven that Sihanouk's overthrow was supported by covert U.S. government assistance.

From Sihanouk's perspective, his frequently changing policies were consistent with his overall objective of keeping his country neutral and sovereign. Cambodia's history has been characterized by the attempts of more powerful neighbors as well as Western imperialists to dominate the country's political life. Therefore, Sihanouk's neutralism reflected his appreciation of historical precedents and his awareness of the rising influence of China and a communist Vietnam in Asia as well as the declining influence of the United States.

The Cambodian National Assembly nevertheless deemed Sihanouk's apparently ambivalent and inconsistent policies regarding the Vietnamese intrusion as an act of treason. It charged him with allowing the North Vietnamese and Viet Cong to operate in sanctuaries on the border. It also charged that the prince had engaged in corruption and had ruined the economy by nationalizing Cambodia's few industries.

These charges used to justify the coup must be seen, however, in a larger context. Before his fall, Prince Sihanouk had lost the loyalty of elite groups in Cambodia. The army united around General Lon Nol and agreed with his view that Sihanouk was not moving strongly enough to remove the Vietnamese from Cambodian territory. Bureaucrats resented Sihanouk's total control over policymaking and personnel decisions; intellectuals opposed his policies of press and speech censorship; and young graduates were frustrated by the lack of job opportunities. Although Sihanouk retained the loyalty of the rural masses, that group wielded little influence in Cambodian politics.

Sihanouk's major failure was his inability to institutionalize a political system in which power relations were not exclusively a function of his own desires and whims. Initially his charisma was the country's primary integrating force; subsequently, however, his total dominance of Cambodian political life undermined the nation's major institutions. The army became the dominant institution in Cambodian politics in March 1970, and for a short time Lon Nol had the support of many Cambodians. There was greater freedom of speech and the press than under Sihanouk, and the economy showed signs of opening and expanding. However, after a few months it became clear that the new government was not only inefficient but corrupt.

At the end of April 1970, U.S. President Richard Nixon, without first informing the Cambodian government, announced an American invasion of Cambodia to protect the lives of U.S. soldiers, to ensure the success of his Vietnamization program, and to gain a decent interval for U.S. withdrawal from Vietnam. He announced that the intervention would clear Cambodia of all major enemy sanctuaries, including the headquarters of the communist military operation in South Vietnam. In fact, the Nixon administration had been secretly bombing Cambodia since 1969, without the knowledge or authorization of the U.S. Congress. U.S. forces dropped an estimated 550,000 tons of bombs on Cambodia, about twenty-five times the explosive force of the atomic bomb that devastated Hiroshima, Japan, and three and a half times as many bombs as were dropped on Japan during World War II. Nearly half the population was uprooted, and Cambodians became refugees in their own country.[1] The bombing had no substantive effect on protecting South Vietnam but only served to create chaos and panic in the Cambodian countryside.

The fall of Sihanouk precipitated five years of total war on Cambodian soil. The U.S.-backed Lon Nol government proved incapable of coping with either international or domestic crises. The regime was corrupt; food shortages occurred for the first time in the country's modern history; inflation was out of control; and hundreds of thousands of Cambodians were displaced—the population of Phnom Penh, Cambodia's capital and largest city, swelled from 600,000 to 2 million. One out of every ten Cambodians was killed in the war—most from U.S. bombings and suicide missions sent by Lon Nol to repel the Vietnamese. From his exile in Beijing, Prince Sihanouk announced his support for the radical rebels, the Khmer Rouge, who opposed the Lon Nol regime. The country fell into a civil war that did not end until April 1975, when the Khmer Rouge took control of the countryside and forced Phnom Penh into submission.

The massive U.S. bombings, the social dislocation, and the corruption of the Lon Nol government attracted support to the formerly weak Khmer Rouge, which many believed was made up of nationalist "peasant reformers." That myth was quickly dispelled when the Khmer Rouge ordered the complete evacuation of Phnom Penh within hours of the takeover.

Pol Pot, the leader of one of several Khmer Rouge factions who eventually became the dominant individual in the new government, headed a tightly disciplined party vanguard called "the organization" (*Angka*), which ruthlessly ran the country. *Angka* represented itself as the leader of oppressed workers, farmers, and peasants against the "feudal, imperialistic, capitalist, reactionary, and oppressor classes" of the former regimes. The name Cambodia was changed to Democratic Kampuchea, and Prince Sihanouk was brought back as the nominal head of state but in reality lived day-to-day under house arrest.

Angka used draconian measures to silence even potential voices of opposition and to reduce to impotency every person believed to be allied with the former ruling groups. The means to this end included strict discipline, total control, terror, and isolation from "impure" societies. The new regime's first undertaking, carried out immediately after the fall of Phnom Penh, was the evacuation of every person from Cambodia's major cities to the countryside. At first it was believed the evacuation was to last for only three days because the new government feared mass starvation in Phnom Penh and other cities, which had very limited supplies of rice. The evacuation, however, was meant to be permanent, to "purify" Cambodian society of decadent urban ways and to ensure internal security by ridding the country of "spies, imperialists, and enemies." The evacuations led to thousands of deaths and the separations of countless families.

Angka also purged persons who were in any way connected to the Lon Nol regime or were believed to harbor the slightest "bourgeois" values. Former residents of Phnom Penh were treated especially harshly by the regime. Cambodians with Chinese or Vietnamese ethnicity, considered impure and untrustworthy, were imprisoned and killed. Temples were closed and Buddhist monks were forcibly disrobed or murdered. In places where displaced people were resettled, high death rates resulted from starvation, illness, and forced labor. An estimated 1.7 million people were executed or worked to death between 1975 and 1979, an act of genocide that has few parallels in history. The country's entire intelligentsia was executed, often in hideous ways.

Further "enhancing" the Khmer Rouge's rule was the policy of forced labor, or collectivization, and the total restructuring of the economy. All Cambodian entrepreneurs lost their money when the regime halted the use of currency and nationalized private businesses. The family unit was replaced by collectives of up to a thousand households, which ate and worked together. Khmer Rouge troops enforced these harsh new policies and made sure that no one resorted to the "bourgeois" values of privatism, hierarchy, individualism, and the nuclear family. For over three years, agrarian idealism in the form of forced labor defined the sum total of economic production. Unlike communist-led countries elsewhere, the Khmer Rouge made no attempt to develop industry, education, or technology.

Survivors reported that Cambodian society was rigidly organized into separate groups of men, women, the elderly, children six to fifteen years of age, and older teenagers. Only small quantities of food were available for communal workers. No schools were open, and no money was in circulation. Buddhist temples were converted into granaries for storing rice, and 80 percent of all books in Cambodia were thrown into rivers. Recalibrating history, the Khmer Rouge declared it "Year Zero"; nothing from the past would be tolerated. Under Pol Pot, Cambodia became one of the most closed societies on Earth. During his three-year rule, only a few diplomats and reporters were allowed to enter the country under tightly controlled conditions for propaganda purposes. The extent of economic hardship and the regime's brutality was foggy to outsiders. Horrific stories retold by traumatized refugees became one of the few windows into Democratic Kampuchea.

The xenophobic ideology that underpinned Khmer Rouge policies included elements of Marxist-Leninism, Maoism, and Khmer nationalism, which romanticized agrarian utopianism. Some of this ideology was laid out in 1950s doctoral theses submitted to French universities written by Hou Yuon and Khieu Samphan. These theses argued that the exploitation of Cambodia's peasants was the source of the country's problems; that only by recapturing the peasantry's agrarian potential could the country achieve self-reliance. Hou Yuon, known to be critical of Khmer Rouge methods, died of uncertain causes in the early period of Pol Pot's rule. Khieu Samphan eventually served as state president of Democratic Kampuchea.

Following the communist victory in Vietnam in the spring of 1975, the Khmer Rouge began raiding Vietnam's border towns, thereby threatening Vietnam's important Mekong Delta region and causing thousands to lose their homes. An estimated 30,000 Vietnamese civilians were killed during these attacks. Pol Pot may have intended to reclaim the territory of the ancient Khmer Empire, which once included most of southern Vietnam. The fighting reflected the historically adversarial relationship between the two nations.

On Christmas Day 1978, a Vietnamese-led invasion overthrew Pol Pot's regime and installed Heng Samrin as president. Heng Samrin was an unknown former Khmer Rouge division commander who had sought refuge in Vietnam when his faction was overpowered by Pol Pot. Heng Samrin was soon replaced by Foreign Minister Hun Sen, who became the nation's most important leader for the next thirty years. Democratic Kampuchea became the People's Republic of Kampuchea (PRK). Vietnamese troops took Phnom Penh after less than two weeks of fighting and forced the Khmer Rouge to flee to the mountains in the western part of the country near the Thai border. Many Cambodians took advantage of the Vietnamese invasion to flee the country. Refugee camps in Thailand became overwhelmed with new arrivals. From these camps, over a million Cambodians would find resettlement in third countries; almost a quarter of a million resettled in the United States.

Vietnam announced that the purpose of its invasion was to end the constant border clashes, which jeopardized Vietnamese citizens, and to expel the hated Pol Pot regime. Certainly, Vietnam also desired a friendly government, not an ally of China, on its doorstep. The Khmer Rouge was Maoist and supportive of China, Vietnam's principal enemy.

The invasion has also been interpreted as a proxy war fought by surrogates of China and the Soviet Union. China provided aid to the Khmer Rouge, and the Soviet Union supported Vietnam; thus, some argue that these two world powers deliberately provoked the confrontation for the purpose of promoting their own self-interest and exercising control over client states in Southeast Asia. This interpretation sees Cambodia and Vietnam as pawns of major powers rather than as nations acting independently. However, historical precedents suggest that more was at issue in this conflict than competition between the major communist powers.

The new Vietnamese-installed government moved to undo the most onerous policies of the Khmer Rouge, and Phnom Penh was slowly repopulated. A market system was reestablished, and piped water and electricity were made available. Marriage and family restrictions were ended, forced collectives were abolished, and the practice of Buddhism was again allowed. Schools were reopened, and universal primary school education was instituted. After four years of the "killing fields," a semblance of normality appeared in Cambodian society.

Despite reforms, the new government faced severe problems. The Cambodians disliked and distrusted the Vietnamese officials and occupation soldiers (who numbered almost 200,000) but nevertheless realized that the Vietnamese were all that stood between them and the return of the Khmer Rouge. In addition, Pol Pot's annihilation of virtually all skilled and educated Cambodians had caused an administrative vacuum. For example, there were only forty-five doctors in the entire country. Few trained administrators had survived, and the country had no currency, no markets, no financial institutions, and no industry.[2]

The new government also faced a famine from 1978 to 1980, in which hundreds of thousands starved to death; to compound the problem, continued fighting between the Heng Samrin and Khmer Rouge forces disrupted the harvest of what little rice had been planted. Farmers were so physically weakened that they could not adequately care for their crops. International agencies were mobilized to provide food, and although thousands of people were saved from starvation, the rescue was only partially successful. As evidence of hoarding, favoritism, and corruption came to light, aid agencies were discouraged, but an even greater problem was the lack of qualified administrative personnel. In general, there was altogether too little food, and it arrived too late.

Affecting poor production, in part, was Cambodia's depleted labor force. If Cambodia had not been drawn into the Vietnam War and had not suffered subsequently from the devastation of U.S. bombing; if Cambodia had not been depleted by genocide under a tyrannical regime, by famine, and by the flight of hundreds of thousands seeking food and freedom, the country's population in 1980 would have been over 10 million. Instead, the total population in 1980 was about half that. Few societies have ever sustained such tremendous losses.

Vietnam's 1979 invasion was not welcomed by Asian countries or the international community at large. Although it freed Cambodians of Khmer Rouge rule, Vietnam's aggression was considered a violation of international law. Cold War politics also influenced the positions of countries in the region. China began a border war with Vietnam as punishment for overtaking their Khmer Rouge allies. Thailand grew nervous with the presence of Soviet-backed Vietnamese troops along its eastern border. The United Nations refused to recognize Heng Samrin's regime and instead gave Cambodia's seat to the Coalition Government of Democratic Kampuchea (CGDK), a government-in-exile formed in 1982 and composed of three disparate factions united solely in their opposition to the Vietnamese-sponsored regime in Phnom Penh.

The three factions of the CGDK included Sihanoukists, led by Sihanouk's son Prince Norodom Ranariddh; the Khmer People's National Liberation Front (KPNLF), an anticommunist group led by Son Sann, a former prime minister; and the ousted Khmer Rouge. Coordinating their work from held territory and camps along the Thai-Cambodian border, the CGDK drew the blessing of the international community as an anti-Vietnamese alliance. Although the Sihanoukists and KPNLF had no affection for the Khmer Rouge, their common goal of ousting the Vietnamese from power produced the uneasy alliance.

Prince Sihanouk was named coalition president largely because he was recognized internationally. The Sihanoukists included a military arm, the Armée Nationale Sihanoukiste, of about 3,000. The KPNLF, with about 5,000 troops, was supported by the noncommunist ASEAN states and the United States. The KPNLF and Sihanoukists enjoyed annual funding of about $7 million from the United States. The Khmer Rouge, fronted by Khieu Samphan, was clearly the largest and most powerful of the three factions, with 35,000 troops loyal to Pol Pot. Supported by China with infantry weapons, rocket-propelled grenades, and mortars, the Khmer Rouge was the best-equipped, most capable, and best-organized fighting force in the country. By virtue of the CGDK's recognition by the UN, the Khmer Rouge, astonishingly, was represented in New York throughout the 1980s.

Years of infighting, resignations, and scheming among the three factions did not come to an end until Vietnam, facing declining Soviet support in the late 1980s, announced plans to withdraw its troops from Cambodia. In an effort to resolve the Cambodian situation, the three coalition partners met with Hun Sen's government in 1991 and agreed to a UN-brokered peace plan signed in Paris.

The historic agreement created a four-party Supreme National Council (SNC) headed by Sihanouk, who would serve as Cambodia's head of state. The agreement also planned for a multinational force of UN peacekeepers and administrators to be stationed in Cambodia: the UN Transitional Authority in Cambodia (UNTAC). UNTAC's purpose would be to manage a cease-fire, disarm factions, conduct free elections, begin the repatriation of refugees, and administer the country's foreign affairs, national defense, and finance. The success of the peacekeeping mission thus depended upon the remarkable notion that foreign troops, unable to able to speak the Cambodian language and ignorant of Cambodian culture, could demilitarize all rebel factions, including the Khmer Rouge.

The UN peace plan could not have been established without the concurrence of the major external players: the United States, Vietnam, China, and the Soviet Union. Vietnam's complete withdrawal from Cambodia and the collapse of communism in Eastern Europe had changed the views of these foreign powers, leading them to the agreement. Moreover, the agreement of the four factions, even though each had its own self-serving reasons, was necessary for the plan to be implemented. When the Khmer Rouge faction resisted, Chinese officials pressured the recalcitrants.

When Prince Sihanouk returned triumphantly to Phnom Penh in November 1991 to become the Cambodian head of state, Cambodians had hopes that the UNTAC experiment could succeed. Shortly thereafter, Khieu Samphan, the Khmer Rouge representative on the SNC, returned as well but was met by a mob that came close to tearing him apart limb from limb. Khieu Samphan was rescued and later returned to participate in the coalition, but the mob action clearly indicated the strong hatred Cambodians still felt toward the Khmer Rouge.

In executing the agreement, UNTAC essentially governed Cambodia from March 1992 to September 1993. About 16,000 blue-helmeted peacekeepers blanketed the country, and over 3,300 civilian administrators took control of Phnom Penh. For a time, Cambodia (a sovereign country) was governed by foreign experts: A Japanese served as UNTAC's chief officer, an American ran the finance ministry, a Pole controlled the foreign ministry, and an Australian oversaw all military forces in the country. Before the mission was completed, one hundred UN member states had contributed peacekeepers, civil administrators, and election monitors to UNTAC. The bizarre nature of the UN program indicated the desperate nature of the Cambodian imbroglio after years of civil war, genocidal rule, foreign aggression, and societal chaos.

It soon became clear that the tasks UNTAC had set for itself were too great to be accomplished in only eighteen months. To run a government, oversee the repatriation of 350,000 refugees, supervise a cease-fire among factions that hated and distrusted one another, and conduct the first Cambodian election in decades were impossible goals even for an organization provided with $2.8 billion, the most expensive and far-reaching plan of this type in world history.

UNTAC, alas, was not able to pacify the nation because numerous violations of the cease-fire occurred, mostly by the Khmer Rouge. Disregarding the Paris agreement, the Khmer Rouge sought actively to expand its zones of influence and thereby control as many people as possible before the elections. The Hun Sen administration in Phnom Penh, which had turned over much of its power to UNTAC, engaged in its own violations and corruption, raising the question of whether any of the factions could run the government once elections had been held.

Despite cease-fire violations, popular support for the National Assembly elections was strong. Hun Sen organized the Cambodian People's Party (CPP), while Prince Ranariddh mobilized the United National Front for an Independent, Peaceful, and Cooperative Cambodia (FUNCINPEC). Both the CPP and FUNCINPEC campaigned on anti–Khmer Rouge platforms. The CPP argued that only the Hun Sen administration was strong enough to prevent a return of the Khmer Rouge. Prince Ranariddh's Sihanoukists, on the other hand, campaigned on the claim that the prince was the only Cambodian alive who had sufficient prestige to reconcile the murderous factions. FUNCINPEC candidates reminded voters that Hun Sen had once been a member of the Khmer Rouge and had been installed in power by the Vietnamese, who were detested by most Cambodians. FUNCINPEC candidates also pointed out the

CPP's blatant corruption, noting that Phnom Penh had become a boomtown catering to the whims of UN troops and foreign advisers.

The Khmer Rouge refused to disarm or demobilize its area. Weeks before the polls, Khieu Samphan unsurprisingly announced the Khmer Rouge would boycott the election and, effectively, the entire peace process. The stated reasons for the boycott were accusations that Vietnamese troops and citizens had remained in Cambodia and would take over the country once elections had been completed, and that UNTAC was biased in favor of the Hun Sen administration in Phnom Penh. No evidence was presented to substantiate these accusations.

The chances for a free and fair election were bleak because of Khmer Rouge intransigence, the absence of Cambodian experience with open elections, reluctance on the part of the ruling Hun Sen administration to give up authority, and a general fear by the populace of the UNTAC foreigners who were essentially administering their country. Nevertheless, between May 23 and 27, 1993, 90 percent of the eligible voters cast ballots for members of a legislative assembly with powers to draft a new constitution. Although the Khmer Rouge did not participate in the elections, they did not sabotage them after it became clear that the overwhelming majority of Cambodians had rejected Khmer Rouge pressure. The largest plurality (45 percent) was won by Prince Ranariddh's FUNCINPEC; Hun Sen's CPP trailed with 38.6 percent of the vote.

The UNTAC authorities declared the elections "free and fair," and the United Nations evacuated its peacekeepers in November 1993, leaving the government entirely in the hands of Cambodians for the first time since 1979. Prince Ranariddh and Hun Sen were designated co–prime ministers after Hun Sen threatened civil war if left out of the top position. (The prince was designated first prime minister and Hun Sen second prime minister.) The elderly Norodom Sihanouk was again named king, but he soon left the country for cancer treatment. The Khmer Rouge was kept out of the assembly and the executive branch. A new era of modern Cambodian politics had begun.

By 1994, Cambodia had achieved a semifunctioning government, and life in the rural areas as well as in the cities had returned to some degree of normality. There was hope that the standard of living would improve with increasing foreign investment and political stability. However, underneath this appearance of normality were deep problems that included ubiquitous corruption, crime, and patronage. Factional struggles between the two prime ministers and their respective parties bogged down the government. The Khmer Rouge continued its terrorist attacks, which placed an immense financial burden on the national budget. The government could not maintain law and order; dissidents were regularly assassinated, and the government was widely blamed for being incapable of stopping the carnage.

The political rivalry between FUNCINPEC and the CPP was ongoing and involved the frequent ouster of prominent ministers; unsuccessful attempts at power sharing at the district levels, a bizarre situation in which all cabinet ministries were run by top officials from each of the rival parties; disagreements over policy issues such as how to deal with the Khmer Rouge; and general anger on the part of Ranariddh's contingent over Hun Sen's forced entry into the government leadership. The rivalry culminated in Hun Sen's coup against First Prime Minister Ranariddh on July 6, 1997—a coup inspired by intrigue occurring within Khmer Rouge holdouts in Cambodia's hinterlands.

Hoping to resolving the outstanding problem of Khmer Rouge presence in the country, both prime ministers attempted to court dissident Khmer Rouge leaders, the most notorious being Ieng Sary and Khieu Samphan. These men, and a few other top Khmer Rouge leaders, sought amnesty and reintegration into Cambodia's new system by announcing they had formed separate political parties. Ieng Sary also pledged to integrate his 3,000 troops (about one-third of the entire Khmer Rouge force) into the national army. Hun Sen feared a Khmer Rouge–FUNCINPEC alliance, which could isolate his CPP and create a formidable force.

The open split among Khmer Rouge factions proved destabilizing. Fighting erupted in Anlong Veng, a Khmer Rouge stronghold along Cambodia's northern border. Rumors swirled about Pol Pot's fate: that he had ordered the killing of one of his longtime cadres, had been captured, was on the run, hiding in exile, or already dead. Determining what was factual proved difficult. Since the Vietnamese invasion in late 1979, Pol Pot had not been seen or photographed at all. Meanwhile, Hun Sen agreed to amnesty for the defector Ieng Sary, hoping to woo him away from the prince's camp. Prince Ranariddh, in a power play against Hun Sen, began to engage Khieu Samphan, hinting that a deal with Khmer Rouge remnants was on the horizon.

In a sense, the relative stability of post-1993 Cambodia had put the Khmer Rouge in a bind. Any real hope they harbored for a return to power had dissipated. Lacking international patrons (due to the end of the Cold War), and unable to hold on to their shrinking territory (due to government troop advances), Khmer Rouge leaders increasingly realized their days were numbered. Hemmed in and desperate, they began to turn on each other. Cambodia's co–prime ministers faced uncertainty as well due to the imminent dissolution of the Khmer Rouge. Neither could agree on terms of amnesty, participation, or criminal prosecution for the scheming Khmer Rouge leaders. Competing for influence, the co–prime ministers turned on each other, and Hun Sen made a bold grab for power.

Prince Ranariddh was out of the country when Hun Sen's coup took place. He charged Ranariddh with a variety of traitorous acts, including unauthorized negotiations with Khmer Rouge hard-liners. King Sihanouk, still ill and out of the country, refused to endorse the new government, but he did nothing to stop the coup and its aftermath. Ranariddh remained in exile, unable to return to Cambodia, because Hun Sen promised to arrest him upon reentry.

The coup reportedly was financed by alleged drug baron Theng Bunma, president of the Cambodian Chamber of Commerce, who publicly stated that he had given Hun Sen $1 million to stabilize the country's political situation. Following the coup, a number of FUNCINPEC supporters were assassinated; others were imprisoned while their homes were ransacked. Although Hun Sen apologized for the breakdown in law and order, the chaos continued for several months; the precarious balance that had emerged through Cambodia's joint leadership had been destroyed.

Twenty days after Hun Sen's coup, Pol Pot was affirmed to be alive and had been brought before a Khmer Rouge "people's tribunal" in Anlong Veng. The trial was held in an open-air, thatched-roof pavilion with dirt floors and bamboo furniture—symbolic of Khmer Rouge achievements. In a stunning turnaround, Pol Pot, the architect and perpetrator of the "killing fields," sat as an anguished old man, accused of murdering a top Khmer Rouge comrade and his family. He was denounced by the crowd, who screamed out "Crush! Crush! Crush!" when his prosecutor identified him. Pol Pot was found guilty and placed under house arrest for life by his erstwhile Khmer Rouge captors.

Pictures of Pol Pot and video of his show trial (taken by the intrepid *Far Eastern Economic Review* correspondent Nate Thayer) were broadcast internationally. It was the first time the outside world had seen Pol Pot since his murderous rule.

The world reacted strongly to Pol Pot's one-day trial. Responsible for the torture and death of millions of people, he appeared like an elderly grandfather. His public statements to Nate Thayer were unrepentant; he asserted that he had a clear conscience. Pol Pot talked about his modesty, his lack of interest in leadership, his unobtrusive style of politics. He claimed his opponents had been executed by the Vietnamese and that the skulls of those tortured and killed at Tuol Sleng prison could not have been Cambodian because they were too small. He seemed most eager to talk about his poor health (he was seventy-two in 1997) and his enjoyment of his new wife and twelve-year-old daughter, the apple of his eye. Pol Pot epitomized the fabled banality of the truly evil person.

Pol Pot's final days were spent under house arrest with government troops closing in on his jungle redoubt. He died of an apparent heart attack on April 15, 1998, supposedly two hours after listening to a Voice of America broadcast that announced his captors were negotiating his handover to international authorities. Some observers suspected suicide, or assisted suicide by his young wife. The truth will remain unclear, as his body was immediately cremated in an ignominious pyre that included automobile tires, old furniture, and debris.

With his death, Pol Pot, one of history's mass murderers, escaped retribution and legal accountability for his crimes. After years of uneasy negotiations involving the UN and representatives of multiple countries, Hun Sen finally agreed in 2006 to set up a court of "extraordinary chambers" as a tribunal for Pol Pot's living colleagues. Prosecution in the tribunal would fall under Cambodian law, inclusive of international crimes. Given the weakness of Cambodia's judicial system and the international nature of the crimes, foreign legal experts were included with Cambodians as lawyers and judges in the proceedings.

Twenty-seven years after the Khmer Rouge was expelled from power, the first Khmer Rouge leader appeared before the court on July 31, 2007. In a pretrial hearing, the onetime director of the notorious S-21 torture center, Kang Khek Ieu, or "Duch," faced the Cambodian people on the following charges: crimes against humanity, mass killings, forced movements, forced labor, inhumane living conditions, and torture. Facing similar charges, Ieng Sary, Khieu Samphan, and a handful of other aged leaders of the Democratic Kampuchea remain in detention awaiting separate trials.

The chaotic departure of the Khmer Rouge from Cambodian politics in the 1990s complicated the country's effort to restore order and develop economically. Hun Sen's 1997 coup was followed by elections for the National Assembly in July 1998, primarily to please donor countries that had withheld funds due to the coup (Cambodia's government's budget is largely dependent on foreign aid monies). The post-coup elections were marred by corruption, intimidation, and candidate assassinations. The CPP received 41 percent of the votes cast, FUNCINPEC 32 percent, and the Sam Rainsy Party 14 percent. Minor parties won the rest of the vote but did not receive seats in the 122-seat National Assembly. Hun Sen was renamed prime minister, and Prince Ranariddh was allowed to return from exile to be the president of the National Assembly under a reborn CPP-FUNCINPEC coalition. Supporters of Sam Rainsy became the opposition in the assembly.

The new millennium saw the beginnings of cooperation among political parties and politicians. No major war was being fought, and the Khmer Rouge was no longer a threat. Hun Sen's grip on power began to focus on his role as the gatekeeper to the Cambodian economy. New Cambodian tycoons linked to Hun Sen emerged. Foreign investors, primarily from Asia, also sought Hun Sen's partnership. Much of the investment centered on forest resources, tourism, and entertainment. Karaoke bars, casinos, and massage parlors popped up all over Cambodia, especially along the Thai border to the west. Garment manufacturers discovered Cambodia's eager and inexpensive labor force. International aid organizations, wielding hundreds of millions of dollars, indirectly took control of the government's agenda. Cambodia's economy grew but it did not experience development. The 80 percent of Cambodians still living in the countryside suffered in poverty.

Politically, Cambodia remains far from democratic consolidation. Elections at local and national levels punctuate the political calendar, but Hun Sen dominates the polling process due to the CPP's elaborate patronage network tied to business elites and local-level leaders. Opposition parties are harassed and human rights advocates risk retribution from those they accuse of committing violations. Cambodia's one-party dominant system resembles electoral authoritarianism and shows few signs of democratic transition. Even so, the trauma of recent decades, combined with the lack of high expectations for democracy, has led many Cambodians to welcome the relative stability established under Hun Sen's tenure.

A degree of resurgent Cambodian nationalism is also emerging under Hun Sen, fueled principally by controversies with Thailand over Angkor-era temples. Anti-Thai riots rocked Phnom Penh in 2003, caused by a Thai celebrity's claim that Angkor Wat belonged to Thailand. Then in 2007, Cambodia submitted a famed temple near the Thai border for United Nations Educational Scientific and Cultural Organization (UNESCO) World Heritage Site status. The dramatically set temple, Preah Vihear, is nestled on a cliff overlooking Cambodia's northern plains and was the subject of a 1962 International Court of Justice case that ruled the temple was indeed Cambodia's. In 2008, even as Cambodian political parties were campaigning for assembly elections, Thai authorities vigorously objected to the details of the 2007 UNESCO proposal, demanding postponement. Cambodian and Thai border troops eventually engaged each other near the temple, drawing the attention of the United Nations Security Council and nearly sparking a full-scale border war.

With events peaking in July 2008, Hun Sen could not have orchestrated events better. In a matter of weeks the Machiavellian strongman scored a political hat trick: official UNESCO designation of Preah Vihear (causing Thai troops to stand down), a landslide CPP election victory, and a reaffirmed image among the populace as Cambodia's tough nationalist. With Cambodia approaching almost two full decades of Hun Sen control, it remains more difficult than ever to imagine the shape of a post–Hun Sen Cambodia, or the arrival of such a period.

INSTITUTIONS AND SOCIAL GROUPS

Prince Sihanouk

After the 1940s, Prince Norodom Sihanouk dominated all aspects of Cambodian society. Although placed on the throne by the French in 1941 (when he was nineteen) and thought by the French to be pliable, Sihanouk became the symbol of Cambodian independence. With his shrill voice, he rallied his people during an era when Cambodia was known as "an island of tranquility in a sea of chaos." Conversant in ten languages, the author of five books, and a stage and movie actor and director, he has been the country's most cosmopolitan citizen. Dogmatic about the value of neutrality, and willing to play any side to survive politically, he is described by observers as temperamental, duplicitous, and inscrutable.

Although Sihanouk ruled autocratically, exercising dominance over the National Assembly, his government was supported by the overwhelming majority of the people. Sihanouk maintained the support of the rural population but eventually lost that of Cambodia's urban elites, who opposed his foreign and economic policies. After he was overthrown by his own premier in 1970, he allied himself with the Khmer Rouge rebels while in exile and, when the Khmer Rouge took power, returned to Phnom Penh as a "ceremonial" leader. Subsequently, he cooperated with the Khmer Rouge, even though it had murdered five of his sons and daughters, fourteen of his grandchildren, and more than a million of his former subjects. Sihanouk is an egotist who was willing to prolong the civil war to maximize his own authority.

Sihanouk denounced the Vietnamese-backed Hun Sen administration; he lived in exile in Beijing and Pyongyang for much of this period, receiving medical treatment for his numerous maladies. His movement in and out of Cambodia solidified his reputation as a mercurial figure. Sihanouk lost much popular support by being out of power for over twenty years and allying himself with the Khmer Rouge. Nevertheless, he remained one of the country's major institutions, eventually returning to Cambodia to become king following the UNTAC-sponsored elections in 1993.

While king, Sihanouk held little formal power and showed regret for some of his actions. He has said that if he were not a Buddhist he would kill himself, believing his life to be filled with shame, humiliation, and despair over Cambodia's past and future.

In 2004, King Sihanouk abdicated in favor of his son Norodom Sihamoni. A bachelor and classical dancer by training, Sihamoni lived most of his life in Prague, Pyongyang, and Paris. As he was a relatively unknown figure to most Cambodians, his appointment came as a welcome move and dampened rumors that Hun Sen might abolish the monarchy upon Sihanouk's death or that the king's more politically ambitious sons, including Prince Ranariddh, coveted the throne. Before his coronation, the apolitical Sihamoni had served as Cambodia's cultural ambassador to the United Nations but otherwise was uninvolved in national life.

King Sihamoni is gradually winning the affection of his subjects but is not as revered as his father. His state visits to China and neighboring countries have served Cambodia's interests. Given the short life of the resurrected monarchy, it remains to be seen whether the institution will endure in coming years. In 2008, Sihanouk, ever erratic, publicly raised the possibility of his son's own abdication only to recant the comments later.

Hun Sen

The opposite of Sihanouk in many ways, Prime Minister Hun Sen has been Cambodia's most important leader in the post–Khmer Rouge period. He was born in a peasant family and did not finish high school. Hun Sen was twenty-four when the Khmer Rouge came to power under Pol Pot. The Khmer Rouge evacuated his family from its rural home, killed his eldest son, and imprisoned his wife. Blinded in one eye by a U.S. cluster bomb, Hun Sen joined the Khmer Rouge as a senior commander and may have become party to its genocidal fanaticism. He defected in 1977, as Pol Pot began his systematic executions of dissident Khmer Rouge members, and escaped to Vietnam.

In 1986, Cambodia was being administered by a Vietnamese-installed government. Hun Sen, the prime minister and foreign minister, had become the most influential figure in the People's Republic of Kampuchea, although Heng Samrin, the head of state, held the highest position. Hun Sen's regime controlled the cities and most of the countryside with the aid of Vietnamese soldiers and advisers. However, few nations recognized this regime as Cambodia's legitimate government despite its control over virtually all aspects of the country's life.

As leader of the Vietnamese-backed PRK, Hun Sen traveled abroad to win foreign aid and support; he was known more as a pragmatist than as an ideologist. His attempts to position his government as being more independent of Vietnam improved his popularity in Cambodia. This popularity, however, was not matched internationally, where he was still viewed as a leader who had come to power from aggression. These global assessments of Hun Sen's aggressive and self-serving nature were reinforced when he demanded a share of the prime ministership in 1993 and when he grabbed power in 1997. Where analysts found Sihanouk to be enigmatic, Hun Sen remains predictably Machiavellian.

Hun Sen, who prefers to be called *somdech* (prince), shrewdly uses his Cambodian People's Party to maintain his hold on power. Employing elections and the trappings of democracy on one hand, and methods of intimidation, harassment, and fear on the other, Hun Sen perpetuates rule best described as electoral authoritarianism. Hoping to challenge the cultural appeal of his royalist rivals, Hun Sen has sought to soften his image by building clinics and schools and by providing special funds for families with triplets. (Some Cambodians believe the lost souls of Khmer Rouge victims find their way into already pregnant women for rebirth.)[3] Thus far, however, Hun Sen's tough image remains as fixed as his grip on power. As the country's most powerful post–Khmer Rouge leader, Hun Sen sits atop Cambodia lacking any serious rivals.

Political Parties

The Cambodian People's Party (CPP) is by far the largest and most broad-based party in Cambodia. With access to government coffers and bureaucratic connections spread through Cambodia's local areas, the CPP is organized as if it were a grassroots structure; functionally, it is anything but a bottom-up "people's party." The CPP is a centralized, patronage-based, hegemonic party that persistently blurs the lines between itself and the state.

Hun Sen and fellow party leader Chea Sim cultivate the CPP's image as a party of stability. Trumpeting fear, the CPP tells the electorate that it stands as the lone bulwark between social stability and a return to disorder. The party operates in the absence of ideology or a coherent political platform. It prefers to paint its opponents as dangerous to Cambodia's future.

To ward off perceptions that the CPP's claims may be true, FUNCINPEC, the party built by Prince Ranariddh, has strategically joined in coalition governments with the CPP. FUNCINPEC, an acronym for its French name, "Front Uni National pour un Cambodge Indépendant Neutre, Pacifique, et Coopératif," grew out of the Sihanoukists in the 1980s tripartite opposition to the Vietnamese-backed Hun Sen. In the 1990s it existed as partner, but potential challenger, to Hun Sen. In the first decade of the 2000s, FUNCINPEC struggles to find its place in the political milieu.

FUNCINPEC's supporters typically are those from urban areas and those partial to royalist influence. The party's popularity has waned because of its reluctance to play a genuine oppositional role to the CPP. Its core leaders pledged pragmatism but the party developed a reputation for political duplicity. Even after its leader was ousted as co–prime minister in Hun Sen's 1997 coup, for example, it joined the CPP in coalition following the 1998 elections. Then, after making a pact with the Sam Rainsy Party, it reneged on a pledge to not join the CPP in a coalition government following the 2003 elections. Prince Ranariddh's decision to break that pledge ended months of postelection wrangling and rewarded the party with cabinet posts, but it subsequently led to FUNCINPEC's decline. In 2006 the party, alleging corruption, sued its own founder and expelled him from the party. The prince formed a new party, the Norodom Ranariddh Party, awkwardly managed from Malaysia, where he remains in exile.

In the midst of the Preah Vihear temple controversy with Thailand, Cambodia held an election in July 2008. Fewer parties competed than did in 2003, and Hun Sen's CPP won 58 percent of the vote, which translated into 72 seats. The Norodom Ranariddh Party won only 7 seats. FUNCINPEC, a shell of its former self, produced a similar meager result with only 6 seats. The Sam Rainsy Party took 27 seats. Other parties occupied the remaining 11 seats.

Cambodia's only genuine opposition party since 1993 has been the Sam Rainsy Party (SRP), formerly the Khmer National Party (KNP). Sam Rainsy served as a finance minister and a member of FUNCINPEC until he was forced out of his position in 1994. His party draws support from liberal segments of society but it struggles to develop a functional apparatus due to harassment from Hun Sen and government officials. For his antigovernment statements, Sam Rainsy has faced defamation lawsuits, stints in exile, a royal pardon, and politically costly deals with Hun Sen. Numerous candidates and activists affiliated with the SRP have been anonymously harassed, shot at, and murdered.

International Aid Community

The Kingdom of Cambodia, as it is known today, was born from international assistance. Few countries have such an intimate history with the broad constellation of the global community's official and private foreign aid organizations. Cambodia, the object of much international sympathy, remains relatively open to government and nongovernment organizations that provide myriad services: resettlement, education, health care, construction of infrastructure, rural development, technical assistance, and human rights promotion. Thousands of foreigners and local Cambodians are employed in 450-plus NGOs and dozens of UN-affiliated agencies and bilateral aid programs, such as USAID, JICA (Japanese International Cooperation Agency), and AusAID (Australian Government Overseas Aid Program).[4]

So pervasive is the aid community that everyday life for many Cambodians is currently interwoven with the many schools, clinics, and infrastructure projects that mushroomed in recent years due to foreign support. A sudden departure of aid flows and aid workers would have a crippling effect on the economy and on Cambodian society in general. In the fifteen years following UNTAC, around 10 percent to 15 percent of GDP has been derived annually from international assistance, leading to worries about "aid addiction." Much of the annual government budget depends on cash flows from Japan and the European Union, creating, in turn, opportunities for official corruption. Donor countries often express concerns over bureaucratic corruption, but many Cambodians believe the wide salary gaps between foreign aid workers and local employees is just as morally repugnant.

With a few exceptions, individuals in the foreign aid community steer clear of direct involvement in Cambodia's political life. Indirectly, Hun Sen's government benefits from the incremental improvements to Cambodian life made possible by aid workers and their programs. The large flows of official development assistance, channeled through Cambodia's government, serve somewhat as a check on government behavior, keeping open repression fairly rare.[5] Unlike Burma, where the military regime functions with relatively little foreign presence in the country, Cambodia's leaders must remain more conscious of who is watching.

DEMOCRATIZATION

Cambodia has never experienced democratic rule. Since the days of ancient Angkor, autocratic rulers have led governments with scarcely any accountability to the ruled. Cambodians have a long history of Hindu-Buddhist notions of the *deva-raja* (god-king) and deference to those in authority. The principles of absolutism, hierarchy, and status, introduced centuries ago, remain important influences on Cambodian politics.

Cambodia's democratization is inhibited not only by a deeply conservative traditional culture but also by the political machinations of the powerful and wealthy. Due to the trauma of the Khmer Rouge and the recent influence of rights-oriented NGOs, interest in individual rights and representative democracy is rising. More and more Cambodians have begun to question the actions of those who hold power and their legitimacy to rule. Nevertheless, Cambodia's political elite have resisted developing democratic institutions that may threaten their own status.

Although relative political stability has been established since 1993, Cambodia is not transitioning to democracy. The Paris Peace Agreement and UNTAC's rapid efforts to secure peace through cease-fire agreements and popular elections set a low baseline for democratic expectations. By using a strategy emphasizing peace building and national elections, the Paris Agreement actually put Cambodia on a course toward electoral autocracy, not democratic institutionalism. The 1993 election launched a pattern where electioneering came to reinforce patronage-based authoritarianism at the expense of developing interest representation, oppositional politics, and civil liberties.

In hindsight, the expectations for democratic transition in the 1990s were naively optimistic. Most Cambodians, bewildered by UNTAC's complex mission, were too inexperienced with popular politics to demand much from representative government. Largely poor, rural, and uneducated, the people had a scope of political expectations at the time that ranged little beyond keeping the Khmer Rouge out of power and receiving help with basic needs. Collective action, public opinion, and exercising individual civil liberties were foreign notions to most Cambodians. Moreover, the educated class experienced with participatory politics had been tragically eliminated by the Khmer Rouge in the late 1970s. In fact, Cambodia's last elected Parliament had been under Sihanouk's patrimonial rule in the 1960s; experienced leaders were scarce. Patronage was more familiar than participation in the country's political culture.

Also reinforcing patronage politics over democratization have been international donors, NGOs, and foreign business tycoons who, by coordinating activities with sitting powers, set the policy agenda and help fund the CPP's patronage coffers, also known as the state budget. With so many foreign actors influencing affairs, the domestic interest groups, associations, and mass organizations that should be applying pressure on elected representatives and shaping the agenda have little opportunity to evolve. With donors providing resources to both state and nonstate actors, the people have yet to wrest democracy from a system of top-down resource allocation.[6]

The continued willingness of the donor community to tolerate rampant government corruption and ineptitude, and balk at demanding serious political reform, exacerbates the continued remoteness of the public from policymakers.[7] Asian industrialists and CEOs, eager to extract Cambodia's natural resources and negotiate deals on state infrastructure projects, also undermine the public interest by habituating Hun Sen and his top men to contract kickbacks and under-the-table favors.

Cambodia's 123-seat National Assembly, an object of tremendous political attention during national elections, falls well short of its democratic function to represent interests. It wields little power. Almost all the assembly's bills are handed down from the government—a rubber-stamp parliament. The elected members do not use the forum to seriously question the prime minister, his cabinet, or government policies.

The assembly's design virtually ensures CPP's dominance in the body for the foreseeable future. Cambodia is thus a hegemonic electoral authoritarian regime. The proportional voting system used to elect the Parliament disproportionately rewards larger parties. In 2003, for example, the CPP won only 47 percent of the vote but occupied 59 percent of assembly seats. Similarly, in 2008, the CPP won 58 percent of all votes but occupied 73 percent of assembly seats. In 2005, Hun Sen engineered a change in the constitutional threshold of assembly seats needed to form a coalition government from 66 percent to a simple majority. Threatening to imprison opposition leader Sam Rainsy, Hun Sen forced the SRP to vote in favor of the amendment.[8]

Although Cambodia's constitution calls for adherence to human rights, a disturbing degree of lawlessness still characterizes political life. Those who champion human rights often risk their personal safety to advance their cause. The politically motivated murders of political radio host Chour Chetharith

(2003), prominent labor rights activist Chea Vichea (2004), and opposition newspaper journalist Khim Sambor (2008)—as well as a dozen activists since the early 1990s—offer chilling reminders of means employed by those in power to silence critics who openly challenge them. Official investigations of political murders distressingly flounder in courts where government judges, using no witnesses, extend guilty verdicts to defendants with no known political ties; honest judges, seeking truthful verdicts, often find themselves removed from the bench.

ECONOMIC DEVELOPMENT

When the Vietnamese-sponsored regime took control in 1979, the government initially favored a command economy based on the Vietnamese model. Private enterprise and private property were not allowed. Beginning in the mid-1980s, however, the PRK regime instituted its own version of Vietnamese-style *doi moi* by liberalizing foreign investment laws, allowing private industries, increasing international trade, returning land to peasant ownership, permitting private transportation enterprises, guaranteeing the end of the nationalization of private enterprises, and legalizing the private sector.[9] This opening of the economy immediately improved the output of the industrial, agricultural, and private sectors.

Initially, about two dozen nongovernmental organizations (NGOs) from Australia, Europe, and the United States provided approximately $10 million per year in relief and development assistance. These NGOs, which supported nutrition centers, hospitals, and artificial limb factories, also oversaw water supply, animal welfare, sanitation, irrigation, and educational projects.[10] Only certain UN agencies that provided emergency relief, such as UNICEF and the World Food Program, were allowed to operate inside Cambodia, whereas the UN Development Program, the World Health Organization, and other development-oriented UN agencies were not.[11] Even so, Cambodia's needs were far greater than what the NGOs provided.

The NGOs built good working relations with their bureaucratic and technical Cambodian counterparts. They were also the country's main contact with the outside world. However, aid providers faced problems with accommodations, communications, travel, and visa relations. Even when a peace settlement was finally negotiated and the embargo was lifted, planning, reconstruction, and development would still be difficult because of severe constraints on the public sector's absorptive capacity. The country's technical and administrative cadres have been few in number, and they have been stretched to the limit.[12] Over time, more NGOs and aid organizations were permitted to operate in the country.

In Phnom Penh, the economy changed dramatically in the 1990s with a boom in consumer goods, mostly from Thailand and China; increased car traffic; out-of-control land speculation; and inflation, driven by a huge supply of money, mostly from the high per diem payments made to foreign aid personnel, whose daily income was often equivalent to Cambodians' average *yearly* income.

By 1997, there were still only about sixty small industries in Cambodia, operating at half capacity. The major investments for foreign exchange at the time were rubber, timber, and tourism. Manufacturing focused on apparel factories that benefited from the Multi Fibre Arrangement (MFA), a globally negotiated country export quota scheme to assist developing countries. By the early 2000s, the number of factories grew to well over one hundred, with many operating at full capacity.

Tourism also began to grow. Academic delegations and adventure travelers were joined by big-ticket travelers on group tours. The magnificent ruins of Angkor, at one time a popular tourist attraction, were unavailable for most of the 1970s and 1980s. By the early 1990s Cambodia was not attracting significant numbers of visitors due to poor roads, rail service, and air transport, and because the Khmer Rouge still controlled nearby land. That changed rapidly in the late 1990s and air service was expanded. Siem Reap, a once small town near Angkor-era temples, now finds itself inundated with large resort-style hotels and busloads of wealthy OECD-country seniors and Asians on package tours.

Under CPP-FUNCINPEC coalition governments, Cambodia experienced modest to low growth rates in the 1990s. Since 2000, however, Cambodia's economic growth has taken a rapid turn upward. Cambodia averaged 9.4 percent annual GDP growth between 2000 and 2006. Over the same period, per capita income increased from $288 to $513; doubling in only six years.[13]

From a domestic perspective, encouragement can be derived from such economic activity. Tourism, industry, and manufacturing are growing rapidly. The apparel industry, in particular, plays an important role in Cambodia's new economy, employing 250,000 workers in more than two hundred factories producing for global brands such as Polo, The Gap, and Banana Republic. The success of the apparel industry continues despite the expiration of MFA in 2005, which many observers predicted would cripple Cambodia's competitiveness. Somewhat surprising, Cambodia has also consented to implementing higher international standards for textile workers and has won praise from the International Labor Organization (ILO). Cambodia now enjoys a positive reputation among socially minded clothing buyers in Paris, New York, and London.

From a comparative perspective, however, the reality is more daunting. Cambodia's economy may be growing but it is so far behind its neighbors that even years of sustained growth will not raise it to regional averages. About four in five Cambodians still live as poor farmers in rural areas. Deficient irrigation works limit Cambodia's agricultural potential, demonstrated by record surpluses of rice in 2006, a particularly good rain year. Where Thai and Vietnamese farmers lead the world in rice exports, Cambodian farmers are only beginning to produce beyond domestic needs. With respect to per capita income, at current growth rates, Cambodians in 2015 will still rank below Filipinos at their 1997 income average: a meager $1,600. Cambodians share a level of development similar to most people in Burma, Laos, and Timor-Leste, where one in three residents remains below the poverty line.

The Kingdom of Cambodia's economic future is now linked to its WTO membership, secured in 2004. A new frontier in oil exploration is being charted with projections estimating peak oil revenues above three times the country's current international aid receipts, raising concerns that Cambodia may substitute one form of revenue addiction for another. Moreover, oil revenues could simply act to replenish current CPP slush funds derived from Cambodia's rapidly depleting forests.[14]

THE CAMBODIAN STATE

In the twelfth century the Khmer Empire, under the great warrior Jayavarman VII, dominated much of mainland Southeast Asia. It was not until the fifteenth century that the empire was reduced in size to approximately the present boundaries of Cambodia. At its height, however, the Khmer Empire was among the strongest states in the world, able to mobilize the citizenry and protect its sovereignty. Modern Cambodia, in contrast, has proven to be among the world's weakest states.

In the analysis of the other Southeast Asian states, massive social dislocation was seen as a necessary condition for a strong state. Cambodia qualifies in this respect but nevertheless has not become strong. Again, modern Cambodian history is the story of monumental dislocation as a result of the Khmer Rouge's systematic destruction of Cambodian social, cultural, economic, and political life. Although a strong state cannot emerge until its society has been weakened, and the latter did occur in Cambodia, a strong state has not evolved because the country has been largely bereft of capable administrative leadership.

The explanation for Cambodia's weakness is thus found in the absence of a group that is both independent of existing bases of social control and skillful enough to execute the designs of state leaders. Cambodia has few experienced technocrats whose loyalty is primarily to the state; the army is weak and undependable; and politically skillful leaders have been practically nonexistent.

In 1993, the United Nations had literally taken over all elements of Cambodia's failed state. UNTAC's departure left a situation similar to that of South Vietnam when the Americans extricated themselves in the early 1970s. In both cases, there was insufficient viability to sustain the state's goals. Fortunately, in Cambodia's case, the ritual of elections did stick. Despite the failure of other democratic institutions to develop, the expectation today is that Cambodian governments are legitimate only if endorsed by election results. The fact that Hun Sen went through with the 1998 election only a year after his coup against his co–prime minister is indicative of this expectation.

The greatest challenges to the legitimacy and viability of the Cambodian state are likely in the past. Internationally, world leaders and donor countries have shown patience with Hun Sen, allowing him the political space—too much perhaps—to restore a state formerly subject to foreign control. Hun Sen's political legitimacy has been derived from three bases: (1) as a Cambodian leader who initially guided Cambodia through the post–Khmer Rouge period; (2) as the leader of a party elected multiple times to take the reins of government; and (3) through his public popularity, which is far from unanimous, but draws support from Cambodia's widest patronage network.

Cambodia, only recently a failed state, is recovering due to tremendous international support and Cambodians' willingness to demilitarize warring factions. Brought to its knees in the late 1980s, and desperate for peace and order, it allowed foreigners to reoccupy the ministries the colonial French once controlled. Though the state's capacity remains weak and the state is too often fused with CPP rule itself, Cambodia's viability looks somewhat promising. Whether the country can produce (or endure) a shift in power from one set of rulers to another, without succumbing to the impulses of violence and militarism, remains an open question.

FOREIGN POLICY

Throughout its modern history, Cambodia has been the target of aggression by its larger neighbors and by Western and communist imperialists. The French, Americans, Soviets, Chinese, Vietnamese, and Thais have all attempted at various times to control Cambodian affairs. During the Cold War, Cambodia was the victim of direct U.S. and Vietnamese intervention as well as Chinese support for antigovernment rebels. The Vietnamese intervention of December 1978 occurred with significant support from the Soviets, who funded the operation and provided much of the weaponry.

After the Vietnamese invasion, the United Nations continued to recognize the Pol Pot regime despite the fact that the Khmer Rouge controlled only about 2 percent of the population and that Pol Pot had been branded as one of history's worst violators of human rights. The vote of U.S. President Jimmy Carter's administration for Pol Pot was based on the view that his opponents, the Hun Sen government, had achieved power by aggression. The vote also reflected Carter's desire to strengthen ties with China and his displeasure with the growing Soviet role in Southeast Asia. The PRK was viewed as a puppet of Vietnam, which in turn was seen as a surrogate of the Soviet Union.

The end of the Cold War brought important international changes in the late 1980s, which affected Cambodia by providing new opportunities for a comprehensive peace settlement after the country had floundered for a decade. Warmer relations between the United States and the Soviet Union were the primary influence on U.S. policy toward Cambodia. For many years, U.S. goals in Cambodia included the withdrawal of Vietnamese military forces; the repudiation of the Khmer Rouge; a political settlement that would permit Cambodians to choose their form of government; and an independent, neutral, and nonaligned Cambodia, protected from outside interference by international guarantees.[15] Before Vietnam withdrew its military from Cambodia, U.S. policymakers argued that the Hun Sen government was essentially a puppet of the Vietnamese, but that argument lost credibility once the withdrawal was completed and when Hun Sen became a partner at the peace talks in Paris.

As the Cold War came to a close, ASEAN was not united on the best means by which to deal with Cambodia. Whereas Singapore took a hard-line stance against the Hun Sen government, Thailand wished to convert Indochina from a battlefield into a marketplace, with the Thais themselves taking the leading economic role in mainland Southeast Asia. Thai Prime Minister Chatichai Choonhavan met with Prime Minister Hun Sen on numerous occasions to negotiate trade programs and a settlement of the Cambodian imbroglio.

After the October 1991 peace accords were signed, the Supreme National Council under Sihanouk became Cambodia's legitimate government. Although part of the SNC, the Khmer Rouge lost Chinese aid when China and Vietnam moved to a rapprochement in 1992 and when China attempted to improve its international reputation following the 1989 Tiananmen Square tragedy. In addition, UN-imposed sanctions against the Khmer Rouge undermined an important source of funding: Thai investors who had engaged the border rebels in deals for timber and gems. To support the peace process, the United States ended its economic embargo against Cambodia. In a matter of a little more than a decade, Cambodia transformed itself from Khmer Rouge pariah state, to a Vietnamese puppet state, to an international experiment, and then a weakling state dependent on international patrons.

Cambodia's international relations evolved further in 1999 when it became a member of ASEAN, only a year after a troubling coup d'état and Hun Sen power grab. Since that time, it has sought to improve its relations with China in particular. Cambodia regards China as its main protector. China has provided military aid to Cambodia and in 2006 agreed to a "comprehensive co-operative partnership," aimed at Beijing consultation on "issues of regional peace, stability, and development" as well as economic matters.[16] In economic relations, the ASEAN–China Free Trade Agreement (ACFTA), signed in Phnom Penh in 2002, included zero tariff classification on certain imports from Cambodia.[17]

Cambodia's biggest foreign relations concerns in recent years have been with its Thai neighbors to the west. In 2003, after a Thai actress supposedly commented that she would not perform in Cambodia until Angkor Wat was returned to Thailand, anti-Thai riots erupted on Phnom Penh streets. Rioters attacked several Thai-owned businesses, causing $50 million worth of damages. No Thais were injured or killed but the incident troubled relations between the two countries. Tensions over the matter reverberated for a time but eventually economic interests triumphed again and the two governments found themselves signing border trade deals and cooperating on oil exploration in the years that followed.[18]

Internationally, the long-awaited tribunal of Khmer Rouge leaders at last became a reality as the first decade of the 2000s came to a close. Although the Khmer Rouge is no longer an organized force, its legacy, alas, continues to define international perceptions of Cambodia and its people. Cambodia's biggest foreign policy challenge going forward is to transcend this image; to create for itself a truly post–Khmer Rouge international identity, much in the same way Vietnam is shedding its "Vietnam War" image by redefining itself as one of Asia's emerging economies.

CONCLUSION

Regime instability, indicated by the country's many name changes, has dictated Cambodia's recent past. No people in Southeast Asia have undergone the magnitude of horrific trauma as what Cambodians suffered from the 1960s to the present. War, holocaust, famine, and oppression have devastated the society once known as an oasis of tranquility. With virtually its entire educated class decimated, Cambodia is attempting to rebuild. However, it is still buffeted by the world's great powers, by its neighbors, and by internal political rivalries. The phenomenal resilience of the Cambodians is the most hopeful sign that the "killing fields" will never return and that Cambodia can develop and remain independent.

Nevertheless, for the foreseeable future Cambodia will continue under weak state institutions, led by a strongman, and threatened by internal political conflict. Without better trained administrators, an improved infrastructure, and continued external aid, the immediate political outlook is bleak. Hun Sen, proven capable of employing any means to ensure power, is unlikely to permit electoral politics, or any other process, to remove him from the apex of power. Patronage, corruption, and disregard for civil liberties are likely to characterize the Cambodian political system for many years to come. Champions of democracy face an uphill battle.

The problems of governing Cambodia and implementing lasting peace have been among the most vexing issues facing contemporary Southeast Asia in the new international era. The demise of the Cold War led to the end of Vietnamese occupation and the final disintegration of the Khmer Rouge, but Cambodia enters the new century far behind its Southeast Asian competitors. It will likely be decades before most Cambodians enjoy the socioeconomic fruits planted by the current generation, a post–Khmer Rouge generation burdened with restoring Cambodia culturally, politically, and economically.

NOTES

1. Eva Mysliwiec, *Punishing the Poor: The International Isolation of Kampuchea* (Oxford, UK: Oxfam, 1988), p. 2.

2. Ibid., p. 11.

3. Duncan McCargo, "Cambodia: Getting Away with Authoritarianism?" *Journal of Democracy*, vol. 16, no. 4 (2005), p. 103.

4. Figures are from home page of Cooperation Committee for Cambodia: www.ccc-cambodia.org.

5. McCargo, "Cambodia," p. 108.

6. Melanie Beresford, "Cambodia in 2004: An Artificial Democratization Process," *Asian Survey*, vol. 45, no. 1 (January/February 2005), p. 137.

7. McCargo, "Cambodia," p. 110.

8. Caroline Hughes, "Cambodia in 2007: Development and Dispossession," *Asian Survey*, vol. 48, no. 1 (January/February 2008), p. 74.

9. Robert J. Muscat, *Cambodia: Post-Settlement Reconstruction and Development* (New York: East Asian Institute, Columbia University, 1989), pp. 88–89.

10. Mysliwiec, *Punishing the Poor*, p. 66.

11. Muscat, *Cambodia*, p. 2.

12. Ibid., p. 83.

13. Figures from the Royal Government of Cambodia, Ministry of Economy and Finance. UNDP figures for 2007 show a GNI of $540.

14. Hughes, "Cambodia," pp. 72–73.

15. Frederick Z. Brown, *Second Chance: The United States and Indochina in the 1990s* (New York: Council on Foreign Relations, 1989), p. 11.

16. Oskar Weggel, "Cambodia in 2006: Self-Promotion and Self-Deception," *Asian Survey*, vol. 47, no. 1 (January/February 2007), p. 146.

17. Robert Sutter, *Chinese Foreign Relations: Power and Policy since the Cold War* (Lanham, MD: Rowman & Littlefield, 2008), p. 268.

18. Weggel, "Cambodia in 2006," p. 146.

Resource Guide

A useful tool for bibliographic and other information on Cambodia is available from Australia National University's WWW Virtual Library: www.gksoft.com/govt/en/kh.html.

The University of California–Berkeley maintains a useful portal for digital and print resources on Cambodia: www.lib.berkeley.edu/SSEAL/SoutheastAsia/seaelec.html. Northern Illinois University's Southeast Asia Digital Library includes a range of useful links that cover government, academic, and research institutions specific to Cambodia: http://sea.lib.niu.edu. The University of Wisconsin–Madison Libraries similarly maintains a list of digital and print resources on Cambodia: www.library.wisc.edu/guides/SEAsia/resarea.html. The Library of Congress maintains an Internet resource guide on Cambodia at www.loc.gov/rr/international/portals.html#t.

The official site of the Cambodian government is www.cambodia.gov.kh. For the party line of the CPP and Hun Sen, visit "Cambodia New Vision" at www.cnv.org.kh. The official Web site of King Norodom Sihamoni is at www.norodomsihamoni.org. An independent organization, the Cambodia Development Research Institute, focuses on development policy analysis: www.cdri.org.kh.

UNTAC provides details on its mission at www.un.org/Depts/dpko/dpko/co_mission/untac.htm. For information on the vast NGO community operating in Cambodia, visit www.ngoforum.org.kh/Core/core.htm and www.devdir.org/files/Cambodia.PDF.

The Cambodian Genocide Program at Yale University, www.yale.edu/cgp, maintains research tools and databases on the Khmer Rouge period. The Web site of the Extraordinary Chambers in the Courts of Cambodia for the Prosecution of Crimes Committed during the Period of Democratic Kampuchea provides information on ongoing judicial action at www.eccc.gov.kh/english, as does the Khmer Rouge Trial Portal at www.krtrial.info. Students may be interested to know that Khieu Samphan's 1959 thesis, "Cambodia's Economy and Industrial Development," is available through interlibrary loan.

11

LAOS

L aos can be described as a quasi-nation. It emerged from maps drawn by European colonialists rather than from a sense of territory and nationhood among a united people. The history of Laos is riddled with constant warfare among contending forces within its borders and the meddling of external powers from without—mainly Thailand, Vietnam, China, France, and the United States. Since it seized power in 1975, the present communist government has faced ongoing problems with little signs of progress: uniting ethnic groups that have fought with each other for decades, resettling large groups of refugees, promoting development amidst an overwhelmingly rural population, educating a citizenry with minimal educational institutions, and protecting the nation's sovereignty against encroachment by neighbors and outside powers.

Laos is landlocked, but uniquely so. Its isolation is exacerbated by the physiographic borders it shares with each of its neighbors. Remote mountains lie along Laos' northern borders with China and Vietnam, and the rugged Annam Cordillera defines its long eastern border with Vietnam (inhibiting overland routes to the South China Sea). The broad and meandering Mekong River separates Laos from most of Thailand and Burma to the west. Culturally, the Mekong supported Lao people on both sides of the river, but the first modern bridge appeared only in the last decade. Laos' access to the Mekong Delta is inhibited by the fact that transport ships must travel through sovereign territory in Cambodia and South Vietnam before exiting. Thus, lowland Laos, inclusive of the Plain of Jars, sits as a land island, disadvantaged in the new international era by the lack of highways, railways, and port access.[1] Given the relative economic dynamism of its neighbors, Laos' economic potential as a modern crossroads for trade and transport is yet unmet.

Contemporary Laos has changed little over the decades. It is still a rural, subsistence, agrarian society of some 6.2 million people divided among over forty ethnic groups, with the dominant lowland Lao consisting of just over 4

CHINA

BURMA

PHONGSALI

VIETNAM

Mekong

Plain
of Jars

LOUANG PHRABANG

XIANG KHONG

Gulf
of
Tonkin

Nam
Theun

Dam

VIENTAINE

Mekong

SAVANNAKHET

THAILAND

LAOS

PAKSE

0 50 100km
0   50   100mi

CAMBODIA

million people. The population density of Laos is the lowest of all Asian countries. Theravada Buddhism, variably blended with local spirit beliefs, predominates among the Lao and among many upland groups. Most ethnic Lao are isolated from both their regional neighbors and the world as well as from upland ethnic minorities within Laos itself. Almost all Lao are poor. The household economy is based on rice and still relies on water buffalo; modern farming techniques and equipment have been slow to reach Lao farmers. In 2007, Laos' per capita GNI was only $580.

Contemporary problems in Laos originate from centuries-old conflicts, when ancient Lan Xang—"the Kingdom of a Million Elephants"—was a battleground for the expansionism of neighboring states. It was not until the fourteenth century that a semblance of national unity emerged. However, dynastic quarrels in the eighteenth century undermined this unity, and the area was divided into the kingdoms of Luang Prabang in the north, Champassak in the south, and Vientiane in the central region.

Vietnam and Thailand periodically plundered Lao kingdoms until the French colonized the area beginning in the late 1880s. In 1899, the French claim of suzerainty consolidated Laos into a single political unit, but French rule did little to modernize or integrate the nation. On the contrary, a small group of elite Lao families was allowed to consolidate its power; thus, the Lao emerged from colonial rule (after World War II) more divided, isolated, and backward than ever.

From 1941 to 1945 the Japanese ruled Laos, although the collaborating Vichy French administered many governmental affairs. At the end of the war, the Gaullist French recaptured Vientiane, the administrative capital, and fought a group called the Lao-Issara (Free Lao), which established a government in Bangkok and became the forerunner and nucleus of the separate pro-communist, anti-French, nationalist Neo Lao Hak Sat (NLHS)—the so-called patriotic front. Lao-Issara was led by Prince Souvanna Phouma and his half-brother, Prince Souphanouvong, who later broke off and joined the NLHS, which was operating in areas held by the Vietminh. By 1953, the NLHS's military force, known as the Pathet Lao, had seized control of the nation's northeastern provinces.

In 1954, France accorded self-government to Laos at the Geneva Conference, which effectively gave Laos complete independence. The aftermath of the Geneva Conference was a period of disarray for Laos, as the competing sides vied for control of the populace and the countryside. Also in 1954, when the Pathet Lao was making significant military gains in large areas of the countryside, the United States sponsored a coup by anticommunists against Souvanna Phouma, who had become premier of the new nation but was considered too much a neutralist by the U.S. government. The coup failed, but Souvanna Phouma was given notice that even neutralist policies were considered intolerable by the United

States. When a right-wing government appeared in 1955, the United States immediately began a $45 million annual aid program.

In 1957, the neutralists, led by Souvanna—this time with backing from the United States—set up a government emphasizing national unity, with cabinet posts for leftists and rightists. In special elections as called for in the Geneva agreements, NLHS candidates won the majority of seats, an outcome deemed intolerable by Souvanna's government and by U.S. diplomats. To overturn the results of the election and reverse the apparent popular trend toward a communist government, the United States—principally through the Central Intelligence Agency (CIA)—extended massive support to right-wing regimes that excluded NLHS representation. There were numerous coups d'état during this period as anticommunist leaders jockeyed for power. However, the major beneficiary of governmental chaos was the NLHS movement, which continued to expand its control as it received increasing amounts of military supplies and support from the Soviet Union.

At the second Geneva Conference in 1961, neutralist Souvanna Phouma, leftist Souphanouvong, and rightist Boun Oum agreed on coalition rule. The United States reversed its policy and supported Souvanna Phouma's appointment as prime minister (after he gave secret permission to the United States to bomb Pathet Lao areas). The coalition collapsed almost immediately, however, as factions maneuvered for power. The NLHS broke from the coalition, and Souvanna Phouma's Royal Lao government, a constitutional monarchy, became a virtual client of the United States.

Escalation of the Vietnam War changed the nature of the struggle between the NLHS and Royal Lao government forces. Hanoi's interest in Laos increased as its need for sanctuaries from U.S. bombing became paramount. Thus, Laos was swept up in the war as Hanoi, in violation of the Geneva agreements, escalated its presence in the northeastern provinces of Laos and as the United States, also in violation of the agreements, began its secret bombing missions in 1964. In the following years, the landlocked nation became one of the most heavily bombed countries in history; some 2.1 million tons of bombs were dropped between 1964 and 1972 (about two-thirds of a ton per Lao).[2] Despite this ferocity, the strategic effect of the bombing was minimal, prompting the CIA to train and supply Hmong and other upland peoples, introduce military advisers, and use the U.S. Agency for International Development as a front for intelligence and training purposes. Laos became the battleground for a neighboring war fought by surrogate powers.

The Laos Peace Accords came in 1973 as the American withdrawal from Vietnam was completed. The accords called for stopping the bombing, disbanding foreign-supported forces, removing all foreign troops, and instituting the coalition Provisional Government of National Unity (PGNU). The new ministries were divided between the Royalists and the Pathet Lao. At the time of the signing of the accords, the NLHS controlled about three-fourths of all Lao territory and one-half of the population. Both sides were allowed to keep their zones of control until elections could be arranged.

The well-organized Pathet Lao (now called the Lao People's Liberation Army) prevailed over the Royal Lao faction in the coalition government, which lacked discipline, was enervated by family feuds, and was considered a puppet of the United States. The Pathet Lao spoke convincingly to the rural people of Laos, who had seen their agricultural base destroyed, their population dislocated, and their villages destroyed.[3] No family had been left unscathed by the civil war and the U.S. bombing.

In December 1975, the Pathet Lao dissolved the PGNU, abolished the 622-year-old monarchy, and established the Lao People's Democratic Republic (PDR). The change in government was preceded by communist victories in Vietnam and Cambodia and by procommunist demonstrations throughout Laos. The rightist ministers fled, and all power was eventually assumed by the communists. Souvanna Phouma resigned and Kaysone Phomvihane, general secretary of the newly formed Lao People's Revolutionary Party (LPRP), became the new prime minister. A Supreme People's Council was set up with Prince Souphanouvong as president and chief of state, while Kaysone Phomvihane— virtually unknown to all but a handful of communist leaders before 1975— assumed political and administrative control of the country. In contrast to Vietnam and Cambodia, where communists came to power as a result of military victory, the change of government in Laos came about relatively peacefully.

The communist victory changed Lao politics fundamentally. For centuries the region had been dominated by a small group of wealthy families that wielded great political and economic influence. Most of those families fled to Thailand, Europe, or the United States, and those that remained underwent "reeducation" programs to cleanse them of their "bourgeois mentality." An estimated 300,000 persons, many of them the most educated in Laos, fled to Thailand following the change in government. The flight of educated Lao and the systematic expunging of civil servants of the former administration created a leadership vacuum that seriously impaired the government's ability to administer and implement new programs.

The new government moved quickly to eradicate the worst vestiges of what they considered bourgeois society by banning nightclubs, massage parlors, and dance halls. Private enterprise was stifled, and the government attempted, rather feebly, to collectivize farms. Most farmers resisted collectivization and continued subsistence production. The government's reeducation programs, affecting thousands of Lao, made the populace wary of the new regime. Refugees reported arrogant bureaucrats and repressive rules and regulations.

Another major change was the withdrawal of the United States as a principal player in Lao politics. Most Western aid, which had funded over 90 percent of the Royal Lao government budget, ended when the communists took power, although the countryside was still devastated from the war. Although the United States did not break diplomatic relations with Laos after the communist takeover, U.S. involvement became peripheral, and the Soviet Union and Vietnam filled the vacuum. In 1979, the leaders of Laos and Vietnam signed a joint revolutionary declaration, a Treaty of Friendship and Cooperation, granting Vietnam the right to maintain some 40,000 troops in Laos. China soon accused Vietnam of working to create an Indo-Chinese federation dominated by the Vietnamese and withdrew its aid to Laos for numerous development projects. The Soviet Union, supplying some 2,000 advisers and $50 million in annual aid, was Laos' superpower patron until 1991, when the USSR collapsed.

The Lao PDR was ruled from 1975 to 1991 without a constitution. When one was finally adopted, it strengthened the presidency (at that time held by Kaysone), although the LPRP retained its position as the primary institution. Civil liberties were allowed "as prescribed by law," but the major advantage of the document was to provide a semblance of stability and predictability with regard to governmental affairs.

President Kaysone's death in November 1992 provided an opportunity for Laos to usher in a new generation of leaders more in tune with the international movement away from communism and toward democracy. However, Prime Minister (and former Defense Minister) Khamtay Siphandone, who was nearly seventy years old, was named leader of the LPRP, and National Assembly Chairman Noahak Phousavan, who was nearly eighty, was named president. Their hard-line conservatism and provincial outlook frustrated those who wanted Laos to look more toward the West for direction.

Beginning in 1990, Laos, like China and Vietnam before it, opened its economy by pursuing a "new thinking," or a market-based approach. Under the "New Economic Mechanism," the government jettisoned failed collectivization policies and centralized economic allocation. By 1995, the twentieth anniversary of LPRP rule in Laos, market economics was in command and party rule was far less doctrinaire. The LPRP also gave new life to Buddhism by restoring temples and encouraging the *sangha*, or Buddhist monastic order, to play a role in development. In what was surely a communist-world first, the funeral services for the regime's first president, the "Red Prince" Souphanouvong, were an entirely traditional Buddhist ceremony, with no ideological overtones.

In 1996, the Sixth Congress of the LPRP further moved Laos toward comprehensive but slow economic reforms. Personalism, conservatism, and nationalism remained the dominant characteristics of the leading party. Military generals held six of the nine positions in the politburo; party leaders viewed the continuation of their unity (in a nation made up of numerous ethnic groups) as the primary national goal. This goal has been difficult to achieve because the economic reforms have made the urban areas wealthier, whereas the rural areas, populated by minorities, have remained poor.

Since the millennium began, the Lao government has continued to liberalize the economy but retained its centralized and oppressive rule. Signs of Asian-style economic dynamism have emerged, mainly in urban areas, but economic reform has yet to modernize or transform the economy to the degree it has in neighboring Vietnam. Laos continues to be both Buddhist and authoritarian, both Marxist and capitalist. Regime leaders, now portraying themselves as the protectors of Theravada Buddhism, now build monuments to legendary Buddhist monarchs of fourteenth-century Lan Xang to prop up their legitimacy.

Khamtay, at eighty-three years of age, was replaced as state president in 2006 by Choummali Sayason, yet another old-line conservative. Other leadership changes produced by the Eighth Party Congress did little to dislodge political hard-liners from the politburo. The post–revolutionary generation leaders who did emerge from the Congress celebrate ties to Laos' communist past. For example, Buoasone Bouphavanh, who became the regime's fifth prime minister, boasts little more than a 1980s education in the collapsing Soviet Union; and among the party's most notable new insiders are the sons of Kaysone and Khamtay.[4] Thus, even as Vietnam and China are handing party leadership to a new generation of educated technocrats, dynastic communist rule may be in embryonic form in mainland Southeast Asia's poorest country.

INSTITUTIONS AND SOCIAL GROUPS

Lao People's Revolutionary Party

Since 1975, the country's dominant institution has been the LPRP, the communist party that emerged from the Pathet Lao leadership. Led by elderly revolutionaries who fought against the French, Japanese, and Americans, the party has practiced democratic centralism, requiring party leaders' unanimous support in all decisions. Policy was formulated and implemented by the party politburo, led by Kaysone Phomvihane. Kaysone had emerged in December 1975 from the caves of a northern province where he and his Pathet Lao colleagues had hidden to escape U.S. bombing. Outside the inner circle of the Pathet Lao, few Lao knew him or knew about him, and Kaysone eschewed a cult of personality, living quietly and making himself available to very few visitors except communist allies. Little was known about his past except for his close association with Vietnam, where he had studied at the University of Hanoi.

Kaysone held the positions of prime minister and then president, as well as general secretary of the LPRP. Surrounded by colleagues from his revolutionary days in the 1950s, he changed his rule little after 1975. Continuity and stability were the themes of governmental leadership until 1979, when reforms were instituted that significantly changed the government's hard-line policies.[5] After that time, and especially after 1986 when the "new thinking" reforms were instituted, Kaysone visited noncommunist countries, and his activities were even reported in the press. Nevertheless, he remained one of the world's least-known leaders up to his death in 1992.

The LPRP, with about 40,000 members—having failed to achieve popular support for its socialist policies—launched a series of reform policies in 1986 to decentralize economic decisionmaking and to liberalize, both economically and politically. In 1989—for the first time—the LPRP allowed elections for the National Assembly, Laos' nominal legislative body. Some 121 government-approved candidates ran for 79 seats, and 65 of the victors were party members.[6] Since the 2006 elections, all but 2 of the now-115 seats are held by members of the party. Assembly elections, little more than Soviet-style plebiscites for preselected LPRP candidates, mean little in a system where the assembly institution enjoys little independence from the party apparatus. To a certain degree, mass organizations that organize youth, women, labor, or minority groups to follow party directives are more connected to the grass roots of Lao society than the LPRP itself. The Lao Front for National Construction (LFNC), for example, is charged with the daunting task of unifying Laos' disparate ethnic groups. Created in 1979, the LFNC's organizational reach extends to every administrative level of government in an effort to co-opt local leaders into the state apparatus.

Unlike Vietnam and China, where the military is increasingly separate from party leadership, military leadership remains integrated with the LPRP. After a decade-long recruitment effort, party membership now stands above 148,000, double the party's size in 1995.[7] It remains to be seen whether a younger generation of leaders will emerge to replace the "revolutionary generation" of the LPRP.

International Aid Community

The Lao PDR government collaborates extensively with the international aid community in pursuing its development policies. International agencies, regional bodies, and bilateral aid programs do not directly control policy but do much to set the policy agenda in Vientiane. A principal international partner, for example, is the United Nations Development Program (UNDP). It ties its current efforts in Laos to achieving UN Millennium Development Goals. Focusing on programs to reduce Laos' poverty rate by half and move the country out of "least developed country" (LDC) status, the UNDP guides a formalized roundtable process of aid coordination with various UN agencies and the network of embryonic civil society organizations (CSOs) now operating in the country.[8]

Other principal partners with the Lao government include the Asian Development Bank (ADB), through its Greater Mekong Sub-Regional Program, the IMF and World Bank, and over fifty bilateral agencies of OECD countries that help prop up the Lao state. The World Bank is particularly influential in supporting the massive hydropower projects the Lao government is undertaking. Antiglobalization critics angrily indict the World Bank for manipulating Lao authorities and the policy agenda.[9]

Lao Abroad

Since 1975, over 300,000 refugees, mostly lowland Lao, have left the country. Ethnic Hmong, Mien, Lahu, and other upland groups recruited by the CIA for its secret war in Laos also compose a large segment of this migrant population. Without U.S. "allies" to protect them, many Hmong and others were subject to genocidal recrimination in the form of chemical-biological toxins falling from Vientiane aircraft in the late 1970s and 1980s. As reported by droves of refugees fleeing into Thailand, whole villages suffered illness and fatal hemorrhaging from "red, yellow, and green gases" dropped from the sky. Disastrous living conditions forced others, including many lowland Lao, to seek refuge as well. Refugees reported forced labor, torture, "seminar camps," and starvation.[10]

After years in Thai border camps, most refugees were resettled in third countries such as the United States, France, and Australia. A vocal segment of the overseas refugee community now actively lobbies foreign governments to exert greater pressure on the LPRP communist regime. Lao refugees regularly target their protests against the governments of the United States and Thailand for failing to address the refugee problem as well as ongoing human rights abuses by Vientiane. The plight of upland minority groups within Laos and the forcible repatriation of refugees from border camps draw the attention of Amnesty International and other human rights groups.

Among the Lao abroad is exiled crown prince Soulivong Savang, grandson of King Vattana. Laos' last king died in a reeducation camp following his overthrow in 1975. Soulivong has held meetings with U.S. government officials and pushed for a more aggressive international isolation of Vientiane. Residing in France, the crown prince remains a dim symbol of hope for Lao seeking regime change and restoration of a constitutional monarchy.

In 2007, Hmong community leader Vang Pao, a former CIA ally, was arrested from his home in California on evidence of plotting to overthrow the Lao government—an act in violation of U.S. law prohibiting Americans from acting violently against foreign governments with peaceful U.S. relations. In support of the legendary seventy-seven-year-old leader, hundreds of Hmong-Americans flocked to the Los Angeles courthouse where Vang stood accused. Vang was eventually released on $1.5 million bond. The alleged plot of Vang Po and his coconspirators included smuggling Stinger missiles into rebel areas and hiring U.S. mercenary forces to launch an offensive on Lao government forces. Hmong rebels have in fact organized attacks within Laos in recent years, producing some fatalities.

An increasing number of economic migrants from Laos, often undocumented, now work in Thailand as laborers. The wages earned and wealth created by these workers, together with the earnings of overseas Lao in third countries, often find their way back to relatives in Laos. In recent years, remittances from abroad, according to Lao government reports, accounted for as much as 28 percent of household earnings in many parts of Laos.[11] The Lao government has also sought, without great success, to entice wealthy and capable overseas Lao back to the country by offering them government jobs, new homes, and other perks.

DEMOCRATIZATION

There is no semblance of democracy in Laos, nor has there ever been. The country's communist leadership has not instituted reforms permitting a representative system or civil liberties. It can be classified as a politically closed regime. Testimony to the Lao people's view that their government is not legitimate is the fact that since it came into power, about one in ten residents have left the country. Indeed, the regime's insecurity regarding its legitimacy is shown by its refusal to allow any kind of opposition or free elections. Civil society is closely monitored, although a 2008 draft law was in motion at the behest of the UNDP to permit CSOs greater autonomy to operate. The government has also experimented with village-level elections.

The fall of communist governments in Eastern Europe as the new international era began did not affect the Lao people because they did not have access to information about these changes. Greater exposure to the world since that time due to increased tourism, new bridges to Thailand, and increased contact with China and Vietnam is a notable change. Nevertheless, the dearth of education in the country inhibits opportunities for a civic consciousness to develop. The country's first university was finally opened in 1996. Television broadcasts from Thailand are the public's main external link to the outside world.

Political liberalization, let alone democratization, is a distant prospect for Laos. Strong economic growth since 2000 is creating a fledgling urban middle class, but those benefiting most are those closest to the regime and least likely to pressure it to reform. Laos' LPRP rulers maintain a monolithic hold on political power and face no overt political opposition.[12] With regime change an unlikely prospect, greater political transformation depends on a generational shift in leadership.

ECONOMIC DEVELOPMENT

Laos is one of the world's poorest countries. With a gross national income (GNI) per capita of $580, and a poverty rate of nearly 40 percent, the standard of living is low. In Laos, only 19 percent of births are attended by a skilled professional, compared to 99 percent in neighboring Thailand and 57 percent in impoverished Burma. About 79 percent of the labor force in Laos remains in agriculture, typically as rice farmers inhibited by poor distribution systems and market coordination. In rural areas, less than four out of ten residents have access to improved sanitation. The spread of HIV/AIDS is growing rapidly, and malaria, tuberculosis, and chronic diarrhea are widespread.

Although such extreme poverty is not new to Laos, the contrast with economic standards in the other ASEAN countries is obvious. Over the past decade, Laos has experienced limited progress in reducing the incidence of disease and improving basic living conditions. Yet, in measures of overall development, Laos annually joins Cambodia, Burma, and Timor-Leste among the bottom third of annual world rankings of the human development index (HDI).

In terms of economic policy, LPRP leaders realized after only four years of rule that their agricultural and industrial policies were failing to revive the economy. In 1979, therefore, a process of decentralization was begun. By the early 1980s, pragmatic policies were formally set forth at the Third Congress of the LPRP. The government's control over the economy was loosened; agriculture began decollectivization; and new technology was introduced, resulting in larger crop output and self-sufficiency in rice for the first time since the revolution. These reforms were called *chin tanakan may* ("new thinking"), Laos' version of the Soviet Union's perestroika or Vietnam's *doi moi*.

The most fundamental changes, however, did not begin until 1986 at the Fourth Congress of the LPRP. These changes, called the New Economic Mechanism, allowed family farms to completely replace the unpopular agricultural cooperatives. Also, market mechanisms generally replaced centralized planning. In 1988, Kaysone admitted that the party's policy of putting private traders out of business, collectivizing farmers, and nationalizing industry had caused the production and circulation of goods to come to a halt, grievously affecting the people's livelihood.[13] The World Bank had been critical of the

government's policy and cited Laos' agricultural inefficiency, declining industrial output, dependency on loans from socialist nations (on poor terms), stagnant exports, and huge balance of payment deficits, all of which acted to
perpetuate underdevelopment.[14]

The reforms emphasized grassroots economic units including factories,
merchants' shops, and construction projects.[15] Rather than move directly from
subsistence to large-scale collective farming, peasant families were encouraged
to join the barter economy, trading their surplus production for commodities. State land was distributed to individual families on a long-term basis, and
consideration was given to making such land inheritable.[16]

The reforms also included a new foreign investment code designed to attract
outside investment to finance the Lao infrastructure, but the results were initially disappointing. Laos did not have a constitution or a civil code, a fact that
frightened off many potential participants. Corruption also discouraged foreign investors reluctant to pay "tea money" to officials. An equally important
problem was administrative capacity: Laos demonstrated little absorptive capability that would allow follow-through on investment and aid projects. Following its neighbors embroiled in the Asian economic crisis, Laos experienced
triple-digit inflation and a currency collapse during the late 1990s. Laos' currency, the kip, fell 87 percent, from 1,080 to over 10,000 per dollar, greater than
any other drop in the region.

Since 2000, however, Laos' economy has experienced rapid GDP growth,
above 6 percent in most years. Inflation has been moderate and the kip has
stabilized, although Thai baht and U.S. dollars remain in wide use. Foreign investment by Asian companies in textiles, food processing, and low-tech assembly is expanding Laos' once pathetic industrial sector. Only 6 percent of
GDP in 1990, industry now accounts for nearly 30 percent of economic activity. Plans to launch a stock market in Laos by 2010 are drawing financial and
technical support from South Korea and Thailand.

Tourism, another recent arrival to the struggling Lao economy, now generates
over $130 million per year with over a million annual tourist arrivals.[17] Laos'
former royal capital of Luang Prabang, nestled along the Mekong in the country's northern mountains, was declared a UNESCO World Heritage Site in 1995.
Tourism, combined with international aid, creates strong incentives for the Lao
government to keep the country open. Contrasting with Burma's military junta,
the LPRP-led Laos depends mightily on international aid in its growth strategy.

Though amounts are not publicly disclosed by the government, most estimates put foreign aid at about 40 percent of Laos' GDP. Since 1989, when the
United States granted its first assistance to Laos since the communist takeover,
by supporting a $1 million antinarcotics project, international aid to Laos has
gradually expanded to a diverse array of intergovernmental, bilateral, and nongovernment sources. In addition to rural development, communications, and

community health projects, the major focus of foreign assistance is on over-coming Laos' unfortunate landlocked geography. Thus, the construction of trans-Mekong bridges and hydroelectric dams gains much attention.

In 1994, Australia financed the construction of a bridge to Thailand near Vientiane, the first along the six hundred miles of river that form much of the Thai border. A second bridge to Thailand, in southern Laos, opened in 2006 and was financed by Japan. A third link across the Mekong is planned to connect northern Thailand and Laos with overland routes to Kunming, China, and plans for a fourth bridge to Burma exist. The new bridges, along with improved land routes to Vietnam, function as globalization lifelines to landlocked Laos. Thai food processing and manufacturing companies, for example, are busily relocating factories to Laos due to the improved infrastructure. Mining, a transport-intensive industry, is also experiencing new private investment from Australian companies, much to the dismay of environmentalists.

Through assistance from the World Bank and Asian Development Bank, the Lao government now pursues an economic growth strategy built on massive hydroelectric projects, aimed to feed the insatiable power grids of Thailand, China, and Vietnam. Twenty-five-year purchase agreements tied to the projects were a welcome arrival to Laos' cash-strapped government. Controversy surrounding resettlement of displaced villagers, environmental destruction, and the distribution of benefits tied to hydropower draws serious international attention. The current construction of the $1.3 billion, 1,070-megawatt Nam Theun 2 Dam, for example, will displace 100,000 people, or nearly one in sixty Lao citizens. At least ten other hydropower dams are in the construction or planning stage. Rumors abound that the government's goal is to construct seventy total dams.

At current growth rates, Laos could graduate from LDC status by 2020. This achievement would meet a joint Lao government–UNDP goal. One sign of rising income is mobile phone use, which went from 29,500 phones in 2001 to 638,200 in 2006—a far greater usage rate than in Cambodia or Burma.[18] Notwithstanding income gains and phone usage, poverty reduction faces significant challenges. Eight in ten Lao residents are still in rural areas far removed from Vientiane's fledgling factories and Luang Prabang's tourist trade. They remain even more distant from export revenues from mining and hydropower that are absorbed by government accounts. Economic opportunity for most rural and upland Lao remains sorely limited.

THE LAO STATE

Laos, like its neighbors Cambodia and Burma, is an example of a state with little capacity to meet the needs of its citizenry or to mobilize its collective strength. Like most Southeast Asian states, it has dual elements of strength and weakness. Certainly, it meets one criterion for all strong states: massive social dislocation. Laos was exploited by a self-serving colonial regime, was occupied by the Japanese and later became a client state of the United States, was bombed during the Vietnam War to an even greater extent than Japan was bombed in World War II, and was finally taken over by a hard-line communist government. Of its 3 million people, about a third were subject to dislocation in the early 1970s caused by the war and subsequent refugee crises.

Laos does not have a societal group that is independent of social controls and capable of executing the designs of state leaders. The LPRP dominates every aspect of Lao political life, having co-opted virtually the entire administrative class and local leadership. Experienced bureaucrats of former governments, having joined the Lao refugee diaspora, remain excluded from state administration. In Laos there is no independent intellectual class capable of competing with the state leaders. The long tradition of student activism seen in Thailand, Indonesia, and Burma is virtually nonexistent. A recent attempt by a small group of student activists led to arrests and exile in Thailand. Internet activism, to the extent it exists, is dominated by second-generation overseas Lao who indicate little desire to return to a country they technically never left.

Additionally weakening the Lao state is the absence of skillful or charismatic leaders. Kaysone Phomvihane's leadership resulted more from his control of the LPRP and from repression than from his capacity to gain the respect and approbation of the Lao people. Subsequent leaders function more as party managers than as mobilizers of popular sentiment or political will.

Political institutions beyond the LPRP are feeble or nonexistent. Whereas Thailand enjoys the symbolic importance of a king to provide overall state legitimacy, Laos has had no parallel institution since 1975. Buddhism is receiving renewed government support but the institutionalization of the *sangha* as a political actor is weak compared to the monastic order in Thailand and even Burma. Moreover, increasing dependency on financial and technical assistance from international aid agencies and wealthy Asian entrepreneurs fosters patronage and corruption—phenomena of state weakness, not strength.

FOREIGN POLICY

As a landlocked nation, Laos has always had to rely on its neighbors for security. Traditionally, Thailand, China, and Vietnam have had the greatest impact on Lao political affairs because these nations share long borders with Laos and control its access to the oceans. After World War II, however, the United States became the paramount power, with almost total control over every aspect of Lao political and economic life.

Until 1975, the United States played the leading institutional role in Laos. By dominating the policies of the Vientiane administrations and financing the Lao military, the United States became the patron and the Lao government became a client of U.S. interests. To secure the continuation in power of pro-U.S. forces, the United States engaged in a secret war in Laos in the 1960s, which cost $2 billion annually. Covert operations and massive bombing raids over Laos were designed to strengthen the anticommunist government in Vientiane, demolish the Pathet Lao infrastructure, and interdict soldiers from North Vietnam. In the long run, however, none of these goals were achieved.

After 1975, the United States no longer had influence over the Lao government, and CIA-supported allies such as the Hmong were left to defend themselves. Not until 1987 did relations with the United States change when the two governments signed agreements for crop substitution programs. Laos had agreed to make a "maximum effort" to stop opium trafficking, and in return, the United States removed Laos from its "decertification list" and reopened its aid program. The irony of these events was the previous tacit U.S. support of upland drug running as a means for upland groups to finance their war efforts.

A major source of tension between the United States and Laos concerned some five hundred U.S. troops from the Vietnam War classified as missing in action (MIA) in Laos who had not been accounted for. The Lao government was bitter about U.S. demands to conduct excavations because it offered no compensation for the thousands of Lao continuing to die every year from miniature land mine bomblets (called "bombis"), full-size land mines, and other unexploded ordnance (UXO) still scattered throughout the Lao countryside. The lasting presence of UXO in Laos continues to hinder rural development, rendering thousands of acres of arable land too dangerous to use.

Vietnam has emerged as the country with the greatest influence on Laos' foreign and domestic policies since 1975, when it placed approximately 50,000 troops in the country. Although there was fear in the 1980s that Laos and Cambodia would be assimilated into a greater Indochina federation under Vietnamese dominance, such a confederation never occurred. All Vietnamese troops were withdrawn by 1990 and Laos began to assert a more independent policy by strengthening its relations with Thailand, ASEAN, and China.

Laos' relations with Thailand have been tense since the Pathet Lao took power, because the Thais viewed Laos as a base for support of insurgency and because the hundreds of thousands of Lao (and Cambodian) refugees who have crossed into Thailand are viewed as an economic burden. In 1987–1988, Laos and Thailand fought a bloody three-month war over a disputed border area. Later, as relations warmed, Thai businesspeople took advantage of the economic reforms in Laos to set up businesses, and border towns became market centers for Thailand. Thai companies are primary investors in the growing sectors of Laos' new economy.

Improved relations have not resolved the centuries-old problem of a strong Thailand versus a weak Laos. As reform began, sentiment from Laos emerged that Thailand, having failed to destroy Laos with its military power, was employing a new domination strategy: attacking Laos with economic power. Although the Lao government later distanced itself from this view, many Lao continued to fear that Thailand—with more than ten times the population of Laos and a history of aggression against its smaller neighbor—might once again intervene. Since the country joined ASEAN, with its strong principle of noninterference, many such fears in Laos have abated in the past decade.

In the new international era, no longer able to rely on Soviet aid, Laos has moved to improve relations with China, which remains an important trade ally and a major supplier of weaponry. Since 1990, China has invested over $1 billion in Laos, and two-way trade has risen rapidly. More important to China, however, are needed overland links through Laos to Thailand and its growing market. In the golden triangle region, increased river trade on the Mekong has created greater incentives for improved overland highways and train routes linking China and Thailand via Laos. With support of the ADB and the six countries of the Greater Mekong Subregion (GMS), a project to complete a 1,800-kilometer (1,110-mile) international road from Kunming, China, to Bangkok, Thailand, was recently launched. Vientiane's government hosted the third GMS meeting in 2008.

Burma and Laos also enjoy improved ties with each other. Leaders have exchanged visits on many occasions. Both party-military regimes share the goal of remaining strongly authoritarian with a nationalist centralized administration and a central role for the military. In addition, both nations also harbor historical distrust and fear of Thailand and China. Notwithstanding similarities between Burma and Laos, the prevailing winds for the LPRP are toward greater relations with China, Thailand, and Vietnam, which offer greater economic opportunity.

CONCLUSION

Laos is the "forgotten country" of Southeast Asia because it is small and is no longer strategically important to the world's major powers. Its total population is far smaller than that of the city of Bangkok. Laos' leadership is unknown to the world, and its military capacity is practically nonexistent. In contrast to Thailand and Vietnam, Laos has changed little over the past several decades. Though the current mini–economic boom is altering Vientiane, and tourists now dot the streets of Luang Prabang, development in most of the country's towns and hill areas has remained largely static. Meeting its stated goal to exit LDC status by 2020 would be a major achievement for Laos. Such a feat, however, will require China-like growth rates and demand that development reaches Laos' diverse and largely rural populace.

Notes

1. The Plain of Jars is a common name for the Xiangkhoang Plateau, where in certain areas hundreds of thick, three meter–tall stone jars lie strewn across the plain. With the jars dating back to 500 BC, their source and purpose remains a subject of Lao legend and of considerable archaeological debate.

2. W. Randall Ireson and Carol J. Ireson, "Laos," in *Coming to Terms: Indochina, the United States, and the War*, ed. Douglas Allen and Ngo Vinh Long (Boulder, CO: Westview Press, 1991), p. 66.

3. Ibid.

4. Geoffrey C. Gunn, "Laos in 2006: Changing of the Guard," *Asian Survey*, vol. 47, no. 1 (January/February 2007), pp. 184–185.

5. Macalister Brown and Joseph J. Zasloff, *Apprentice Revolutionaries: The Communist Movement in Laos, 1930–1985* (Stanford, CA: Hoover Institution, Stanford University, 1986), p. 165.

6. Geoffrey C. Gunn, "Laos in 1989: Quiet Revolution in the Marketplace," *Asian Survey*, vol. 30, no. 1 (January 1990), p. 84.

7. Gunn, "Laos in 2006: Changing of the Guard," p. 185.

8. Geoffrey Gunn, "Laos in 2007: Regional Integration and International Fallout," *Asian Survey*, vol. 48, no. 1 (January/February 2008), p. 64.

9. Merial Goldman, *Imperial Nature: The World Bank and Struggles for Social Justice in the Age of Globalization* (New Haven, CT: Yale University Press, 2005).

10. Jane Hamilton-Merritt, *Tragic Mountains: The Hmong, the Americans, and Secret Wars for Laos, 1942–1992* (Bloomington: Indiana University Press, 1993).

11. Bertil Lintner, "Laggard Laos Turns Economic Corner," *Asia Times Online*, January 10, 2008, www.atimes.com/atimes/Southeast_Asia/JA10Ae01.html.

12. Bertil Lintner, "Political Dissent in Laos," *The Irawaddy*, vol. 8, no. 6 (June 2000), www.irrawaddy.org/article.php?art_id=1903.

13. *Asia Yearbook, 1990* (Hong Kong: Far Eastern Economic Review, 1990), p. 161.

14. Charles A. Joiner, "Laos in 1987," *Asian Survey*, vol. 28, no. 1 (January 1988), p. 104.

15. Ibid., p. 96.

16. Martin Stuart-Fox, "Laos in 1988," *Asian Survey*, vol. 29, no. 1 (January 1989), pp. 81–82.

17. Gunn, "Laos in 2007: Regional Integration and International Fallout," p. 66.

18. Lintner, "Laggard Laos Turns Economic Corner."

Resource Guide

A useful tool for bibliographic and other information on Laos is available from Australia National University's WWW Virtual Library: www.gksoft.com/govt/en/la.html.

The University of California–Berkeley maintains a useful portal for digital and print resources on Laos: www.lib.berkeley.edu/SSEAL/SoutheastAsia/seaelec.html. Northern Illinois University's Southeast Asia Digital Library includes a range of useful links that cover government, academic, and research institutions specific to Laos: http://sea.lib.niu.edu. The University of Wisconsin–Madison Libraries similarly maintains a list of digital and print resources on Laos: www.library.wisc.edu.guides/SEAsia/resarea.html. The Library of Congress maintains an Internet resource guide on Laos at www.loc.gov/rr/inter national/portals.html#t.

Under the direction of the Ministry of Culture and Information, the *Vientiane Times* offers English-language news: www.vientianetimes.org.la. A similar news agency with closer connections to the LPRP is the Lao News Agency at www.kplnet.net/index.htm. The UNDP Lao provides useful economic development information: www.undplao.org. To appreciate the significance of hydroelectric power and its rising impact on Laos, visit the Nam Theun 2 Dam Web site at www.namtheun2.com.

Among the Lao abroad, useful Web sites include Global LaoNet at www.global.lao.net and the Hmong International Human Rights Watch at www.hmongihrw.org.

12

TIMOR-LESTE

O ccupying only half of a small island in the expansive Indonesian archipelago, the 1.1 million people of Timor-Leste (commonly called East Timor) have drawn considerable worldwide attention in recent decades. Regrettably, East Timor joined the post-Holocaust, "never again" narrative in 1975 when it experienced its first spate of politically motivated mass killings at the hands of Indonesian invaders. The world did nothing to stop the violence then, but it responded with measured effectiveness in the face of a genocide-style reprise in 1999 and internal chaos in 2006. Although episodic bloodshed has continued to torment East Timor in the new international era, foreign occupation and meddling have bedeviled the small island for over five hundred years. Timor-Leste's story, both sad and triumphant, is of a long, painful struggle for political freedom, independence, and unity.

Facing Indonesia to the north and Australia to the south, Timor Island sits prominently in the Timor Sea. It is home to rugged terrain, timber resources, and mountains that reach upward to 9,000 feet. Three times the size of Cyprus in the Mediterranean, the island is similarly divided into two political entities. East Timor occupies the island's eastern half; Indonesia enjoys sovereign control over its western half (excluding a small East Timor–controlled enclave).

The division of the island runs centuries deep. Portuguese friars first arrived on its eastern flank during the sixteenth century, followed by the Dutch, who gained control of the island's western reaches. By the late eighteenth century, East Timor was under full Portuguese control, although it remained only a minor star in a global empire that celebrated Brazil in the Americas, Mozambique in Africa, and Goa in India. Portuguese rule of East Timor followed a pattern of general imperial neglect, although Catholicism developed deep roots in many areas of the island.

For 460 years, the Portuguese dominated affairs in East Timor. Change did not arrive until World War II, when Dutch and Australian troops, ignoring Portuguese neutrality, overwhelmed the colonists and established East Timor

Banda
Sea

INDONESIA

DILI

BAUCAU

PANTE
MAKASAR

SUAI

INDONESIA

Timor
Sea

TIMOR-LESTE

| 0 | 50 | 100 km |
| 0 | 50 | 100 mi |

as an Allied military staging ground. Their presence invited Japanese forces, who defeated the Allies in a 1942 battle on the island. As its next occupiers, Japan's warriors brutally demanded submission by East Timor's residents. Tens of thousands were killed and many islanders were forced into sexual slavery as comfort women. At the end of the war, Timorese leaders attempted independence but without success. The Portuguese subsequently returned to East Timor for an unwanted three-decade encore of colonial rule.

Independence almost came to East Timor in 1975. In that year, half a world away in Lisbon, a coup d'état led by leftist military officers unleashed widespread Portuguese sentiment to decolonize overseas territories. Timorese aspirants encouraged by these events established *Fretilin*, an acronym for the "Revolutionary Front for an Independent East Timor." Its goal was full independence and statehood. Even as Portuguese administrators experimented with local elections and the planned decolonization of the territory, rival groups claiming leadership of the independence movement sparked a civil conflict. *Fretilin* forces eventually overcame internal challengers and established control of Dili, the administrative capital. With their plans of an orderly transfer thwarted, Portuguese officials retreated in a messy withdrawal. On November 28, 1975, *Fretilin* declared East Timor independent—a "democratic republic." Nine days later, however, shortly after a visit to Jakarta by U.S. President Gerald Ford, Indonesia invaded East Timor, drawing support from some anti-*Fretilin* groups within the territory. Jakarta's purpose was full annexation and unification of Timor under the Indonesian flag. Decades later, declassified government documents released in Washington, D.C., confirmed the Ford administration's knowledge and support of the invasion.[1]

Driven by fears of *Fretilin*'s Marxist orientation, and communist victories in Vietnam, Cambodia, and Laos months earlier, General Suharto's armed forces employed vicious tactics in executing Indonesia's annexation of East Timor. The 35,000 Indonesian "volunteer forces" maliciously attacked Timorese civilians, tortured prisoners, and sprayed chemical napalm on villages to ensure the population's complete submission. During the pacification campaign following the takeover, leftists and refugees were placed in camps or otherwise interned for "reeducation." Out of an original population of 650,000, an estimated 100,000 Timorese (about one in six) lost their lives at the hands of the Indonesian military during the invasion, making it among the worst mass atrocities in modern history in terms of loss of life per capita.[2]

Suharto declared East Timor as Indonesia's twenty-seventh province only months after his forces had occupied it. Although most countries refused to recognize the annexation and condemned Indonesia's actions, Suharto's government experienced only minor international repercussions. The United States and many of its Cold War allies in the region were deafeningly silent on the matter. Australia, a key regional player, formally recognized the annexation as legitimate. Alternatively, the United Nations condemned the takeover and granted observer status to *Fretilin*, inviting its representatives to the General Assembly. However, as with the Palestinian Liberation Organization, observer status in the world's premier organization of nations had little effect on dislodging the occupiers or forcing a political settlement.

The ensuing years of Indonesian control of East Timor were marked by continued suppression. Thousands of Timorese resisting Indonesian control were imprisoned or executed. From 1974 to 1999, almost 20,000 Timorese died as a result of armed clashes with Indonesian troops or from extrajudicial killings by occupation authorities; an additional 80,000 Timorese died from preventable illness or starvation.[3] In total, close to one-quarter of East Timor's pre-1975 population died during the twenty-five years of Suharto's occupation. Armed resistance continued during the period, led principally by *Fretilin*'s military wing *Falantil* (*Forces Amadas de Libertação Nacional de Timor Leste*). Over time *Falantil* weakened and *Fretilin* turned increasingly to political means, nonviolence, and efforts to raise international awareness of East Timor's plight.

To dampen foreign sympathy and thwart his critics, Suharto closed the annexed territory to outsiders for many years. The tight control on information worked. During the 1980s the issue of East Timor largely disappeared from the international consciousness.

Suharto's attempt to integrate East Timor with Indonesia failed miserably. Not only did the Catholic population differ with Indonesia's Muslim majority, but there also was too little by way of shared history, language, or culture to bind the disparate populations together. Neither did East Timor's impoverished, battle-scarred populace share in the rapid economic growth sweeping Indonesia. Economic conditions improved marginally in the 1980s with meager sums of development aid trickling in from Jakarta, but Java's economic dynamism was worlds away from the Timorese experience. Rather than look to Suharto's New Order government, Timorese turned to their local communities and to Catholic leaders for unity and direction.

In 1988, East Timor was finally reopened by Suharto. It was a significant shift in policy. Pope John Paul II seized the opportunity to visit a year later, a landmark event that sparked pro-independence demonstrations, which were forcibly suppressed by Indonesian security forces. Following the papal visit, a pattern of popular protest and harsh military repression emerged. In 1991, an especially appalling massacre of defenseless protesters occurred at the Santa Cruz cemetery in Dili. Congregating themselves to memorialize the death of Timorese students killed days earlier by security forces, scores of young people were suddenly targeted in a vicious melee of bloodshed resulting in seventy dead and countless wounded. Much to the dismay of Indonesian political and military leaders, disturbing video images of the slaughter were smuggled out of East Timor by foreign journalists and broadcasted internationally. Suddenly, East Timor's long saga of occupation drew renewed global attention.

Although never a cause célèbre on the scale of the anti-apartheid movement or the ongoing campaign for Tibetan autonomy, East Timor retained a solid core of champions abroad. Throughout the 1990s, numerous international human rights groups stepped up pressure on Suharto's government. The independence movement received a major boost in 1996 when two longtime Timorese leaders, Bishop Carlos Filipe Ximenes Belo and Jose Ramos-Horta, were jointly awarded the Nobel Peace Prize. The movement also featured an important Mandela-esque face for its cause, that of imprisoned poet-warrior Jose "Xanana" Gusmao, known for his leadership of *Fretilin* guerrillas and his impassioned prison writings during long years of confinement.

In the end, it wasn't renewed international activism, Nobel-level attention, or Xanana's growing status that triggered events that led to independence. In the new international era, the powerful forces of globalizing markets and Asia's financial collapse put into motion events that would end Suharto's occupation.

In May 1998, amidst the financial contagion rocking Southeast Asia, Suharto's government collapsed in spectacular fashion. The economic crisis and IMF rescue programs ignited public anger and revealed the depth of Suharto's mismanagement and his family's corrupt dealings. Social disruption lasting for weeks culminated with intense anti-Suharto street protests in Jakarta and elsewhere. Succumbing to the loss of international legitimacy and facing unyielding domestic pressure, the once-invincible Suharto resigned in political disgrace. Consequently, East Timor's fate followed a new course.

Only weeks after Suharto's resignation, B. J. Habibie, Indonesia's new president, floated the idea of a "special status" for East Timor. A few months later he announced plans for a UN-supervised referendum where Timorese could choose between "autonomy within Indonesia" or "independence." It was a political gamble. Not only might the vote fall in favor of independence, but doing so could fuel separatist aspirations held by other groups within Indonesia. Smoldering irredentist movements in Aceh and Irian Jaya in particular seemed prone to such trajectories. Undeterred, President Habibie pursued the referendum believing that Indonesian goodwill on the East Timor controversy could foster international respect for his post-Suharto reform agenda. Desperately enmeshed in Indonesia's worsening economic crisis, Habibie saw East Timor as a mechanism to restore confidence among international observers and foreign investors.

In negotiations over the UN's role in the planned referendum, Habibie refused to allow foreign peacekeepers as part of the international mission. The civilian authorities of the United Nations Assistance Mission in East Timor (UNAMET), a $50 million endeavor, carried the mandate to train local officials and educate the public in preparation for the referendum. UNAMET officials would thus rely on local security to see the plebiscite through. For anxious Timorese, Habibie's promised referendum was all that stood between them and independence.

On August 30, 1999, after two disorganized postponements, the residents of East Timor finally went to the ballot box to cast votes on their new political status. The run up to the referendum was marred by various hostilities and dreadful acts of violence perpetrated by pro-autonomy militias (backed by elements within the Indonesian military). Despite security concerns, the turnout for the referendum was remarkable, surpassing 98 percent of registered voters. The results were equally overwhelming: Nearly four out of five residents (79 percent) voted for full independence.

Reactions to the vote were intense on both sides. Fearful of militias, independence supporters were cautious rather than jubilant. Pro-Indonesia militias, as they had warned, launched a bloody campaign against independence supporters. East Timor suddenly turned chaotic. Enraged thugs attacked civilians with cold brutality. Dili was set ablaze and disturbing reports of torture and murder surfaced, only to be followed by evidence of mass graves. Fears that political genocide was unfolding grew. Outside Dili, rampaging militias looted and destroyed village after village. Horrific acts of rape and sexual assault accompanied the chaos.[4] The armed militias even attacked UNAMET personnel, killing three staffers and exciting fear among the sizable but defenseless foreign personnel. From Jakarta, Habibie called on the Indonesian military to restore order, but his estranged generals acted slowly while claiming no responsibility for instigating or participating in the turmoil.

International concern developed further as a refugee crisis mushroomed, sending 250,000 Timorese into Indonesian territory and elsewhere over a matter of days. Among those fleeing were leading independence figures such as Nobel laureate Bishop Belo, who fled to Australia for safety. Alindo Marcal, a well-known Protestant leader, was less fortunate—his corpse was found hacked into pieces in a militia-run refugee camp. In two weeks of post-referendum violence, the death toll had risen to well over a thousand. The extent to which Indonesian generals had armed the local militias or Indonesian soldiers had otherwise participated remained unclear. Most observers believed it was significant.

From his New York office, UN Secretary-General Kofi Annan warned the Indonesian government and its military about "crimes against humanity." He then flew to Jakarta to address the situation personally. Lingering feelings of imperial responsibility reverberated in Portugal. Citizens across Lisbon flooded city streets, forming a six-mile human chain and demanding a forceful international response to end the unrest and killings. East Timor's crisis then grabbed the attention of the UN Security Council but, alas, the United States and China, still reeling from recent events in Kosovo, initially balked at authorizing a coordinated intervention.

As events escalated by the day, a solution surfaced in the form of an Australian-led peacekeeping force. The International Force for East Timor (INTERFET) included troops from Australia, Thailand, Singapore, Bangladesh, Brazil, and other willing countries. Conceding his own ineffectiveness on the matter, Habibie granted permission for INTERFET to enter East Timor. With unprecedented speed in the history of assembling and deploying international peacekeepers, INTERFET troops found themselves in East Timor only five days from their initial authorization. Unwilling to relent, the militias pledged death to all outsiders but soon found themselves overwhelmed by the presence and power of the Blue Berets.

With the violence in check and the refugee crisis under international control, the referendum's results were eventually allowed to follow their intended path to Timorese self-rule. In mid-October 1998, the Indonesian Parliament publicly declared the 1976 annexation of East Timor void. INTERFET was also terminated, replaced by a new UN mission designed to manage East Timor's transition to statehood: the United Nations Transitional Administration in East Timor (UNTAET). In the months that followed, UNTAET successfully governed the country, resettled refugees, and managed elections for a new parliament and president. The UN's highly respected Brazilian-born diplomat Sergio Vieira de Mello functioned during this period as East Timor's chief executive.

On May 20, 2002, at midnight, Timor-Leste was reborn as a sovereign, independent nation. The nighttime fireworks and celebrations matched the soaring expectations and aspirations of the Timorese people. Present in Dili to memorialize the event were the world's leaders—Kofi Annan, former U.S. president Bill Clinton, and Australian Prime Minister John Howard. In a show of goodwill, Indonesia's new president, Megawati Sukarnoputri, uncomfortably attended as well. Presiding at the ceremonies was indefatigable freedom fighter and longtime political prisoner Xanana Gusmao, now a free man and the country's first president.

Simultaneous with independence, the United Nations Mission of Support in East Timor (UNMISET) replaced UNTAET to assist the country in early statehood. The new mission included 5,000 security forces and almost 500 foreign advisers. UNMISET, designed to last only one year, stayed three. It expired in 2005 and was replaced by a smaller UN presence of nonsecurity personnel, the United Nations Office in East Timor (UNOTIL).

Timor-Leste's statehood allowed for new opportunities but also created unprecedented challenges. Since its independence, Southeast Asia's newest country has struggled with political infighting, regime instability, and endemic poverty. After a few short years of relative calm, political conditions deteriorated markedly in 2006, less than a year after UNMISET's security forces had left the country. In a sad iteration, political violence returned and Timor-Leste experienced another round of traumatic street-level chaos, vandalism, mass dislocation, and loss of life. Summoned again to restore peace was an Australian-led peacekeeping contingency, this time under the name Operation Astute. The United Nations followed this event by establishing yet another new mission, the United Nations Integrated Mission in Timor-Leste (UNMIT). Its mandate, authorized through early 2009, included measures to institutionalize democracy with the assistance of civilian advisers and the presence of 1,600 armed UN police officers.

A new round of political hostilities after parliamentary elections in 2007 and a double assassination attempt on the president and prime minister in early 2008 underscored the depth of Timor-Leste's ongoing political fragility. The necessary presence of international authorities and security forces renders the Timorese's hard-won right to self-rule an unfulfilled promise. True independence remains elusive.

INSTITUTIONS AND SOCIAL GROUPS

Catholic Church

The most significant colonial legacy of the Portuguese was religion. Ninety-six percent of Timor-Leste's population is Roman Catholic, in contrast to the Muslim presence that characterizes much of the surrounding region. Catholicism in East Timor actually strengthened under Indonesian rule due to *Pancasila*'s monotheistic imperative (which required citizens to indicate their religious identification). It was also strengthened by active local leaders, whose work was acknowledged by Pope John Paul II and his decision to visit the troubled island in 1989. As the moral voice of Timorese society and the arbiters of Timorese interests, local Catholic leaders fueled the territory's resistance movement during the pre-independence period and continue to shape the country after statehood.

Today, the debate over church-state relations is among the central elements of postindependence politics. Timorese political figures are divided on where church-state lines should be drawn. Prime Minister Mari Alkatiri's proposal to restrict religious education in public schools sparked indignation among church authorities and was ultimately defeated upon the threat of social disorder. Tensions between church leaders and Alkatiri, a *Fretilin* veteran and religious Muslim, persisted until he resigned under great pressure in 2006. Although *Fretilin*-led governments did not pursue a socialist agenda while in power, church leaders often characterize party leaders, including Alkatiri, as Marxists.

In recent years, the church has developed avenues for a more forceful role in electoral politics. Church policy disallows bishops and priests from formally endorsing parties or candidates during services, but outside church walls they are encouraged to speak openly about their preferences. State funds are also used to support the church, an action justified, in President Ramos-Horta's words, "as an obligation of the State to the oldest and most credible institution in our Nation."[5]

Independence Leaders

Many of East Timor's most prominent independence leaders continue in pivotal leadership roles in the postindependence period. Having emerged from a seminary-trained class of *mestizo* elites, intellectuals, and civil servants, these leaders took their cues from the political Left in Portugal during their formative years in the 1970s.[6] Less ideological today than before, veteran independence leaders now jockey for positions in government as partners and rivals hoping to navigate the young country through its seemingly impossible challenges.

Chief among Timor-Leste's leaders is Jose "Xanana" Gusmao, elected as the country's first president and currently serving as its prime minister. Known best by his pen name, "Xanana," the journalist-turned-revolutionary found himself atop *Fretilin* in the early 1980s following a massive Indonesian offensive that eliminated many of the group's leaders. Xanana then worked with Catholic leaders and *Fretilin*'s rivals to create a broad political coalition and an effective clandestine rebel operation. To many Timorese, his legend is part Che Guevara, part Nelson Mandela. When he rejected offers for liberty in exile during his long imprisonment in Jakarta, Xanana became the international face of Timorese courage. Suharto honored Nelson Mandela's request to visit Xanana in prison, and Xanana thanked Suharto with repeated requests to allow an independence referendum.

Jose Ramos-Horta, *Fretilin*'s founder, has also bridged the pre- and postindependence eras as a powerful political actor. In what proved to be entirely consequential, he fled East Timor only days before the Indonesian takeover in 1975. While abroad, he drew attention to East Timor's plight, serving as its observer-representative in the United Nations. Ramos-Horta lobbied governments, legislatures, and human rights organizations in singular fashion to generate international pressure on Suharto's regime. In 1988, he broke with *Fretilin* to pursue a path of nonviolent resistance. A joint Nobel laureate with Bishop Carlos Ximenes Belo in 1996, Ramos-Horta now serves as the country's second elected president. Constitutionally, as head of state, he holds only limited powers to dissolve Parliament and veto legislation. Nevertheless, as a nonparty independent and because of his legendary ambassadorial history,

Ramos-Horta wields unparalleled moral authority both inside and outside the new country.

Mari Alkatiri, also a *Fretilin* founder, remains another prominent figure. He served a tumultuous four-year stint as prime minister, a position with greater constitutional authority and policymaking power than the presidency. Inter-party divisions and rivalries with Gusmao, Ramos-Horta, and Catholic leaders forced him to resign in 2006 but he remains active as a *Fretilin* party leader in Parliament.

National Parliament and Political Parties

Though weak as institutions, the national Parliament and the country's political parties are important vehicles for political expression and contestation in Timor-Leste's embryonic democracy. The promise of a healthy democracy rests on how well these institutions develop. The extent to which political figures involved in parliamentary politics choose to stay within the bounds of peaceful conflict is among the crucial questions facing the country.

The sixty-five-member unicameral National Parliament currently seats seven of the fourteen parties that contested peacefully in its most recent poll, held in 2007. A proportional representation party-list ballot determines seat allocation. By law, at least one in four of all candidates on party lists are required to be women. *Fretilin*, now a political party, won 29 percent of the total vote and a plurality of twenty-one seats, but it is no longer the most influential faction in Timorese politics. *Fretilin*'s postindependence leadership under Prime Minister Mali Alkatari weakened the party's overall position in electoral politics. Dampening *Fretilin* dominance has been the party work of Xanana Gusmao, who founded the National Congress for Timorese Reconstruction Party (CRNT) prior to the 2007 national elections. The CRNT won 24 percent of the popular vote and eighteen seats in the 2007 polls, and currently leads the government in a coalition alliance, the Parliamentary Majority Alliance (AMP), that includes like-minded parties with fewer elected seats.

Before the CRNT-AMP coalition emerged, difficulties surfaced in forming a parliamentary government and choosing a prime minister. *Fretilin*, with the most seats, was unable to find a partner and attempted to form a minority government. A minority government was unacceptable to other seated parties, including Xanana's CRNT. The possibility of a unity government of all parties later surfaced but talks broke down along *Fretilin*-CRNT lines, despite President Ramos-Horta's attempts at mediation. When a CRNT-AMP alliance government emerged with Xanana Gusmao as prime minister, President Ramos-Horta decided to recognize its authority. *Fretilin* protested the decision and Dili streets exploded with angry house burnings and vandalism; this time, however, no deaths were reported. Alkatari appealed to *Fretilin*'s supporters to protest using civil methods, but he maintained for months that Xanana's government was illegitimate.

DEMOCRATIZATION

Institutions of democracy in Timor-Leste are weak and underdeveloped. The greatest threat to the consolidation of democratic institutions is not antidemocratic sentiment, authoritarian impulses, or the threat of occupation; it is, rather, the likelihood of institutional failure to produce the needed functions of government. An ethos for democracy is taking root in Timor-Leste but the country's history is short and its dependence on international support for regime legitimacy remains considerable. Moreover, the nagging threat of social disorder and violence that characterizes Timorese political passion also inhibits confidence in assessing the country's democratization as anything but tenuous. The country fits the definition of what might be called an "ambiguous" regime.

Indicative of Timor-Leste's weak democratic institutions were the events of 2006 when, less than four years into its democratic experiment, Dili slid into another episode of political chaos. A large number of disgruntled government soldiers from the interior west, on strike over low wages and alleged discrimination, were fired by Prime Minister Alkatiri. In turn, the soldier-petitioners spurred riots, looting, arson, and clashes with local police and military loyalists. Multiple deaths occurred and the homes of military officials were set on fire. The risk of general social disorder grew quickly. Xanana Gusmao, then president, added fuel to the fire by publicly indicating sympathy for the soldiers.[7] Echoing earlier incidents, over 150,000 Timorese fled in fear. As the country braced itself for another wave of bloody turmoil, some government ministers began to distribute weapons to civilians. Only the arrival of another Australian-led peacekeeping force was able to bring calm to Dili's streets.

In terms of democratization, the events of 2006 were especially troubling because this time political violence could not be blamed on Indonesia, outsiders, or some foreign entity. Rather, blame lay within suggesting evidence of a growing regional cleavage and a political culture prone to violent conflict.

The fragile state of Timor-Leste's democracy was further demonstrated in 2007 by parliamentary elections, which produced another cycle of disorder and chaos. When *Fretilin* supporters initially refused to recognize a parliamentary majority coalition, street-level havoc occurred yet again. By early 2008, rebels sought President Ramos-Horta's life in an assassination attempt that left him hospitalized, induced into a coma by doctors to help him survive gunshot wounds to his abdomen. Prime Minister Gusmao narrowly missed a similar fate with an attempt on his life during the same thwarted coup. Ramos-Horta recovered and rejoined Xanana to lead the struggling country, but the damage the assassination attempts had inflicted on democracy remained.

Hopeful observers saw the death of Alfredo Reinado, the estranged army major who launched the 2006 mutiny and the 2008 assassination coup, as the beginning of the end of a destabilizing rebel movement and hope for democracy.[8] Nevertheless, an end to political violence in Timor-Leste's young democracy has yet to be realized. Whether a generational change of leaders will improve or further challenge the country's democratic development remains an open question.

ECONOMIC DEVELOPMENT

Among the most serious problems Timor-Leste faces are grinding poverty and massive unemployment. Independence did not transform economic deficiencies Timor-Leste inherited from its past. In fact, the 1999 referendum chaos that destroyed much of the country's physical infrastructure set back the new country from its birth. New autonomy and authority to allocate state resources has spawned infighting because there is so little to allocate. Aside from promising revenues derived from oil extraction in the Timor Sea, the young country enjoys few economic prospects. A 1996 report from the UNDP tragically describes Timor-Leste as Asia's least developed country—a county "chained to poverty."[9]

At $358, Timor-Leste's GDP per capita is the lowest in Southeast Asia. Moreover, the vast majority of Timorese produce and earn income in the non-oil economy where growth has even been negative in recent years. The indicators of overall human development in Timor-Leste are most disheartening. Only twenty-seven countries in the entire world (all in Africa) rank lower than Timor-Leste when measured using the Human Development Index (HDI). In Southeast Asia, the citizens of Laos, Cambodia, and Burma (on average) enjoy higher levels of human development and lower levels of poverty incidence than do those living in Timor-Leste.[10]

Weak private investment and slow job creation plague the economy. Because half of the population is under twenty years old, demographic stress will extend employment pressures well into the future. Seasonal food shortages also afflict much of the island's populace who farm for subsistence. Almost a quarter of the population depends on food assistance during lean months of the year. Coffee production and vanilla, palm oil, and other commercial crops await more intensive investment before the country's agricultural sector functions profitably in Southeast Asia's trade-based economy. Timor-Leste, a net importer that suffers chronic trade deficits, is just as dependent economically as it is dependent politically. Government expenditure stimulates most of the country's economic growth, which tends to range between 1 percent and 5 percent.

After hard-fought treaty negotiations with Australia over rival claims, government revenues from oil extraction in the Timor Sea have begun to flow in recent years. By agreement, the Joint Petroleum Development Area (JPDA) set aside boundary disputes for fifty years and sends 90 percent of reserve revenues to Timor-Leste and 10 percent to Australia. In 2007, over $2 billion from oil revenues was funneled through government accounts, resulting in a welcome budget surplus.

Wise allocation of oil-generated wealth through the Petroleum Fund (created by the Alkatiri government) is designed to help boost other productive sectors as well as education and social services. Increasing alongside rising hydrocarbon-driven revenues, however, are the risks of falling into the "oil curse." Common to many small petrostates, the oil curse leads to high-stakes elite conflict, authoritarian impulses, and corruption. Without wealth from oil, however, Timor-Leste's economic future would appear extremely bleak. At the moment, oil is a blessing, not a curse.

Added to the political effects of oil dependency is economic vulnerability. High volatility in global fuel prices in 2008 exacerbated Timor-Leste's economic instability and revealed more risks tied to dependence on oil revenues. The drop of crude oil prices during the global financial crisis of late 2008, from a high of over $140 a barrel to a low near $40, sorely impacted expected revenues.

Dollarization of the country's monetary system, virtually imposed upon Timor-Leste by the IMF, was designed to encourage a predictable investment environment and mitigate the risk of domestic economic crises. However, the strength of the U.S. dollar is itself affected by the fact that global trade in oil is priced in dollars. Thus, when high demand for crude oil combines with a weakening dollar (as it did before the 2008 global financial crisis), Timor-Leste's rising oil revenues do not go as far in purchasing the many imports the country needs for a functioning economy. On the other hand, a drop in oil demand combined with a strengthening dollar (experienced with the onset of the 2008 global financial crisis), allows Timor-Leste to buy more imports with marginally lower oil revenues.

THE TIMOR-LESTE STATE

Timor-Leste's state is dependent and fragile. Technically sovereign, it can be described (somewhat singularly) as an "infant state"—a state engaged in a needy, agnatic relationship with the international community through its

UN parentage. Although sometimes classified as a failed state, Timor-Leste is so new as a political entity it is difficult to equate it with countries that genuinely experienced a measurable loss of sovereign control, central authority, or capacity for self-governance (such as Somalia, Zimbabwe, or Afghanistan). Having yet to achieve a measurable degree of state autonomy or capacity in the first place, Timor-Leste, an infant state, is disproportionately dependent on foreign support for its very being.

Threats from external political forces and massive social dislocation generally foster the rise of a strong state. In the Timorese experience, however, it was the UN that accreted and concentrated power to manage sociopolitical disorder. Over the past decade, virtually all functions of the Timor-Leste state (security, government, social services, and justice) have been or continue to be performed by UN operations: UNAMET (1999), INTERFET (1999), UNTAET (1999–2002), UNMISET (2002–2005), UNOTIL (2005–2006), Operation Astute (2006), UNMIT (2006–present), the East Timor Tribunal (2000–2006), and the CAVR Truth and Reconciliation Commission (2002–2005). Essential as these missions have been to the country's emancipation and stability, Timor-Leste's future as a fully sovereign state depends on how it is weaned from UN paternalism. President Ramos-Horta, ever conscious of this fact, has vocally encouraged the United Nations to maintain its presence in Timor-Leste for at least a decade to lead the country out of its infancy.

Countless non-Timorese members of the international community have expended an immeasurable amount of human effort, attention, and resources to assist Timor-Leste in its independence and statehood. Although the bulk of this effort has come from the United Nations, other multilateral and nongovernmental organizations now function in the country and, paradoxically, deepen the state's dependency on foreign assistance. Given the country's low level of development, foreign assistance is likely to continue long after the last UN mission leaves Dili. Timor-Leste is perhaps decades away from creating a strong state with the autonomy and capability to function independently and effectively.

Lastly, with respect to the state's legitimacy, questions persist about how Timorese willingly consent to authority. The cultural and moral authority of the Catholic Church and particular independence figures remain intact, but a respect for and submission to the state and its embryonic political institutions remain questionable. Growing regional divisions between east and west, known locally as the *firaku-kaladi* divide, suggest an added challenge to the legitimacy of the state and its territorial integrity.

FOREIGN POLICY

Timor-Leste's relationship with the United Nations remains its most crucial foreign policy priority. Nevertheless, the young country's evolving politics is producing a coherent foreign policy agenda and debate. Dili's principal bilateral relations are with Indonesia, Australia, and (increasingly) China.

Among Timorese, relations with Indonesia remain controversial due to past resentments of Suharto's occupation and the postreferendum mayhem in 1999. A bilateral initiative of the two states, the Timor-Leste Commission of Truth and Friendship (CVA), was launched in 2005 to smooth relations. For many Timorese who suffered at the hands of Indonesian perpetrators, the creation of a commission smacked of impunity. Xanana, a supporter of the commission, drew the ire of church officials, UNMIT, and international NGOs that questioned the CVA's establishment.[11] At the state-to-state level, however, CVA has allowed current governments to distance themselves from the sins of the past.

Timor-Leste's relations with other major partners reflect a more forward-looking posture. Its ties with Australia are complex, multilayered, and asymmetrical. Disputes over territorial waters damaged relations after independence but Australia willingly returned its peacekeepers to Dili in 2006 to quell civil unrest. Certain parties within Timor-Leste fear Canberra has neocolonial designs to ensure Dili serves Australian interests. Ramos-Horta and Xanana show less concern for this possibility than do *Fretilin* and Mari Alkatiri, who looks to China and Portugal as patrons. Portugal remains Timor-Leste's largest aid donor, with Australia a close second.

China, a permanent member of the UN Security Council and long sympathetic to *Fretilin*'s objectives, sent troops to support UNTAET and was the first country to establish diplomatic relations with Timor-Leste. While early support of *Fretilin* reflects Cold War priorities, more recent moves have sought to preempt Taiwan from courting the new Asian country. China's interests in Timor-Leste may be more economic than political. Oil and resource hungry, China seeks a partnership with Timor-Leste as part of its grand strategy to secure energy sources. Evidence of a deepening relationship between the two countries includes increasing foreign aid from Beijing; the financing of government buildings, including the construction of Timor-Leste's new presidential palace in Dili; and a $1.6 million seismic study for oil and gas in Timor-Leste's interior.[12] In a reversal of roles, as a show of goodwill, the government of Timor-Leste donated $500,000 to China in 2008 in support of recovery efforts following the massive Sichuan earthquake.

With respect to international organizations, Timor-Leste's key relations are with the Asian Development Bank, where membership was established in 2004, and ASEAN, where membership hopes are seriously inhibited by the criterion that Dili establish foreign embassies in all ten ASEAN capitals (Timor-Leste has only a handful of diplomatic missions worldwide). WTO membership is an even more distant hope, although membership with the IMF and World Bank has resulted in a proliferation of project-based aid initiatives.

CONCLUSION

The full dignity of independence celebrated by Timor-Leste in 2002 came at a heavy price—achieved after 460 years of Portuguese control; three merciless years of Japanese occupation; a thirty-year return of Portuguese rule following World War II; a failed attempt at independence in 1975; twenty-five years of a brutal occupation by Indonesia's Suharto; an independence referendum; a scorched-earth campaign by anti-independence militias; a refugee crisis; a dramatic Australian-led peacekeeping operation; and an ambitious UN mission that governed East Timor's final transition to statehood. Elections, democratic institutions, and membership in international organizations have since followed but political stability and economic development have remained elusive.

The "never again" narrative of which Timor-Leste's history is inseparably woven has recently adopted a new term: *Chega*, Portuguese for "enough!" or "stop." The title of a UN-commissioned report on the atrocities committed under Indonesia's occupation, *Chega!* might as well be a mantra for independent Timor-Leste as it seeks full self-governance. Realizing an end to episodic disorder, killing, and refugee flows seems requisite for the infant state to experience genuine independence and stability. Political order, elusive today, is the keystone in the delicate bridge that may someday lead Timorese to the economic and human development they so sorely deserve.

NOTES

1. Tom Regan, "Report: Gerald Ford Disagreed with Bush's Iraq Policy," *Christian Science Monitor*, December 28, 2006, www.csmonitor.com/2006/1228/dailyUpdate.html.

2. Michael Leifer, "Timor, East (Indonesia)," *Dictionary of the Modern Politics of South-East Asia* (London: Routledge, 1995), p. 236.

3. *Conflict-Related Deaths in Timor Leste 1975–1999: The Findings of the CAVR Report*, commissioned by UNTAET and the Timor-Leste National Parliament, available at www.cavr-timorleste.org/updateFiles/english/CONFLICT-RELATED%20DEATHS.pdf.

4. Ibid.

5. Extracted from a campaign speech by presidential candidate Jose Ramos-Horta, March 23, 2007, Dili, available at www.pm.gov.tp/speeches.htm.

6. Michael Leifer, "Fretilin, (Indonesia)," in *Dictionary of the Modern Politics of South-East Asia* (London: Routledge, 1995), p. 97.

7. Joseph Nevins, "Timor-Leste in 2006: The End of Post-Independence Honeymoon," *Asian Survey*, vol. 47, no. 1 (January/February 2007), pp. 162–167.

8. Simon Montlake and Nick Squires, "After Foiled Assassination, Timor Rebels' Sway May Lessen," *Christian Science Monitor*, February 12, 2008.

9. Nevins, "Timor-Leste in 2006," p. 163.

10. Refer to comparison indicators following the last chapter of this book.

11. Jose Cornelio Guterres, "Timor-Leste," *Southeast Asian Affairs, 2008*, p. 369.

12. Ian Story, "China and East Timor," Association for Asian Research, August 15, 2006, www.asianresearch.org/articles/2920.html.

RESOURCE GUIDE

The University of California–Berkeley maintains a useful portal for digital and print resources on East Timor: www.lib.berkeley.edu/SSEAL/SoutheastAsia/seaelec.html. Northern Illinois University's Southeast Asia Digital Library includes a range of useful links that cover government, academic, and research institutions specific to East Timor: http://sea.lib.niu.edu. The Library of Congress maintains a resource guide on East Timor at www.loc.gov/rr/international/portals.html#t.

The government's official Web site is www.easttimorgovernment.com. The "useful links" provided on the front page of this site are comprehensive for governmental and non-governmental organizations. UNMIT's address is http://unmit.unmissions.org/. The Timor-Leste Commission for Reception, Truth and Reconciliation (CAVR), and its report, *Chega!*, are available at www.cavr-timorleste.org. Wikipedia's list of political parties in East Timor provides links to home pages of active political parties. The East Timor Action Network (ETAN), at www.etan.org, is an excellent source for the many dimensions of East Timor's past and present. For current news in English, the monthly magazine *Guide Post* is available online: www.guideposttimor.com.

Southeast Asia

SELECT INDICATORS

	Total population 2007	Gross National Income (GNI) per capita ($US) 2007	Gross Domestic Product (GDP) per capita ($US) 2007	Gross Domestic Product (GDP/PPP) per capita ($US) 2007	Poverty rate: percentage below national poverty line 1990–2004	Births attended by skilled professional 1997–2001
Brunei	390,000	26,930	17,121	51,005	N/A	99%
Burma	51,500,000	N/A	235	1,039	33	57%
Cambodia	26,000,000	540	440	2,727	35	32%
Indonesia	228,000,000	1,650	1,302	3,843	27	72%
Lao PDR	6,200,000	580	485	2,039	39	19%
Malaysia	26,200,000	6,540	5,142	10,882	16	97%
Philippines	85,900,000	1,620	1,192	5,137	43	60%
Singapore	4,400,000	32,470	26,893	29,663	N/A	100%
Thailand	65,300,000	3,400	2,750	8,667	14	99%
Timor-Leste	1,100,000	1,510	358	2,506	42	18%
Vietnam	86,400,000	790	631	3,071	29	85%

	Percent of rural population 1975	Percent of rural population 2005	Human Dev. Index (HDI) value: 0.0–1.0 2005	Human Dev. Index (HDI) ranking (of 177 countries) 2005	Freedom Rating Index 2008	Corruption ranking (of 179 countries) value: #1=least 2007
Brunei	38	26	0.89	#30	partly free	N/A
Burma	76	69	0.58	#132	not free	#179
Cambodia	90	80	0.60	#131	not free	#162
Indonesia	81	52	0.73	#107	free	#143
Lao PDR	89	79	0.60	#130	not free	#168
Malaysia	62	33	0.81	#63	partly free	#43
Philippines	64	37	0.77	#90	partly free	#134
Singapore	0	0	0.92	#25	partly free	#4
Thailand	76	68	0.78	#78	partly free	#84
Timor-Leste	85	73	0.51	#150	partly free	#123(tie)
Vietnam	81	74	0.73	#105	not free	#123(tie)

Sources: UNFPA; UNDP; World Bank; IMF; CIA; Freedom House; Transparency International

Index

Abdul Rahman, Tunku, 6, 135–136, 146, 153, 155, 161–162
Abdul Razak, Tun, 136–137
Abu Sayyaf, 85–86, 94
Aceh, 110–111, 297
Afghanistan, 10, 16, 116, 175, 201
AFTA (ASEAN Free Trade Area), 17, 60, 154
Aguinaldo, Emilio, 79
Ahmad, Zakaria Haji, 156n6, 156n8, 156n11, 156n13, 156n14
Alagappa, Muthiah, 131n19, 156n20, 176n7, 215n14, 242n11
Albritton, Robert B., 63n6, 63n8
Alkatiri, Mari, 300, 302, 303, 307
Allen, Douglas, 291n2
All Burma Monks Alliance, 199, 205
Al-Qaeda, 85, 94, 109, 147, 174
Amnesty International, 166, 231
Anand Panyarachun, 29, 31–32, 34, 43, 44–45
Anata, Aris, 130n1
Anderson, Benedict, 130n2
Angka ("the organization"), 249–250
Angkor Wat temple, 59, 245, 259, 267, 271
Annan, Secretary-General Kofi, 298
Anwar Ibrahim, 139, 141, 144
Antara News, 131n14
Aquino, Benigno, Jr., 68, 69, 80, 82, 89
Aquino, Corazon "Cory," 69–70, 71–74, 78, 91, 95
  communism and, 72, 84

domination of dynastic family, 87
"Freedom Constitution" of 1986, 79–80
last-minute U.S. support for, 92
political parties in support of, 80–81
as woman, 83
Arifin, Evi Nuridya, 130n1
Aris, Michael, 197
Arndt, H. W., 131n16
ASEAN (Association of Southeast Asian Nations), 7, 16
  Brunei, 187
  Burma, 59–60, 140, 154, 200, 208, 211, 212–213
  Indonesia, 127, 140
  Malaysia, 153
  Philippines, 74, 94
  Singapore, 171
  Thailand, 58
  Timor-Leste, 308
  Vietnam, Laos, and Cambodia, 59, 140, 154, 239, 241, 270, 290
ASEAN Free Trade Area (AFTA), 17, 60, 154
ASEAN Plus Three process, 60–61
ASEAN-China Free Trade Agreement (ACFTA), 60–61, 271
Asian Development Bank (ADB), 90, 283, 287, 290, 308
Asian values debate, 12, 15, 140, 149, 155, 163
Asia-Pacific Economic Cooperation (APEC), 241

313